The Christian Coalition

The Christian Coalition

Dreams of Restoration, Demands for Recognition

Justin Watson

MACMILLAN

First published 1999 by
MACMILLAN PRESS LTD
Houndmills, Basingstoke, Hampshire RG21 6XS
and London
Companies and representatives
throughout the world

ISBN 0-333-77231-8 paperback

A catalogue record for this book is available
from the British Library.

10 9 8 7 6 5 4 3 2 1
08 07 06 05 04 03 02 01 00 99

Printed in the United States of America by
Haddon Craftsmen
Bloomsburg, PA

To Caroline

CONTENTS

ACKNOWLEDGMENTS

This book began as my doctoral dissertation at Florida State University (FSU). I am grateful to the entire faculty and staff of the Department of Religion for the opportunity to work with them over the years. I am also grateful for a fellowship provided by FSU's Office of Graduate Studies during the 1995-1996 academic year that made it possible for me to finish my basic research and writing in a timely fashion. The Department of Religion graciously provided me with employment as an instructor during the 1996-1997 academic year while I prepared this manuscript for publication. I would also like to thank a former member of the FSU faculty, Dr. Richard Rubenstein, and his wife, Betty, for their kindness during my days in Tallahassee.

Special thanks must go to the members of my dissertation committee, Dr. Leo Sandon (Director), Dr. John Kelsay, and Dr. Neil Jumonville, for their wise counsel and encouragement. And I am deeply indebted to Dr. Sandon for the support and friendship he and his wife, Marvel Lou, extended to me throughout my graduate school years.

Many organizations, publications, and individuals aided in this project by providing materials and information that otherwise would have been unavailable to me. These include the Christian Coalition, People for the American Way, Americans United for Separation of Church and State, *Christianity Today*, Kim Lawton, Public Research Associates, *The Washington Times*, The Chalcedon Foundation, Jay Rogers, and the librarians of the Strozier Library of FSU. A special thanks goes to Judy and Jahan Shahi, who welcomed me into their home during my three research trips to Washington, D.C.

I am grateful also to my editor at St. Martin's, Karen Wolny, whose enthusiasm and professionalism made this book possible.

Finally, I must also thank all of my friends, near and far, for the support and kindness that sustained me throughout this endeavor.

CHAPTER 1

"BUT WHAT DO THEY *REALLY* WANT?"

SEVERAL YEARS AGO, when I first started to investigate the Christian Coalition (CC), Pat Robertson's controversial political organization, a friend of mine heard about my research and asked, "What do they want?" I gave a brief summary of what I thought were the major issues that concerned the CC and its constituency. My friend was not satisfied and asked, "But what do they *really* want?"

After several years of research, I have found that the answer to that question is not as straightforward as I once thought it was, or as simple as the CC's opponents or defenders would have us believe.

The complexity of the goals and purposes of the CC can be illustrated by two experiences I had while attending the CC's 1995 national convention, experiences that occurred only minutes apart. I went to a panel discussion on proposals for a "Religious Equality Amendment" to the U.S. Constitution. When the discussion, which had touched on rather complex legal and constitutional issues, was opened up for questions from the audience, one man stood up and said earnestly, "I don't know about all this legal talk. What I want to know is 'Will this bring our nation back to God?'" The answer he received, which was couched in the complexities of "legal talk," probably did not answer his simple and heartfelt inquiry.

During a coffee break that followed this meeting, I was approached by a friendly gentleman who noticed from my name badge that I was, like him, from Florida. He inquired how my organizing efforts on behalf of the CC were going. When I told him that I was an academic doing research on the CC, his friendly demeanor changed. "Do you think," he asked with an edge of suspicion and defiance in his voice, "we have a right to do this?" By "this" he obviously meant the political activism of conservative evangelicals. And just as obviously he expected me, an academic (probably a secular humanist and political liberal), to reject their right to get involved in politics. After I stammered out an unconvincing platitude affirming the right of all Americans to engage in political activity, he turned away. The conversation was over.

These two questions, "Will this bring our nation back to God?" and "Do you think we have a right to do this?" embody two pervasive themes that I have found in the literature of the CC. The first theme, the necessity of restoring America to its status as a Christian nation, is reflected in the first man's earnest desire to "bring our nation back to God." This theme fits with conventional wisdom about the CC—that it is attempting to impose the values and beliefs of conservative evangelicals on American society. It is not difficult to find in the writings and speeches of Robertson numerous calls to "reclaim America," to "take back our nation," and to "restore our Christian heritage," along with strong denunciations of non-evangelical lifestyles and worldviews. This restorationist rhetoric is so persistent that the antipluralistic and antidemocratic intentions of the CC have become unquestioned commonplaces in social and political commentary. The question "Will this bring our nation back to God?" is exactly what we have been led to expect, and often get, from the CC and its members.

There has been far less serious attention paid to a second theme that has become common, if not pervasive, in the literature and activities of the CC and its allies—the victimization of evangelical Christians by a hostile secular culture. "Do you think we have a right to do this?" is the question of a defiant victim demanding recognition for the rights, interests, and identity of evangelicals through political action.

This image of "the evangelical as victim" is not part of the conventional wisdom about the CC's goals and purposes. Not surprisingly, critics of the CC flatly reject the reality of so-called anti-Christian bigotry. Barry Lynn of Americans United for Separation of Church and State asserted, "What they are really complaining about is the failure of government to help them promote their faith."[1] Sociologist Steve Bruce and political scientist Matthew Moen, for instance, noted the adoption of the rhetoric of "victimization" by politically active conservative evangelicals. But neither Bruce nor Moen saw this rhetoric as more than, in the words of Moen, "a clever and calculated ploy to tap the reservoir of positive sentiment for victims of American society."[2]

Unlike these two scholars, however, I have come to believe that the theme of victimization merits more serious attention than simply dismissing it as a "ploy." Serious attention means entertaining the possibility that claims of victimization, and the concomitant demands for recognition, are as important to adherents of this movement as their dreams of restoring Christian America. Notions of persecution by the "world," after all, run deep in the Christian tradition. For evangelicals who read the New Testament as an inerrant history of the primitive church, the understanding that to be a Christian is to be persecuted is obvious, if not inescapable. The ways these notions have been and will continue to be used in contemporary American politics need to be understood, not simply dismissed.

Giving serious attention to the CC's claims of victimization and demands for recognition does *not* mean accepting those claims and demands at face value. To understand the CC it is not necessary for us to accept their beliefs as true, but merely to appreciate that supporters of the CC may hold them as true. Whether or not evangelical Christians have been discriminated against in particular instances should be a question for the courts. My concerns are different. As intellectual historian Perry Miller once wrote, "I am not, let me insist, concerned with events, but with ideas, for history is often more instructive as it considers what men conceived they were doing rather than what, in brute fact, they did."[3] By taking the CC's demands for recognition seriously, we can understand that what they conceive they are doing is more complex and more deeply rooted than they have often been given credit for.

There is an obvious and fundamental tension between the calls for the restoration of a Christian America and the demands for recognition of evangelical Christians as a persecuted group. The calls for restoration involve a rejection of the legitimacy of social and religious pluralism as an accepted norm of American society. The demands for recognition, in contrast, depend on the norms of pluralism for legitimation.

Many, of course, suspect that the demand for recognition is but a cynical tactic to gain political power, a "Trojan horse" for the CC's real goal, an evangelical *reconquista* of American society and culture. The

CC would use pluralism, this interpretation holds, to destroy pluralism. If this is so, however, the leaders of the CC would be wise to eliminate the restoration theme from the organization's rhetoric in order to keep their true objective hidden. But the two themes are often stated side by side, with little apparent awareness of what seems to be an obvious contradiction. Is this just stupidity? Or is there some more complex interrelation that has made the contradiction less than obvious to adherents of the CC? Nevertheless, as the CC seeks to influence public opinion and implement certain public policy initiatives, it will have to deal with the perception, if not the reality, of contradiction between restoration and recognition. The way it deals with this tension may determine its future and its impact on American political life.

An understanding of the goals and purposes of the CC is only possible within two related contexts, which I attempt to describe in Chapter 2. The first and most general context is the complex stream of American religion from which the CC emerged, evangelicalism, and the long and ongoing struggle of evangelicals to come to terms with their place within the pluralistic ethos of modern America. The most immediate context for understanding the CC is that of the political mobilization of conservative evangelicals since the late 1970s. The emergence and development of this political and social movement, which I have elected to call the "Christian Right,"[4] have prompted an outpouring of scholarly and journalistic attention, as well as a mountainous body of polemical literature by both its supporters and opponents. There has been, however, considerable disagreement about how to assess its development, impact, and prospects for the future.[5]

Those readers who are already familiar with this literature may find it more convenient to turn directly to Chapter 3, in which I examine the two figures who have stood at the center of the CC, Pat Robertson and Executive Director Ralph Reed. I sketch their lives, careers, and thought prior to the founding of the CC in 1989; I also discuss Robertson's unsuccessful run for the Republican presidential nomination in 1988. In Chapter 4, I detail the history, structure, activities, and accomplishments of the CC, concentrating on how that organization has moved toward "adjustment" to "the secular norms and practices of American politics."[6]

In Chapter 5, I turn to the restoration theme. The desire to return to a lost golden era has been pervasive in the literature of the CC but has been expressed in different ways by Robertson and Reed. While

Robertson preaches an old-fashioned jeremiad for the restoration of a covenanted Christian nation, Reed calls for the restoration of a civic religious consensus that has been lost in recent decades. I also attempt to make clear that Robertson and Reed are not pursuing a state-imposed religious establishment or a totalitarian theocratic order but a renewal of the cultural influence and prestige that evangelicalism once enjoyed in American society.

In Chapter 6, I explore the CC's claims of victimization and demands for the recognition of the rights of evangelicals. I carry out this exploration through an extended comparison between the methods of the CC and those of the contemporary social and political movement most identified with the rhetoric of victimization, multiculturalism. Despite coming from opposite ends of the political spectrum, both movements utilize invocations of shared victimization, create politically usable histories, offer a critique of the oppressive forces supposedly arrayed against them, and advance a public agenda based on demands for what philosopher Charles Taylor has called "recognition."[7]

Many readers might find any comparison between disadvantages suffered by women or minorities, and the experience of the white middle-class evangelical constituency of the CC, to be ludicrous, if not deeply offensive. The purpose of my comparison, however, is not to endorse the reality or nonreality of "anti-Christian bigotry," but to explore the nature and function of the recognition theme in the CC. I am not urging my readers to accept or reject the victim identity of the CC's constituents but to understand how the CC is promoting that identity for its constituency.

In the final chapter, I try to make sense of the tension between restoration and recognition, between the rejection of pluralism and appeals to the pluralistic ethos. I consider three interpretations of this tension, and, while there is substantial evidence to support each interpretation, I conclude that both themes, although intellectually incompatible, will continue, for the time being, as essential elements of the CC's appeal to its constituency.

My understanding of the CC is informed by a study of the interrelated historical, religious, and political contexts that I outlined above, but my analysis of it is based on critical reading of primary source materials—material produced or distributed by the CC, as well as public statements of CC leaders reported in the mass media. Study of this material cannot tell us what the rank and file of the CC believe, or what is said behind closed doors at the CC headquarters. Analysis of this material *can* tell us what the CC leadership sees as important to communicate to the CC membership in order to strengthen loyalty and to motivate action.

I must also explain that I have restricted my research to one organization, the CC, rather than the more common practice of dealing with the Christian Right as a whole. What we call the Christian Right is actually a multitude of organizations with a variety of concerns and approaches. It is rooted in a sector of American Christianity that is characterized by organizational diversity and the lack of any central authority. The Christian Right does not speak with a single voice.

By studying a single organization I avoid two difficulties. First, I avoid the task of defining which organizations and figures should or should not be included in the Christian Right, as well as the monumental task of devoting sufficient attention to all of them. Second, I avoid incorrectly attributing the views of one organization, or the dominant opinion in the movement, to every organization associated with the movement. While this narrowing of focus will necessarily limit the applicability of my findings, I hope that my concentration on the CC, currently the most influential and visible Christian Right organization, will increase the significance of this project.

Concentration on the CC, however, has an unavoidable drawback. The CC is a "moving target," a currently functioning organization that is constantly responding to events. It is impossible to have the kind of closure necessary to create a definitive portrait of its goals and purposes. This was demonstrated in the clearest possible fashion when on April 23, 1997, Reed unexpectedly announced that he would be stepping down as Executive Director. Claiming that his work at the CC was done, Reed said that he would be starting his own campaign consulting firm, Century Strategies, to help "pro-family, pro-life, and pro-free enterprise candidates at every level of government."[8] Robertson issued a statement expressing his gratitude and said that Reed would continue to serve on the CC's Board of Directors.[9]

On June 11, the CC announced at a press conference that Reed's successor as executive director would be Randy Tate, a thirty-one-year-old Gingrich Republican who represented the 9th District of Washington state in the 104th Congress (1995-96). At the same time, Robertson made the unexpected announcement that he was leaving his post as president to become chairman of the CC's board, a newly created position. Donald Hodel, a sixty-two-year-old business executive and former Secretary of

Energy (1982-85) and Secretary of Interior (1985-89) in the Reagan administration, was named as the organization's new president. But Hodel will actually be assuming Reed's responsibilities, the day-to-day management and strategic direction of the CC. Tate will operate as Hodel's assistant.[10]

As of this writing, it is simply unknown whether Hodel and Tate will maintain the course Robertson and Reed set or head off in a new direction. It is also unknown if Robertson will be as closely involved in the CC as he has been in the past. Reed's relationship with the CC, despite his seat on its board of directors, is just as unclear. Discussions of the future of the CC, therefore, run the risk of being guesswork. Yet the potential significance of the CC is such that I believe a balanced and in-depth study of its formative years, the Robertson-Reed years, remains imperative.

When I was young, my father gave me some good advice that I have consistently failed to follow. "Boy," he said, "don't talk about religion or politics. It'll only get you into trouble." And as I have discovered, talking about religion *and* politics has gotten me into even more trouble. I ask my readers to remember that my intention in this study is not to advance any particular religious or political agenda— except the promotion of reasonable and civil discourse about matters of religion and politics. My task as a scholar of religion is not to judge the CC but to understand it. Yet judgments are inevitable because collective decisions and actions upon the pressing issues of our day are inescapable. I can only hope that what follows will make a fair and decent contribution to fashioning well-informed judgments, decisions, and actions.

CHAPTER 2

A REVOLUTIONARY CONSERVATISM

AMERICAN EVANGELICALISM

WHEN THE CHRISTIAN RIGHT FIRST EMERGED, it was identified with fundamentalism. Its most visible leader, Jerry Falwell of Moral Majority, proudly wrote in 1981, "I have always made it clear that I am a Fundamentalist—big F!"[1] "Fundamentalist" became a common designation in popular discourse for all theologically, politically, and socially conservative Protestants, even when some of those Protestants found that label insulting.

Supporters of the Christian Right have designated themselves as members of specific denominations, such as "Baptists" or "Presbyterians," or as "evangelicals," "pentecostals," "charismatics," or simply as "Christians" as well as "fundamentalists." While self-designations are not privileged, the variety of self-designations requires a historically accurate and conceptually precise coordinating term that is sufficiently inclusive, but not unnecessarily offensive to those it purports to describe.[2] The coordinating term I will use is "evangelicalism." Fundamentalism, neoevangelicalism, and the pentecostal-charismatic movement will be understood as the basic subtypes within the larger evangelical movement.

The terms evangelicalism and evangelical are derived from the Greek *euangelion,* meaning "good news." In Anglo-American usage, historian George Marsden told us, evangelical came to be the name of the revival movements that swept across the English-speaking Protestant world in the eighteenth and nineteenth centuries.[3] These revival movements, in America often called the First and Second Great Awakenings, developed a particular form of mass evangelism, "revival meetings," in which emotionally charged preaching and singing where used to arouse in those present an immediate experience of conversion or rededication to the Christian faith. The broad Protestant transdenominational religious heritage that emerged from those revivals is called "evangelicalism." The diversity of this heritage, which historian Timothy L. Smith has likened to a kaleidoscope, should not be underestimated.[4] Evangelicals have been divided not only by theological differences and denominational groupings, but also by regional and ethnic-racial variations. But given this diversity, can we really speak of evangelicalism as a unified phenomenon? Marsden has proposed three senses in which American evangelicalism has unity: as a consensus on certain doctrines, as an organic movement, and as a transdenominational community.[5]

First, while there has been no single authoritative evangelical creed or confession, there has been, according to Marsden, a general consensus consisting of an emphasis on five doctrines: "(1) the Reformation doctrine of the final authority of Scripture; (2) the real, historical character of God's saving work recorded in Scripture; (3) eternal salvation only through personal trust in Christ; (4) the importance of evangelism and missions; and (5) the importance of a spiritually transformed life."[6]

Second, American evangelicalism has also possessed unity as an organic movement. By this Marsden meant that evangelicals have shared common historical roots, have faced similar experiences, and have developed parallel and interrelated practical tendencies. In particular, Marsden pointed to a common ambivalence toward the larger American culture. On the one hand, evangelicals have shared in the American democratic, optimistic, individualistic, pragmatic, and market-driven ethos. On the other, evangelicals have resisted dominant cultural trends that they felt undercut "traditional supernaturalistic understandings of the Bible message."[7]

The third, and most specific, sense in which American evangelicalism has been a unified phenomenon has been as a transdenominational community. Evangelicalism developed as an informal coalition of denominational and independent organizations, which cooperate to support missions, revivals, evangelism, publishing, charity, and education. The coalition and its activities have provided a wider religious fellowship in addition to loyalty to a particular denomination. Sometimes, this transdenominational community has been more formally organized, such as the Evangelical Alliance in the nineteenth century and the National Association of Evangelicals in the twentieth century. Contemporary evangelicalism, in all three senses, has sometimes been regarded as a distinct subculture outside the "mainstream" of American life. This was not always so. In the view of many historians of American religion, evangelicalism dominated nineteenth-century American culture. Marsden, in particular, has argued that it is essential to understand this loss of dominance, the transition from being cultural insiders to being outsiders, and the persistence of insider identification among evangelicals in order to grasp the origins, nature, and significance of the Christian Right.[8]

The antebellum period was, according to historian Sydney E. Ahlstrom, "the great time of evangelical triumph."[9] Evangelicalism played a special role in American life. The evangelical revivals of the Second Great Awakening provided the basis of national values, identity, and unity in an era when what it meant to be an American was an open question.[10] Historian Martin E. Marty described the evangelicalism of this period as "a kind of national church or national religion."[11] This was not because all Americans were evangelicals. "Antebellum America was 'evangelical,'" wrote historian Mark Noll, "because so much of the visible public activity, so great a proportion of the learned culture, and so many dynamic organizations were products of evangelical conviction."[12]

These activities and organizations were focused on two intimately related enterprises: revivalism and social reform. Beyond the conversion of individuals, revivalism also had a greater social and cultural significance. As historian Perry Miller observed, if the antebellum configuration of sectional tension and religious diversity "posed a threat of centrifugal force, then that had to be countered by the centripetal power of the Revival."[13] Antebellum evangelicalism did not sunder the conversion of individuals from social reform. This reformism was supported by and grew out of the optimistic postmillennial eschatology of most evangelicals. Postmillennialists expected Christ's second advent to occur *after* the millennium, a long era of peace and righteous in which Christians had thoroughly Christianized society, culture, and politics. Based on this millennial call to Christianization, as Ahlstrom observed, "the 'Evangelical United Front' took up the manifold causes of moral reform, missionary advance, and humanitarian reform—with revival preaching almost always leading the way."[14] Because evangelicals became involved as partisans in many politicized causes, the always thin line between religion and politics in America became, as Noll characterized it, "virtually nonexistent."[15]

Evangelicalism was as pervasive in the antebellum intellectual world as in the social world. The evangelical worldview had two pillars. The first was the traditional Protestant doctrine of the authority, reliability, and perspicuity of scripture. The second was Scottish.Common Sense Realism, a philosophical tradition that held that human beings can have direct and reliable knowledge of reality, religious truth, and morality. Educated evangelicals of the nineteenth century used Common Sense Realism to synthesize their understandings of the Bible, science, morality, democracy, and social progress into a single worldview.[16]

The evangelicalism that entered the last half of the nineteenth century was, in the words of Ahlstrom, "extraordinarily well adapted to the popular ideals and patterns of American life."[17] But in the half century after the Civil War evangelical Protestantism also faced fundamental challenges both socially and intellectually.[18] Socially, the patterns of American life to which evangelicals had so successfully adapted were changing. Rapid industrialization and urbanization, combined with massive immigration, began shifting the center of gravity of national life away from the social world of evangelical Protestantism. Beyond the poverty and social pathologies that made the expanding cities seem dark and threatening places, the rapid growth of the Roman Catholic Church and other non-Protestant religious communities made the cities seem also alien.

While the social hegemony of evangelical Protestants was slipping away, there were also changes in the intellectual world. Evolutionary notions in biology (Darwinism) and history (Historicism and biblical criticism) undercut the stability and intelligibility of the evangelical worldview. Their religious truth was displaced from the center of intellectual life and became merely one of many non-privileged ways of making sense of the world.

The social and intellectual crises that confronted American evangelicals in the late nineteenth century can be understood as a confrontation with modernity and the process of secularization. Sociologist James Davison Hunter identified three elements of modernity as having a particular secularizing impact on American evangelicalism: functional rationality, cultural pluralism, and structural pluralism.

Functional rationality undermined the supernaturalistic basis of the evangelical worldview, especially the authority of the Bible. Cultural pluralism threatened evangelicalism's ability to provide American culture with a commonly held set of values. Structural pluralism, especially the differentiation of public and private spheres of life, helped deprive evangelicalism of a public and political role.[19] All three elements aided secularization, which sociologist Peter Berger defined as "the process by which sectors of society and culture are removed from the domination of religious institutions and symbols."[20]

This process of removal meant a profound shift in the role of evangelicals in American life, a transition from cultural insiders to cultural outsiders. How have evangelicals responded to these changes? Hunter outlined three general, but not mutually exclusive, responses of evangelicals to secularized modernity: withdrawal, accommodation, and resistance.[21]

Withdrawal, according to Hunter, involves "avoiding the confrontation with modernity entirely by refusing to participate in the modern social world and in modern culture in every way possible."[22] Withdrawal implies, of course, an acceptance of the privatization and depoliticization of religion, as well as an acceptance of an outsider identity. While total isolation is for the very few, the withdrawal response can be practiced to a lesser degree, such as by creating alternative institutions. Sociologist Nancy Ammerman observed that in their churches, otherwise modernized fundamentalists have "taken back from modernity a social territory in which to live."[23] Some degree of withdrawal or separation has always been an option for American evangelicals.

Accommodation involves revising a religious worldview and its practices in order to make it more compatible with contemporary conditions. Protestant liberalism, for example, has been willing to modify supernatural beliefs and exclusive or universal truth claims in order to keep Christianity relevant to the modern world. Its relevance, of course, has been based on persuasion or utility, rather than authority, since religion has become a private matter. There has been the danger, however, that something essential may be bargained away for the sake of relevance. But as Hunter pointed out, *any* religious group that continues to live within the social structures of modernity must inevitably practice some degree of accommodation and are to some degree modernized and secularized. Ironically, religious opponents of secularization who become involved in politics on behalf of religious values run an even greater risk of "secular contamination" by that very political activity.

The third option, religious resistance to modernity, defends supernaturalism, maintains universal and exclusive truth claims, and rejects the privatization and depoliticization of religion. But resistance is not simply conservatism, the continued adherence to traditional beliefs and practices. Traditionalism can easily take the form of withdrawal and passivity. Resistance is more active, militant, and even politically aggressive in its opposition to modernity. Resistance movements may also be less than strictly conservative in their innovative and selective use of resources within a given tradition.[24]

The fundamentalist movement of the 1920s was an example of such militant resistance to modernity by American evangelicals.[25] Or, as Marsden humorously put it, "A fundamentalist is an evangelical who is angry about something."[26] In the 1920s these "angry evangelicals" fought against modernism in the churches and Darwinism in the schools. They initially met with success. "Fundamentalism," Ammerman observed, "offered a vision of civilization restored. For a few years, early in the decade, many Protestants found that vision appealing."[27] Within a few years, however, the fundamentalists were defeated in both the churches and the schools. In the major denominations, fundamentalist factions failed to win over the less militant theological conservatives who were afraid of schism.[28] After early state and local successes, the national antievolution cause collapsed after William Jennings Bryan's humiliation at the 1925 Scopes trial. The credibility of fundamentalism also collapsed. "After 1925," wrote Ammerman, "the culture ceased taking fundamentalists seriously as social and religious reformers."[29] The fundamentalists had led evangelicalism into cultural exile.

If resistance was the most visible response of theologically conservative evangelicals to modernity in the 1920s, an uneasy mixture of withdrawal and accommodation became the dominant theme for the next several decades. Fundamentalists withdrew into a subculture based on what became an extensive alternative network of nondenominational agencies for education, missions and evangelism, publishing, and broadcasting. While some new denominations and independent congregations were established, most fundamentalists remained within the major denominations while supporting the fundamentalist network.[30]

Over the next several decades, American culture was interpreted differently by those who continued to identify themselves as fundamentalists and by those who came to call themselves neoevangelicals, and later simply evangelicals. The distinction remained fluid for decades, but fundamentalists were those who maintained a greater and more uncompromising separation from the surrounding culture. It was a style and stance suited to withdrawn and angry cultural outsiders.[31]

The neoevangelicals were also outsiders, but outsiders who "still entertained," in the words of Marsden, "at least lingering aspirations to a wider social, spiritual, and moral influence such as evangelicals had enjoyed only a generation before."[32] With hopes of regaining cultural relevance, and with it a wider audience for the fundamental truths of Christianity, the neoevangelicals were less willing to make separation from the major denominations a test of faith.[33] It was a strategy of limited affirmation and accommodation of modern American culture, but a strategy that remained wary of the "slippery slope" of liberalism. A nonbelligerent attitude of "cooperation without compromise" was, they felt, necessary for evangelism and cultural influence.[34]

It is hard to say just when and how the parting of the ways between separatist-fundamentalism and accommodationist-evangelicalism occurred, but by the 1960s the distinction was clear.[35] Whether the distinction has remained relevant is another matter. For Hunter, all but a few remnants of militant "1920s fundamentalism" have been brought into accommodationist "mainline Evangelicalism."[36] Marsden, in contrast, emphasized evangelical fragmentation over doctrine and politics since the 1960s. Neither the fundamentalists nor the neoevangelicals, nor any other faction, have been able to dominate or hold together the entire movement. "Perhaps," Marsden suggested, "it [evangelicalism] will continue to develop in the form of sympathetic parallel manifestations of related traditions."[37]

Another outgrowth of evangelicalism's confrontation with modernity was the pentecostal-charismatic movement. It has paralleled, yet until recent years has been distinct from, the fundamentalist-evangelical development I have described. Pentecostalism, with its emphasis on religious experience, can be understood, like fundamentalism, as a "conservative innovation" in response to modernity.[38] Pentecostalism, however, was rooted primarily in the Wesleyan-Methodist-Holiness stream of American evangelicalism rather than the Calvinist-Reformed background of the most prominent fundamentalist leaders. Even though pentecostals often adopted dispensationalism and stressed the literal truth of the Bible, their distinctive emphasis on the experience of Spirit Baptism and other gifts of the Spirit, as well as the enthusiastic worship style that grew out of that emphasis, made them suspect among the more doctrinally oriented and reserved evangelicals. Non-pentecostal evangelicals were particularly alarmed by the claims of some pentecostals to extra-biblical spirit-led revelation.

In addition to differences in faith and practice, the first pentecostals were not cultural insiders being displaced as the fundamentalists felt themselves to be, but outsiders from the lower levels of society.[39] So it is not surprising that pentecostals did not mimic 1920s fundamentalist resistance to modernity, but they instead anticipated and paralleled the mixture of withdrawal and accommodation practiced by other theologically conservative Protestants. The early pentecostals withdrew from other denominations into separatist sectarian organizations that encouraged indifference or hostility to the surrounding culture. Despite primitive pentecostalism's "regressive and disruptive strain," according to historian Grant Wacker, "the entire movement has undergone a slow but remarkably uniform acculturation toward the values of middle-class, mainstream Protestantism."[40] In other words, over the course of several decades the pentecostal sects became pentecostal denominations that were less hostile to, if not affirmative of, much of the surrounding culture.

Not only did pentecostals become more like other Protestants, starting in the 1960s some middle-class Protestants in mainline and non-pentecostal denominations (as well as a striking number of Catholics) adopted elements of pentecostalism's worship style, experiential emphasis, and interest in charismatic gifts. Rather than create separate denominations as the pentecostals had, the neopentecostal or charismatic movement was organized as loose decentralized networks of independent congregations, parachurch organizations, and prominent independent ministries. Like the neoevangelicals, charismatics have been unwilling to accept the role of alienated cultural outsiders and have pursued a more affirmative and accommodating stance toward American culture. Despite continuing tensions with other evangelicals and fundamentalists, the pentecostal-charismatic movement, in the words of historian Richard Quebedeaux, "finally became an acceptable minority variant within the Christian mainstream by the early 1980s."[41]

All varieties of evangelicalism experienced a popular resurgence during the 1960s and 1970s, an era marked by social and cultural upheaval. This resurgence, according to Marsden, was based on "a deeply rooted ideological spiritual heritage, vigorous institutions, skills in promotion, and an era when people were open to spiritual answers to national and personal crises."[42] Not only were there more evangelicals, but the prospering institutional network of evangelicalism possessed a new self-confidence, especially in the face the decline and disarray of the mainline Protestant churches. Given this resurgence, it was not surprising that politics once again became a matter of concern to many evangelicals.

Evangelicalism, and its constituent submovements, has displayed a variety of approaches to the political realm in the twentieth century. As I noted above, nineteenth-century evangelicals participated in a wide variety of social reform efforts. They reflected, in general, the political views, interests, and assumptions of American society as a whole.[43] In the early decades of the twentieth century, in combination with the rise of fundamentalism, what has been called the "Great Reversal" took place. This was the disappearance of the long tradition of evangelical support for progressive social reform and a clear turn toward political conservatism.[44] Sometimes this is attributed to the rising popularity among evangelicals of a pessimistic eschatology, premillennialism. Premillennialists expected that society would grow worse and worse until finally Christ returned to establish a thousand-year period of holiness described in Revelation 20. In the face of Christ's imminent return, reforming a declining and doomed society was like polishing the brass on a sinking ship. But this political change is better explained, Marsden argued, as the fundamentalist reaction to the theological liberalism of the Social Gospel movement within the major protestant denominations. Advocates of the Social Gospel or "social Christianity," such as Baptist theologian Walter Rauschenbusch, seemed to place greater emphasis on social reform projects than on saving lost souls through evangelism.[45] As revivalist Billy Sunday once put it, "We've had enough of this Godless social service nonsense."[46] This turn to political conservatism was not so much of a matter of deliberate choice but the natural result of an attempt to preserve the religion, culture, morals, and especially the individualism of late nineteenth-century America.[47]

The fundamentalists of the 1920s took their militant resistance to modernity into the political realm in a variety of ways. Prominent fundamentalist evangelists and leaders often made political pronouncements on prohibition, communism, and Catholicism.[48] Fundamentalists of the 1920s were best known for their efforts to prohibit the teaching of evolution in public schools. But after the 1925 Scopes trial decisively damaged the public and political credibility of fundamentalism, most fundamentalists withdrew to the sidelines of American political life. "Either they lapsed into political inactivity," Marsden observed, "or blended in with conservative Republicans in the North, or birthright Democrats in the South."[49]

Not all fundamentalists, however, conformed to this pattern. In the 1930s a handful of colorful fundamentalist preachers, whom Ahlstrom dubbed "apostles of discord," vehemently opposed the New Deal.[50] Of more importance were the activities and career of fundamentalist Carl McIntire, a student of the Princeton inerrantist J. Gresham Machen. Through his American Council of Christian Churches, McIntire appealed to those suspicious of liberal theology, the ecumenical movement, Catholicism, and New Deal "socialism." He made the communist conspiracy to destroy America the central concern of political fundamentalists.[51] In the 1950s, McIntire helped launch the careers of several well-known preachers who continued to warn fundamentalists of various communist plots into the 1970s.[52] While usually dismissed as the lunatic fringe, the anticommunist fundamentalists were seen by historian Richard Hofstadter as an important element in the "pseudo-conservative" coalition supporting Senator Barry Goldwater in the presidential election of 1964.[53] More important for this discussion is that McIntire and his protégés kept the flame of politicized resistance to modernity burning through decades of cultural exile.

Where the politicized fundamentalists were seen, and proudly saw themselves, as outside the pragmatic consensus of American political life, the neoevangelicals sought to accommodate that consensus and, to the extent that they could, Christianize it. Theologian Carl F. H. Henry argued, in his *The Uneasy Conscience of Modern Fundamentalism* (1947), for a return to the more transformationist stance toward culture that he thought characteristic of evangelicalism in the nineteenth century. Evangelism came first, believed Henry, but evangelism must be followed by the improvement of society.[54] While this social program may have seemed startling to apolitical fundamentalists, it was actually quite modest. The neoevangelicals, as Marsden observed, "assumed it would be a Christianized version of Republicanism."[55] *Christianity Today* and similar evangelical publications reflected a moderate to conservative politics that was well within the American mainstream.[56] Billy Graham, the most notable figure in neoevangelicalism's attempt to leave behind the angry outsider legacy of fundamentalism, associated himself with the political mainstream through a ministry to various occupants of the White House. The 1960s and 1970s saw the appearance of many books and publications urging evangelicals to become involved in politics, as well as the election of a number of openly professing evangelicals to national office, a trend that culminated in the election of Jimmy Carter to the presidency in 1976.[57]

Although, as Marty observed, "it has always been more difficult to get them into focus,"[58] pentecostals largely anticipated and paralleled the mixture of political withdrawal and accommodation practiced by most other theologically conservative Protestants in this century. Their early apolitical stance of radical withdrawal has moved steadily, as I noted above, toward accommodation of the values, including presumably the political values, of the middle-class evangelical mainstream. The more elevated social background of many in the charismatic movement was probably instrumental in lessening resistance toward political involvement.

THE NEW RIGHT AND THE CHRISTIAN RIGHT

The mobilization of various types of evangelicals on behalf of conservative political causes that began in the 1970s was rooted in a broader conservatism that became prominent with the 1964 presidential campaign of Republican Barry Goldwater. This form of conservatism was quite different from the elite intellectual conservatism that emerged in the 1940s and 1950s and the traditional "mainstreet" conservatism of midwestern Republicans. Goldwater conservatism, appealing to southern and western popular resentment against the northeastern liberal elites, "represented an insurgency," according to political analyst Kevin Phillips, "not an attempt at traditional Republican preservationism."[59]

Despite the defeat of Goldwater, the electoral recovery of populist conservatism was remarkably rapid and robust.[60] Populist conservatism grew on what Phillips called the "two decade breakdown" of the 1960s and 1970s. This breakdown involved not only social and moral upheaval but declining economic opportunity, military and diplomatic weakness, and a loss of faith in public institutions.[61] As a result, much of the middle class turned toward a "center extremism"— an ideology that, according to Phillips, "fitted neither liberal nor conservative prescriptions but linked the economics of frustration with indignant social conservatism and suspicion of rich and poor alike."[62] In a backlash against the 1960s, the center extremism of the 1970s was a "reaction of traditionalism, (white) ethnicity, pro-family sentiment and religious fundamentalism—a Counter Reformation on the heels of the Reformation."[63]

The conservative activists, such as Richard Viguerie and Paul Weyrich, who came to prominence in the 1970s by stressing these social issues called themselves the "New Right" in order to differentiate themselves from an older and less effective conservatism.[64] Though the leaders of the New Right proudly called themselves conservatives, the New Right was *not* an attempt to preserve the status quo. "Bluntly put," Phillips wrote in 1982, "we may live in a time in which conservatism cannot conserve, and so must reach back for *lost* truths and practices." Supporters of the New Right were "nostalgic nationalists" who were not interested in maintaining the status quo but were seeking to "restore the *status quo ante* of fifteen, twenty-five or even sixty years earlier."[65]

The counter reformational thrust of the New Right was especially congenial to the fundamentalist-evangelical attempt to preserve the religion, culture, and morals of late nineteenth-century America. Both fundamentalism and evangelicalism are forms of what historian Fritz Stern called "a revolutionary conservatism" that seeks "to destroy the despised present in order to recapture an idealized past in an imaginary future. . . . They sought a breakthrough to the past, and they longed for a new community in which old ideas and institutions would once again command universal allegiance."[66]

The first highly visible return of evangelicals to the political mainstream, however, was associated not with the New Right but with the election of Jimmy Carter to the presidency. While Carter received a higher proportion of evangelical support in 1976 than democratic candidates had in 1968 and 1972, his administration had alienated many evangelical voters by 1980.[67] According to Viguerie, this happened because, "Not only did the Carter administration ignore the born-again Christians, it actively and aggressively sought to hurt the Christian movement in America."[68] Particularly inflammatory was a 1978 Internal Revenue Service (IRS) policy that threatened the tax-exempt status of all-white Christian academies.[69] More generally, the stance of the Carter administration on abortion, prayer in schools, busing, the Equal Rights Amendment (ERA), gay rights, and other issues did not live up to the expectations that many evangelicals had of "one of their own."

After two generations of withdrawal and quiet accommodation, many evangelicals were, as Ammerman described it, "tired of being ignored."[70] During the 1970s, evangelicals had become involved in several grassroots New Right single-issue campaigns, such as the anti-ERA movement.[71] A turning point came in 1978 and 1979 with the formation of several organizations, most notably Moral Majority, meant to mobilize large numbers of evangelicals, especially fundamentalists, as part of a general attempt by the New Right to develop a conservative political majority, and a particular attempt to elect Ronald Reagan to the presidency in 1980.

When the Christian Right emerged as a political force, it was quickly accused of wanting to use government to impose intellectual, moral, and religious uniformity on the American people. "[T]heir declared goal," said a brochure issued by People for the American Way, "is the enactment of laws that will prohibit everything which goes against their narrow interpretation of the will of God."[72] While accusations that Jerry Falwell was a Baptist Ayatollah were clearly excessive, the Christian Right does want to use the law for moral reformation of society. The Christian Right wants to restore the public role and authority of evangelical morality and belief, values that modernity has defined as private matters with no standing in public life. Rejection of the public-private distinction, a basic feature of evangelical resistance to modernity, is the basis of what legal scholar John H. Garvey called the "offensive agenda" of the Christian Right. But, as Garvey noted, the Christian Right also has a "defensive agenda."[73]

Politicized evangelicals felt themselves to be under attack by the forces of modernity. "In other words," sociologist Nathan Glazer observed in 1982, "it is the great successes of secular and liberal forces, principally operating through the specific agency of the courts, that has in large measure created the issues on which the Fundamentalists have managed to achieve what influence they have." According to Glazer, the Christian Right saw itself as engaged in a "defensive offensive."[74] Beyond judicial decisions on school prayer and abortion, the expanding network of evangelical colleges and broadcasting enterprises had to be "defended" against interference by various regulatory agencies of the federal government. Many evangelicals felt the federal government's further expansion of the public sphere through increased regulation of education and family life had to be resisted.[75]

For the emerging movement of politicized evangelicals in alliance with the New Right, the family became an important symbol of both the idealized restorable past and what was presently under attack. The "traditional" American family, which as Hunter pointed out was really "the prototypical nineteenth-century bourgeois family," has been invested with tremendous religious, personal, social, and political meaning.[76] The "pro-family" coalition sought to defend a traditionalist concept of the family against the challenges explicit or implicit in the sexual revolution, no-fault divorce, birth control and abortion, the feminist and gay rights movements, and the recognition of children's rights, as well as the economic conditions that required many mothers to return to the work force. The "anti-family" forces, so easily identified as the product of secularist political liberalism, seemed the latest incarnation of the social and intellectual evils of modernity that had threatened evangelicalism since the late nineteenth century. The family provided evangelicals with a potent and multifaceted symbol of many of their concerns, as well as common ground with non-evangelicals on the political right.[77]

The most powerful symbol of the threat to the family was the Supreme Court's 1973 decision in *Roe v. Wade*. The emergence of abortion as a central issue for evangelicals has often been attributed to the influence of writer Francis Schaeffer, a one-time protégé of Carl McIntire. Schaeffer's many popular books provided evangelicals with a dualistic intellectual framework in which to see abortion as the inhuman end product of materialistic humanism, the antithesis of theistic Christianity.[78] Schaeffer tied together opposition to abortion, objections to secular modernity, defense of traditional evangelical morality, and the notion of America as a Christian nation in an urgent appeal to evangelicals to become involved in politics and social activism before it was too late.[79] "More than anything else," wrote evangelical scholar Ronald H. Nash, "Schaeffer's influence may have led conservative Evangelicalism to embark on a crusade to turn America around."[80]

America itself also became an important symbol of what was under attack and what must be restored, an important symbol in both the defensive and offensive agendas of the Christian Right. Like most politically conservative movements, the Christian Right was deeply concerned with the international threat of communism. But America, according to the Christian Right, was also under attack internally through moral and religious corruption. An ever-growing litany of national sins was recited by leaders of the Christian Right in their jeremiad for the 1980s. This litany was followed by a call for national repentance and a renewal of traditional morality through political involvement. Not a few observers of the Christian Right were struck by the irony, if not the flat contradiction, of premillennialist preachers, such as Falwell, trying to "save" America through politics rather than merely awaiting the imminent return of Christ. If anything, the logic of premillennialism dictated an outsider role in relation to a culture and a political system that was about to be destroyed by God's wrath. Perhaps, as Marsden suggested, premillennialism was not the decisive influence on the attitudes of Christian Right evangelicals toward American culture and politics. What was at work was a deeper insider identification with American culture.[81]

The Christian Right's jeremiad was based on the memory of evangelicalism's lost cultural dominance. "All but the most radically alienated fundamentalists," in the words of Wacker, "have embraced the notion that Christians, especially evangelical Christians, ought to be the moral custodians of the culture."[82] This custodial ideal is most clearly expressed in Christian Right appeals to notions of a national covenant with God, Deuteronomic interpretations of American history, and depictions of evangelicals as a faithful saving remnant. According to evangelical authors Peter Marshall and David Manuel, "Our forefathers have broken the trail for us, and shown the way. Their call *is* our call. If just a fraction of us Americans choose to go the Covenant Way, it will suffice."[83] This restoration of a covenanted Christian America has been one of the most durable, consistent, and politically troublesome themes in Christian Right literature. It has also been at the heart of the Christian Right's "revolutionary conservatism"—the recapture of an idealized past in an imaginary future.

The emergence of the Christian Right was not expected by observers of religion and politics in America. "Of all the shifts and surprises in contemporary political life," wrote political scientist Kenneth Wald, "perhaps none was so unexpected as the political resurgence of evangelical Protestantism in the 1970s."[84] The surprise of its rapid emergence, as well as the rhetoric of figures such as Falwell, stimulated the formation of a network of organizations and activists critical of the Christian Right. The rhetoric of opponents of the Christian Right has sometimes been as strident and apocalyptic as the fundamentalist-style political preaching being denounced.[85] Such shrill public discourse may have led to a generally negative public perception of the Christian Right, despite some sympathy for many of its social and moral concerns.[86]

Social scientists have developed various ways of explaining support for the organizations of the Christian Right. Political scientist Clyde Wilcox enumerated the basic explanations as personality, alienation, social status, symbolic politics, belief and value congruity, politicized group consciousness, and resource mobilization theories. He conceded that any of these explanations may be useful in understanding the motives of individuals. But Wilcox drew the general conclusion that supporters of Christian Right groups "are those who find the religious and political values and positions expressed by the groups congruent with their own." Support for the Christian Right should be understood with the rational-choice perspective that was used to explain support for any other political group or movement. Wilcox was particularly critical of those explanations that portray support for the Christian Right as the irrational product of psychological maladjustment or social-status anxiety. He found little empirical evidence to support these explanations, which often have been used to discredit that movement.[87]

Political scientist Matthew Moen argued that certain scholarly interpretations of the Christian Right contributed to popular suspicion of the movement. Some scholarship, often mimicked by journalists, understood the Christian Right as the creation of manipulative televangelists rather than the product of popular discontent. This "top down" explanatory mechanism also led to the mistaken expectation that the movement would disappear if certain leaders were discredited or withdrew from politics. Another stream of scholarship regarded the Christian Right as the product of the authoritarian personality tendencies of its supporters. "The larger point," according to Moen, "is that Christian Right was placed very early into established frameworks that often reflected a liberal understanding of the conservative mindset." The concerns of Christian Right supporters were explained away rather than "taken at face value."[88]

Making a similar point, historian Alan Brinkley noted, "The resurgence of right-wing fundamentalism in the United States has unsettled many liberal and left-oriented scholars because it has seemed to contradict some of their most basic assumptions about modern society." Despite substantial evidence to the contrary, the supporters of the Christian Right have been depicted "as a group somehow left behind by the modern world—economically, culturally, psychologically—

expressing frustration at their isolation and failure."[89] The political activity of theologically conservative evangelicals has been seen as a temporary, and ultimately futile, irrational, and illegitimate rebellion against secularization and modernization.

British sociologist of religion Steve Bruce, for example, argued that the failure of the Christian Right is inevitable because what it objects to about the modern world (particularly the secularity of the public realm) "is a near-inevitable consequence of cultural pluralism in a democratic industrial society." There is, Bruce argued, a fundamental conflict between an exclusivist approach to religion and the inclusivism necessary for success in American coalition politics. Because of the exclusivism of adherents of the Christian Right, potential Catholic, Jewish, and secular allies have remained suspicious. The only way to create cooperative alliances across religious lines has been to treat specific religious beliefs as a private matter.[90] Falwell, for instance, described Moral Majority as "a political organization providing a platform for religious and nonreligious Americans who share moral values to address their moral concerns in these areas. Members of Moral Majority, Inc. have no common theological premise."[91] For the sake of political success, Falwell was willing to accept the public-private distinction regarding religion—a feature of modernity that the Christian Right fundamentally rejects. Such an essential contradiction disappoints and disillusions movement adherents, Bruce argued, and makes the evangelical-fundamentalist venture into politics unsustainable.

Bruce excluded the possibility that the Christian Right may work out some tolerable degree of accommodation to cultural and structural pluralism within the context of its basic resistance to modernity. Bruce seemed to assume that modernity must be accepted or rejected as a whole. The adherents of the Christian Right, in his view, have been too rigid to adapt to, or compromise with, certain features of modernity, while rejecting others outright. Bruce therefore expected an inevitable, if not imminent, collapse of the Christian Right.

If we accept Bruce's interpretation, the demonstrated ability of the Christian Right to rise repeatedly from the deathbed of political failure is quite inexplicable. Moen, in contrast, offered a framework within which we can understand change within the Christian Right as well as its persistence. His central argument was that "the Christian Right has gradually reconciled and adjusted itself to the secular norms and practices of American politics."[92] (It is a reconciliation that has not, at least in the short term, required the modification of religious beliefs and morals.) He traced this transformation of the Christian Right through three periods of development.

The first, or expansionist, period lasted from the inception of Christian Right organizations in 1978 until 1984. During this period of rapid growth and high public visibility, figures such as Falwell of Moral Majority and "God's Angry Man," James Robison of Religious Roundtable, influenced the political agenda by bringing moral and family issues to the forefront of public discussion. Despite its influence, the Christian Right failed to get much of its legislative agenda enacted and did not seem to secure much more than rhetorical support from the Reagan administration. Moen attributed this to their "political amateurishness"—a lack of adjustment to the norms and practices of politics. During this period the heavily fundamentalist leadership of the movement made overt religious appeals with strong moralistic overtones. While this strident rhetoric was apparently attractive to a core of supporters, it may have alienated many other evangelicals and confirmed the claims of opponents of the Christian Right.[93]

In 1985-1986, the Christian Right, according to Moen, went through a period of transition and retrenchment. Almost every major organization of the expansionist period faded from public view or folded entirely. The direct-mail base upon which these organizations depended was eroded by an ironic combination of early success in setting the political agenda and tactical blunders by Christian Right leaders. The donor base also may have been weary of constant appeals for money. Organizational retrenchment brought lower public visibility and less ability to influence the public agenda. Some observers wrote obituaries for the Christian Right. But retrenchment was actually the beginning of what Moen calls a "strategic reorientation."[94]

The third period was one of institutionalization. By 1987 leaders of the Christian Right had, according to Moen, "examined their mistakes, assessed the existing political situation, commissioned polls to outline appropriate strategy, and then restructured the movement in major ways." The "retooled" Christian Right, according to Moen, had four characteristics. First, Christian Right organizations have moved toward financial stability by establishing themselves as genuine membership organizations, rather than relying on direct mail to raise funds. Second, the constituency of the Christian Right has expanded beyond the fundamentalist core of the early movement to a "greater representation of theological orientations." Third, the Christian Right's discussion of issues has been recast in the more inclusive liberal rhetoric of "rights," "equal access," and "discrimination." Fourth, the Christian Right has reoriented itself to grassroots political activity, particularly in school boards and the local-state structures of the Republican party.[95]

According to Moen, this newly institutionalized Christian Right "has adjusted itself to the traditional practices of American politics." While the difficulty of balancing religious purity and political pragmatism will remain, the ability of the Christian Right to change and adapt probably means that this movement will be with us for some time.[96]

The CC, as I will demonstrate below, has clearly attempted to institutionalize the Christian Right. Pat Robertson's campaign for the Republican presidential nomination in 1988, according to Moen's chronology, should be part of the period of institutionalization. But I think this campaign, and the candidate himself, is better understood in terms of transition and strategic reorientation.

CHAPTER 3

ROBERTSON
AND REED

PAT ROBERTSON AND RALPH REED, the two men who have stood at the center of the CC, are very different individuals. They are of different generations and social backgrounds. One is a religious leader who turned to politics, while the other is a political operative who became religious. When Robertson ran for president, Reed backed another candidate. Despite the unlikely nature of their partnership, they share the experience of having their lives unexpectedly transformed by what they understand as a personal encounter with Jesus Christ. And more importantly, they share that experience with millions of other Americans—millions who Robertson and Reed hope will come to agree with their politics as well as their faith.

PAT ROBERTSON

Marion Gordon "Pat" Robertson,[1] the founder of the CC, was born in Lexington, Virginia, on March 22, 1930. He was the second son of A. Willis Robertson, a conservative Democrat from Virginia who served in the U.S. House of Representatives (1932-1946) and in the U.S. Senate (1946-1966). Raised as a Southern Baptist by his devout mother, he graduated magna cum laude from Washington and Lee University in 1950 with a reputation as a young man who knew how to party. After service as a Lieutenant in the Marine Corps from 1950 to 1952 in Korea,

Robertson earned a J.D. from Yale Law School in 1955. He did not, however, pass the New York State bar examination. During a brief and disappointing business career in New York City, Robertson found his life meaningless and empty. In April 1956, Robertson had a conversion experience, and within a few months he decided to go into the ministry. He attended The Biblical Seminary (now called New York Theological Seminary), a small evangelical school in New York City. After graduating in May 1959 with a Bachelor of Divinity degree, Robertson began a brief ministry to the poor in the Bedford-Stuyvesant section of Brooklyn. Robertson returned to Virginia and in 1960 was ordained a Southern Baptist minister.

In 1961 he started WYAH-TV in Norfolk; it was quite possibly the first television station completely devoted to religious programming. Despite financial, technical, and personnel problems during its early years, Robertson built his one dilapidated station into the nonprofit tax-exempt Christian Broadcasting Network (CBN). Its success was based on the generous financial donations of viewers during periodic telethons, as well as on Robertson's shrewd management. Since 1966, Robertson has also served as the host of CBN's flagship program, *The 700 Club.* Expanding on the success of CBN, Robertson has created what has often been described as an "empire" of business, ministry, and educational projects, including a relief agency, a successful commercial cable TV channel, and Regent University, an accredited graduate school with programs in communications, business, counseling, theology, education, law, and public policy.[2]

When Robertson decided to run for president, he was not initially considered a serious candidate for the 1988 Republican nomination, but his surprising strength in the February 8, 1988, Iowa caucuses established him as a national political figure. However, within weeks Robertson was soundly defeated in a succession of primaries, and he was forced to end his campaign. Robertson returned to *The 700 Club* and leadership of CBN, but he did not abandon involvement in politics. He supported the Republican nominee, Vice President George Bush, in the general election. In 1989 he founded the CC and hired Ralph Reed as its executive director. As I will show, the CC has grown rapidly and established itself as a major political organization.

Robertson's religion has been hard to characterize. He has been called, with varying degrees of justification, a pentecostal, a charismatic, an evangelical, and a fundamentalist. He was raised as a Southern

Baptist, an experience that he later described as "primarily social, not spiritual."[3] Much to his mother's dismay, Robertson apparently gave little thought to religion during his Marine Corps and Yale Law School years. Robertson described his experience with the "legal realism" of the Yale faculty as deeply disillusioning.[4] He attributed his failure of the Bar examination to this disillusionment. "Looking back now," wrote Robertson in 1986, "I wonder if it could have been my way to register a protest against what had happened to the historical roots of the entire legal system."[5]

In April 1956, while trying to start his own electronics business in New York City, he encountered Cornelius Vanderbreggen, a fundamentalist minister and a friend of Robertson's mother. This meeting triggered Robertson's conversion experience, and within a few months Robertson left the business world for the ministry. While at seminary, Robertson came into contact with leaders of the neopentecostal, or charismatic renewal, movement. He avidly pursued and finally experienced various gifts of the Holy Spirit, including glossolalia, the gift of "speaking in tongues." Historian David Edwin Harrell saw this as the key period in Robertson's religious formation. "During the three-year period from 1956 to 1959," wrote Harrell, "when Pat Robertson attended The Biblical Seminary and migrated from casual Christian, to fervent evangelical, to pioneering charismatic, his fundamental religious personality was formed."[6]

Robertson, however, in my opinion, should not be described as a pentecostal. He never joined any of the traditional pentecostal denominations but instead was ordained a Southern Baptist minister. His background, son of a U.S. Senator and a Yale Law graduate, can be considered an excellent example of how the charismatic movement was socially different from traditional pentecostalism. Robertson's innovative television ministry also demonstrates the charismatic movement's greater willingness to adapt to contemporary culture.

Robertson's *The 700 Club* was originally a Christian talk show that emphasized charismatic worship and teaching, with on-air demonstrations of gifts of the spirit. Since 1980, the show has evolved toward a magazine format presenting what is referred to as "news from a Christian perspective."[7] *The 700 Club*, however, has retained an emphasis on divine healing and other miracles. Robertson's particular *charismata* has been the "word of knowledge." Robertson has offered on-air prayers during which he has discerned information about healings or miracles in the lives of unnamed viewers. Books authored or coauthored by Robertson have also promoted charismatic belief in miracles, healings, and divine intervention.[8]

Yet his affirmation of the supernatural has been shaped by a thoroughly pragmatic approach to spirituality. He has explained the miraculous and the spiritual in terms of a rationally understood system of laws that are "as valid for our lives as the laws of thermodynamics."[9] Those who apply these laws will find success, happiness, prosperity, health.[10] These universal spiritual laws are to be discovered in the Bible, which Robertson described as "a workable guidebook for politics, government, business, families, and all the affairs of mankind."[11] Robertson's attempt to rationalize the supernatural reflects a widespread tendency in evangelicalism to accommodate the cognitive style of modernity.[12]

Despite clear justification for regarding Robertson as a charismatic, it should be noted that he no longer identifies himself publicly as such.[13] In 1982, for instance, Robertson described himself as "an evangelical who believes in the gifts of the Holy Spirit."[14] Whatever his inner convictions, as a religious broadcaster with a national and international audience, and as a political figure with national ambitions, Robertson has probably found it wiser to avoid intra-Christian particularism as much as possible.

Robertson has often been called a "fundamentalist," but this is really a misuse of the term. He can be considered "fundamentalist-like" because of his militant resistance to the secularizing features of modernity.[15] But popular usage of the term "fundamentalist" is seldom so nuanced. More often, especially in Robertson's case, it is used as a pejorative label for political purposes. Robertson does not identify himself as such, and the hard core of "classic" fundamentalists— inerrantist, separatist, and Baptist—would be profoundly suspicious of Robertson's charismatic "word of knowledge" extra-biblical revelations. Fundamentalist suspicion of Robertson has affected the political support Robertson has been able to gather. Based on surveys conducted during the 1988 primaries, political scientist Clyde Wilcox observed: "Those who attended fundamentalist Baptist churches—the core base of the Moral Majority—were less supportive of Robertson than other whites."[16]

The best reason to regard Robertson as an evangelical is his active involvement in the transdenominational evangelical network. Beyond Robertson's participation in events sponsored by evangelical figures such as Billy Graham and Bill Bright, his daily TV program, *The 700 Club,* has evolved into a public forum for evangelicals of all types, not just for charismatics. Robertson's movement toward this broader self-identification was carried out in the context of a greater general acceptance of pentecostals and charismatics by other evangelicals since the late 1970s. Like many evangelicals, Robertson is a premillennialist who expects an imminent and literal fulfillment of biblical end-time prophecies. "I firmly expect to be alive," he wrote in 1984, "when Jesus Christ comes back to earth."[17] In fact, between 1977 and 1982, Robertson's sense of expectation was so strong that it led him, according to historian Mark G. Toulouse, "to predict that events leading to the end of the world would more than likely begin in earnest in the fall of 1982."[18]

While his expectations about 1982 were disconfirmed, Robertson has continued to expect end-time events to unfold in a particular sequence foretold in scripture. This raised fears during his presidential campaign that, if elected, Robertson would use his power to bring about the fulfillment of prophecy, even to the point of instigating a nuclear war.[19] It should be noted that, unlike most premillennialists, Robertson believes in a post-tribulation rapture.[20] According to this view, Christians will have to live through the sufferings of the seven-year tribulation on Earth before they reign with Christ on Earth during the millennium. Thus a "post-trib" President Robertson probably would not want to incinerate the planet with nuclear weapons.

Robertson also believes that the current behavior of American Christians, the remnant that has held fast to the national covenant with God, will mitigate the tribulation.

> Yet God in my feeling is not going to judge America as harshly as He might because of the large numbers of Christians. Because of His elect in this nation He is going to spare the nation the kind of judgement that some of the activities might deserve.[21]

Therefore, it has been the duty of "His elect" to spread the gospel and to work for as righteous a social-political order in America as possible during whatever time is left. Robertson has been characterized as postmillennial in terms of his practice, but has remained premillennial in his theology and in his basic assumptions.[22]

Robertson's turn to politics came through a long and uneven process. As the son of a U.S. senator, he was exposed to politics throughout his early life. He expected to follow in his father's footsteps and run for public office after practicing law.[23] But after his religious conversion, Robertson rejected involvement in politics and refused, on the basis of divine guidance, to become involved in his father's unsuccessful reelection campaign in 1966.[24]

By the mid-1970s, however, he displayed a renewed interest in politics and social issues. Like many evangelicals, he was initially hopeful about the candidacy of the born-again Jimmy Carter in 1976, but deeply disappointed with Carter as president.[25] In the late 1970s, Robertson edged toward politics. In 1978 he was involved in an unsuccessful attempt to make his friend G. Conoly Philips the Virginia Democratic Party's nominee for a U.S. Senate seat.[26] A year later, Robertson told *U.S. News & World Report* that, counting both Catholics and Protestants, "we have enough votes to run the country. And when the people say, 'We've had enough,' we are going to take over."[27] On April 29, 1980, Robertson served as cochairman of the "Washington for Jesus" rally, an event that drew hundreds of thousands of participants to the Washington, D.C., mall.[28] Speakers included a wide array of evangelical leaders, although not Billy Graham, Oral Roberts, or Jerry Falwell.[29] While its organizers denied at the time that it was a political event, Robertson, who also disavowed any political purpose, described the assembled Christians as "the great silent majority."[30] And in 1986, Robertson called the "Washington for Jesus" rally "the beginning of a spiritual revolution" that he hoped "would sweep the nation."[31]

The possibilities of a Christian political movement may have been clear to Robertson at "Washington for Jesus,"[32] but his involvement in Christian Right politics in the early 1980s was inconsistent. In 1980 he resigned from the board of directors of Religious Roundtable, a prominent early Christian Right organization, and severed all formal connection to Christian Right organizations.[33] Also in 1980, Robertson was quoted by *Newsweek* as a critic of evangelical politics. "God isn't a right-winger or a left-winger," he said. "There's a better way. Fasting and praying . . . appealing, in essence, to a higher power."[34]

There are several possible explanations for this political retreat. Robertson was apparently expecting the premillennial tribulation to begin in 1982. "[A]t least for the next couple of years," wrote Robertson in 1980 to supporters of CBN, "the church of Jesus Christ should concentrate on the salvation of the lost, rather than taking over temporal political power."[35] Perhaps Robertson, known as a charismatic, had difficulty working with the heavily fundamentalist leadership of the early 1980s Christian Right. And quite possibly, he found these leaders to be naive sheep among the political wolves. "The evangelists," he told *Newsweek,* "stand in danger of being used and manipulated."[36] Harrell argued that Robertson remained sympathetic to the Christian Right but wished to distance himself from their mistakes in order to preserve his own political future.[37]

The idea that Robertson was sympathetic but playing a waiting game has merit. Throughout the 1980s, *The 700 Club* was a valuable and consistent forum for Christian Right figures.[38] In 1981 Robertson created his own nonpartisan political organization, The Freedom Council. Unlike Moral Majority, The Freedom Council was intended as a low-profile, grassroots organization. Appealing to evangelical Christians, its mission was to "encourage, train, equip Americans to exercise their civil responsibility to actively participate in government."[39] The Freedom Council only existed for five years, but it has sometimes been seen as laying the groundwork for Robertson's presidential campaign.[40]

Rumors that Robertson would run for president surfaced as early as 1980.[41] According to Robertson's 1989 book *The Plan,* in the summer of 1984 "numerous conservative, highly-placed friends" began urging him to run for president. He also wrote that he was resistant to the idea even after he began to believe it was God's will.[42] Also in 1984, Robertson changed his party registration to Republican and attended the Republican national convention in Dallas.[43] In 1985, a supportive article in *The Saturday Evening Post* launched his unofficial candidacy and depicted him as a successful broadcasting executive who would be a natural successor to Ronald Reagan.[44] He officially entered the race on October 1, 1987, after supporters supposedly gathered 3.3 million signatures on a petition urging him to run.[45] While Robertson scored some early successes, he was out of the race after the "Super Tuesday" primaries on March 8, 1988.

Robertson's campaign can be understood as part of what Moen termed the transition, retrenchment, and strategic reorientation of the Christian Right in the mid-1980s. Reed once described Robertson as "a midwife that took what was largely a social protest movement and transformed it into a political movement that elects candidates."[46] In short, the Robertson campaign exemplified the painful transition from political amateurishness toward political sophistication.

Not only was Robertson a first-time candidate, many of his supporters were quite literally political amateurs—people who got involved in their first political campaign out of ideological or religious enthusiasm. This enthusiasm, however, proved offensive to many party regulars.[47] The campaign itself seemed an amateur production because of its many self-inflicted wounds. Robertson's unusual beliefs and assertions, alleged misrepresentations in his campaign biography, war record, and associations with scandal-ridden television evangelists led the campaign to take a defensive, if not adversarial, posture in relation to the news media.[48] As journalist Garry Wills observed, "What slickness the campaign has tends to undo itself out of distrust for the rest of the world."[49] On a deeper level, the inability of the Robertson campaign to reach beyond its base constituency of charismatics and pentecostals to other evangelicals was a fundamental failure.[50] Most important, despite efforts to "repackage" Robertson as a conservative Christian business-man,[51] there was a lack of realism about the candidate. Robertson had such consistently high negative ratings in opinion polls that expectations of success must have been based on a faith in miracles.[52]

Yet the Robertson campaign did display some important indications of increasing sophistication among politicized evangelicals. Robertson made a substantial effort to present the full array of policy positions expected of a serious presidential candidate. While Robertson's positions—fiscal conservatism, an aggressively anti-Communist national defense, tax relief for families, sweeping welfare and education reform, and getting tough on drugs and crime—centered around his notion of morality, his standard stump speech did not use biblical citations and tried to maintain a Reaganesque optimism.[53] The organizational and financial effort to mount a presidential campaign was a quantum leap in complexity beyond anything the Christian Right had previously attempted. While Robertson's organization could not in the end outdo Bush's party regulars, it did much better than expected and, in fact, better than several other Republican campaigns.[54] Contrary to expectations, the Robertson campaign did its best in caucus contests in which careful local organization was important.[55] And as Wilcox observed, "his campaign succeeded in establishing footholds in state party committees throughout the country."[56] Ironically, the failure of the Robertson campaign demonstrated what sociologist Jeffrey K. Hadden called, "an enormous progression to political sophistication" among politically conservative evangelicals. Rather than giving their support to Robertson, the longshot "Christian" candidate, most evangelicals backed more electable "secular" candidates during the primaries.[57]

This brief summary of the successes and failures of his campaign has not done justice to the strong passions elicited by Robertson's candidacy. For his strongest supporters, the campaign was a labor of love, a virtual crusade for God and country.[58] Yet Robertson's opponents seemed to view his campaign as a threat to American freedom and democracy. For example, Robertson's speech formally announcing his candidacy was shouted down by protesters who carried signs such as "Hitler in '39, Robertson in '88."[59]

These polarized responses can be understood by examining the fundamental theme of the Robertson campaign: "Restore the Greatness of America Through Moral Strength."[60] For Robertson, morality meant self-restraint and immorality meant self-indulgence.[61] These notions of morality and immorality were clearly linked to religion. In 1982 he described the contemporary "tailspin in morality" as the emergence of the "antichrist spirit." "[T]he people in a society begin to throw off the restraints of history," wrote Robertson, "then the restraints of written law, then accepted standards of morality, then established religion, and, finally, God Himself."[62] Restoration of morality functioned as a "code word" for the restoration of religion. Both his supporters and his opponents seemed to understand that he was not only calling merely for a renewal of traditional morality, but a restoration of "Christian America."

This was clear in Robertson's 1986 jeremiad, *America's Dates With Destiny*. In the first section, "Beginning Our Journey," he outlined "the central role of Christian faith and biblical truth" in early American history.[63] According to Robertson, because of the spiritual commitment of the founders, God blessed America with freedom, prosperity, and strength. But in the second section, "Losing Our Way," he described the abandonment of that spiritual commitment, the withdrawal of God's blessing, and the consequent slide into irreligion, immorality, social anarchy, and national impotence. "Can we endure," Robertson asked rhetorically, "if we forsake the God of our fathers and strip from the national consciousness the teachings of the Holy Bible?"[64] Robertson blamed America's tragic decline on the unchecked influence of a tiny minority of secular humanists and political liberals. In the third and final section, "Finding Our Way Again," Robertson argued that, like the biblical Israelites, our only hope for the renewal of God's blessings was through national repentance and a return to righteousness. Repentance should take the form of evangelical involvement in politics before it was too late.[65]

With this redemptive understanding of American history, it was not surprising that Robertson was repeatedly asked about his views of church-state relations. When asked on *Meet the Press* in 1985 if he believed in the separation of church and state, he said simply and without qualification, "Certainly."[66] In another 1985 interview, he held that government and the church, "as an institution," should not influence one another. "But I do think there should be moral influences, and I do think that those who are deeply dedicated, religious people of all faiths should be involved in the governmental process. I certainly don't think the Constitution in any way intended to protect the government from religion."[67]

Robertson recognized the widespread fear that he would use the power of government to force people to accept religious values. "I would never," he told *U.S. News and World Report* in 1986, "see the power of the sword—the secular state—being used to enforce spiritual values on people."[68] He even resigned his ministerial ordination and left his post at CBN in an attempt to placate those who believed that the election of a clergyman would be "tantamount to a preference of one religious denomination over all others."[69] "The president," he told *USA Today* in 1986, "is the president of all the people."[70]

Yet other statements by Robertson during his campaign were not so reassuring to those who were wary of him. In a key speech at Washington's Constitution Hall, September 17, 1986, he pointed to a public, if not a political, role for religion. The founders, he argued, "knew all too well that there was only one source of our liberty." He then quoted Washington, "Reason and experience forbid us to expect public morality in the absence of religious principle." Robertson called current church-state jurisprudence "a tortured view of the establishment of religion clause" and an "intellectual scandal." He also urged his listeners, "For the sake of our children, we must bring God back to the classrooms of America." While atheists have "every right of citizenship," Robertson did not believe that "the ninety-four percent of us who believe in God have any duty whatsoever to dismantle our entire public affirmation of faith in God just to please a tiny minority who don't believe in anything."[71]

Statements Robertson had made on *The 700 Club* also excited fears that he did not believe in religious equality. For example, on January 11, 1985, he said, "Individual Christians are the only ones really—and Jewish people, those who trust the God of Abraham, Isaac and Jacob—are the only ones that are qualified to have the reign, because hopefully they will be governed by God and submitted to him."[72] When a co-host

asked if he was saying that only Christians and Jews were qualified to
be in government, Robertson said, "Yeah, I'm saying that. I just said that.
You can quote me." He later explained that he said this as a minister
rather than as a candidate for president.[73]

Robertson's dual personas were reflected in a common reaction
to his church-state views. As the *Wall Street Journal* put it in 1986, "Mr.
Robertson's message is different when addressing broader audiences
than when addressing his narrower Christian constituency."[74] To opponents such as Jim Castelli of People for the American Way, it was "clear
that Robertson pays lip service to 'the separation of church and state'
while simultaneously trying to smear the concept as a communistic
notion."[75] Even potential allies had their doubts. Secretary of Education
and prominent conservative William J. Bennett told Robertson in a letter,
"I am not alone in sensing some ambiguity in your position on the role
of religion in politics."[76]

This ambiguity was also present in his typical answer when asked
if the United States was a Christian nation. "It used to be, but it's not
anymore. I don't think anybody realistically expects it to become one
anytime soon."[77] On one level, Robertson was trying to reassure voters
by saying that he would not attempt to impose his religion on America.
On a more implicit level, this remark makes two things clear: 1) America
was at one time a Christian nation, even though it is not anymore; and,
2) America really *ought* to be a Christian nation in the future, even though
it would not be realistic to expect that anytime soon.[78] Robertson, as one
campaign volunteer told the *New York Times,* was working "to return
America to what it's supposed to be."[79]

Robertson is what I have called a "revolutionary conservative."
He has called for the restoration of an "idealized past in an imaginary
future." This apparently struck a responsive cord among those who, in
the words of Fritz Stern, "despised the present."[80] As Richard Cizik of
the National Association of Evangelicals observed, "Those who follow
Robertson tend to feel discriminated against. They have a bunker
mentality. They feel modernity is against them—in matters dealing with
sex, crime, pornography, education."[81] Indeed, as I will show, the
accusation of religious discrimination, or "anti-Christian bigotry," was
a consistent and essential theme of his campaign.

This became apparent in early 1986 when Democratic National
Committee Chairman, Paul G. Kirk, Jr., sent out a fund-raising letter
attacking Robertson's "extremist values and views." Robertson in turn

accused Kirk of "virulent anti-Christian bigotry."[82] Besides the Democrats, Robertson also accused People for the American Way of attacking him in order to "destroy all the faith and all the beliefs of the evangelical people in this country."[83] On several occasions, he drew parallels between the anti-Catholic sentiment in the 1960 presidential campaign and his own situation. During the 1988 Iowa caucus campaign, Robertson told supporters, "What they said in 1960 about Kennedy was bigotry. What's being said about me in 1988 is bigotry."[84]

I have already noted Robertson's difficulties with the news media, so it is not surprising that he charged, "There's an incredible amount of religious bigotry . . . anti-Christian bigotry in the press."[85] Robertson felt reporters were fixated on his religion and gave little serious attention to his entire record or policy views.[86] In 1988, NBC's Tom Brokaw asked Robertson if he was being guided by "God's advice" in his presidential campaign as he had been when he was a television evangelist. Robertson said the question reflected "religious bigotry."[87] A consistent point of conflict was Robertson's insistence that he be called a "religious broadcaster," not a "television evangelist."[88] Few media outlets acceded to this request. Writers on the op-ed pages of the *New York Times* made a special point of continuing to call him a "televangelist" or a "TV evangelist."[89] An upset Robertson told a *Newsweek* reporter in 1988, "It's like calling a black man a nasty word that begins with an 'N'. . . . It is this incredible arrogance of the liberal media and guys like you who . . . label me contrary to my desires."[90]

Robertson was not the only presidential candidate in 1988 to have bad relations with the news media. Colorado Senator Gary Hart's campaign, for instance, was effectively ended by press reports of an extramarital affair. And Vice President George Bush got in a verbal shoving match on national television with CBS anchorman Dan Rather. While Robertson's adversarial relationship with the press probably limited his ability to reach the broader electorate, Robertson's battles with the media seemed to strengthen his connection with some voters. One woman told *Newsweek*, "What turned me on to Pat is that the press seemed so against him."[91] I would argue that when the press seemed to mock Robertson's religion, those who shared his beliefs also felt ridiculed. Resentment against the news media was a staple of Robertson's campaign. Crowds would come roaring to their feet when Robertson ended speeches with, "Give me the chance to see the look on Dan Rather's face when he has to say, 'Pat Robertson won Iowa.'"[92]

Robertson and his supporters also felt unwelcome within the Republican Party. Party regulars were quoted in the press as calling Robertson supporters "Fascists," "Nazis," "wackos," "Robertson Moonies," "right-wing religious nuts," and "scary."[93] Robertson alleged "Watergate style underhanded tricks" and pointed to "anti-Christian bashing that is going on by the Bush forces—such things as calling evangelicals 'cockroaches.'"[94] At one point, Robertson accused the Bush campaign of leaking news of the scandal surrounding fellow "televangelist" Jimmy Swaggart in order to hurt Robertson's chances in upcoming primaries.[95]

Although Robertson was clearly angry over his treatment by Democrats, liberals, the news media, and other Republicans, their supposed "bigotry" may have provided Robertson with confirmation of the righteousness of his cause. In 1984 Robertson wrote, "But we must recognize also that the devil and his emissaries despise Christians. . . . Persecution is simply part of living as a Christian in this world."[96] *Newsweek,* I would argue, was only partly correct in 1988 when it observed that, "His [Robertson's] skill at playing the victim is almost unrivaled in public life."[97] Claiming victimhood was probably not a mere exercise of acting skill for Robertson. Facing the contempt of the "world" was a part of his identity and that of his supporters, and an experience that helped to bind them together. As one campaign worker told *Charisma* magazine in 1988, "Christians are the only people in this country who are persecuted. It's time we stand up and be heard."[98]

Given Robertson's emphasis on persecution, his denunciations of "liberal elites," and his apocalyptic calls for action, he can easily be seen as a populist practitioner of what historian Richard Hofstadter called "the paranoid style of American politics."[99] Some of Robertson's public policy ideas are unusual, such as his suggestion, based on the biblical "year of Jubilee," that all debts be canceled and accumulated property be redistributed each fifty years to prevent the excessive concentration of wealth.[100] And he does indeed demonstrate many of the characteristics of earlier populist movements in American history. It would be, however, a mistake to dismiss him as a "crackpot populist."[101] Political scientist Allen D. Hertzke found in Robertson's harsh moralistic critique of elite-led secularization an important expression of deep popular discontent with the direction American culture has taken.[102] The small but dedicated following Robertson gathered in 1988, as journalist William Schneider put it, "show that there are causes and resentments that lie beyond the boundaries of a carefully managed national consensus. Attention must be paid."[103] Robertson's subsequent involvement in politics has seemed directed toward getting that attention. Some observers felt that Robertson had never really been running for president, but for leadership of the Christian Right.[104] There were also hints that Robertson's purposes were much more ambitious. In 1986 Robertson told the *National Review,* "The overall secularization of society . . . [is] an issue on which none of us has ever had a vote. Evangelicals are going to *put* it on the agenda."[105] "This campaign is not a one-shot attempt to win one office," said a Robertson campaign official in 1988, "though that is the focal point of our efforts. It is designed to start a permanent restructuring of American politics, especially Republican politics. There are a lot of folks out there who want to reclaim control over their lives and their government. And we're determined to help them succeed."[106] After his defeat in the "Super Tuesday" primaries, Robertson told reporters, "We are going to place Pat Robertson people on city councils, school boards and legislatures all over this country. . . . That's His plans for me and for this nation."[107]

In some ways those plans have succeeded through the CC. But before I examine the structure and activities of that organization, I need to discuss the CC's other guiding personality.

RALPH REED

The Executive Director of the CC, Ralph Eugene Reed, Jr.,[108] was born on June 24, 1961, in Portsmouth, Virginia. Due to his father's career as a U.S. Navy flight surgeon, the Reed family moved repeatedly. Reed grew up in such places as Miami, Florida, Louisville, Kentucky, and Toccoa, Georgia. "Buddy," as he was nicknamed, was raised as a Methodist by Republican parents who voted for Goldwater and Reagan. He showed an early and intense interest in history and politics. When a reporter asked Reed's mother what her son had always wanted to be, she said, "In charge."[109]

Reed attended the University of Georgia from 1979 to 1983 and was active in campus Republican politics. He also wrote a weekly political column for the college newspaper. "He was a fire-eating Republican," recalled one fellow staffer in 1993, "on the far right of every issue. But he was provocative and entertaining, like Rush Limbaugh today."[110] Reed later described himself as "a libertarian, an economic conservative, and a low-tax activist."[111] His politics led him to the campus chairmanship of the College Republicans, and eventually to a statewide leadership position in that organization.

Reed did volunteer work in 1980 for Ronald Reagan's presidential campaign and for Mack Mattingly, the Republican nominee for a U.S. Senate seat in Georgia. In the summer of 1981, Reed served as a Senate intern for Mattingly and then remained in Washington for the fall 1981 semester to work with the National College Republicans and the Republican National Committee. "I came to Washington," he later wrote, "as an eyewitness to the Reagan Revolution."[112] Reed returned to the University of Georgia politically ambitious and driven. "He was more concerned with the end result," recalled one classmate, "than the path by which he got there."[113] He had to leave his position at the college newspaper, for instance, over accusations of plagiarism.[114] Reed has said of that period in his life, "My goal was to be the next Lee Atwater—a bare-knuckled, brass tacks practitioner of hard-ball politics."[115]

Reed graduated from college in 1983 with a B.A. in History. He was awarded the 1983 prize for best senior essay in history at the University of Georgia. The essay was published in the Winter 1983 issue of *Georgia Historical Quarterly* as "'Fighting the Devil with Fire': Carl Vinson's Victory over Tom Watson in the 1918 Tenth District Democratic Primary." Reed's account of this primary contest in the "Bloody Tenth" reveals his fascination with the drama and tactics of wild southern politics.[116] I suspect that Reed was seeking the same drama of politics when in 1983 he took a job with the National College Republicans in Washington, D.C. Eventually he became that organization's executive director. His "mentors" were veteran Republican organizers such as Grover Norquist, Jack Abrahmoff, Morton Blackwell, and, to a lesser extent, Lee Atwater.[117] Reed was considered, as one associate said, "the best practitioner of kiddie politics."[118]

Despite his ambition to become a "bare-knuckled" political operative, Reed became disillusioned. "The lofty ideals that I brought to the nation's capital," recalled Reed, "were shaken by the reality of life in Congress." Not only did Reed see "votes sold to the highest bidder," but he also observed an admired "profamily, traditional values" politician carrying on an extramarital affair. "I learned quickly," wrote Reed, "that the pursuit of power is an empty and unsatisfying exercise without a moral compass to guide one's journey."[119]

Reed apparently found that moral compass in September 1983. "One Saturday," wrote Reed, "after an evening of socializing with friends, I felt a gentle tugging in my conscience that I should start attending a local church." Using a phone book in "Bullfeathers," a popular bar-restaurant close to Republican headquarters on Capitol Hill, Reed found a listing for Evangel Assembly of God, a church in Camp Springs, Maryland.[120] "The next day," Reed continued, "following the morning services, the pastor led an altar call for those desiring to have a closer relationship with Christ. I raised my hand in affirmation and began a new life of faith."[121]

Reed has described this new life as "a dramatic change." He gave up smoking, drinking, and the use of profanity. Reed, however, has said little about how his religious views or practices have developed since his conversion. In a 1992 interview Reed described the church where he answered the altar call, Evangel Assembly of God, as "charismatic."[122] In his 1996 book, *Active Faith,* he mentioned that while a graduate student at Emory University he attended "Mt. Paran Church of God, a large evangelical church in Atlanta."[123] This congregation is affiliated with the Church of God (Cleveland, Tennessee), a holiness-pentecostal denomination.[124] In 1995, it was reported that he had become "a Presbyterian."[125]

His new identity as an evangelical Christian brought about no shift in his positions on public policy, but he felt "the way I treated people,"[126] and his attitude toward the political enterprise, did change. "Since 1983," he has said, "I haven't been involved with anybody in politics for whom I bear a grudge in my heart."[127] For Reed, politics was still like boxing, a matter of getting hit and hitting back, but now he was "not going to throw a kidney punch."[128] In a letter apologizing to an old opponent, Reed wrote, "Politics for me had degenerated into a cheap play for power. I now realize that politics is a noble calling to serve God and my fellow man."[129]

Reed continued to work with the College Republicans until 1984, when he left to work for the reelection bid of North Carolina Senator Jesse Helms. Reed has claimed that he was not employed directly by the Helms campaign but worked for an independent organization, Students for America (SFA).[130] Reed's move from Washington may have been partially the product of his disillusionment, but probably more important was Reed's desire to help Helms, a perennial favorite of both the New Right and the Christian Right.[131] For young conservatives, and especially for a newly minted evangelical like Reed, the hard-fought Helms race was where the action was in 1984. In a 1993 C-SPAN interview, Reed waxed nostalgic about the experience of his generation of college Republicans who "got in our cars and drove down to North Carolina and helped Senator Helms."[132]

In a 1993 profile on Reed, *Time* described SFA as "a conservative organization with an evangelical tint."[133] Reed described it as "a conservative Judeo-Christian campus organization."[134] "We are," read one SFA pamphlet, "patriotic conservative students dedicated to the advancement of Judeo-Christian values." Founded in 1984 and head-quartered in Raleigh, North Carolina, SFA claimed to be "the vanguard of the conservative movement on the college campuses," and "the fastest growing youth political movement in the nation."[135] According to the 1986 edition of the *Encyclopedia of Associations,* SFA, with Reed listed as Executive Director, claimed 7,000 members. In subsequent editions, however, Reed's name did not appear in the SFA's description.[136]

The degree to which Reed and the SFA became involved with the Christian Right's network of organizations is unclear. In *Active Faith,* Reed described asking Falwell for a few minutes on the program of a 1984 Raleigh, North Carolina, fund-raising event in order to promote a local pro-life march. "He generously agreed," wrote Reed, "wrapping his arm around my shoulder as I spoke at the podium."[137] It has been reported that Reed was arrested in 1985 during a demonstration at a Raleigh women's health clinic where abortions were being performed.[138] Despite these connections and activities, Reed has written that "I did not consider myself a 'Christian activist,' but I shared many of the values of the movement and wanted to see religion play a more vital role in the public life of the nation."[139]

Reed may have been hesitant to get too involved with other Christian Right organizations because of what he later described as their amateurishness. "When evangelicals started getting involved in politics," said Reed in 1992, "they didn't even know how to get a call through to Capitol Hill."[140] This evaluation may have contributed to Reed's support for Jack Kemp, not Robertson, in the 1988 presidential race. Reed has argued that the leaders of the early Christian Right did not understand the limits or nature of politics. "Seduced by the allure of politics," wrote Reed, "they were sometimes naive about its vanity and false pretense. Like first-time investors who sink everything they own into a high-risk venture, they poured all their aspirations for the reformation of society into politics."[141] Involvement in politics sometimes fostered what Reed called "an arrogance and a self-righteousness that was poorly suited to the rough-and-tumble of politics."[142] Reed has also pointed to the Christian Right's "blind faith in Reagan" that allowed the Republican operatives to get evangelical votes while largely ignoring their concerns about abortion and school prayer.[143]

Reed contrasted the early leaders with those, such as himself, who have come to prominence since the late 1980s. "These leaders tended to be young (under forty), enjoyed extensive Washington experience, boasted impressive academic or legal credentials, and were generally political professionals rather than pastors or preachers."[144]

While he remained involved in politics, including work in a 1986 California senate race and Jack Kemp's 1988 run for the Republican presidential nomination, Reed decided to leave behind the instability of politics for an academic career.[145] In the fall of 1985, he entered Emory University's doctoral program in history and decided to specialize in the American South. Reed received his Ph.D. in the spring of 1991. The presence of an earned doctorate on Reed's resume added to his credibility, but Reed found historical training useful in another way. "Most political operatives think in two-year cycles. I think in quarter centuries."[146]

While in graduate school, Reed published an article that demonstrated an awareness of the often harsh mechanisms of social control, as well as the importance of religious worldviews in accepting or challenging those mechanisms. "Emory College and the Sledd Affair of 1902: A Case Study in Southern Honor and Racial Attitudes" appeared in the *Georgia Historical Quarterly* in 1988. Sledd, a professor at Emory, published an essay in 1902 in the *Atlantic Monthly* that was critical of some aspects of southern race relations, particularly the savagery of lynch-law. As a result, Sledd was hung in effigy, forced to resign from Emory, and driven into temporary exile in the North. He was not condemned, Reed argued, "for his rather unremarkable racial views, but rather for his broader attacks on the values and social conventions of the South, particularly the code of honor." Sledd's criticism of lynch-law, so closely associated with the defense of the traditional white family, was seen as "a threat to the entire social order." The social mechanisms used to punish Sledd effectively silenced him on racial issues for the rest of his life. Reed observed that the Sledd affair demonstrated the "hazards of speaking one's mind in a culture that valued conformity over conscience."

Reed found that the "Southern Methodist world-view" of Sledd contributed to his willingness to conform and suffer in silence. This worldview "stressed Christ on the cross as the central metaphor in the believer's life." This metaphor viewed suffering as the "sum and substance of the Christian life" and encouraged "silent acquiescence to the most severe forms of injustice and persecution." Challenging or reforming the social order was *not* part of this worldview. "While Quakers and many evangelical sects in the North trumpeted warnings of coming judgment for national sins, and spawned reform movements fueled by their faith in God, Southern Methodists carefully avoided even the appearance of radicalism."[147]

Reed's doctoral dissertation, directed by Dan T. Carter, was entitled *Fortresses of Faith: Design and Experience at Southern Evangelical Colleges, 1830-1900.*[148] Given his intense interest in politics, Reed's choice to do a detailed study of nineteenth-century southern denominational colleges may seem surprising. Reed's conversion to evangelical Christianity and his decision to become an academic, of course, provide obvious explanations for the marked shift in his area of intellectual interest. But Reed's nonpolitical dissertation was not irrelevant to his work at the CC. Reed's dissertation displayed an awareness of and willingness to grapple with the challenges facing evangelicals in American society.

According to Reed, evangelical colleges were important not only because of their prominent role in southern higher education but because "their growth and development reflected the changing social aspirations and motivations of Southern Evangelicals."[149] Reed found that some historians have interpreted evangelical college-founding as rooted in the sectarian motive of protecting evangelical youth against evil social influences. Other historians saw in these colleges a desire for greater influence in society. Reed wanted to transcend this dichotomy by understanding the motivation for evangelical college-founding as ambivalent, encompassing both the sectarian and social impulses. "Evangelicals sought protection from society's excesses," wrote Reed, "yet hungered [for] prestige and power."[150]

Reed used the classic *Gemeinschaft* ("community," based on more informal natural bonds of kinship, friendship, or shared faith)– *Gesellschaft* ("society," based on formal, impersonal, and contractual relationships within a capitalist system) formulation of German sociologist Ferdinand Tonnies to describe the evolution of evangelical colleges.[151] In the antebellum era, church colleges were distinct, tightly knit *Gemeinschaft* communities based on a shared faith. Reed devoted considerable time and effort to exploring and illustrating the nature of these college communities.

Because they were the South's leading educational institutions after the Civil War, these colleges became useful bases from which evangelicals could influence and elevate southern culture. The evangelical effort to gain social and cultural leadership was largely successful. The South became, according to Reed, "the most distinctly religious and Protestant section in the nation."[152] But this influence came at a price. In order to be influential, evangelical schools had to train their students for technical and professional careers and adopt the more impersonal *Gesellschaft* ethos of the commercial New South. As evangelicals gained prestige and influence, they wanted their educational institutions to be prestigious and influential. Eventually, many of these schools came to view themselves as secular enterprises serving the wider society, and they severed their ties to the churches that had founded them. Reed found in this evolution a greater significance. "This transformation of the church colleges was a microcosm of the broader evolution of Southern Evangelicalism."[153]

Quoted in a 1993 profile of Reed, Emory Professor James Roark said of Reed's dissertation, "It was a first-rate piece of work, but I'm not sure Ralph would want it published today."[154] Any reluctance Reed might have about publishing his dissertation would probably stem from the stark differences between his academic approach to history and the approach to history found in the literature of the Christian Right. Reed would be hard pressed to explain these differences to the constituency of the CC.

Reed, reflecting the assumptions of an academic historian, found complexity, ambiguity, and irony in the historical process. In contrast, the Christian Right's covenantal framework of American history is singular, simple, and unambiguous. According to the covenantal framework, Americans either have conformed to the God-given original purpose of the founding fathers and been blessed by God, or they have deviated from that purpose and been punished. Only full realization of the original purpose is legitimate. But in Reed's dissertation, the college founders did not start with a single, simple, unambiguously good purpose. Instead they had dual purposes. Both were good purposes, but there was an inherent contradiction between them. Thus, both could not be fully realized. One must be sacrificed for the other, or a pragmatic balance between them must be arranged. Only partial realization of either was possible.

Reed would be especially hard pressed to explain to the constituency of the CC the ironic outcome of evangelical efforts to extend their social influence. In their attempt to elevate southern society, the *Gemeinschaft* evangelical community paid the price of becoming more like the *Gesellschaft* larger society. In their attempt to extend their purity, they became less pure. Even more ironic is the evangelical loss of control of their instruments of influence, the colleges and universities they had founded. "What evangelicals gained in modernity," wrote Reed, "they painfully discovered, cost them dearly in their loss of control over their institutions of higher learning."[155] Although Reed does not make this point, it is obvious that this loss of control made the evangelical community less influential in society in the long term.

I find it easy enough to apply this same ironic pattern to the Christian Right. Will the attempt to extend evangelical influence result in the loss of religious purity and eventually in a loss of influence? This would be a particularly sharp question for Reed, who has led the CC in the direction of adaptation to the norms and practices of secular politics. Perhaps Reed feels that the extension of evangelical influence in contemporary American society is so urgently needed that the potential negative consequences are a price that has to be paid. Or perhaps Reed feels that he and the new generation of Christian Right leaders will escape the mistakes of the past and navigate successfully between the Scylla of religious purity and the Charybdis of political pragmatism. It is also possible that Reed has simply put his dissertation on a shelf, not permitting himself to entertain the troubling questions that it would raise.

CHAPTER 4

INSTITUTIONALIZING THE REVOLUTION

THE POST-REAGAN 1980s were particularly difficult times for the Christian Right. As Reed put it, "When Ronald Reagan got on that helicopter [to return to California] a great deal of the pro-family political capital went with him."[1] Not only had Robertson's 1988 presidential campaign ended in failure, but Moral Majority, once the movement's flagship organization, went out of existence in 1989. The demise of the Christian Right became the conventional wisdom of the day. "Rarely in modern times," one writer in the *New Republic* expressed it, "has a movement of such reputed potential self-destructed so suddenly. Free thinkers may want to reconsider their skepticism about divine intervention."[2] But the Christian Right did not collapse or die. Robertson's campaign, as Reed once said, "will be for evangelicals what Barry Goldwater's run was for conservatives in 1964: a defeat that provided the seeds of ultimate triumph."[3]

ORIGINS

Robertson probably first became aware of Reed when *The 700 Club* did a story on Reed's 1983 conversion.[4] According to Reed, he first met Robertson at Dartmouth College during the 1988 New Hampshire primary campaign.[5] They next met in January 1989, when they were "coincidentally" seated next to each other at a dinner in Washington, D.C.[6] At that dinner Robertson was receiving a "Man of the Year Award" from Reed's old organization, Students For America (SFA).[7] Robertson invited Reed to join the staff of a political organization that he wanted to form.[8] He also asked Reed to write a memo sketching out what such an organization should be like. Reed reported that after sending the memo he heard nothing until he was invited to an organizational meeting in Atlanta on September 25, 1989.[9] "Pat introduced me," wrote Reed, "as the first staff member of a group that as yet had no name, a development that surprised me as much as everyone else."[10] Reed also reported that most participants in this meeting favored the creation of an "American Congress of Christian Citizens," which would be what Reed described as "a kind of political Billy Graham crusade that would fire up the troops and draw massive media attention."[11] Less well-received, according to Reed, was the Reed-Robertson proposal to create an organization for grassroots activism. In the end, it was decided to follow both approaches simultaneously under the name Christian Coalition.[12] But by March of 1990, Robertson and Reed decided to concentrate exclusively on grassroots organizing.[13]

Reed has depicted the origins of the CC as distinctly humble. Its first office was in a warehouse filled with the detritus of Robertson's campaign for the presidency. "Phones jangled all day," recalled Reed, "with disgruntled vendors still owed money by the defunct campaign."[14] The CC was able to get off to a fast start, however, by using the Robertson campaign's mailing list of donors and activists to solicit funds and recruit members for the new organization.[15] As Reed explained to *Christianity Today* in 1990, "We believe that it is God's will that those people stay involved [in politics] for the long haul, not just for a single campaign."[16] Reed was also able to obtain a one-time contribution of $64,000, which he later called "seed money," in October 1990 from the Republican Senatorial Committee.[17]

PURPOSE, STRUCTURE, AND ACTIVITIES

The basic purpose of the CC was to "make government more responsive to the concerns of Evangelical Christians and pro-family Catholics."[18] This purpose was elaborated as a fivefold mission to:

1. represent Christians before local councils, state legislatures and Congress;
2. speak out in the public arena and in the media;

3. train Christian leaders for effective social and political action;
4. inform Christians about timely issues and pending legislation;
5. protest anti-Christian bias and defend the legal rights of Christians.[19]

In 1989 the CC applied for tax-exempt status as a nonprofit "social welfare" organization under Internal Revenue Service (IRS) code 501(c)(4). As of this writing, the CC's application is still pending with the IRS. (If that application is rejected, the CC will be liable for back taxes. But until then, the CC can continue to function as a tax-exempt organization.[20]) The CC itself has been tax-exempt, but donations and membership fees have not been tax deductible for the contributors. Such organizations have a relatively wide latitude for action. They can engage in voter education, produce voter guides, be advocates for public policy, and even lobby public officials. Their primary purpose, however, cannot be partisan politics. For this reason, CC literature states, "The Christian Coalition is not affiliated with any political party and does not endorse any candidates."[21] And as a 501(c)(4) "social welfare" organization, the CC is not required to comply with the Federal Election Commission's (FEC) restrictions on funding and expenditures, or registration and disclosure requirements.[22]

The CC has a national headquarters in Chesapeake, Virginia.[23] According to its 1994 tax return, its Board of Directors consisted of Robertson (president), Reed (executive director), Judy Liebert (chief financial officer), and two directors, Billy McCormack and Dick Weinhold. Only Reed and Liebert were full time and salaried. In 1994, Reed was paid $146,009 and Liebert $80,176.[24] In 1995, Reed's salary had risen to $197,077, but Liebert was not listed on that year's tax return as a member of the Board.[25] In June 1996, Liebert was reportedly suspended from her position after going to the U.S. Attorney in Norfolk, Virginia, with information about "financial irregularities" and "potential criminal activity" involving a vendor providing direct-mail services to the CC.[26] As of this writing, federal prosecutors have not announced any action against the CC or the vendor in connection with this matter.

The CC is organized as a network of state affiliates and local chapters. Each state affiliate is incorporated in its state and has to secure its own tax-exemption from the IRS. Affiliates, which retain a separate legal identity and are not funded by the national organization, must obtain a charter from the CC Board of Directors. These charters must be renewed annually. Local chapters, usually organized on the county level, are not incorporated but are merely units of the state organization.[27] These state affiliates have been described as "franchise-style operations." The chartering requirement gives the national CC the power to cut off an affiliate that does not follow directives from national headquarters.[28]

The CC grew quickly. "We're the McDonald's of American politics," said Reed in 1995.[29] When the CC was first noticed by the press in the spring of 1990, it claimed a membership of 25,000.[30] By the end of 1990, the CC claimed 57,000 members, 125 local chapters, and an annual budget of $2.8 million. By 1992, the CC's budget had risen to $8.5 million and it reported 250,000 members and 1,000 local chapters.[31] The CC claimed its one millionth member in February 1994.[32] In May 1995, when the CC announced its *Contract with the American Family,* it claimed 1.6 million members, 50 state affiliates, 1,600 local chapters, and a $25 million annual budget.[33] In an August 1995 mailing, Robertson told CC members that he hoped to double the organization's membership to 3 million in the next six months.[34] But a year later, the CC was still claiming only 1.7 million members.[35] When Reed announced his resignation on April 23, 1997, he offered the figures 1.9 million members and 2,000 local chapters.[36] While the CC's membership claims have often been seen as exaggerations, the fact that these claims have not continued to increase would seem to indicate that they are not total fabrications. And in addition to the leveling off of membership growth, the CC has also faced diminishing donations. According to the organization's tax return for the non-election year of 1995, the CC received $18.7 million in donations— 12 percent less than in 1994,[37] and far less than the $25 million budget it had been claiming. Donations seem to have substantially increased, however, during the election year of 1996. The CC claimed that a record $24.9 million had been received by December 7, 1996.[38]

The CC has three publications. *Religious Rights Watch,* a one page flyer, is published monthly and reports violations of the legal rights of Christians. Readers have been encouraged to become involved by contacting public officials to protest or by reporting such incidents to the CC. A second publication, *Congressional Scorecard,* produced semiannually, presents the voting record of Representatives and Senators on issues selected by the CC. Similar materials regarding voting in state legislatures are published by state affiliates.

The CC's third, and perhaps most important, publication is *Christian American.* It first appeared in the spring of 1990 as a quarterly four-page newsletter. In 1991, it became a monthly thirty-two-page tabloid newspaper featuring news stories, analysis, and editorials. Each issue featured "Pat's View," a question and answer column by Robertson, columns by Reed and other staff members, as well as syndicated columns by such writers as Cal Thomas and Phyllis Schlafly. In September 1995, *Christian American* began to be published six times a year in a thirty-four-page magazine format. Much of the content is similar to the tabloid format, but the absence of trumpeting headlines indicated a shift to a softer, less confrontational style. In a 1996 letter to subscribers, Reed claimed *Christian American* "has become the nation's leading provider of news and information for conservative Christian pro-family readers."[39]

In addition to these publications, the CC has made use of electronic media. It has maintained an Internet Web site (http://www.cc.org) from which it is possible to download press releases, position papers, voter guides, and electronic versions of the CC's print publications. Visitors to this Web site are able to register for upcoming events sponsored by the CC, send an e-mail message to members of Congress, or become a member of the CC, as well as purchase books, videos, and gift items.

The CC also has a monthly television broadcast called *Christian Coalition Live*. Hosted by Reed, viewers call in on a toll-free line to ask questions and discuss issues with Reed and guests such as William Bennett, Newt Gingrich, and Bob Dole. The first half-hour is carried by National Empowerment Television (NET), a cable TV network created by conservative organizer Paul Weyrich. After the first half hour, *Christian Coalition Live* is "narrow-casted" via satellite downlinks to the monthly meetings of CC local chapters, which are scheduled to coincide with the broadcast. This latter portion of the program is described by the CC as a "national strategy session." The narrow-casted portion of the show presents "'action items'—brief presentations on the most current issues that matter to the profamily movement, and offers specific guidance on what local activists can do to move public policy in the right direction."[40]

Reed has been enthusiastic about what he called the "electronic Godzilla" of technopopulism. "A combination of legislative savvy," wrote Reed, "voter anger, and technologies like fax machines, microcomputers, and talk radio is making it possible for the average person to affect government as never before." He also noted that when Robertson urges viewers of *The 700 Club* to contact their Congressmen and

Senators, the Capitol Hill switchboard is often overwhelmed. The larger point for Reed is that "alternative media," dominated by conservatives, "now rivals or eclipses the establishment press in shaping the nation's political agenda."[41]

In early 1993, the CC opened a lobbying office, or "Command Center," on Capitol Hill in Washington, D.C.[42] Now called the Governmental Affairs Office, its purpose is to monitor legislation and federal agencies, lobby Congress and administration officials, and represent the CC before the national media, as well as work in alliance with other lobbying groups.[43] In the first six months of 1996, the CC reportedly spent $5.9 million on Washington lobbying activities.[44] This Washington office is also able to provide information and direction for the CC's grassroots activists directly through *Christian Coalition Live,* "burst fax alerts," e-mail, the Internet, automated calling lists, and computerized direct mail. The same message often comes more indirectly through the influence of Christian and conservative talk radio and TV programs.[45]

Reed's enthusiasm for technology that will further the CC agenda was demonstrated by the elaborate communication system set up by the CC at the 1996 Republican National Convention. To effectively mobilize the estimated 500 CC members among the 4000 delegates and alternates, the CC distributed wireless "personal digital assistants" with specially designed software that would link 102 floor whips to the centralized CC "Communications Command Center." This system allowed whips to canvass delegates, communicate the information to the Center, and relay voting instructions back to the convention floor. This system allowed rapid and continual coordination by CC leaders. Reed may have made a point of publicizing the CC's communications systems in order to intimidate those Republicans who considered starting a floor fight over the abortion plank.[46]

Beyond communications technology, the CC also uses national and local training sessions to brief the membership on the strategy and tactics decided upon by the leadership. In November 1991 and September 1992, the Christian Coalition held two-day "Road to Victory" conferences at CBN's Founders Inn Conference Center in Virginia Beach. At these meetings, CC members heard addresses by prominent conservative politicians and activists, as well as presentations on various issues ("The Homosexual Agenda"), and they attended "how to" workshops ("Lobbying Your Legislator"). Attendees also met in state caucuses to facilitate state organization and action. Representatives of other Christian Right and politically conservative organizations set up information booths and display tables. Beginning in 1993, these annual "Road to Victory" conferences have been held at the Washington, D.C., Hilton hotel, and they are open to members of the news media and televised by C-SPAN. The CC claimed that 4,600 people had registered for the 1996 meeting.[47] In 1997, however, the CC announced plans to hold "Road to Victory" in Atlanta, Georgia.[48]

Beyond these national meetings, the CC has sponsored an extensive program of one- and two-day seminars held in cities across the United States. While these seminars have been advertised with a slogan that mixes the sacred and the secular, "Think like Jesus. Lead like Moses. Fight like David. Run like Lincoln," their aims have been mostly the practical and the possible.[49] These seminars introduce CC members to the "nuts-and-bolts" of grassroots political activism, as well as to the outlook, structure, and methods of the CC. While the CC holds seminars to train candidates for school boards,[50] most of the training seminars have a different focus. "We teach people how to establish a voter registration drive in their church," said Reed, "how to lobby legislators, how to set up a grass roots phone tree. It's very activist driven. Most of our members will never run for office. Most of them will write a letter, make a phone call, or send a letter."[51] In an August 1995 mailing, Robertson told CC members that the organization hoped to hold "more than 300 Citizen Action Training Schools across America in the next 12 months."[52] These training objectives have been part of a much more ambitious long-term plan. "Our goal," said Reed in 1992, "is to have 10 trained activists in each of America's 175,000 precincts by the end of the decade."[53]

One of the most important activities that CC members are trained in is the identification and mobilization of "pro-family voters" on the precinct or neighborhood level. Identification of sympathetic citizens is aided by obtaining computerized lists of registered voters, those who signed petitions on certain issues, and church membership lists, as well as names referred by other CC members active in local churches.[54] Prospects are then contacted using an informal phone survey. A standard "Voter Identification Script" includes questions on sex-education and abortion, as well as an open-ended question about a local issue important to the respondent.[55] CC volunteers also engage in door-to-door canvassing to contact prospects who have not been reached by phone and to meet neighborhood residents whose views are unknown. Survey information is compiled in computer databases used to contact pro-family voters to urge them to participate in elections and referenda, attend city council or school board meetings, write letters, or contact public officials. In September 1996, Reed promised that before the November elections CC activists would contact "between two and three million households by letter and by phone and get them to the polls" as a part of what he called "the most ambitious voter-education, get-out-the-vote program in the history of American politics."[56]

These efforts are organized through a precinct-based structure rather than through local churches. Precinct organization is seen by the CC as a more effective use of resources to target particular districts and officeholders.[57] This has not meant, however, that churches have been ignored by CC activists. Evangelical congregations represent a rich pool of potential pro-family votes. "The churches are the nexus points for tens of millions of Americans," observed a CC training manual, "who share a conservative, pro-family philosophy. No other cultural structure represents such a vast reservoir of potential help for the pro-family movement."[58]

Members of a CC local chapter act as "Church Liaisons" to the individual churches they attend. A principal function of Church Liaisons is to organize voter registration drives. In September 1996, the CC announced that it would attempt to register one million new voters by the November elections.[59] Given the character of the congregations in which CC members are generally active, these new voters are likely to enlarge and strengthen the religious conservative voting bloc.

Church Liaisons also organize the distribution of information about upcoming elections in the form of "voter guides," simple comparisons of candidates on issues selected by the CC. Based on a questionnaire completed by the candidates, these guides do not *explicitly* endorse certain candidates—although it is often easy to infer which candidate the CC perceives to be "more pro-family." Critics have accused the CC of *implicitly* endorsing certain candidates, usually conservative Republicans, by misrepresenting the positions of other candidates or by selecting issues for comparison that favor one candidate. The guides are usually distributed on the last Sunday before the election, giving candidates little time to refute what they may feel are misrepresentations.[60] Reed has argued that the CC's voter guides are not only nonpartisan, they are similar to voter-education literature distributed by liberal groups for decades.[61] He claimed the CC's only innovation is to distribute tens of millions of these guides and to create them for the kind of local races, such as school board elections, that previous voter education efforts had ignored.[62]

On July 30, 1996, the FEC filed a civil lawsuit in a U.S. District Court against the CC for illegally aiding various Republican political campaigns in the 1990, 1992, and 1994 elections. Based on complaints by the Democratic National Committee, the FEC alleged that CC activities, especially the distribution of voter guides, constituted "in kind contributions and independent expenditures on behalf of Republican candidates." The FEC also charged that the CC had acted in coordination, cooperation, or consultation with leaders of those campaigns. If the court finds against the CC, it could be fined and prohibited from engaging in similar activities in the future.[63]

The FEC did not pursue, however, a second allegation that the CC's primary purpose was partisan—an allegation that, if proven, could have jeopardized the CC's tax-exempt status and its freedom from regulation by the FEC.[64] The CC leaders also took some comfort in the fact that similar cases have been decided against the FEC.[65] But the more immediate problem was the effect of the FEC lawsuit on CC activities in the upcoming 1996 election. Organizations critical of the CC, such as Americans United for Separation of Church and State, began publicizing the notion that churches distributing CC voter guides might have their 501(c)(3) tax-exemption challenged or revoked by the IRS.[66] Invoking the specter of the IRS was meant to make ministers reluctant to permit the distribution of CC literature. The extent to which this tactic was effective is unknown and may be impossible to determine. President Clinton's reelection campaign, however, felt it necessary to air television ads that cautioned, "Don't be misled by last-minute voter guides distributed outside our churches."[67] The CC maintained that these efforts to suppress dissemination of voter guides failed. It claimed that it "distributed 46.3 million voter guides in more than 100,000 churches nationwide" just before the 1996 election.[68]

In order to avoid misunderstandings or suspicion, Church Liaisons are advised to get permission from the congregation's leadership before engaging in voter-education activities. The recommended method of doing this, according to a CC manual, is to offer to start a "Civic Concerns Ministry" as a service to the congregation, which will "educate the body of Christ about public policy and train Christians for effective citizenship and leadership." The advantage of creating such a ministry is that it "allows churches to be involved in the Christian Coalition without asking pastors to assume any role with which they may be uncomfortable."[69] Such a lay-led ministry can accomplish its political purposes without disrupting the religious focus and function of the congregation. In contrast to the early Christian Right's preacher-led model of political mobilization, this lay-led ministry within a congregation allows for, in Reed's words, "a professionalization of the church's civic involvement." Reed regards this as "one of the main differences between the old religious right and the new pro-family movement."[70] Reed noted, for instance, that all the state chairmen of Falwell's Moral Majority in the 1980s were preachers. "By contrast," observed Reed, "of the fifty state chairmen of the Christian Coalition, only one is an ordained minister."[71]

Not only does the Civic Concerns Ministry provide what the CC regards as a service to the congregation, it also can identify voters sympathetic to the CC, as well as find and develop potential CC activists. The names of these voters and potential activists are given to the appropriate precinct coordinator who can mobilize their votes or efforts when needed. The precinct coordinator then passes on these names to the county, state, and national organizations of the CC.[72] The Church Liaison–Civic Concerns Ministry functions within congregations as a parallel structure to the precinct organization of the CC. This congregational structure provides the CC with a receptive audience for its message and fruitful ground for recruiting support.

INSTITUTIONALIZATION

Reed's clear intention was that the CC not be tied to the cycle of elections alone but should be a permanent organization "that would represent people of faith in the same way that the Chamber of Commerce represents business or the AFL-CIO represents union workers."[73] In short, the CC was intended to be what Moen called the "institutionalization" of the Christian Right. He listed four characteristics of institutionalization: 1) achieving financial stability by building a genuine membership base; 2) appealing to a broader constituency; 3) using more inclusive rhetoric; and 4) being oriented toward grassroots political activity.[74]

How does the CC display these four characteristics?

Financial Stability

The CC has been accused of many things, but never of being poorly funded. But whether this financial health has come from the creation of a genuine membership base is unclear. The CC's 1994 tax return, for instance, claimed total revenues of nearly $22 million, with about 96 percent of this amount coming from "Direct public support."[75] It is possible this amount came from hundreds of thousands of relatively small contributions, but until there is a detailed disclosure of particular sources or contribution amounts, it will be unknown what proportion of the "Direct public support" came in large amounts from corporations or wealthy individuals. The *Wall Street Journal* reported in 1996 that the CC had a low-profile "big-donor" fund-raising program similar to those of many other political organizations. Individuals who donated $1000 or $5000 were invited to special receptions and events where they met prominent politicians, celebrities, and CC leaders such as Robertson and Reed. CC officials refused to provide the *Journal* with information on these activities. An unnamed CC "insider" told the *Journal* that $750,000 was raised in this fashion at the 1996 Republican National Convention, and that the 1996 big-donor program was ten times larger than in 1995.[76]

A likely candidate for such large contributions is Robertson and his extensive business empire. Reed claimed in 1990, however, that there was "no financial relationship *per se* and no cash transfers" between the CC and Robertson's Christian Broadcasting Network (CBN).[77] Even if the CC has gotten no direct cash gifts from the Robertson business enterprises, the CC has received enormous amounts of free promotion from Robertson's *The 700 Club.*[78]

In addition to direct donations from individuals and corporations, the CC and some of its state affiliates receive funds through LifeLine, a long distance telephone service that contributes 10 percent of customer payments to a Christian nonprofit organization chosen by the customer.[79] The CC also solicits donations through selling books, video tapes, and gift items carrying the CC logo through advertisements in *Christian American* and at the CC's Web site.[80]

Like many nonprofit organizations, the CC has regularly sent out direct-mail letters making urgent appeals for money. In a 1993 interview, Reed described the mailing lists he uses as "Catholic churchgoers, pro-life citizens, evangelicals, . . . people who are in favor of tougher laws against crime and drugs."[81] The computerized databases of voters and local activists that the CC works so hard at creating are undoubtedly utilized for direct-mail purposes. Despite the CC's consistent and apparently effective use of direct mail, Reed has been wary of fund-raising becoming an end in itself. In his 1994 book, *Politically Incorrect,* he quoted former Moral Majority staff member Cal Thomas, who argued that in the early 1980s the chance "to transform the culture was quickly squandered when it was decided to emphasize fund-raising instead of building the political machinery to exercise real power."[82]

Other than these scraps of information, relatively little is known about the finances of the CC. The decline in income the CC experienced in 1995 has been the first indication that it too can suffer the boom-and-bust funding problems that killed off the direct mail–driven organizations of the early Christian Right. Donations increased once again during the 1996 election season but with the apparent leveling off of CC membership growth, it will be interesting to see what happens to CC revenues and its financial viability.

Grassroots Activism

Moen's fourth characteristic of the institutionalized Christian Right, an orientation to grassroots activism, has been one of the most consistent themes of the CC. (I will return to Moen's second and third characteristics below.)

Despite the populist themes of Robertson's 1988 campaign,[83] he proved to be a rather unpopular populist in the primaries. His only successes came in straw polls and caucuses where careful local organization and mobilization were at a premium. Reed saw this so-called invisible army in action in a 1988 Republican precinct caucus in DeKalb County, Georgia. Robertson supporters, though most had never participated in such an event before, acted in complete unison. This resulted in what Reed termed "the political equivalent of a total shutout." Party regulars were "swept aside by the religious tidal wave." Reed, whose candidate, Jack Kemp, had been soundly defeated, called this experience an "epiphany." Reed's own dream of bringing "religious values and conservative principles back into the political arena" finally seemed possible. "I had seen the beginning of a new political era in that Georgia courthouse, and its seeds lay in the precincts." Religious conservatives, concluded Reed, only needed "guidance and direction."[84]

Since joining forces with Robertson, Reed has preached the grassroots gospel relentlessly. "The Christian community got it backwards in the 1980s," said Reed in 1990. "We tried to charge Washington when we should have been focusing on the states. The real battles of concern to Christians are in the neighborhoods, school boards, city councils and state legislatures."[85] Reed, of course, was not alone in this insight. The myriad of groups, organizations, and activists that compose the Christian Right began to concentrate on local issues and activism in the late 1980s.[86] But unlike many of these organizations, the CC has acquired the resources and visibility to give selected local issues national attention. And with support from the national organization, local CC activists can attempt to enact a national agenda at the grassroots level.[87] "If we do that," Reed once wrote of building local organization, "America will continue in a more conservative, profamily direction no matter who wins the White House."[88] In a 1996 speech at the National Press Club, Reed claimed, "There are an estimated 2,000 religious conservatives who now serve on school boards, city councils, state legislatures and in Congress."[89] He did not say, however, how many were associated with the CC.

The CC described the objective of its local efforts as that of building, "a permanent, non-partisan, issues oriented grass roots precinct organization." Organizing in precincts, "the most basic unit of the American political structure," was seen as "vital to providing pro-family citizens with a permanent voice commensurate with their numbers." Such organization "can serve as a vehicle for whatever issue or project the leadership and members deem necessary."[90] The grassroots organizing efforts of the CC have proven so effective that their political opponents learn from them. Kevin Mack, an official with the Virginia Democratic Caucus, told political scientists Mark Rozell and Clyde Wilcox in 1993 that he and his colleagues "get the Christian Coalition training manuals, read them and appropriate things that are good, and now we go back to our people and try to teach them the same things."[91]

But organizing the nation's 175,000 precincts is a long and slow path to power. As one CC pamphlet told members, "There is an old expression that goes 'How do you eat an elephant? One bite at a time.'"[92] The image of eating an elephant one bite at a time is an apt one for the growing power of the CC within the Republican party. The Christian Right has always been associated with the Republicans, of course, but the CC has been far more intentional in developing this relationship.

Political scientist Duane M. Oldfield observed that, "Whereas previous movement groups had had incidental dealings with the party, the coalition, from its beginnings, made organizing within the party a central focus of its overall activity."[93] At the 1992 Republican National Convention, some 300 of the 2,000 delegates were reported to be members of the CC.[94] Four years later, the CC claimed more than 500 delegates—the result of a reported $2 million expenditure.[95] A much-noted article in the September 1994 issue of *Campaigns & Elections* reported that the Christian Right was "dominant" in 18 state Republican parties, and its strength was "substantial" in 13 more.[96] And since the CC is usually recognized as the flagship organization of that movement, Robertson and Reed claimed the lion's share of credit. The CC's success at the grassroots has fueled fears of a "takeover" of the GOP by the "radicals" of the CC, but Reed dismissed these objections. "If moderates complain," said Reed, "they have to keep in mind that we're the ones licking the envelopes and burning the shoe leather. The only crime that the Christian Right has committed is the crime of democracy."[97]

Critics of the CC, however, charge that it is not practicing grassroots democracy, but undermining democracy through grassroots "stealth campaigns." Such stealth campaigns have often been associated with the so-called San Diego model, named after tactics developed by religious conservative activists in the 1990 elections in San Diego, California. These tactics were typically used in local races, such as school board elections, that usually generate low voter turnouts. "Stealth" candidates avoid all public and media attention and only seek the support of targeted "pro-family" voters. A high turnout of these targeted voters can win low-turnout elections.[98] One critic of the San Diego model said, "It's really the collapse of the democratic process if they are able to walk into office by lying and not saying what they truly believe."[99]

The CC has denied that it advocates or practices "stealth" politics. According to Reed: "We believe pro-family candidates should run unapologetically on who they are and what they believe because the public shares their viewpoint."[100] But, according to one report, at the "Road to Victory" conference in 1991, the CC Field Director Guy Rodgers bluntly explained the rationale behind stealthy methods: "We don't have to worry about convincing a majority of Americans to agree with us. Most of them are staying home and watching *Falcon Crest.* They're not involved, they're not voting, so who cares?"[101] In a 1991 interview, Reed told political scientist Allen D. Hertzke that the genius of identifying and mobilizing sympathetic voters is that it allowed the CC to "use a 'stealth' approach as opposed to the Falwell approach of media events, rallies, and endorsements."[102] And in an oft-quoted statement, Reed compared politics to guerrilla warfare. "It's better to move quietly," said Reed, "with stealth, under cover of night."[103]

Reed has maintained that his comments on guerrilla warfare were quoted out of context and that he was not advocating stealth tactics, but merely commenting on the strategic shift of the Christian Right toward low-profile grassroots activism. "I was," said Reed, "speaking in broad historical terms."[104] He argued that repeated accusations of stealth are really liberal attempts to demonize religious conservatives. "The left gets upset when our people do not run as theocrats, which is what they would like for them to do. That is a caricature of a person of faith."[105] The San Diego model, charged one CC document, "was not a 'model' at all, just a threadbare scare tactic whipped up by conspiracy theorists."[106] Whatever the truth of these accusations in the past, the high visibility of the CC on the national scene has made it much harder for local CC activists to move "under cover of night." As writer Sidney Blumenthal observed in 1994, "For the religious right, invisibility is no longer possible."[107]

A Broader Constituency

Reed has hoped to overcome the image of religious conservatives as sneaky extremists by trying to broaden the CC's constituency and issues agenda, as well as making the rhetoric of the CC more inclusive. This effort clearly demonstrated Moen's second and third characteristics of the institutionalization of the Christian Right. "Casting a wider net," as Reed dubbed the new strategy, emerged in the aftermath of Republican defeat in the 1992 presidential election. Reed has often rejected the charge that religious conservatives and their "culture war" rhetoric at the Republican convention were responsible for the Democratic presidential victory in 1992. "Blaming evangelicals for Bush's loss," wrote Reed, "is like blaming the sinking of the Titanic on the people shoveling coal in the boiler room."[108] Religious conservatives, according to Reed, were unfairly made into scapegoats by other Republicans and by the media.[109]

But Reed knew that simply denying these charges would not be enough. His wider net strategy was instead a proactive way of overcoming the image of the Christian Right as too small, too extreme, and too fixated on divisive moral issues. "The key to success for the pro-family movement," wrote Reed in 1993, "is to discuss a broader issues agenda in the language of the target audience—churchgoers and families with children. In doing so, a social movement until now composed largely of white Evangelicals can win natural allies among Catholics and racial minorities."[110]

Creating a broader constituency has been a perennial goal of Christian Right activists, and one toward which some progress has been made. As I noted above, in 1988 the Robertson campaign brought many pentecostals and charismatics into a movement long dominated by fundamentalists. Wilcox argued for the broadening potential of this influx: "By embracing the support of evangelicals, conservative Catholics, and other Christians the charismatic Right may have the potential to build a coalition of conservative Christians which the intolerance of the fundamentalists has prevented."[111] A 1994 poll by the *New York Times* and CBS News found the Christian Right to be a "far more diverse group in terms of geography, politics and even religious doctrine than is generally suggested by either its critics or its most vocal proponents."[112] In addition to this unexpected breadth, a 1996 study conducted for the American Jewish Committee found that this movement still had considerable potential for growth within its current social base. "As conservative evangelicals learn more about the religious right, they are more favorable," explained sociologist Tom W. Smith. "If the Christian Coalition and similar organizations can expand their familiarity among this group, they will gain more adherents."[113]

Despite its broadening membership base and potential for growth, Reed has made it clear that he does not believe the CC can realistically claim to represent more than a minority of Americans. Estimates of the size of this minority vary widely. A 1996 survey conducted by the Pew Research Center found that "Only 7 percent of voters think of themselves as members of the 'religious right.'"[114] Yet according to exit polls conducted by the Voter News Service on election day 1996, 17 percent of voters identified themselves as members of the religious right.[115] And Reed claimed that "pro-life and profamily voters" are "a third of the electorate."[116] Whatever the size and shape of this constituency, Reed stated that it was a "major marketing error" by Falwell's Moral Majority to claim to speak for everyone. "Politics in the '90s," according to Reed, "is about niche marketing, finding and targeting your audience. Not broadcasting, but narrowcasting."[117]

This does not mean, however, that Reed has eschewed expanding the CC's niche in the political marketplace by appealing to constituencies that religious conservatives have ignored, threatened, or offended in the past. "For too long," said Reed in early 1997, "our movement has been predominantly and frankly almost exclusively a white, evangelical, Republican movement with a political center of gravity centered in the safety of the suburbs."[118] Reed pointed to the potential for political cooperation with other socially conservative "people of faith"—Catholics, Jews, Latinos, and African-Americans—groups traditionally affiliated with the Democratic party.[119] Robertson also articulated this cooperative vision at the 1996 "Road to Victory" conference: "We are going to work with people of good will all over this nation. We are not going to be exclusive but inclusive. We are going to bring people together into a vast winning coalition to bring back the values that we care about in America!"[120]

From the beginning, the CC has attempted to enlarge its "marketshare" by including "pro-family Catholics" in its statement of purpose. In October 1995, the CC formed the Catholic Alliance, a division of the CC geared specifically to Catholic voters. "If Catholics and evangelicals can unite," Reed told the first meeting of the Catholic Alliance, "there is no person who cannot run for any office in any city or any state in America that cannot be elected."[121] When Catholic Alliance was first formed, Reed told the conservative Catholic magazine *Crisis* that according to an internal survey, 16 percent of CC members were Roman Catholic. He wanted to raise this to 25-30 percent, the percentage of Roman Catholics in the general population.[122] Reed also expressed the hope that the new organization would boost the Catholic membership of the CC to "more than 2 million by the end of the decade."[123]

During its first year, however, only 30,000 people joined the Catholic Alliance, and a number of Catholic bishops prohibited the distribution of CC and Alliance literature in the parishes under their supervision.[124] Perhaps in response to these problems, in September 1996 the Catholic Alliance was reorganized as a corporation separate from the CC, with its own all-Catholic board of directors and an advisory board.[125]

The CC has also attempted to reach out to the Jewish and African-American communities. Reed has repeatedly called on white evangelicals to recognize and repent for a long history of anti-Semitism and racism, and to take steps toward building a multiracial movement free of bigotry.[126] Prominent Jewish and African-American conservatives have addressed the annual "Road to Victory" conferences, where they seem to have been warmly received.[127] Despite the Anti-Defamation League's critical 1994 report, *The Religious Right*,[128] and widely publicized accusations in 1995 that Robertson had made anti-Semitic statements in his 1991 book *The New World Order*,[129] Reed has been so optimistic about the potential for political cooperation with Orthodox Jews that he considered "the possibility of launching a Jewish Coalition as a sister organization in future years."[130]

Because the Christian Right has been stereotypically identified with southern white racism, Reed has perceived outreach to African-Americans as crucial to the future of the movement. Reed claimed in November 1995 that about 3 or 4 percent of CC members were African-American. He noted that this was lower than the percentage of African-Americans in the general population but added "it's higher, frankly, than we thought it might be."[131] Reed has taken steps to increase African-American involvement in the CC. His co-host on *Christian Coalition Live* was at one time an African-American woman, Star Parker.[132] In July 1995, the CC sponsored a conference on racial reconciliation attended by more than one hundred African-American ministers and conservative activists.[133] In 1996 the CC named Rev. Earl Jackson, a conservative African-American minister and radio talk show host, as national liaison to African-American churches.[134] In April 1996, the CC offered a $25,000 reward for information regarding a series of arson attacks on African-American churches in the South.[135] In June, when these arsons became front-page news, the CC held a meeting with twenty African-American pastors in Atlanta. The CC announced that it would raise $1 million for a "Save the Churches Fund" by asking the 100,000 churches on its mailing list to take a special collections during Sunday services in July.[136] But by an October 17 ceremony, at which Reed gave a $25,000 check to the pastor of a burned-out black church in Richmond, Virginia, the CC had raised only $750,000. "We are saying loud and clear," said Reed as he presented the check, "that we are one in Christ and that we are not going to allow the racial divisions that parted us in the past to do so ever again."[137]

An appeal to the African-American and Latino communities of the inner-city was at the center of "The Samaritan Project," which Reed presented on January 30, 1997, as the CC's legislative agenda for the 105th Congress. This agenda was a combination of many familiar conservative anti-poverty proposals. These included: federally funded scholarships for low-income public school children to attend private or parochial schools, "empowerment zones" to stimulate new inner-city businesses, the removal of restrictions against funding of church-related drug treatment programs, and a $500 tax credit for those who do volunteer work to help the poor. In addition to these initiatives, which would cost the federal government an estimated $3 billion, Reed announced that the CC planned to raise $10 million by the year 2000 to assist 1000 inner-city youth ministries.[138] To advance the Samaritan Project, the CC held a Congress on Racial Justice and Reconciliation in Baltimore on May 10, 1997. Approximately 300 black churchgoers attended the one-day event.[139]

Not surprisingly, some were wary of the CC's motives. The CC's credibility on racial reconciliation was not strengthened when, in October 1996, it had to apologize for sending out a sample voter guide that used a photo of a black man as a fictitious candidate who opposed the CC's views on every issue.[140] Regarding the CC aid to burned-out churches, Howard University political scientist Ronald Walters observed, "You have to think they are doing this for some political motive."[141] Laura Murphy, an African-American official with the American Civil Liberties Union, compared "The Samaritan Project," to attempts by cigarette manufacturer Philip Morris to boost sales in the black community. "This is just a new marketing effort," she said.[142]

Reed has tried to sound upbeat about the possibilities of "a Rainbow Coalition on the right," but negative responses by leaders in each of these social groups have forced Reed to recognize that attempts by the Christian Right to go beyond its current social base "will take a generation."[143] Some of Reed's fellow conservatives were perplexed by his efforts in this area. One conservative strategist, Bill Pascoe, told the *New York Times* that outreach to minorities has usually failed. "At the same time you're not picking up new friends," observed Pascoe, "you're alienating old friends."[144] Despite the lack of much concrete progress in these communities, the mere fact that the CC has made these overtures is useful in countering the "anti-Catholic, anti-Semitic, racist" stereotype associated with the white evangelical constituency of the CC. And beyond the level of short-term public relations, the possibility exists that Reed *really* believes in the interreligious and multiracial future of religious conservatism and that he is trying to lead his constituency in that direction. It remains an open question whether they will follow.

Reed, however, has not found it necessary to create any outreach program to women voters. In contrast to its lack of Jews and African-Americans, the CC already has women in several visible leadership positions.[145] And if attendance at "Road to Victory" conferences is indicative, women seem as likely as men to be grassroots CC activists.[146] According to a 1993 survey commissioned by the CC, the average voter who attended church twice or more a month—the CC's target constituency—was "a career-oriented, baby-boomer woman with children."[147] This was confirmed by a 1996 survey conducted for the American Jewish Committee, which found that 57 percent of those "aligned with the Religious Right" were female.[148] An analysis of the 1994 vote conducted by political scientist John C. Green and others found that "Evangelical men and women voted for the GOP at the same (high) rate."[149] Reed explained the much-discussed "gender gap" in the 1996 presidential vote as "more of a lifestyle issue than a gender issue." Based on exit polling, Reed claimed that while Clinton won single women by 21 percent, and divorced women by 33 percent, Dole "tied Bill Clinton among marrieds with children."[150] According to Reed, within the CC's niche of the political market, churchgoers and families with children, there is no gender gap to overcome.

Another form of narrowness that Reed has sought to overcome, at least on the level of appearance, has been the CC's barely disguised identification with the Republican party.[151] To show that the CC has a separate and independent agenda, Reed cited regulations on the availability of tobacco to children and the legalization of gambling as issues on which "we strenuously disagree with the national Republican party."[152] If for no other reason than to protect the CC's tax-exemption, Reed has sought to keep the CC at least officially nonpartisan.[153] But Reed has also recognized the strategic danger of partisan identification and urged that "The pro-family movement must not become a wholly owned subsidiary of the Republican Party, and it must be willing to mobilize its troops for independent or Democratic candidates who advocate its views."[154] If the CC cannot do this, the Republicans will take the votes of religious conservatives for granted, and the CC will have less leverage to enact its agenda.

The CC, however, has found only a few "pro-family" Democrats, such as former Pennsylvania Governor Robert Casey and Rep. Charles Stenholm of Texas, willing to participate in CC events. In addition, many notable figures and leaders in the Democratic party are openly hostile to the Christian Right in general, and the CC in particular.[155] Reed puts the blame for the exclusively Republican character of the CC on the Democrats. "For its part," claimed Reed, "the pro-family movement would frankly prefer a more bipartisan posture but has so far found the national Democratic party both unwilling and unable (given its domination by liberal special interest groups) to work with it."[156]

To demonstrate its bipartisanship, the CC held a "Celebration of Life" rally in Chicago during the 1996 Democratic National Convention. The event was meant to call attention, according to Reed, to the pro-life views held by 37 percent of Democrats. Four Democratic members of Congress appeared at the rally. Speaking to an audience of several hundred, Reed called the Democrats "the party of censorship . . . on the central issue of our time: abortion."[157] At the rally Reed claimed that one-quarter of CC members identified themselves as Democrats, but CC spokespersons were either unwilling or unable to have CC members who were convention delegates meet with reporters. In contrast to Reed's extensive involvement in the Republican's San Diego convention, he reportedly flew into Chicago for this rally and flew home as soon as it was over. The *Washington Post* characterized Reed's stay of seven hours in Chicago as "the sort of visit Yasser Arafat might make to Tel Aviv."[158] Given the mutual hostility of Democratic leaders and the leaders of the CC, and the incompatibility of their politics, it should not be surprising that the CC has no political home but the Republican Party.[159]

As part of casting a wider net, Reed has also felt it important to reach out to Perot voters. While this constituency has little interest in the social and moral issues that move CC activists, Reed regarded Perot's movement as a "secular analog to the pro-family movement." In his 1996 book, *Active Faith,* Reed sounded optimistic about cooperation with the Perot movement on shared goals such as "balanced budgets, lower taxes, choice in education, term limits, and political reform."[160] Perot's speech at the CC's 1996 "Road to Victory" conference was marred, however, by the negative reception given him by CC delegates. Not only did many regard him as someone who helped elect Clinton in 1992, Perot tried to ignore the issue of abortion. Throughout his speech, many individuals held up 12' x 18' signs reading "PRO-LIFE PRO-FAMILY" or shouted, "What about abortion?"[161]

Perhaps the most important way Reed has sought to broaden the constituency of the CC has been through broadening its issues agenda. According to Reed, the Christian Right has not lived up to its potential because "We have allowed ourselves to be ghettoized by a narrow band of issues like abortion, homosexual rights, and prayer in school."[162] Reed did not want to abandon the value-laden issues that have energized the movement's activists, but "the cluster of pro-family issues must now be expanded to attract a majority of voters."[163] Such an expansion was necessary because "Without specific policies designed to benefit families and children, appeals to family values or America's Judeo-Christian heritage will fall on deaf ears."[164] Reed has called for the development of a policy agenda that deals with the concerns of the average voter. And as the 1997 formulation of the minority-oriented "Samaritan Project" legislative agenda demonstrated, Reed was also willing to adopt issues of interest to particular communities. In advocating this "wider net" strategy, Reed often cited Paul in I Corinthians 9:22: "I have become all things to all people so that by all possible means I might save some."[165]

This call for a broadened agenda was not new within the Christian Right.[166] In his presidential campaign, for instance, Robertson sought, with limited success, to discuss a broad range of policy issues rather than just his religious and moral views. And in 1990, Robertson told CC members, "People care about their pocketbook. Jobs, taxes, educational issues are important to them. We can't just focus on abortion, gay rights, pornography, and prayer in schools without being labeled a fringe group identified with single issues."[167]

To show his commitment to a wider conservative agenda, Reed supported the 1994 Republican *Contract with America,* despite its notable lack of provisions dealing with the Christian Right's traditional issues.[168] Reed also stayed "on message" even when Republican leaders didn't. Just after the 1994 election, when Republican leader Newt Gingrich unexpectedly suggested a school prayer amendment, Reed quickly distanced himself from Gingrich's proposal. "I want to make it perfectly clear that this is not our top priority," Reed told the *New York Times.* "I, for one, don't think we'll turn the country around by having public acts of piety. Our priorities are tax relief and welfare."[169]

Reed denied that his broader agenda represented a strategic abandonment of the Christian Right's traditional issues: "The economic and cultural issues are a seamless web."[170] Tactically, Reed was very concerned that the CC not disrupt its alliance with other conservatives. In 1993, he told the conservative journal *Human Events,* "Look, we're not saying that everybody has to make the social issues *the* most important issue. We're simply saying you shouldn't *exclude* them from being part of the breadbasket of issues that we talk about."[171] In the aftermath of the Republican congressional victories in 1994, Reed declared, "We have no intention of doing to the new [104th] Congress what the unions, feminists, and the gay lobby did to President Clinton when he took office. They presented an extremist agenda and forced this administration out of the mainstream on many issues."[172] But Reed's support of the Republican *Contract* was not disinterested. "Our objective was to win a big victory on the Contract with America," explained Reed, "thereby building up political capital that we could later spend on social issues."[173]

Like the Republican *Contract,* the CC's social issues legislative agenda, the *Contract with the American Family,* consisted of ten proposals that were developed through polls and focus groups. The CC even hired the same pollster, Frank Luntz, who had worked with Gingrich on the Republican *Contract.*[174] Predictably, when Reed did unveil the *Contract with the American Family* on May 17, 1995, critics such as Ira Glasser of the American Civil Liberties Union denounced the CC proposal as "Dangerous and radical."[175] But a closer study of this document reveals, especially in comparison with earlier manifestos of the Christian Right, a striking avoidance of radical positions. When the American Jewish Congress (AJC) issued a sharply critical report on the *Contract,* it found, "Most noticeably, the extreme ideas of sectors of the conservative Christian movement are simply missing from the Contract." The AJC report attributed the lack of extremism to "Political and organizational expedience."[176] Reed's allies had a similar evaluation. Gary Bauer of the Family Research Council called it "unduly modest."[177] Pat Buchanan made a similar evaluation: "The Coalition has given away any boldness in a search for popularity and consensus."[178]

Reed's perceived tendency toward "expedience" brought much more bitter condemnation from other Christian Right leaders. In 1994, Randall Terry, the founder of the anti-abortion group Operation Rescue, called the CC's cooperation with pro-choice Republicans "treachery": "We cannot—in the name of the Christian Coalition—sell out the law of heaven for short-term political gain. To do so is an abomination."[179] Martin Mawyer of the Christian Action Network complained that the CC was "so locked into Republican politics, they are continually forced to re-define themselves based on the current political climate and who's in charge of the Republican party."[180] Mawyer also called the CC's attempts to cast a wider net "unprincipled" and said they were based on "deceiving the American public."[181] Judy Brown of the American Life League attacked the limited anti-abortion proposal in the CC's *Contract,* comparing it to pledging "to close one-third of the Nazi concentration camps."[182] When Reed declined to vigorously attack the possible presidential candidacy of the pro-choice General Colin Powell, James Dobson of Focus on the Family told Reed in a letter, "This posture may elevate your influence in Washington, but it is unfaithful to the principles we are duty-bound as Christians to defend."[183]

Criticism of Reed's "mainstreaming" of the CC has centered on the bedrock issue of abortion. In 1993, Reed, for instance, argued for a broader issues agenda based on 1992 exit polls that showed that "Only 12 percent of voters indicated that abortion was a key issue in their voting decision."[184] This did not endear him to his pro-life allies. But to make matters worse, at the 1994 "Road to Victory" conference Reed seemed to suggest that he would accept revision in the language of the abortion plank of the Republican platform, so long as it remained pro-life.[185]

The perception that Reed was "soft on abortion" was exacerbated in 1996 by his apparent coolness toward the fervently pro-life presidential campaign of Pat Buchanan and the implicit support many observers saw Reed giving the lukewarm-on-abortion Bob Dole campaign.[186] Reed also refused to join other Christian Right leaders in actively trying to keep Powell off the Republican ticket.[187] On May 3, 1996, Reed did not appear with representatives of other Christian Right organizations at a press conference organized by the Buchanan campaign to denounce attempts to change the abortion plank of the Republican platform.[188]

Even worse for Reed's relations with his anti-abortion allies was the release in early May 1996 of a *Newsweek* excerpt from his new book, *Active Faith,* in which Reed appeared to advocate a revision of the abortion plank.[189] Rather than calling for a right-to-life amendment to the constitution, he suggested that the Republican plank state: "We seek by all legal and constitutional means to protect the right to life for the elderly, the infirm, the unborn, and the disabled."[190] His ostensible reason for the suggestion seems to have been a naive pragmatism: "Amending the Constitution may be the least practical and most remote weapon at our disposal at this time."[191] He may also have been trying to position himself as the most reasonable pro-life leader—the leader with whom the Dole campaign could most easily deal.[192]

Reed undoubtedly knew his suggestion would be controversial, and he was careful to say that these words were his own and "do not reflect the policy of the Christian Coalition."[193] But he did not seem to realize that he was touching the third rail of Christian Right politics. Angela "Bay" Buchanan, manager of her brother's 1996 presidential campaign, said, "Ralph Reed is sending up the white flag of surrender," and she called his suggestion "an absolute retreat" that provided "aid and comfort to the pro-abortionists."[194] Reed, she said, was "no longer a legitimate leader of social conservatives in this country."[195]

Reed explained that his attempt at writing a new pro-life plank was meant "to provoke a discussion."[196] But when the response was denunciation rather than discussion, Reed quickly shut up and fell in line with other pro-life leaders in stopping Dole and other Republicans from changing or weakening the abortion plank. He could not afford to become isolated on this bedrock issue. In the July/August issue of *Christian American,* Reed took a much harder line: "We will oppose with every fiber in our being any effort to include a rape and incest exception in the pro-life plank, or to drop a call for constitutional and legal remedies such as an amendment to the Constitution."[197] During the platform committee struggles before the Republican convention, Reed worked closely with Schlafly, Bauer, and Bay Buchanan—the group came to be known as the "fearsome foursome."[198]

Reed's difficulties on abortion in 1996 show how Reed has pursued the broadening and "mainstreaming" of the CC agenda through a Clintonesque strategy of "triangulation." On the advice of political consultant Dick Morris, in 1995 President Clinton began to distinguish himself from both liberal Democrats and conservative Republicans in Congress. Clinton's third position, thus the name triangulation, was meant to be perceived as centrist and above the usual partisan bickering—a stance that proved popular with the electorate.[199] Reed, however, has not taken positions that place the CC in the center of the ideological spectrum but merely positions that will be attacked from the left *and* from the right. Spokespersons for various left, liberal, and moderate political organizations have issued predictable, and occasionally hysterical, streams of criticism of the CC agenda as extreme, dangerous, radical, and theocratic. By receiving attacks from those on the right, Reed was able to encourage the perception that his positions were not extreme but part of the mainstream. "Thunder from the right," from Terry, Schlafly, Bauer, Dobson, or the Buchanans, made charges of the CC's right-wing extremism less credible. In *Active Faith,* Reed seemed to relish recounting attacks from both ends of the political spectrum. "We did not mind dodging bullets from the far left and right," he explained, "because it placed us right where we belonged: in the mainstream of the debate. It also kept our critics off balance and prevented us from being pigeonholed as a fringe movement, as some had attempted to do for years."[200]

Reed's disagreements with others in the Christian Right have been interpreted as signs of the movement's disunity and potential disintegration. This interpretation may be partly the product of wishful thinking by its opponents, but Reed's triangulation did have risks—as his troubles over the abortion plank demonstrated. While Reed has established himself as the religious conservative leader most likely to be considered "mainstream," borrowing tricks from "Slick Willie" Clinton may not help Reed among many religious conservatives. Bauer, for instance, observed that "Ralph is probably a bit more interested in being an inside player in the Republican party."[201]

Reed, however, dismissed these suspicions as the price of progress. "Any leader of a social-reform movement who is on the cutting edge of tactical and strategic shifts by that movement is going to experience some level of ambivalence, and sometimes opposition, from others in the movement. And that is not a sign of anything other than the fact that you're moving the ball down the field."[202]

Inclusive Rhetoric

Reed's ability to broaden the issues agenda of the CC, and to position that agenda in the perceived mainstream, has depended upon his apparent acceptance of the realities of social diversity and his recommendation of civility in public discourse. The overall course that Reed has set for the CC, at least for its rhetoric, seems to be toward what Moen called "the secular norms and practices of American politics."[203]

When the CC first began to attract public attention, its rhetoric often had a strident tone as it identified itself with controversial figures and causes. For example, in 1990, in a full-page ad in *USA Today,* Robertson put himself in the role of actor Clint Eastwood's "Dirty Harry" character. He dared members of Congress to "Vote for the NEA [National Endowment for the Arts] appropriation just like . . . the gay and lesbian task force want. And make my day."[204] Also in 1990, the CC gave its implied support to the reelection campaign of Senator Jesse Helms by distributing 750,000 voter guides.[205] A 1991 editorial in *Christian American* called Clarence Thomas, "a perfect choice to fill the Supreme Court vacancy," and the CC launched an intense lobbying effort on his behalf.[206] Reed later identified the raucous and divisive battle over the Thomas nomination as the moment when the CC "catapulted on to the national political radar screen."[207]

In the early years of CC activity, Reed and Robertson said things that have been used against them repeatedly. Second only to his comments on guerilla warfare and stealth politics, Reed's most infamous quotations are the following: "We think the Lord is going to give us this nation back one precinct at a time, one neighborhood at a time, and one state at a time"[208] and "I honestly believe that in my lifetime we will see a country once again governed by Christians . . . and Christian values."[209]

Robertson confirmed fears about the ambitions of the CC when he wrote in a 1991 fund-raising letter, "THE CHRISTIAN COALITION WILL BE THE MOST POWERFUL POLITICAL ORGANIZATION IN AMERICA."[210] In his televised speech at the 1992 Republican National Convention, Robertson accused Bill Clinton of having "a radical plan to destroy the traditional family and transfer many of its functions to the federal government."[211] And Robertson's most memorable statement from 1992 was, "The feminist agenda is not about equal rights for women. It is about a socialist, anti-family political movement that encourages women to leave their husbands, kill their children, practice witchcraft, destroy capitalism and become lesbians."[212]

In the aftermath of the 1992 elections, however, Reed's wider net strategy emerged in an attempt to give the Christian Right what *Time* called, "a gentler, more catholic visage."[213] Strident rhetoric, especially in CC fund-raising letters, did not by any means cease in November 1992, but since that time the CC has adopted a new public style that can be traced to Reed's rise to prominence. Beginning in 1993, Reed's was the face that the CC preferred to present to the wider public.[214] Robertson has been taking what he called, "an elder statesman's role."[215] For instance, when the CC publicly presented the *Contract with the American Family,* Robertson was in Africa.[216] And direct-mail pieces have come to bear Reed's signature as well as Robertson's.

The face Reed tried to present to the public was smiling and reasonable. In the January 1993 issue of *Christian American,* Reed advised members to "avoid hostile and intemperate rhetoric."[217] "When stating our own convictions," he urged readers, "we must acknowledge the opinion of others and the sincerity of their beliefs. We must emphasize inclusion, not exclusion. We must adopt strategies of persuasion, not domination. We must be tolerant of diverse views and

respectful of those who express them."[218] And Reed, who did not
originally like the name "Christian Coalition" because he knew it would
be criticized,[219] denied the notion that the CC claimed that those who
hold differing views were not good Christians, or that the CC claimed to
represent all Christians.[220] Reed has been careful to criticize any notion
that religious conservatives speak for God in matters of public policy.
"There may be only one way to get to heaven according to one's
theology," wrote Reed, "but there is probably more than one way to
balance the budget or reform health care."[221]

Reed also disclaimed any exclusivist notions of a "Christian
America." "America is not solely a Christian nation," explained Reed,
"but a pluralistic society of Protestants, Catholics, Jews, Muslims, and
other people of faith whose broader culture once honored religion, but
which today increasingly reflects a hostility toward faith in the public
sphere."[222] In his speech before the Anti-Defamation League in April
1995, Reed acknowledged the burden of the long history of Christian
anti-Semitism. He referred to "the blatant wrongs of a few—those who
claimed that 'God does not hear the prayers of Jews,' those who said that
this is a 'Christian nation,' suggesting that others may not be welcome,
and those who say that the only prayers uttered in public school should
be Christian prayers."[223] Even *New York Times* columnist Frank Rich,
who accused Reed of fronting for the anti-Semitism of Robertson, wrote
of Reed's speech, "There isn't a sentence . . . with which any fair-minded
person, Jew or gentile, can disagree."[224]

When Reed presented the *Contract with the American Family* he
went out of his way to make it seem unthreatening and reasonable. Reed
assured his listeners, "These provisions are the ten suggestions, not the
Ten Commandments. . . . Our goal is not to legislate family values, it is
to ensure that Washington values families."[225] Significantly, the text of
Contract with the American Family did not cite the Bible even once, and
only occasionally cited materials published by Christian Right organizations. It did, like any other public policy proposal, cite public opinion
polls, government documents, journalists, and scholars.[226] Also, unlike
the House Republican *Contract with America,* Reed did not set any
deadline for the passage of these proposals. "This contract is designed,"
said Reed, "to be the first word, not the last, in developing a bold and
incremental start to strengthening the family and restoring values."[227]

One area in which the rhetoric of Reed and the CC has remained
strident is its criticism of anti-Christian bigotry and the victimization of

"people of faith." But even this rhetoric, which I will examine in detail in Chapter 6, has been cast in the more inclusive liberal rhetoric of "rights," "equal access," and "discrimination." The CC's *Contract,* for instance, did not call for the restoration of pre-1962 compulsory school prayer but for protection of the right of voluntary religious expression. CC literature has often appealed to the precedent of the religiously based civil-rights movement to justify the activities of the Christian Right. During his speech at the 1995 "Road to Victory" conference, Reed distributed a seven-point "Christian Coalition Pledge Card." This pledge was supposedly based on one drafted by Martin Luther King, Jr. for the Southern Christian Leadership Conference. Citing the seventh point of the pledge, Reed urged CC members to "Refrain from the violence of fist, tongue, or heart."[228] Reed argued that King's healing and inclusive rhetoric was crucial for the success of the civil rights movement. According to Reed, the pro-family movement has needed a similar rhetoric. "The American people," wrote Reed, "need to know that we do not desire to exclude our political foes, only to gain our own place at the table."[229]

In his 1996 book, *Active Faith,* Reed continued to emphasize a rhetoric of civility. "How we say things," declared Reed, "is frequently more important than what we say. In short, our words are at times as powerful a witness of our faith as our beliefs—for good or ill."[230] He has been quite critical of the rhetorical excesses of the leadership of the early Christian Right. According to Reed, their "high-octane message stuck in the throats of the general public like a chicken bone."[231] Reed stressed how much today's religious conservatives have learned from past mistakes. "Over time, we have learned to understate rather than overstate our influence, resisting the temptation to shout when speaking in a soft voice will more than suffice."[232]

Nevertheless, in the final chapter of *Active Faith,* Reed criticized certain rhetorical excesses of the contemporary Christian Right. "Every word we say and every action we take," declared Reed, "should reflect God's grace. . . . Nowhere is this principle more important than in our opposition to Bill Clinton."[233] Criticism of the policies of Clinton's administration and his official conduct were completely legitimate. "But those who are identified as followers of Christ," cautioned Reed, "should temper their disagreements with Clinton with civility and the grace of God, avoiding the temptation to personalize or demonize their opponents."[234] Reed was also critical of gay-bashing: "I have found some of the religious conservative movement's discourse on homosexuality disturbing." While Reed regards homosexuality as a "deviation from normative sexual conduct and God's laws," he also argued that the assertion that AIDS is a divine punishment on gay "perverts" was "inconsistent with our Christian call to mercy."[235]

Whether Reed's call for civility was motivated by personal conviction or political expedience is unknown. But both his usual critics and his usual allies found fault with him. The predictable criticism from the left concentrated on how Robertson's extremism made Reed's appeal for civility an obvious sham. Barry Lynn of Americans United for Separation of Church and State found it "particularly hypocritical for Ralph Reed to remain silent when the boss of his organization uses the same shrill rhetoric Reed claims is inappropriate for others."[236]

Criticism of Reed's call for civility also came from the right. As Reed noted, "I had some of my dear friends in the conservative community who were very upset about it. But I'm glad I said it."[237] The "thunder from the right" came from Jerry Falwell, whom Reed singled out for both Clinton- and gay-bashing. Falwell responded to Reed with dismissive irritation, predicting that as Reed "gets older he'll be more careful about questioning the persons in his own movement who may have been at it longer than he."[238] In a similar vein, Bauer told a reporter that he had no problem with civility but that he had a problem with being "lectured by someone who seems to think he is noble in this regard and everyone else needs lecturing."[239] On a more tactical level, Schlafly found Reed's call for civility toward Clinton to be "strange advice" in the face of the Democrat's "no-holds-barred media advertising campaign of Republican-bashing."[240] As with Reed's attempt to position the CC's agenda within the mainstream, Reed's reputation for using "mainstream" rhetoric has only been strengthened by these attacks. But Reed's call for civility may also alienate him from his natural allies and supporters.[241]

THE CHALLENGES OF 1996 AND BEYOND

This discussion of the purpose, structure, and activities of the CC has demonstrated that the CC has been an attempt to institutionalize the Christian Right. While this attempt has not met with unqualified success so far, the CC's financial strength and membership size, its orientation toward grassroots activism, and its broader constituency and issues agenda, as well as its more inclusive rhetoric, have allowed it, in a short period, to become a "player" in national politics.

In the aftermath of the congressional elections of 1994, Reed was hailed as the "wunderkind" who delivered the evangelical vote to the victorious Republicans.[242] When the CC presented its *Contract with the American Family* in 1995, many of the Republican leaders pledged their support.[243] And at the CC's annual conference in September 1995, almost all of the Republican presidential candidates came to "court" the support of the CC membership in the upcoming primaries.[244] At that same conference, Reed could announce, "We have gained what we have always sought, a place at the table, a sense of legitimacy."[245]

One year later, at the 1996 conference, Reed did not repeat that proud announcement. Instead, he sounded embattled and defiant. He warned both the CC's friends and foes that "you had better get used to the Christian Coalition, because we're going to be around for a long long time."[246] This change was, of course, linked to the collapse of the so-called Republican Revolution of 1994. And the lawsuit by the FEC, filed just six weeks earlier, threatened the CC's primary means of electoral influence, the distribution of voter guides in the upcoming November election. But it was the surprising events of the 1996 race for the presidency that revealed most clearly how far the CC still has to go to have a secure place at the table of the political mainstream.

With the early withdrawal of former Vice President Dan Quayle and Bill Bennett from the presidential race, there was no nationally known Republican who was able to claim to be *the* consensus Christian Right candidate in the 1996 primaries. Reed and other religious conservatives adopted a strategy of "wait and deliver." In other words, religious conservatives should remain neutral for as long as possible in order to maximize their bargaining power.[247] But as the race developed there emerged a division in the movement. Reed described it as a disagreement "as to whether you should go with a pragmatic choice who can win or whether you can go with the choice of your heart."[248] The "choice of your heart" candidate who emerged from the pack was Buchanan. Unlike the boomlets for Powell and Forbes, which divided religious conservatives only over the tactics of opposition, the successes of the Buchanan campaign posed a fundamental threat to Reed's mainstreaming of the CC.[249]

Buchanan's militant rhetoric and "scary" persona represented what Reed had been trying to overcome since the 1992 Houston convention. Indeed, Buchanan's infamous "religious war" speech in Houston had provided the critics of religious conservatism with a stick with which to beat the movement. Reed did not want the CC to wear the label of "extremist" that he knew would be slapped on Buchanan. And if Buchanan was able to win the nomination, his almost certain defeat in the general election would be blamed on the "lunatic fringe" of religious conservatives. Buchanan's adoption of an "outsider"—"peasants with pitchforks"—stance toward the Republican party also represented a threat to the future of the religious conservative movement as Reed envisioned it. In Reed's view, religious conservatives were increasingly party "insiders" with positions of responsibility. And as insiders, "they must do more than 'send a message.' . . . They must win elections. They must govern."[250]

Throughout the primaries, Reed frequently stressed the diversity of views among religious conservatives, indicating his desire to put daylight between the CC and Buchanan. Yet an overt rejection was out of the question because of the strong support Buchanan's views on abortion had within the CC constituency.[251] Understood this way, the Buchanan campaign had a silver lining for the CC. As Reed put it, "We knew that the activism and energy represented by the Buchanan campaign was a critical part of our broader effort to preserve the pro-family and pro-life stands of the Republican party."[252]

Therefore, Reed could not attack Buchanan, even though he did not want to support him. Reed described this as "the delicate dance we performed throughout the primaries."[253] After the New Hampshire primary, for instance, when some Republicans began to call Buchanan an "extremist," Reed issued a warning. "When you attack those candidates who stand up for our values," said Reed, "you are attacking us."[254] Yet in warning that "extremist" was an antireligious conservative "code word,"[255] Reed was really trying not to defend Buchanan, but to defeat him. "Using those kinds of terms," explained Reed, "will only drive more religious conservatives toward Buchanan, and potentially propel him to the nomination."[256]

Almost by default, Senator Bob Dole emerged as the candidate for the more pragmatic "insider" religious conservatives. Dole barely survived the successive challenges of publisher Steve Forbes and Buchanan, and he might not have done so without the barely disguised support of the CC. Dole owed Reed, as *Wall Street Journal* columnist Paul Gigot put it, "big time."[257] Despite Reed's repeated claims of neutrality, Dole's comeback win in the South Carolina primary, in which he got 22 percent more of the CC vote than Buchanan,[258] represented a victory for Reed's brand of insider pragmatism.

If Dole's victory over Buchanan demonstrated the commitment of many religious conservatives to an insider identity, that identity was tested by their treatment as outsiders at the 1996 Republican National Convention. With an estimated 1000 delegates, over 500 of whom were supposedly CC members, religious conservatives were able to win decisive platform victories and make rules changes on future delegate selection.[259] But Dole, who had been embarrassed repeatedly by pro-life resistance to his suggestions for tolerance language in the platform, let it be known that he had not read the platform and that he wasn't bound by it.[260] Dole made only a passing mention of abortion in his acceptance speech. Vice presidential nominee Jack Kemp was pro-life, but it was his economic views that were emphasized by the campaign.[261] Perhaps most striking was the almost complete absence of religious conservatives speaking from the podium in San Diego.[262] *Newsweek,* for instance, summarized the conventional wisdom about Reed: "Christian Coalition leader wins platform battle, sent to back pew when the cameras roll."[263]

Dole, of course, went down to the defeat everyone, even Robertson, had been predicting for months.[264] Critics were quick to point out the losses suffered by the CC. People for the American Way claimed that the CC had been "severely chastised" by the defeat of at least eight Republican Congressmen who had earned 100 percent ratings in the CC's *Congressional Scorecard,* and by the "stunning defeat" of a Parental Rights Amendment in Colorado.[265] Americans United's Director Barry Lynn observed, "The Christian Coalition isn't a toothless tiger, but it sure needs dental work."[266] Some CC activists were also dismayed by the election results. Sara DiVito Hardman, Chairman of the California CC, was quoted by the *Los Angeles Times:* "I'm asking whether we have lost the ability to read the public's mind."[267]

Reed was quick to put a different spin on all this. He stressed that both houses of Congress remained in Republican hands, something for which the CC could claim some credit. According to Reed, "Conservative evangelicals were the firewall that prevented a Bob Dole defeat from mushrooming into a meltdown all the way down the ballot." The "margin of victory" in the first reelection of a Republican Congress in sixty-eight years, according to Reed, was provided by "conservative people of faith."[268] Reed also argued that, "More important than the quantity elected is the *quality* of these pro-family legislators." Of the 96 members of the House who had earned 100 percent ratings on the CC *Congressional Scorecard,* 87 were reelected. And 9 of 10 Senators with the 100 percent rating were reelected.[269]

Reed also started work on the 1998 election by pointing out that parties not holding the White House usually win the congressional midterm election of a president's second term. This pattern, combined with the continued shift of southern voters toward the GOP, allowed Reed to predict "Republican dominance of Congress at least to the end of the decade—and perhaps beyond."[270]

Despite putting the best possible spin on the 1996 results, Reed did not paint it as a victory. As he said on *The 700 Club* the day after the election, "Sometimes elections are about victory or defeat and sometimes they are about survival. And for religious conservatives and deeply committed Christians in America this election was about survival."[271] Reed, of course, had seen this coming long before November 5. In the September issue of *Christian American,* Reed demonstrated that he understood the disappointment of many CC members with Dole and the failure of the 104th Congress. But "politics is poker, not chess," wrote Reed. "We must play with the cards we have, doing the very best we can with the resources and candidates at our disposal."[272]

Robertson, however, did not care much for the cards he had been dealt in 1996. On the November 6th edition of *The 700 Club,* he blamed the defeat on Dole and incompetent "inside-the-beltway" consultants who "muted social issues in favor of money issues."[273] In a post-election interview with the *New York Times,* Robertson warned, "We're not going to sit by as good soldiers and take whatever is given us." In contrast to the CC's "wait and deliver" strategy of 1996, Robertson announced a "coalesce early" strategy for 2000. He said that he would convene a meeting sometime in 1997 of Republican conservatives to settle on an agenda and a presidential candidate—"someone," he was careful to point out, "who's electable."[274] Reed, although he did not mention any plans for a meeting, echoed Robertson's strategy in a TV interview on November 10th. He referred to "a growing consensus among religious conservatives" to "find someone, in the model of Ronald Reagan, who will run unapologetically on this agenda."[275] Or as Reed later told columnist Cal Thomas, "We are going to have to invent a presidential candidate for the year 2000."[276]

While the CC emerged from the 1996 elections somewhat damaged and disappointed, the obituaries many would like to write for that organization might be more the product of wishful thinking than of sober analysis. The CC did not live up to its invincible image, but one could argue that many of the political reverses the CC suffered were the product of Republican blunders. Some on the Christian Right will undoubtedly blame Robertson and Reed for supporting the "wrong" candidate for president, or for supporting him too strongly for too long.[277] Yet only those who care nothing about election results can argue with Reed's answer: "It's hard to make the argument that this race would have been significantly closer if the nominee had been someone else."[278] In the longer term, the FEC lawsuit may pose a serious threat to the CC's methods and tax-exempt status, but any final resolution, given the possibility of appeals, may be years away.

The most serious question facing the CC is posed by the departure of Reed to start his own political consulting firm, Century Strategies. In a prepared statement, he explained that "I never intended to stay in this job forever. I believe that institutions such as the Christian Coalition, like the rest of the political system, are energized by new blood and new ideas."[279] Despite the inevitable speculation, there is little evidence so far that Reed's resignation was forced by any fundamental disagreement between Robertson and Reed, or by any revolt against Reed within the CC. Robertson, of course, stressed his "gratitude and support" for Reed.[280] Reed remained on the CC's Board of Directors and Robertson reportedly offered Reed the presidency of Regent University in order to keep his services.[281] One unnamed conservative activist, however, said that Reed had grown frustrated with his role of junior partner to Robertson. "In many respects, he's eclipsed his boss, and that's going to cause some friction."[282] Others saw in Reed's resignation an attempt to get out before the CC's problems, such as the FEC lawsuit, came to a head.[283] But others saw Reed taking the opportunity to shape the message and direction of campaigns from the inside, rather than having to react to them from the outside, as in 1996.[284] By leaving the CC, Reed may have found a way to "invent a presidential candidate for the year 2000" who will speak for the CC's constituency.

Robertson's decision to take a new role as chairman of the CC's board was unexpected but easier to understand in terms of his broader goals. On the same day the changes in the CC were announced, media mogul Rupert Murdoch made public a $1.9 billion deal to buy half of the Family Channel, Robertson's cable TV network. By scaling down his business and political responsibilities, Robertson may be preparing to devote more of his attention to WorldReach, an international evangelization ministry that he started in 1995. Using communications technology, WorldReach means to bring 500 million people to Christ by the turn of the century.[285] Critics of the CC, however, doubt that a changed job title will make any difference in Robertson's control of the CC. As Barry Lynn of Americans United observed, "You could put Jesus, Moses and Mohammed on the board and he'd still be the one calling the shots."[286]

Whatever the reason for these changes, the challenges facing the CC's new leaders, Hodel and Tate, will be great. Reed's departure has left a big hole. He built the CC's organization from scratch and gave it the style, if not the substance, of mainstream politics. And if Robertson, whose name and personal charisma helped attract much of the CC's constituency, takes a less visible and less active role, Hodel and Tate will be left to take up the slack in motivating the rank-and-file. Hodel, an experienced administrator and an expert on energy and environmental issues, has clear mainstream credentials but is not known for an ability to mobilize grassroots activists on social issues.[287] And Tate, a genuine grassroots religious conservative who got into politics as a Robertson supporter in 1988, has relatively little experience in national politics.[288] If Hodel and Tate cannot hold onto the CC's precarious mainstream status *and* effectively mobilize religious conservatives, then the CC will be headed for hard times.

Despite these difficulties, the resources and assets, especially its network of activists, that contributed to the rise of the CC are still in place. Oldfield found the Christian Right as a whole to be "deeply rooted in the American social structure, drawing its strength from a vibrant, well-politicized constituency and from that constituency's impressive organizational infrastructure."[289] Unless there has been a profound and pervasive disillusionment at the grassroots with Reed's type of pragmatism, the CC will still provide the most developed vehicle within the Christian Right for taking concrete political action. As Rozell and Wilcox observed, those active in politics the longest "may become socialized into the norms of politics and learn to compromise to achieve at least part of their policy goals."[290] Newer activists, such as those mobilized by the 1996 Buchanan candidacy, will tend to be more doctrinaire and more prone to abandon politics entirely in disgust. Those who remain, according to Rozell and

Wilcox, "will eventually become more willing to compromise and more skilled in political bargaining." But the ongoing processes of socialization and institutionalization will be "chaotic, because there have been multiple, overlapping waves of mobilization."[291]

Given this chaos, and the general volatility of contemporary American politics, predictions about the future of the CC are a hazardous, if not foolish, enterprise. Yet, I believe the CC's attempt to institutionalize religious conservatism still has the potential for enduring success. But like the nineteenth-century southern evangelicals in Reed's dissertation, the CC may find that the methods that bring success can have unintended and ironic consequences. In the next two chapters, I will examine two themes in the literature of the CC that have been central to the appeal and success of that organization. In the final chapter, I will discuss the strained, if not contradictory, relationship between these themes and speculate on the possible consequences for the future of the CC.

CHAPTER 5

DREAMS OF RESTORATION

As I noted in Chapter 1, a perennial question about the Christian Right in general, and the CC in particular, is "What do they want?" or more precisely, "What do they *really* want?" One way of answering that question is to focus on the "offensive agenda" of the Christian Right. This agenda is one of aggressively reasserting, through political and legal means as well as by persuasion, the public authority of evangelical belief and morality. Evangelicals who adopt this stance are interested in the restoration of a lost past in which life was better and more godly.

The urge to return to a lost golden era is not an innovation of the Christian Right or the CC. The restorationist impulse grows out of the fundamental religious desire to reactualize what historian of religion Mircea Eliade called "sacred time," a paradigmatic and mythic time of origins in which the power and reality of the sacred was fully manifest.[1] This fundamental religious desire to transcend the corruptions of history has been readily apparent in American religion and culture. Restorationism has been essential to various American sectarian traditions, such as the Campbellites, the Mormons, and the Landmark Baptists, that have sought to restore the pattern and purity of the primitive church, the Christianity of the very first followers of Christ.[2]

But the significance of the restoration ideal is much broader. According to historian David Edwin Harrell, "it may be the most vital single assumption underlying the development of American Protestantism."[3]

American restorationism receives far less scholarly attention than millennialism, but the two are intimately related. As historians Richard T. Hughes and C. Leonard Allen argued, "most millennial visions elaborated a very specific content drawn from a first age whose perfections had been lost or obscured in a fall but that might be recovered in the millennial dawn."[4]

American restorationism or primitivism did not suddenly develop in the nineteenth century but was an important feature of Anglo-American Puritanism.[5] Puritanism's interest in "primordial reform" was based on three influential sources: Christian humanism's desire to go "back to the sources" of the Christian faith; the continental Reformed tradition's emphasis on "biblical precedent"; and the covenant theology of William Tyndale, which understood England as a "new Israel." These influences contributed to Puritanism's drive to replicate the primitive church within the context of a national covenant with God.[6]

The other great formative influence on the American mind, the Enlightenment, also appealed to restorationist themes. Enlightenment restorationism had, however, a different focus. "The quest for the primordium persisted;" wrote Hughes and Allen, "the rationalists simply substituted one book—the book of Nature—for another and exchanged the primordium of the early church for the primordium of Eden."[7] Jefferson's Declaration of Independence, for instance, asserted that unalienable rights are not the product of history, but come directly from the Creator. America, as a "new order for the ages," leaped over history to recover what was found originally in nature.

Despite their deep differences, Puritanism and the Enlightenment did share a common quest for a primordial paradigmatic time—a commonality that had important consequences in the eighteenth and nineteenth centuries. Because of this, argued Hughes and Allen, "the primordium of the primitive church and the primordium of nature could become so thoroughly amalgamated in the thinking of so many of this period."[8] The God of the Bible and nature's God of the Enlightenment came to be identified, despite their differences, as did the teachings of Christ and the laws of nature. And "nature's nation," the United States, came to be regarded as a uniquely "Christian nation" with a universal mission to spread the blessings of liberty and Christianity. The nation itself came to be identified by some with the purity and innocence of Eden, and therefore with a millennial destiny.

The lost golden age that the Christian Right and the CC wish to recover is, strictly speaking, neither the primitive church nor Eden.

Instead they hope for a restoration of "Christian America." But like the sacred primordial time of religious myth, the historicity of an era when America was a "Christian nation" is doubtful. In their 1984 book, *The Search for Christian America,* historians Mark A. Noll, Nathan O. Hatch, and George M. Marsden specifically rejected the Christian Right's version of America's lost Christian heritage. This rejection was based not only on the flawed historical methods of the Christian America advocates, but on an analysis of their substantive claims. "We feel," wrote Noll, Hatch, and Marsden, "that a careful study of the facts of history shows that early America does not deserve to be considered uniquely, distinctly or even predominately Christian, if we mean by the word 'Christian' a state of society reflecting the ideals presented in Scripture. There is no lost golden age to which American Christians may return."[9] There was too much, argued the authors, in American history and in the history of American Christianity that contradicted, or that subverted, scriptural ideals.

Christian America advocates admit the distance between ideals and historical realities but regard such instances as sinful aberrations, exceptions to the rule. "The stories in our nation's history," wrote Robertson in 1986, "about cruelty to the Indians, misuse of the land, racial and class prejudice, and bigotry and injustice are often true. But those moments that illustrate our forefathers' failures happened not because those men *kept* Christ's commission, but because they *wandered* from it."[10] Robertson's use of the word "moments" reflected an attempt to minimize what has been shameful in American history while recalling the positive achievements of America's Christian culture. These idealized achievements, especially in comparison with the hard reality of contemporary failures, have been offered as proof that there was indeed a golden era in American history. "Histories" of America's Christian origin and heritage, although they have not conformed to the standards of academic historians, have been important in justifying and articulating the restorationist impulses of the Christian Right.

It should be remembered that the assertion "America is a Christian nation" is a statement of faith about God's special relationship to America. Faith in a national covenant with God, or in the providential role of America, can neither be proved nor disproved, only accepted or rejected. Such assertions are not statements of historical fact, but part of a vision about the meaning of the national experience. But this vision of the meaning of America is not undisputed. As historian Arthur

Schlesinger, Jr. pointed out in *The Cycles of American History,* there has been "a continuing tension between two divergent conceptions of the nation: does America mean a commitment to a national experiment? or consecration of a national destiny?" While Schlesinger was unapologetically a proponent of the experimental conception, he recognized that "Both have dwelt within the American mind and struggled for its possession through the course of American history. Their competition will doubtless continue for the rest of the life of the nation."[11]

The desire to restore a golden age in which the nation was fulfilling its original consecrated destiny is a perennial one in the American mind. This desire can be seen in fundamentalism's resistance to modernity in the 1920s and the revolutionary conservatism of the politicized evangelicals of the Christian Right. But the object of this study, the CC, has given this perennial desire a particular shape in response to contemporary conditions. It is to the particular character of the CC's restorationist impulse that I now turn.

THE CC'S RESTORATION OF CHRISTIAN AMERICA

Critics and opponents of the Christian Right use the exclusive and antipluralistic implications of "Christian America" rhetoric to discredit and demonize the intentions of the movement and its leadership.[12] According to Reed, however, the movement's Christian nation rhetoric is not really a call for theocracy but is indicative of "the cognitive gap separating evangelical speakers and secular ears." Unlike other recent movements, he argued, the early Christian Right "lacked friendly media to interpret the nuances of the community and elevate its more responsible leaders."[13]

The Christian Right's pursuit of political sophistication and effectiveness requires greater circumspection about the use of such rhetoric. This circumspection has been apparent in Reed's comments on the notion of America as a Christian nation. When an ABC television reporter asked, "You don't want a Christian nation?" Reed replied, "Not in any official sense. No. What we're looking for is a pluralistic democracy that welcomes faith into its politics and into its government."[14] In *Politically Incorrect,* Reed asserted that historical statements by presidents and Supreme Court justices indicating the Christian or religious character of America, "reflected a consensus on civil religion that united Americans for the first three centuries of their history." "None of this," argued Reed, "adds up to the conclusion that America is a 'Christian nation' in the sense of a theocratic state or a unicultural society." Labeling America as solely a Christian nation, he was careful to note, "not only ignores the enormous contribution that Jews have made to America but it is something of an anachronism." Just as Massachusetts can no longer be described as a Puritan commonwealth, argued Reed, America can no longer be called a Christian nation. "What religious conservatives want," Reed explained, "is to accommodate the historic role of faith in American civil life. In short, they seek to restore the time-honored tradition of civil religion—not to establish Christianity by law or create an official church."[15]

Robertson also has a non-threatening answer to the "Christian nation" question asked by journalists. During a television interview in 1995, Robertson quoted a 1892 Supreme Court decision in which a Justice wrote, "This is a Christian nation." Robertson then said, "But subsequent to that, of course, right now we're not a Christian nation. I think that it would be an affront to the Almighty to claim America, as it currently exists, is a Christian nation. And I have never imagined political action which would make that happen. I can't conceive of it."[16] In a 1995 *Wall Street Journal* article written to refute charges of anti-Semitism, Robertson wrote, "Despite claims to the contrary, I have never suggested or even imagined any type of political action to make America a 'Christian nation.'"[17]

Reed and Robertson have distanced themselves from "Christian nation" rhetoric in different ways. For Reed, the reason America is no longer a "Christian nation" was largely demographic—a greater non-Christian population. To Robertson, in contrast, American is no longer Christian because of grave moral and religious failures. "I don't believe," Robertson told CC members in 1993, "a Christian nation would permit the slaughter over 20 years of 30 million helpless unborn babies. . . . And certainly no Christian nation would forbid its little children to learn the Bible or pray to God."[18] His bitterness over the moral decline of the nation is not hard to detect in such statements as, "We had in America a Christian nation. It has been taken away from us."[19]

Reed has not seemed as concerned with the loss of the particular label, "Christian nation," as with the loss of a workable moral and civic consensus. The realities of contemporary religious and ethnic diversity might make the achievement of such a consensus more difficult, but consensus is still possible, Reed argued, as long as people of faith are not excluded. "We are of different faiths," said Reed of Americans in 1996, "different ethnic backgrounds, different colors, and different creeds. This diversity is not a weakness; it is our greatest strength."[20] Reed's rhetorical embrace of diversity was, of course, undercut by the implied particularism of the name *Christian* Coalition. In a similar fashion, Robertson's disclaimers of ambitions of making the nation Christian again have been hard to believe. Through the CC, Robertson has been working to end the very moral and religious failures that have disqualified America from being a Christian nation. Efforts by Robertson and Reed to distance themselves and their organization from the negative connotations of "Christian America" rhetoric, I would argue, have been only partially successful.

Despite these differences and disclaimers, the literature of the CC demonstrated the restorationist impulse in a remarkably clear fashion. *Christian American* editor Michael Ebert, for instance, in a column on the Fourth of July, quoted Washington's 1789 inaugural address: "'The propitious smiles of Heaven can never be expected on a nation that disregards the eternal rules of order and right which Heaven itself has ordained.'" Ebert then observed: "When we restore those eternal rules of order Washington spoke about, our nation will truly be free. That's an independence day worth working for."[21]

The CC's "Citizen Action Seminar" training manual, for instance, stated, "One link at a time, little by little, we must rebuild the faith and integrity of the foundation of government that once upheld the morality and spirituality of our political system."[22] A typical CC fundraising letter, signed by Robertson, asked, "will America return to the vision of our nation's founding fathers—of limited government, respect for family, reverence for God, and an affirmation of the moral and spiritual values which made America great?"[23]

Many of the proposals of the CC's *Contract with the American Family* also appealed to the theme of restoration.[24] A Religious Equality Amendment was needed because "It is time for people of faith in America to restore the right to freedom of religious expression. It is time to reilluminate the meaning of the First Amendment and the fundamental liberties it offers to all of [our] citizens. It is time to reclaim for religious expression the free speech protections it never should have lost."[25] Enactment of a School Choice program would "restore to parents the vital role that school bureaucrats have assumed in recent decades."[26] In arguing for tax-relief for families, the *Contract* proposal presented tax rates and exemption levels of the 1950s as the norm to which we should return.[27] Restrictions on late-term abortions and on federal funding of abortions were presented as "Restoring Respect for Human Life."[28] Legal reforms, asserted the *Contract* proposal, "will help restore faith in the judicial system and make the streets safer again for American families and their children."[29]

Robertson, whose 1988 presidential campaign slogan was "Restore the Greatness of America Through Moral Strength," has often articulated the desire to return America to the way he believes it once was. In 1990, Robertson said, "We are in [politics] until we see America brought back to its founding principles. Back to the Bible, back to the Constitution, back to the greatness that it knew through faith in God, through individual self-reliance, through moral restraint."[30] In the conclusion of his 1993 book, *The Turning Tide,* Robertson urged his readers, "But let us not stop short until there is a complete restoration of the time-honored traditions of this nation, the complete fall of liberalism, and God's blessings are once again upon the land."[31] At the 1994 CC "Road to Victory" conference, he concluded his keynote address with a call "to bring America back to the promise of its inception. . . . A moral nation, once again, a good nation."[32] In a 1995 speech at the William and Mary Law School, Robertson said, "We want our history back. We want our tradition back. We want our constitution back. And we want God back in the schools of America." He concluded that speech with a call to "work for a time when this nation is once again one nation under God."[33]

The desire to return to a better past was also apparent, though expressed in more nuanced terms, in statements by Reed. In a 1993 speech at the Ethics and Public Policy Center, Reed said, "What most religious conservatives really want is to reclaim some strengths of the America that most of us grew up in, the post–World War II America that was proud, militarily strong, morally sound and looked up to by the rest of the world." Reed claimed that this America existed "until the nation's cultural fabric was torn apart" by various social upheavals of the 1960s and 1970s. He was careful, however, to note, "Many of the social changes of the past thirty years are advances that must be preserved." He cited the civil-rights movement and greater equality for women in the workplace as such advances.[34]

While Reed has said that religious conservatives have "a vision of an expansive future, not an intolerant past"[35] and that "Religious conservatives want to move forward not backward,"[36] Reed's nostalgia for a better past extended beyond the postwar era. In a chapter of *Politically Incorrect,* he describes at some length the "religious conservative vision for America." "America," wrote Reed, "would look much as it did for most of the first two centuries of its existence. . . . Our nation would once again be ascendant, self-confident, proud, and morally strong. Government would be small, the citizenry virtuous, and mediating institutions such as churches and volunteer organizations would carry out many of the functions currently relegated to the bureaucracy."[37] Reed idealized this past in contrast to the harsher realities of the present. At one point, he made the astonishing statement that in nineteenth-century America, "everyone was accountable to parents, neighbors, church or synagogue, and the community."[38] It was this idealized vision of the American past that Reed referred to when he has spoken of "restoring traditional values."

Like Robertson, Reed often ended his speeches on a restorationist note. He usually did this by citing an anecdote about Lincoln. When a clergyman assured Lincoln that "God is on our side," Lincoln replied, "I know that the Lord is always on the side of right, but it is my constant anxiety and prayer that I and this nation should be on the Lord's side." Reed then concluded, "If that is our motto and that is our prayer, then with God's help we can heal our land and restore America to greatness. Thank you, and God bless you."[39] By using Lincoln, a profoundly unifying figure in the American civil religion, as a model, Reed identified his movement with the very best of America's past—a time when we were on God's side. Identification with Lincoln's humility also refuted accusations that the CC has arrogantly claimed to speak for God.

The larger rhetorical framework in which the CC makes its appeals for restoration is that of the jeremiad. The jeremiad, or the "political sermon" as it was called by the Puritans, first reminds its audience of the original promise and obligations of the community. It then laments, sometimes in a painful degree of detail, how far the community has departed from that original promise by neglecting its obligations. Finally, the jeremiad warns of the dire consequences that will soon come if the community does not repent, fulfill its obligations, and restore its original purity.[40]

As I noted in Chapter 2, the Christian Right's jeremiads have usually appealed to the notion of a foundational national covenant with God. These jeremiads usually begin with an account of America's religious founding by the Pilgrims and/or Puritans of New England.[41] Robertson's rhetoric has also operated within this covenant framework, but he located the religious founding of America in Cape Henry, Virginia on April 29, 1607.[42] According to Robertson, men from ships of the Virginia company came ashore, planted a cross on the beach, and joined in a prayer—"the first public prayer of the first permanent settlement in America"—led by Robert Hunt, the Anglican chaplain of the expedition. "Together," Robertson told his readers, "the men of the Virginia Company thanked God for their safe journey and recommitted themselves to God's plan and God's purpose for this New World."[43]

Robertson has given great significance to this event and this date. In his 1990 book *The New Millennium*, Robertson wrote, "In God's eyes the United States of America did not begin on July 4, 1776 but on April 29, 1607."[44] Although Robertson has not explicitly called this event the sealing of a national covenant with God, it has played that role in his thinking. The 1980 "Washington for Jesus" rally, at Robertson's suggestion, was held on April 29th. "What better day," wrote Robertson, "could there be to remember the nation's spiritual heritage and to call the people to pray that God might renew His blessings upon us?"[45] Despite the importance of this date to Robertson, it does not seem to have received attention in CC literature or in the writings of Reed. More important for the outlook of the CC has been Robertson's generalized insistence on the reality and consequences of a national covenant with God. The power, wealth, and freedom enjoyed by Americans were neither accidental, nor a result of intrinsic merit. "It happened," according to Robertson, "because the men and women who founded this land made a solemn covenant that they would be the people of God and that this would be a Christian nation."[46]

A national covenant has not often been explicitly mentioned in CC literature. One notable instance was a *Christian American* editorial that depicted President Clinton's 1993 inauguration as a rejection of the national covenant. True to the pattern of the jeremiad, the editorial first reminded readers that "America was a covenant nation." The editorial quoted "prominent Christian author and legal scholar Gary Amos," who asserted that this covenant was embodied in the Declaration of Independence, "which acknowledges God as Sovereign over these United States," and in the Constitution. This was followed by Amos's lamentations over America's departures from the way of the covenant.

On January 20, 1993, our new President, joined by many in the land,
will formally 'break' the covenant of our Fathers if he and the
affirming electorate demonstrates [sic] allegiance to his 'new
covenant' and promotes as 'contitutional' [sic] those things which
God condemns.[47]

Finally, the editorial called on Christians to "'present themselves
before the Lord, mourn and renounce the idolatries, abominations and
worship the true Sovereign of these United States,' Jesus Christ."[48]

This editorial showed a remarkable fusion of the civil and the
religious, or secular and sacred, history. The Declaration of Independence
and the Constitution, two documents of significance within an
entirely secular understanding of history, were imbued with religious
significance. They represent the national covenant with God.[49] This
fusion was also evident in how seriously Clinton's "New Covenant" 1992
campaign theme was taken by Amos.[50] Clinton's "New Covenant" was
not merely a label for a political program like the "New Deal" but an
evocative symbol for America's sinful turn from the God of its Fathers.

Aside from the revealing admission that Jesus Christ is the "true
Sovereign of the United States"—so much for the full partnership of Jews
with Christian conservatives—the call to renew the covenant obviously
drew on the biblical histories of Israel. The resonance of this call
depended on a parallel between the old Israel and the new Israel,
America—one of the most enduring themes in the American mind from
colonial times onward.[51]

This parallel has resonated deeply with Robertson. "It is no
coincidence," he wrote in 1994, "that Israel has been the most resilient
nation in the history of the world and America the most powerful. Both
are established on principles laid out by God."[52] "I cannot help,"
Robertson wrote in the final chapter of his 1993 book *The Turning Tide,*
"but think of the images in the Book of Deuteronomy . . . wherein God
laid out for the people of Israel two contrasting images of the future: one
promising great hope, the other threatening grave consequences. . . . I
believe we stand at a similar moment in history with the opportunity to
choose between two opposite views of reality."[53] In the remainder of the
chapter, Robertson explained how every blessing and every curse
promised to Israel in Deuteronomy had come to pass, or was coming to
pass, in the history of the United States. "As an evangelical Christian I
believe," declared Robertson, "that this is more than a biblical metaphor,

and I am convinced that it is a faithful analysis of what is taking place in this land today."[54] Given this Deuteronomic framework, it was not surprising that Robertson understood the 1980 "Washington for Jesus" rally as an American fulfillment of the classic call to repentance in 2 Chronicles 7:14.[55] Reed, who has avoided any mention of a national covenant, also made a connection between Israel and America, although in a different fashion. "Unique among all nations in history," wrote Reed in *Politically Incorrect,* "with the exception of Israel, America was settled by persons of faith."[56] In a 1994 speech to the National Press Club, he cited a *U.S. News & World Report* poll to support the point that "apart from Israel, America is the most religious nation in the world."[57] While Reed shared Robertson's tendency to place Israel and America in a special category of nations, his basis for doing so was different. The similarity between the two was not a covenantal relationship with God, but a high degree of religiosity that can be ascertained by use of historical documents and polling data—the artifacts of secular rather than sacred history.

Consistent with his "wider net" strategy, Reed has used the perspective of secular rather than redemptive history. He has not spoken of a national covenant, attributed providential significance to events, or claimed special insight on the basis of faith. This did not mean, however, that Reed was not preaching a jeremiad to America. The framework of the jeremiad—reminder of original goodness, lamentation over deviations, and exhortation to return to the original state—was a basic pattern in Reed's public statements.

Reed has described the original goodness that must be restored as a socially beneficial religious-moral consensus, a non-sectarian "civil religion." This consensus, according to Reed, "has been the glue that held American society together, bridging ethnic and racial differences by expressing the common attributes of faith while assiduously avoiding the European practice of established churches."[58] Reed, who has been prone to quote Alexis de Tocqueville's more approving observations on religion in America, argued that this common "civil religion" has been a source, if not *the* source, of all that has been good in American history. Beyond the social glue religion provided, Reed stressed the religious roots of the American revolution, the nineteenth-century reform movements that culminated in the abolition of slavery, the Populist and Progressive movements, the temperance and labor movements, the civil rights movement, and the social ferment of the 1960s. "This spirit of compassionate volunteerism," wrote Reed, "animated by faith in God and love of our fellow man is what made America great, not government programs out of Washington."[59] Reed went so far as to argue that "if America has a national political tradition, it is that of religious activism firmly rooted in millennialism."[60]

Reed was concerned to show that religious involvement in politics has not only been persistent but that it has been a distinctly positive influence. His argument for religious involvement in politics, however, remained within the framework of secular history. Reed did not argue that religion was good for America because God blessed America for its faith. Instead, he argued that religion was good because it created good social effects. "Civil religion" provided a shared symbology that provided the basis of national unity and social harmony. It also inculcated the socially positive values and behaviors that made a free political and economic order possible. America was great because it was good. And it was good because it was religious.

One can, of course, find similar social utility arguments scattered throughout Robertson's writings. (This will be especially apparent when I discuss Robertson's church-state views below.) One should expect this, given his pragmatic approach to spirituality and his insistence that the Bible is "a workable guidebook for politics, government, business, families, and all the affairs of mankind."[61] My point is not that Reed wrote within a secular and Robertson within a sacred framework. My point is that Robertson has tried to fuse secular and sacred understandings of American history, whereas Reed has not.

To say that Reed's argument remained within the framework of secular history does not mean that it was a particularly good historical argument. Reed's historical presentation, for instance, can be criticized for giving far less attention to the divisive and negative effects—such as anti-Catholic nativism—than he does to the unitive and positive effects of fervent religiosity in American history.[62] (Reed, of course, was not writing scholarly history but using history to make a political point.) His description of "civil religion" also failed to take note of the inevitable tensions between the particular beliefs of the denominations and the generalities of a shared "civil religion." Despite these serious flaws, Reed attempted to present the CC's call for restoration in a way that did not require an evangelical frame of reference. If one wants a moral, prosperous, free, and well-ordered society, Reed argued, then work to restore the historic influence of religious faith in American life. Reed's jeremiad was tailored for the mainstream, but it remained a jeremiad.

The similarities and differences between Robertson and Reed in their depiction of America's lost golden era extend also to their understandings of how that era came to be lost. Robertson, with his explicit Deuteronomic-sacred history framework, has been likely to see this loss as a breaking of the covenant, or a fall from grace through sin. Robertson, however, has advanced no single consistent understanding of when the United States ceased to be a Christian nation.

Sometimes he has located this change, as have many Christian Right spokespersons, in the last three decades. Changes in moral standards, certain judicial decisions, and the growth of the welfare state since the 1960s have been favorite subjects in Robertson's lamentations over American decline. He depicted, for instance, the supposed "extraordinary" increase in social pathologies since the Supreme Court's school prayer decisions of 1962-1963 as "a sign of the lifting of God's blessing from our land."[63] On a different level of causation, Robertson has argued that "the court-mandated removal of religious restraint from our schools has been the major contributing cause of the moral breakup in our society."[64] Robertson's utilitarian arguments, however, have functioned within a larger spiritual framework. Prohibition of prayer in school, for instance, was not merely the "removal of religious restraints" leading to moral confusion and social disorder, but an act that incurred God's wrath.

On other occasions, Robertson has depicted the degradation of Christian America as a much longer process involving the interplay of a series of particular events and general long-term trends. This is the pattern in Robertson's 1986 work, *America's Dates with Destiny,* but its three-part structure gave the impression that the trend toward American decline began with America's 1917 entry into World War I.[65] In his 1990 book, *The New Millennium,* Robertson seemed to confirm this: "It has taken the left some 70 years to reduce us to this level."[66] But on another occasion, Robertson noted that from the eighteenth century onward there was conflict between the worldviews of "those who believed that this was a nation ordained by God and those who leaned more toward the views of the French Enlightenment, which put religion and politics at odds."[67] This war of worldviews was raised to new heights in Robertson's 1991 book, *The New World Order.* He described the assault on Christian America as part of an international conspiracy spanning millennia, directed by Satan himself, and aimed at establishing a secular humanist world government ruled by the Antichrist. "Such a world government," Robertson explained, "can come together only after the Christian United States is out the way."[68]

Robertson's lamentations over America's decline have fused secular and sacred history. God, Satan, and the Antichrist were as much a part of his historical narrative as George Washington, the American Civil Liberties Union, and FDR. This fusion, however, when connected to his sharply dualistic conspiracy theory of history, has some troubling implications for the practical level of politics. These elements of Robertson's jeremiad have led to a depiction of his political or intellectual opponents as the enemies of all that is decent and good. Such a view is not conducive to the negotiation or pragmatic compromise necessary in American politics.

Reed, so often criticized for his tendency toward pragmatic compromise,[69] advanced his lamentations within the framework of secular history. He explained the nature and causation of American decline in terms that can be understood, if not accepted, by those who do not share his religious views. This is not to say that Reed's picture of America's problematic present and future is any less serious than Robertson's. Reed, however, has not pulled God and Satan onstage as players in his historical drama.

The critique of American society advanced by Reed and echoed in the *Contract with the American Family,* relied heavily on social scientific literature and statistical information about various social pathologies. Reed, however, located the root of these problems not merely in the expansion of the federal government, though that is part of his analysis, but in the declining role of religion in American public life. While he admitted that the reasons for the "sudden rise of social pathologies beginning in the mid-1960s" are complex, he also asserted, "there can be no doubt that there is a correlation between a decline in the role of religion in our society and the rise of social pathologies of every kind." Judicial decisions that Robertson said angered God or broke the national covenant, Reed termed "signposts along the road to a declining role of religion and faith in American culture." This cultural trend was accompanied by increasing bias in government policy "against the valuable social role religion plays in stabilizing marriages, nurturing young people, and knitting together communities."[70] This "valuable social role" of religion has been central to Reed's analysis of what was right with America originally, what has gone wrong recently, and what can be done to solve our social problems.

In *Active Faith,* Reed argued that the liberalism that dominated American intellectual and political life from the New Deal to the Great Society almost always advanced its ideas in moral terms and religious language. But the liberalism of the Democratic party, according to Reed, lost its moral core in the 1960s, when it became captive to contending special interests with demands for a never-ending proliferation of government programs. Consequently, liberalism has become uncomfortable with, and even hostile toward, the use of religious and moral language in politics. "The religious left lost its soul," wrote Reed, "and we stepped into the vacuum."[71] In Reed's view, the contribution of religious conservatives to contemporary politics is "their insistence that, in the end, the answers to moral decline can be found only with a return to faith in God."[72]

Unlike Robertson, whose historical speculations regarding American decline range over the centuries, the focus of Reed's analysis and lamentations are trends since the 1960s. On occasion, such as in a speech to the Economic Club of Detroit in 1995, Reed has made reference to the expansion of government since Roosevelt's New Deal. "It took us sixty years to get into this mess, and we will not get out of it overnight."[73] But Reed, in contrast to Robertson, did not depict these changes as part of some conspiracy to destroy America. Rather than demonizing historical actors and contemporary political opponents, Reed recognized the corrosive effects of social trends that have made religion less influential and families less important in the wider culture. These trends include immigration, secularization of education, expansion of the welfare state, rising standards of living, declining birth rates, and the rise of mass media.[74] The results of these impersonal trends were regarded by Reed as problematic rather than evil, and were certainly not regarded as the product of intentional and personal evil. A sharply dualistic historical framework, which makes political negotiation and pragmatic compromise difficult for Robertson to justify, was not part of Reed's outlook. Reed has even described liberalism—*the* evil influence in the eyes of some religious conservatives—as a force, up until the 1960s, for justice and morality. By not fusing secular and sacred history in his jeremiad, and by not making his opponents the embodiment of evil, Reed has not robbed himself of a legitimation of the tools he needs for effective political action.

Reed's lamentations of the dire state of American society lacked the rhetorical power of Robertson's. Reed, after all, cannot threaten America with the wrath of God, or warn of the onset of the Tribulation, as can Robertson. But Reed did manage to paint a frightening picture. "To look at America today," he wrote in 1996, "is to witness a nation struggling against forces as dangerous as any military foe it has ever faced. The threats, however, come not from without but from within." He pointed to the disintegration of families, the prevalence of abortion and drugs, rampant illegitimacy, children being shot by "marauding carloads of juvenile gang members." "There is no economic solution to this social chaos" asserted Reed, "it is a collection of moral problems that require moral solutions."[75]

Depictions of the choices facing America in absolute life-or-death terms have been common in CC fund-raising letters, which have usually born Robertson's signature. The following is a sampling of such letters from 1993-1995.

By standing together, we can turn America back from its headlong plunge into moral chaos.

I am sending you this [Congressional] Scorecard because I need your help to stop (or at least slow down) the anti-family *train of destruction* coming down the tracks.

The Clinton [1993 tax] plan is *a dagger aimed at the heart of the American family.*

If Christians and pro-family Americans fail to take strong and unified action today, we won't recognize America tomorrow.

This [1996] is a crossroads election year that, I believe, will determine America's direction for generations. *In fact, it may be the most important election of our lifetime.*

IN OTHER WORDS, YOU AND I CANNOT AFFORD TO RELAX OR BECOME COMPLACENT EVEN FOR A MINUTE . . . OR ALL THE GAINS WE MADE THIS PAST YEAR WILL BE LOST.[76]

These letters convey the fearful urgency of the CC's jeremiad to America. A *Christian American* editorial conveyed the same urgency: "Unless America will repent and return to God, our perilous descent into violence and anarchy will not be stopped."[77]

The CC's call to restore the "historic" role of faith in American culture has often raised concerns that this organization wants to abolish the separation of church and state and impose evangelical beliefs on America through the power of government. I now turn, therefore, to an examination of the relationship between church and state as presented by Robertson and Reed.

CHURCH AND STATE

Is the CC's restorationism really a call for an established state religion? Robertson has denied this. "What the Christian Coalition is trying to do," asserted Robertson, "is change the context of the current debate over church-state issues, to put things back into their natural and historic perspective."[78] For Robertson, this normative perspective is that of the founders. "The wisdom of our biblically based Founding Fathers," wrote Robertson, "gave the United States of America the finest concept of ordered liberty the world has ever known."[79] Like other conservatives, Robertson has rejected evolving constitutional standards and has advocated a return to, in his words, "a government elected by the people under a timeless constitution to be interpreted according to the clear intention of the framers."[80]

In a 1995 article in the *William & Mary Bill of Rights Journal,* Robertson argued that the intention of the framers of the Establishment Clause was limited to preventing the creation of a state church. Its purpose was only the *institutional* separation of churches from the apparatus of government. According to Robertson, "It means that government should not set up an official sect or denomination on which it bestows its special blessing. It means that government should not control or intervene in the internal affairs of religious institutions. And it means churches, as in the case of the Anglican Church in the United Kingdom, should not have *official* representation in government."[81]

Such institutional separation is what Robertson meant when he said, "I believe in the separation of church and state as it was defined in the first 150 years of this nation."[82] When Robertson denounces the separation of church and state he is referring to the broader notion of separation dominant in contemporary church-state jurisprudence. Robertson characterized this broader separationism as the product of "a determined effort to radically alter the historical understanding of separation."[83] He has been particularly concerned with the consequences of the three-pronged Establishment Clause test developed by the Supreme Court in *Lemon v. Kurtzman* (1971).[84] Robertson described the "secular legislative purpose" prong of the *Lemon* test as "an invitation to mischief."[85] The requirement of a secular purpose, Robertson argued, may make governmental accommodation of religious practice impossible. Requiring secularity of legislative purpose may also lead to constitutional challenges based on the religiousness of the motives of legislators.[86] Rigorous application of the secular purpose test, Robertson asserted, "could lead to the removal of the religious world view from the political process."[87] Such hostility toward religion in the "public square," according to Robertson, was never intended by the founders.

The Establishment Clause, for Robertson, allows not only for the accommodation of religion in the public realm, but for governmental support of religion. The institutional separation was not intended to mean, in Robertson's words, "that religious ideals and ideas are to be excluded from the political and lawmaking processes. Nor should it mean that government is (or should be) disabled from generally endorsing, promoting, or encouraging religious belief and practice, from acknowledging God, or even from giving certain forms of aid (including financial) that advance the cause of religion."[88] Robertson pointed to actions of the founding generation of legislators, such as provisions in the Northwest Ordinance of 1787 for religious education, that support his interpretation of their intentions.[89]

Robertson has made even more ambitious claims for the public role of religion. Beyond being accommodated and encouraged by government, religion has been fundamental to the American public order. "Without question, they [the founders] believed that although no one Christian denomination should dominate the nation, the principles of the Bible and Christianity should underlie our government and American education as well."[90] Robertson found these principles in the Declaration of Independence and the Constitution.

Citing Amos's *Defending the Declaration*, Robertson held that the basic concepts of the Declaration of Independence— "self-evident truth" and "unalienable rights"—are "traceable back to medieval

Christian theological and legal thought, and ultimately to Scripture."[91] But in this article, Robertson did not discuss the Declaration's phrase "the laws of nature and of nature's God," a concept that Amos argued contains the legal theory of the Declaration.[92] This was surprising because in his 1986 book, *America's Dates with Destiny,* Robertson claimed "our forefathers appealed to God's laws as revealed in nature and in the Bible ('the Laws of Nature and Nature's God') as the foundation upon which everything else was built."[93] Robertson, of course, has wanted to restore this merger of natural and revealed law as the objective basis of morality and rights in American law.[94]

Robertson also argued that human rights cannot be secured by reliance on a social consensus. Such reliance would open the door to moral relativism and to a legal positivism that could be used to make even the most barbarous acts "legal." Robertson argued that some "objective basis of morality" is necessary to provide security for human rights. That objective basis, according to Robertson, can be found only in a religious framework.[95]

Religion, in Robertson's view, the *only* secure basis for morality (that is, individual self-restraint), is necessary for the continued survival of the American form of government. Robertson's favorite quotation, perhaps, has been that from Washington's Farewell Address: "reason and experience both forbid us to expect that National morality can prevail in exclusion of religious principle."[96] But Robertson has also made it apparent that only a particular type of religion can serve the nation in this way. "[L]imited government such as ours," Robertson said in a 1993 speech, "can only work if there is a code of behavior such as only our Judeo-Christian tradition, our faith in God and God's Word can provide."[97]

Like Robertson, Reed has been concerned to refute accusations of religious authoritarianism. He argued that unlike Islamic fundamentalist political movements, American religious conservatives are "an interest group within a democratic order." "If they gained power," asserted Reed, "they would not repeal the Constitution or attempt to impose their religion on others through the state."[98] Reed also echoed much of Robertson's views on the Establishment Clause, while adding distrust-of-government-bureaucracy rhetoric. Reed wrote, "I strongly support the separation of church and state in order to protect the church, not the state. I favor church-state separation because I would not entrust the sacred tablets of my faith to the same government that . . . delivers a first-class letter with the efficiency of a nineteenth-century stagecoach."[99]

But Reed apparently had no objection to the posting of the Ten Commandments on a county courtroom wall in Alabama. He was a principal speaker at a "Save the Commandments Rally" held in April 12, 1997, to support Judge Roy Moore's refusal to obey a state appellate court order to remove the Commandments.[100] Wouldn't Judge Moore's actions be an example of "entrusting the sacred tablets of faith" to government, an impermissible establishment of religion? Reed probably did not find any constitutional problem because, like Robertson, he interpreted the Establishment Clause narrowly. "The Establishment Clause," wrote Reed, "prohibited the federal government from foisting upon the populace (many of whom subscribed to dissenting faiths) a national religion. It did not contemplate hostility to religion in general."[101] Thus in Reed's view, Judge Moore was not establishing a particular religion but was instead the victim of the appellate court's hostility to religion in general.

Like Robertson, Reed found fault with *Lemon v. Kurtzman*'s supposed exclusion of religion from the public sphere. According to Reed, "The 'lemon test' is a lemon."[102] Reed also criticized the judiciary's inconsistent application of this test. The CC *Contract* echoed this criticism. "So the *Lemon* test, in practice, turns out not to be a test at all," stated the *Contract,* "but a way for the courts (particularly the Supreme Court) to cloak contradictory outcomes in seemingly objective terms."[103]

Reed even proposed, but did not elaborate, an alternative three-part test: "No law should be held unconstitutional that does not establish a state religion, prefers no denomination over another, and has an essentially secular purpose."[104] His inclusion of "essentially secular purpose" in this test is in conflict with Robertson's characterization of the secular purpose prong of the *Lemon* test as "an invitation to mischief."[105] Without more elaboration by Reed on church-state issues it is impossible to say whether this was a serious difference between Robertson and Reed, or simply a statement that Reed did not examine carefully enough.

Like Robertson, Reed asserted that religious influence is necessary for the health of the body politic. "A secular government informed by sacred principles," wrote Reed, "and open to the service of persons of faith not only poses no threat to the constitution, it is essential to its survival."[106] Allegiance to a power higher than any human government is a bulwark against tyranny. "Faith as [a] political force," asserted Reed, "is not undemocratic; it is the very essence of democracy."[107]

Yet Reed's emphasis on the restoration of the religio-moral consensus of America's past stood in conflict with Robertson's demand for an "objective basis of morality." Unlike Reed's possibly minor disagreement with Robertson over the secular purpose prong of the *Lemon* test, Reed's emphasis on consensus is central to his version of restorationism. Reed may, of course, have adopted this language of consensus, with its risk of subjectivism and relativism, only to avoid the criticisms that have always been leveled at the Christian Right's "offensive agenda"—criticisms confirmed by Robertson's demand for an "objective" basis for morality. But perhaps this was an issue on which Robertson and Reed had a real and fundamental disagreement.

THEOCRATIC INTENTIONS?

Closely related to these establishment clause questions is the common accusation that the *real* purpose of the CC is theocratic. "I have no doubt," Barry Lynn of Americans United for Separation of Church and State said in 1993, "that the goal of Pat Robertson's organization is to create what amounts to a theocracy in America."[108] Robertson and Reed, of course, have been concerned to deny this accusation. In the conclusion of his *William & Mary Bill of Rights Journal* article, Robertson stated, "Nothing I have said here should be interpreted to be a call for theocracy."[109] Reed offered an alternative interpretation: "In fact, though liberals regard our focus on abortion and school prayer as aspects of a theocratic agenda, they are best understood as the modern form of a perennial Christian concern for justice and equality."[110]

A notoriously slippery term, the word theocracy, from the Greek *theokratia,* or "rule by God," was coined by the historian Josephus to describe the political system established by Moses for the Jewish people. It has been applied to a wide variety of regimes, including pharaonic Egypt, the Papal States, Calvin's Geneva, Buddhist Tibet, Puritan New England, early Mormonism, and the Islamic Republic of Iran. Unlike democracies or monarchies, theocracies do not necessarily possess some common institutional structure. Instead "theocracy" can refer to any form of government in which God is the ultimate locus of sovereignty and authority. The will of God is enacted through revealed laws and through divinely commissioned agents—a sacred monarchy, a clerical aristocracy, or the collective rule of the faithful.[111]

Historian Jerald C. Brauer observed that the most profoundly influential example of theocratic thinking in American history was that of Puritan New England in the seventeenth century. Based on the assumption of God's universal sovereignty, the Puritans believed that God's will for human social and political life could be known through scripture, reason, and Christ. God's political will was enacted through "the rule of the saints" in both church and state.[112]

While the specific legal and institutional arrangements that embodied New England's theocratic ideal did not survive, Brauer argued that the ideal of the rule of the saints was recast by church-state separation and revitalized by voluntarism. The theocratic ideal lived on in the conjunction of revivalism and the voluntary societies of antebellum evangelicalism. The rule of the saints, enacting God's political will, was achieved through persuasion and cultural dominance, not legal coercion or ecclesiastical establishment.[113]

Rather than a return to Puritan New England, Robertson and the CC have seemed to advocate a restoration of the evangelical quasi-establishment, the voluntaristic version of the American theocratic ideal. In this limited sense, one can call Robertson's ambitions "theocratic." But when opponents of Robertson and the Christian Right use the word "theocracy," they usually are not pointing to Brauer's voluntaristic version of the theocratic ideal. They instead are invoking fears of a totalitarian state enforcing religious law. These invocations of religious totalitarianism have been supplied with substance by the activities, teachings, and influence of Christian reconstructionism.[114]

The reconstructionist movement grew out of the teachings of Rousas J. Rushdoony, a former Orthodox Presbyterian minister. Since the 1960s, Rushdoony has called upon Christians to assert "dominion" over both the natural *and* the social world in accordance with the "dominion mandate" in Genesis 1:26-28. Because of this emphasis on "dominion," another name for this movement is "dominion theology."[115]

As historian Bruce Barron observed, "Reconstructionism has affinities with the Christian Right but its scope and goals are much broader."[116] The people of God, according to the reconstructionists, should exercise dominion using biblical law as the "blueprint" for a totally "reconstructed" and holy social order. Reconstructionists propose a society that would be not merely reformed, "but rather razed and rebuilt,"[117] as sociologist Anson Shupe put it. This radical program of social reconstruction is based, according to reconstructionist Greg L. Bahnsen, on three central concepts: presuppositionalism, theonomy, and postmillennialism.[118] Rushdoony attended Westminster Theological Seminary and not only adopted the Presbyterian fundamentalism of its founder J. Gresham Machen, but the presuppositional approach to apologetics of Cornelius Van Til, a Dutch Reformed professor at Westminster. In contrast to evidentialist apologetics, which is based on Common Sense Realism and seeks to prove the truth of Christianity through factual evidence, Van Til held that facts did not speak for themselves but were only meaningful within some presupposed framework of interpretation. Since God alone was sovereign, only God's framework of interpretation, as revealed in scripture, was true. The attempt by nonbelievers to create their own coherent interpretation of reality was necessarily doomed to failure. And because truth was a matter of presuppositions, there can be no common intellectual ground, no compromise, and no social or political cooperation between Christians and nonbelievers.[119]

The necessity of the second central concept, theonomy, or "God's law," grew out of the consequences of presuppositionalism. Van Til rejected the possibility of basing human life on our autonomous reason or on conceptions of natural law, but he offered no constructive alternative.[120] Rushdoony found an alternative in the revealed law of the Bible. "Neither positive law nor natural law," wrote Rushdoony, "can reflect more than the sin and apostasy of man: *revealed law* is the need and privilege of Christian society. It is the *only* means whereby man can fulfil his creation mandate of exercising dominion under God."[121] As Bahnsen expressed it, "*Every* single stroke of the law must be seen by the Christian as applicable to *this* very age between the advents of Christ."[122] Some reconstructionists have advocated, based on specific Old Testament texts, punishing homosexual behavior, adultery, blasphemy, and "habitual criminality" with the death penalty.[123]

While the ceremonial laws of Moses were abrogated by the coming of Christ, the moral and civil laws of the Old Testament have continued to be valid as God's "blueprint" for the social, legal, and political order of all nations and for all time.[124] Reconstructionists have admired the theocratic "law-order" of Puritan New England as an important, albeit unsuccessful, attempt to build a Christian commonwealth on biblical law.[125] In fact, some reconstructionists have described themselves as "Puritans" or "neo-Puritans."[126]

Reconstructionists are also postmillennialists because, as Rush-doony wrote, "Man is summoned to create the society God requires."[127] The fulfillment of the Genesis 1:26-28 dominion mandate, the reestablishment of a theonomic Kingdom of God on earth, has always been the purpose of salvation history. The second coming of Christ will be the culmination, rather than the sole act, of the progressive establishment of God's kingdom.[128] Unlike premillennialists, who believe time is always running out, reconstructionist leaders have urged their followers to prepare for an indeterminately long struggle to establish a godly society. Because of this, the reconstructionists have emphasized patient, gradual, uncompromising, and grassroots efforts in evangelism, education, and politics.[129] Because the sovereign God of history has willed their victory, time is not running out. As reconstructionist David Chilton expressed it, "Time is on our side."[130]

The full implications of these ideas are too extensive to consider here.[131] But it should be clear that reconstructionists point to an exclusively Christian conception of society that has no room for religious diversity or toleration. As Rushdoony has argued, the legal system of any culture is the practical expression of its religion, its ultimate authority, and therefore "there can be no tolerance in a law-system for another religion. Toleration is a device used to introduce a new law-system as a prelude to a new intolerance."[132] Because there can be no common ground between Christians and nonbelievers, between the sharp duality of true and false presuppositions, there can be no legitimate possibility of cooperation. And because time is on the side of the Christians, reconstructionists have no need of the democratic and pluralistic politics of compromise and accommodation to advance their goals.[133]

Few evangelicals have become reconstructionists. But reconstructionism's critique of the presuppositions of humanism, secularism, and modernity have provided politically active evangelicals with useful ideological and rhetorical tools. Reconstructionism's emphasis on a Christian dominion over society has clear affinities with the desire of many other evangelicals to reassert the public authority of their own beliefs and morality. The reconstructionists have been tactically influential as well. Many evangelicals, as Barron pointed out, "have moved beyond selective, periodic, issue focused lobbying and adopted the patient, long-term, bottom-up, all-encompassing approach to change that the Reconstructionists have been advocating all along,"[134]

Opponents of the Christian Right have emphasized the connections and affinities between the two movements. Reconstructionism, according to journalist Sara Diamond, "has become the central unifying ideology for the Christian Right."[135] The Anti-Defamation League's 1994 report The Religious Right highlighted the seminal influence of reconstructionism on the Christian Right. "If it weren't for [Rushdoony's] books," a leader in Moral Majority, Robert Billings, allegedly said in 1980, "none of us would be here."[136] The original source of the Billings quotation, it is interesting to note, was not a secularist expose but an essay by Gary North, one of the most prominent reconstructionist writers.[137] The reconstructionists, always interested in promoting their own movement, have emphasized their intellectual influence on the leadership of the Christian Right.[138] But Christian Right leaders have not been willing, possibly due to the radical nature of reconstructionist ideas, to acknowledge that influence.[139]

There have been many reports and allegations of connections and affinities between Robertson and the reconstructionists. Rushdoony and North, for instance, have appeared on Robertson's The 700 Club.[140] Robertson's Regent University has hired professors with reconstructionist ties and views. These professors have used reconstructionist books in their classes at Regent.[141] Robertson's book The Secret Kingdom, with a chapter on "The Law of Dominion," has been called "a primer on dominion theology."[142] Robertson's ministry and political activities have been seen as good examples of what reconstructionism or dominion theology has wanted to accomplish.[143] Robertson created Regent University, according to its catalog, to train Christian leaders in "disciplines that play a dominant role in the world—those areas that significantly affect the way man thinks and conducts his affairs."[144] Even the name "Regent" is significant. "A regent is one who represents a king in his absence."[145] Until Christ returns, in other words, God's people should rule as His representatives.

Both Robertson's presidential campaign and the CC have been seen as the product of dominionist "Christians should be in charge" thinking.[146] A 1992 Christian American editorial, for instance, clearly stated the dominionist viewpoint that "God has charged us with the awesome responsibility of exercising stewardship over His creation. Part of that creation is the government of our society." The editorial went on to quote Proverbs 29:2, "'When the righteous are in authority, the people rejoice: but when the wicked beareth rule, the people mourn.'"[147]

Given reconstructionism's radicalism, it is not surprising that Robertson, like other Christian Right leaders, has distanced himself from its teachings. In 1992 he told *Christianity Today* that "I don't agree with reconstructionism, although I do believe that Jesus is Lord of all the world."[148] In a letter to *Christianity Today,* reconstructionist writer Gary DeMar claimed to be confused by Robertson's rejection of that movement while at the same time professing "the heart and soul of Reconstructionism," the universal dominion of Christ. "At the very least," wrote DeMar, "Pat Robertson, as I've always suspected, is an operational Reconstructionist."[149]

DeMar's evaluation of Robertson and, by implication, of Reed and the CC, should not be accepted at face value. While the basic affinities that make possible cobelligerency against a common enemy should be recognized, Robertson, Reed, and the CC have exhibited important, if not crucial, differences, from reconstructionism.

Reconstructionists, using triumphalist rhetoric based on their presuppositionalism, insist on an exclusively Christian approach to rebuilding society. "Many evangelicals want to change the world," observed Barron, "but only the dominionists insist they must run it."[150] Reconstructionists have therefore adopted a policy of non-cooperation with those who are not, in their eyes, Christian. Despite an ambivalence toward diversity, which I will discuss in more detail below, Robertson and the CC have not put into operation the major practical result of reconstructionist presuppositionalism—the refusal to compromise or cooperate with nonbelievers.

Robertson's 1988 presidential campaign was disappointing to reconstructionists, Barron observed, because of Robertson's willingness "to compromise ideological purity for the sake of short-term victory."[151] The CC has continued and extended this willingness to compromise by actively seeking political cooperation with persons who do not share specifically evangelical presuppositions, such as Catholics, Jews, and nonreligious conservatives. Reed's "wider net" strategy is based on the possibility of common or neutral ground between people of different worldviews—a possibility that reconstructionist presuppositionalism categorically rejects.

A one-page flier, signed by reconstructionist writer John Lofton and quietly distributed at the 1996 "Road to Victory" conference, contained a "shocking" quotation from an unpublished news interview with Reed. Reed was quoted as saying, ". . . it's less important to me what somebody's personal religious faith is than where they stand on the issues." Reed reportedly went on to say that he would support an atheist with whom he agreed on the issues over a Christian with whom he disagreed. Lofton then asked, "How can a Christian, under any circumstances, say he would vote for an unbeliever—a 'fool,' according to God (Psalm 14:1)—to rule over us? Why is Ralph Reed, obviously, seeking to be all things to all people when our Lord warns, clearly: 'Woe unto you, when all men shall speak well of you! For so did their fathers to the false prophets' (Luke 6:26)."[152]

Even worse than supporting non-Christian candidates, Reed's willingness to reject "Christian nation" rhetoric was seen by DeMar as a "preemptive surrender" of the CC's "Christian emphasis" for the sake of "political expediency." DeMar asked, "With what does Reed want to replace our 'Christian social order'? Neutrality is impossible. If Christian values are not adopted as the standard of righteousness for a nation, then whose values will be chosen? If not God's law, then whose law? Reed and the Christian Coalition need to give us an answer."[153] In a review of Reed's *Active Faith,* DeMar pointed to Reed's "intellectual and theological schizophrenia" in using the Bible to say homosexuality is immoral while affirming the equal rights of homosexuals to participate in the political process. According to DeMar, "Reed takes the biblical *prohibitions* against homosexuality but does not want to have anything to do with the biblical *sanctions.*" And the sanction for homosexuality, DeMar reminded his readers, is the death penalty.[154]

In a similar vein, when Reed's *Politically Incorrect* was reviewed in the reconstructionist publication *Chalcedon Report,* the writer, Jay Rogers, observed: "*Politically Incorrect* is an excellent study on exactly what is wrong with the Christian conservative movement. According to *Politically Incorrect,* the ideology of the Christian Coalition is antinomian (anti-biblical Law) and pluralistic." Rogers accused the CC of "bowing to the idol of 'pluralism,'" which gives everyone an equal voice in politics. "But most politically active Christians," wrote Rogers, "don't want equal time with homosexuals, abortionists, animal worshiping pagans, witches, radical feminists and pornographers. We want them silenced and mercifully disciplined according to the Word of God." Because Reed "seeks to soothe the frightened pagans," Rogers charged, he "flatly refuses to stand for the moral Law of God."[155]

Robertson's "operational" embrace of the second pillar of reconstructionism, theonomy, or biblical law, has also been more apparent than real. Much has been made of the influence upon Robertson of supposedly theonomically inclined professors, especially Herbert Titus, at Regent University's Schools of Law and Government.[156] But the form of theonomy, what Barron calls "constitutionalism," that has been taught at Regent differs significantly from the "Mosaic law is the only alternative" approach of Rushdoony. The Regent constitutionalists have embraced another basis for law— "the laws of nature and nature's God." According to Barron, this concept, rooted in Romans 1-2, "refers specifically to the generally perceptible knowledge that affirms special revelation provided by 'nature's God' *through Scripture.*"[157] The constitutionalists, while hardly part of the American legal mainstream, only advocate a return to a legal system based on the biblically informed original meaning of the Declaration and the Constitution, not a reinstitution of "every single stroke" of biblical law.

I have already noted how Robertson adopted Titus's constitutionalist position in *America's Dates with Destiny* in 1986 to explain his view of church-state relations.[158] It would be hard, however, to argue that Titus continued to influence Robertson after the former's controversial departure from Regent in July 1993.[159] Titus has attributed his firing to Robertson's desire for Regent to project a more mainstream theological, legal, and political image. "This indicates to me," Titus told an interviewer, "that they [Robertson and Regent officials] were trying to bring this change in the university to coincide with the change in the Christian Coalition to appeal to a broader range of people."[160] A desire to distance himself from Titus may account for Robertson's failure in his 1995 article on church-state relations to use Titus's concept of "the laws of nature and nature's God." Rather than Robertson being led toward theocratic radicalism by Regent professors, it seems he has moved in the opposite direction.

Given Reed's drive to mainstream the CC, it is not surprising that in *Active Faith* he denounced "the 'Christian nation' or Reconstructionist community, which argues that the purpose of Christian political involvement should be to legislate biblical law." Reed admitted that reconstructionist ideas had certain precedents in American religious history. "But those currents did not reflect the mainstream of Christian thinking then," asserted Reed, "and they certainly do not today." He warned that "Reconstructionism is an authoritarian ideology that threatens the most basic civil liberties of a free and democratic society." For Reed, the pro-family movement "must unequivocally dissociate itself from Reconstructionism and other efforts to use the government to impose biblical law through direct political action."[161]

Reed apparently was willing to back up this stance toward reconstructionism with action. Howard Phillips, the presidential candidate of the reconstructionist-influenced U.S. Taxpayers Party (USTP),[162] was not permitted to speak at the 1996 "Road to Victory" conference, and his campaign was given no space in the conference exhibition area. The USTP claimed that CC leaders had promised to introduce Phillips at a general session but failed to do so. "And so that is something to keep in mind," advised the writer for the USTP, "as you deal with the Christian Coalition; that promises don't necessarily mean anything to the leadership of that organization."[163] In a press release, Phillips noted that "pro-abortion" presidential candidates, Clinton and Perot, had been invited to speak, while the "only real pro-life Presidential candidate" had been excluded. Phillips asked, "What exactly is the nature of the 'Victory' the Christian Coalition is seeking?"[164] The CC's "exclusion" of USTP from the 1996 "Road to Victory" conference may also have been rooted in Reed's much-discussed political realism. Every religious conservative vote that went to Phillips and the USTP was a vote lost to the Republicans. And on a more petty level, the USTP may have been excluded because its vice-presidential candidate was Herbert Titus—the same Herbert Titus fired from Robertson's Regent University amid controversy in 1993.[165]

Another supposed indication of Robertson's "dominion theology" and theocratic intent is the chapter on "The Law of Dominion" in his 1982 book *The Secret Kingdom*.[166] Yet Robertson's discussion dealt entirely with reasserting human dominion over the physical world—in terms of overcoming base physical passions, and in healings, miracles, and achieving prosperity. The chapter was devoid of political references. Demands for Christian control of social and political institutions have apparently been read into Robertson's "Law of Dominion" in view of his later entry into politics.

When Robertson published a revised edition of *The Secret Kingdom* in 1992, he included this pointed statement: "The Law of Dominion should not be confused with the teachings of what is sometimes called 'dominion theology' or 'reconstructionism.'"[167] He specifically rejected reconstructionism because of its postmillennialism. He characterized reconstructionism as "the idea that man, through his own efforts, is going to reconstruct the fallen earth and bring in the millennial kingdom. While there are elements of this belief which are biblical, in general this view is mistaken." He went on to emphasize the vital importance of teaching "the Law of the Lord," especially in post-communist Eastern Europe. "If indeed all men would walk according to His Law," Robertson concluded, "it would be a whole new world we would be living in, but obviously they are not. The idea that we are going to bring in the millennium by ourselves is, in my estimation, false theology."[168]

Given the strength of these statements, it is surprising that Robertson's continued advocacy of a premillennial eschatology has been ignored or discounted.[169] It is especially surprising given the fact that "The Law of Dominion" chapter in *The Secret Kingdom* was followed by the book's concluding chapter, "The Coming King," which presented a clearly premillennial eschatology.[170] As I noted above, Robertson's post-tribulationist version of premillennialism can be used to justify, even require, social-political activism. While his eschatology may allow Robertson to cooperate with postmillennialists, he does not share the reconstructionist assurance that "time is on our side." If Robertson's 1995 novel, *The End of the Age,* which depicted the onset of the Great Tribulation in the year 2000, illustrated anything, it was Robertson's conviction that time is running out.[171]

Robertson's supposed postmillennialism can also be seen in his system of "kingdom laws,"[172] which if practiced will allow the blessings of the Kingdom of God—success, happiness, prosperity, and health—to be "experienced in large measure right now."[173] For this reason Robertson has sometimes been seen as an advocate of the "kingdom now" movement—a reconstructionist-like movement within pentecostal-char-ismatic circles.[174] Yet Robertson's pragmatic spirituality has been kept within premillennialism and he has maintained the classic Christian tension between the disclosure and the fulfillment of the Kingdom of God. "Only God will inaugurate the visible reign on earth of His Son and those who will rule with Him," Robertson told readers of *The Secret Kingdom,* "but His word for the last two thousand years has been to 'prepare the way.'"[175]

Because Reed has not operated as a religious leader in the way that Robertson has, it is not surprising that he has made few pronounce-ments on the subject of eschatology. Yet he has made it clear that he is no postmillennialist. In *Politically Incorrect,* Reed wrote: "We must be faithful in seeking to establish goodness today while remembering that only God's Kingdom contains true peace and harmony, and His Kingdom is not of this world."[176] In his speech at the 1995 "Road to Victory" conference, Reed told CC members that the name of Christ in their organization's name gave them a responsibility. "The responsibility is not, ultimately, to win. It is to be found faithful when He returns."[177] And in a speech at the 1996 "Road to Victory" conference Reed affirmed his belief that "He is coming back again very very soon! Amen."[178] Reed, however, did not specify what he meant by "very very soon."

Robertson and Reed should not be regarded as reconstructionists. While they may cooperate with reconstructionists within the Christian Right, they do not preach or practice the central ideas of reconstructionism. The possibility exists, of course, that reconstructionists have been active in the rank-and-file and local leadership of the CC.[179] Rogers's critical review of Reed's first book asserted, "Is there hope for the Christian Coalition? Yes! *Politically Incorrect* does not speak for all members of the Christian Coalition. Many of its leaders on the grassroots level stand for the moral Law of God."[180] This may be true, but I wonder how long a consistent and self-conscious reconstructionist would be able to accept the current tactics or strategy of the CC. Reconstructionist leaders are beginning to develop their own political vehicles, such as the USTP, which unlike the CC, as DeMar put it, do not "water down their message to appeal to the masses."[181]

RESTORATIONISM AND THE PLURALISTIC ETHOS

While Robertson and Reed have not advocated the legal establishment of a national religion or a reconstructionist theocracy in the United States, the logic of restorationism implies a rejection of diversity and the pluralistic ethos of contemporary American society. A restoration of America's solemn covenant to be a Christian nation would mean that the best a non-Christian could hope for would be resident alien status and tolerance.

Reed, as evidenced by his avoidance of "Christian nation" and "sacred history" rhetoric, has been more aware than Robertson of the offensive antipluralistic implications of such statements. His calls for the restoration of a religious-moral consensus have included the recognition that greater equality for women and minorities have been "advances" of the last thirty years that must be preserved.[182] But the logic of restorationism is against such selectivity. If the true genius of America was contained in the original order established by the founders, then *any* change must be regarded as an indication of deviation and decline. Reed would no doubt argue, and rightly so, that the founders made room for the evolution of American polity, society, and culture through the constitutional amendment process.

Yet the admission of historical evolution and the selective embrace of social-political "advances" have undermined Reed's restorationist argument. If the original intent of the founders can be questioned, relativized, and even rejected on race and gender, why should their views on religion and morality remain unquestioned and absolute? I suspect that Reed has appealed to the supposed original intent of the founders on religious and moral questions because he has found support for his own position there. In the selective use of the founders to buttress his arguments, Reed is like political activists from across the political spectrum. But Reed has let the camel of pragmatic relativism get its nose into the tent of restorationism. This is the root of the criticism directed at Reed from within the Christian Right. For short-term pragmatic political purposes, such relativism is necessary, but in the long-term, it threatens Reed's intellectual justification of his political agenda.

Robertson, who has remained willing to justify his vision for America in terms of sacred as well as secular history, has been far less troubled by the antipluralistic implications of his restorationist views. In fact, Robertson has demonstrated a remarkable hostility to diversity in American culture. He has stressed that the founders of the nation, "were all basically from one common stock and one common philosophy."[183] But, according to Robertson, "Today, the United States struggles under a social philosophy of 'diversity' and 'pluralism.' . . . Unity is no longer the goal of secular society, but disparity, difference, and diversity. Consequently, confusion is triumphant."[184] Respect for social and cultural diversity, because it has tended to undermine an idealized and monocultural view of American history, is seen as part of secularism's "de-Christianizing of America."[185] Pluralism for Robertson is not a fact of life but "the name we give the transition from one orthodoxy to another."[186] Robertson has no intention of accepting any new de-Christianized orthodoxy. Instead, he wants a return to the old orthodoxy.

For Robertson and Reed, appeals for the restoration of Christian America have not been directed toward governmental establishment of a national church or toward a reconstructionist theocracy—although those who hope for such things may be encouraged by the success of the CC. I would argue that what Robertson and Reed "really want" is a return to the de facto or quasi-establishment of evangelical Protestantism of the nineteenth century. The anti-Catholic nativism and anti-Semitism of that era would be dismissed by Robertson and Reed because they define their enemies in terms of hostility to religion rather than by different religious beliefs. Catholics and Jews with a conservative or traditionalist orientation are seen as cobelligerents against secularism.

What Robertson and Reed want is a return to a supposed golden era in which it would not occur to anyone to question the propriety of public school prayer, the Ten Commandments on the wall of a government building, unabashed mixtures of evangelical piety and patriotism, or the assertion that this is a Christian nation. Although this evangelical ethos was protected and reinforced in some ways by law, what Robertson and Reed hope for is more powerful and pervasive than mere legality—the restoration of a culture in which evangelicals are insiders, not outsiders.

CHAPTER 6

DEMANDS FOR
RECOGNITION

IF THE CC EMPLOYS AN "OFFENSIVE AGENDA" of restoring "Christian America," it also advances a "defensive agenda" that calls for the recognition and protection of the rights of evangelicals against a hostile secular culture. This is not new. This defensive element has long been part of the Christian Right—accusations of "anti-Christian bigotry" were common in Robertson's presidential campaign rhetoric. The CC, however, is notable for the degree to which it has embraced and aggressively promoted this image of evangelicals as a disadvantaged group.

The basic purpose of the CC—"to make government more responsive to the concerns of Evangelical Christians and pro-family Catholics"—is based on the judgment that government has become less responsive, or unresponsive, to these groups. The fifth mission of the CC—"to protest anti-Christian bias and defend the legal rights of Christians"—is based on the notion that such protests and defenses have become necessary. Accordingly, the CC's publications and literature often appeal to the theme of victimization. One of the CC's monthly publications, *Religious Rights Watch,* has been entirely devoted to reporting incidents of discrimination against Christians.[1]

The CC's major publication, *Christian American,* has often carried news items, feature stories, or editorials on anti-Christian bias. The front page of the September 1994 edition bore a banner headline, "ASSAULT ON FAITH," that was subtitled, "Liberals Launch Campaign of Bigotry." This cover article alleged that "The anti-Christian attack strategy recently adopted by liberal organizations like the Anti-Defamation League and high-ranking Democrats, as well as their media counterparts, is an orchestrated offensive against people of faith in the political arena."[2] This anti-Christian offensive was seen as part of the Democrats's strategy for the 1994 congressional elections to paint Republicans as "radicals" and "extremists."

The same issue of *Christian American* also carried an article denouncing a report released in June 1994 by the Anti-Defamation League (ADL) entitled *The Religious Right: The Assault on Tolerance and Pluralism.*[3] The article, "ADL Guilty of Defamation," included many quotations from Jewish conservatives critical of the ADL's report and was a brief version of "A Campaign of Falsehoods: The Anti-Defamation League's Defamation of Religious Conservatives," a twenty-nine-page response to the ADL's criticisms of the CC. The CC claimed that "The ADL report is filled with fabrications, half-truths, innuendo, guilt by association that are reminiscent of the political style practiced by Joseph McCarthy in the 1950s."[4]

Other CC literature has also utilized the anti-Christian bigotry theme. One CC pamphlet, entitled "Christian Americans Are Tired of Getting Stepped On," had on its cover a picture of a flag decorated with a cross. The flag was lying on the ground and covered with muddy footprints. The pamphlet bore endorsing quotations from Charles Stanley, Beverly LaHaye, D. James Kennedy, and Father Michael Scanlan, as well as from Robertson. Every quotation mentioned bias, censorship, discrimination, or ridicule directed against Christians.[5] Periodic fund-raising letters have also discussed a general victimization of Christians. America, according to one letter signed by Robertson, "has become a largely anti-Christian pagan nation—and our government has become a weapon the anti-Christian forces now use against Christians and religious people."[6] In another letter, Robertson pleaded for an immediate contribution by writing, "Please don't let the Left's *politics of division, fear and anti-Christian bigotry succeed.*"[7]

Other letters have pointed to more specific threats. In a December 1995 letter, for instance, Reed claimed, "the Federal Election Commission is likely to take action in the next few days or weeks that is nothing short of an attempt to *shut down the Christian Coalition* and silence Christians in politics."[8] When in July 1996 the FEC finally did sue the CC for illegally aiding various Republican campaigns, a letter co-signed by Robertson and Reed asserted, "The FEC action is a dagger aimed at the heart of America's churches. . . . They are using the power of the federal government to muzzle Christians and make us second-class citizens."[9] In his speech at the 1996 "Road to Victory" conference, Reed proclaimed, "I've got news for our critics, the radical left, and yes, the liberal bureaucrats of the Federal Election Commission. We will not be harassed, we will not be intimidated, and we will not be silenced! We are Americans too!"[10]

The CC's proposal for a Religious Equality Amendment in the *Contract with the American Family* claimed that "Examples of hostility toward religious values and those who hold them abound."[11] The *Contract* asserted that this hostility has been encouraged by judicial interpretations of the Establishment Clause. "In 1962, the Supreme Court banned organized prayer from public schools. Since then, federal, state, and local courts and officials, including public school administrators, have joined in a nationwide search and destroy mission for student religious practices."[12]

Robertson has also depicted the Supreme Court's 1962-63 prayer and Bible-reading decisions as premier examples of what he called a "vicious vendetta against religious values in the schools of America."[13] His 1993 book *The Turning Tide* had an appendix entitled "The War Against Christianity," which contained "horror stories" of supposedly rampant anti-Christian bigotry.[14] In one memorable 1995 speech, Robertson compared the liberal attack on religious freedom in America to a brutal gang rape.[15]

Reed has pointed to what he called the "marginalization of religion." Part of this has been based on contemporary church-state jurisprudence. The "First Amendment," asserted Reed, "has been twisted into a weapon that billy-clubs people of faith into submission and silence."[16] Critics of the Christian Right, according to Reed, "scrawl a harsh caricature" depicting religious conservatives as "the final and ugly backwash of George Wallace's and David Duke's politics of rage."[17] He also charged that the news media and the entertainment industry have consistently represented religion and religious persons with demeaning stereotypes.[18] "Religion has become equated with fanaticism," observed Reed, "orthodox faith with fascism, and politically involved people of faith are painted as zealots."[19]

The CC's rhetoric of victimization, and the apparent willingness of its constituency to embrace it, has depended in part on elements in the Christian tradition itself. Those who have suffered for the faith, especially to the point of martyrdom, have provided the Christian tradition with a potent image of heroism.[20] For evangelical supporters of the CC, who read the New Testament as an accurate, if not inerrant, history of Christ and the primitive church, the image of Christians as those who are hated by the "world," just as Christ was hated, is almost inescapable.

Robertson has appealed to such images of heroic suffering by Christians. In describing the spread of Christianity within the Roman Empire, Robertson used the aphorism, "The blood of the martyrs had been the seed of the church."[21] "It has been true throughout the ages," Robertson wrote in 1984, "that those who are God's messengers are often set upon and hurt by the people they have tried to warn. That kind of suffering is virtually unavoidable as long as we live in a wicked world of superstition, hatred, and ignorance."[22] For Robertson, "Persecution is simply part of living as a Christian in this world."[23] He has urged American Christians to expect more such suffering in the future. "There has always been a struggle between the people of God and those who serve Satan. Throughout history there have been successive martyrdoms of Christians, and it is the height of arrogance to assume that only twentieth-century Christians in the United States of America will be spared any kind of persecution. That goes against the flow of history for the last two thousand years."[24] Robertson's expectations of inevitable and escalating persecution were echoed in "Hate Crimes Against Christians," a 1992 *Christian American* editorial. "None of this should surprise us. Jesus told His disciples to expect tribulation and persecution in the world." The editorial concluded, "It will get worse."[25]

Inevitable conflict with the world has also been part of Robertson's eschatological expectations. Robertson has consistently affirmed the notion that Christians will have to endure persecution and even martyrdom during the Great Tribulation and the rule of the Antichrist.[26] Using this framework, Robertson has been able to elevate disrespectful remarks and incidents of discrimination to the level of events in salvation history. These remarks and incidents, no matter how trivial and isolated they may seem, have functioned as confirmations of biblical prophecies, harbingers of the eschaton, and a summons to heroic faith. Those who suffer these evils for the sake of Christ will become the human protagonists at the center of the drama of history, a drama that is just about to reach its climax.

Yet the CC's "defensive agenda" cannot be understood as only a product of Christian belief. The tradition of suffering for the faith has certainly provided a framework for understanding and accepting the inevitability of secular hostility, but that tradition has *not* provided a rationale for political activism or agitation for the recognition of "rights" that are being denied.

PARALLELS TO MULTICULTURALISM

The CC's defensive agenda, its emphasis on the victimization of evangelicals and demand for recognition of their rights, was paralleled in another controversial movement that rose to public prominence in the early 1990s, multiculturalism.[27] While considering these parallels, it is necessary to keep in mind the fundamental differences, and the deep antagonisms, between the Christian Right and multiculturalism. The parallels between these movements are not in their goals or vision for America, but in their tactics and rhetoric—parallels in form, not in substance.

Like many controversial "isms," multiculturalism is seldom defined even when it is being heatedly debated. Even its proponents have difficulty agreeing upon a single meaning for the term.[28] It has served as an amorphous banner under which disparate emphases and interests have cooperated for similar ends and against common opponents. Multiculturalism has most often been discussed in the context of education, but its significance has been far broader. Multicultural education has been a reaction to what was called the "melting pot" theory, which held that cultural diversity among immigrants should be eliminated through "Americanization," assimilation into the white middle-class mainstream of American society and culture. But the massive social and political changes of the 1960s, especially those related to the civil rights movement, led to a more basic, and affirmative, reassessment of the meaning of cultural diversity in the schools. This new approach, multicultural education, argued "that schools should be oriented toward the cultural enrichment of all children and youth through programs rooted to the preservation and extension of cultural alternatives."[29] Multicultural education goes beyond mere acceptance and accommodation of cultural differences to a recognition of the right of diverse groups to exist, survive, and thrive.

This affirmation of cultural diversity in education has been applied to the entirety of American public life in the form of multiculturalism. In the words of political scientist Richard M. Merelman, multiculturalism "not only asserts the viability, merit, and durability of multiple cultures, but also calls for public support of these cultures within a democratic framework."[30] Beyond the affirmation and support of the cultures of racial and ethnic minorities, multiculturalism has been embraced by advocates for the rights of women, homosexuals, and people with disabilities—groups that have been disadvantaged, victimized, or excluded by the mainstream or dominant culture.[31] Merelman observed that multiculturalism was a "novel form of political compact" since it was based on the acceptance and promotion of group differences rather than on group or individual similarities.[32]

Much of the criticism leveled at multiculturalism has been based on its supposed promotion of differences. Historian Arthur Schlesinger, Jr. warned of multiculturalism's potential for "the fragmentation, resegregation and tribalization of American life."[33] Philosopher Richard Rorty criticized multiculturalism's repudiation of national identity. "This repudiation," wrote Rorty, "is the difference between traditional American pluralism and the new movement called multiculturalism." Pluralism was the attempt, according to Rorty, to make America a "community of communities." Multiculturalism's "politics of difference" has been "the attempt to keep these communities at odds with one another."[34]

Other critics have made separatism the basis for a distinction between "good" and "bad" multiculturalism. Historian of education Diane Ravitch, for instance, distinguished "pluralistic multiculturalism" from "particularistic multiculturalism."[35] The pluralistic form, which Ravitch endorsed, sees America's common culture as having been formed by the "interaction of its subsidiary cultures"—a common culture that was multicultural. In contrast, particularistic multiculturalists "insist that no common culture is possible or desirable." They reject interaction or accommodation among groups. "The brand of history they espouse," wrote Ravitch, "is one in which everyone is either a descendant of victims or oppressors."[36] Like Schlesinger and Rorty, Ravitch saw in particularistic multiculturalism, "the way to unending racial antagonism, as well as disintegration of the sense of mutuality on which social progress depends."[37]

Robertson's hostility to what he calls multiculturalism has a similar source. For Robertson, multiculturalism's rhetoric of sensitivity, tolerance, and respect for diversity has been part of a methodical program "to undermine authority and to bring down the structures that contribute to the cohesiveness of society."[38] More fundamentally, an emphasis on diversity strikes at the heart of Robertson's vision of restoring Christian America. Reed, despite his rejection of Christian nation rhetoric, has also called for the restoration and maintenance of a single shared culture. Despite these fundamental differences between multiculturalism and the CC, there are notable parallels between them. These parallels, it should be remembered, are not in substance or goals, but in form and tactics. How did these parallels come about? While there may be specific instances of tactical borrowing, a more basic explanation may be the common cultural, social, and political context of the early 1990s in which both have emerged and operated. Because of this common context they may have chosen similar paths to power and to the accomplishment of their particular political goals.

Invocations of Shared Victimization

The first parallel is a reliance on notions of shared victimization. The social groups that are associated with multiculturalism claim to be victims of various forms of oppression, discrimination, disempowerment, and exclusion. This association has been so strong that critics, such as conservative author Dinesh D'Souza in his 1991 bestseller, *Illiberal Education,* have characterized multiculturalism in higher education as "a revolution on behalf of minority victims" that seeks "to advance the interests of the previously disenfranchised."[39] Proponents of multiculturalism in education, who object to the dismissive tone of D'Souza's work, have laid no less stress upon the centrality of oppression for the multicultural enterprise. "African Americans, Asian Americans, Puerto Ricans/Latinos, and Native Americans," stated a 1989 report on educational reform in New York state, "have all been the victims of an intellectual and educational oppression that has characterized the culture and institutions of the United States and the European American world for centuries."[40]

African-American literary scholar Henry Louis Gates, Jr., however, noted that the emphasis on victimhood in academic circles has sometimes been overdone. What Gates has referred to as the "routinized production of righteous indignation"[41] can fail those it purports to aid. "Once the invocation of oppression became another move in a game of academic one-upmanship," observed Gates, "it was easy to lose sight of what's happening on the streets outside."[42]

Yet this "invocation of oppression," whether on behalf of a particular group, or on behalf of all who have been marginalized, remains a powerful means of creating group solidarity and cooperation among otherwise disparate groups. "[R]epression and hostility by outsiders," observed sociologist Keith A. Roberts, "tend to create a feeling of common plight and common destiny."[43] And as sociologists Luther P. Gerlach and Virginia H. Hine argued, opposition is a key factor in the strength and growth of social movements.[44] Opposition is not necessarily "objective" in the sense that those outside the movement would assent to its reality. "The dynamic that motivates movement growth, however, does not depend directly on the amount of 'real' opposition or the type of risk, but on participants' subjective perception of these influences."[45] The substance of the invocation may or may not be accurate, but the *purpose* of the invocation is to strengthen the perception of oppression or opposition among adherents and thus strengthen the movement.

A second important function of invocations of oppression is to lay claim to "the moral clout that comes with victimhood."[46] Victimhood carries a moral force because of a deep association of victims with innocence, and thus with entitlement and power. As African-American essayist Shelby Steele observed, "Our innocence always inflates us and deflates those we seek power over. Once inflated we are entitled; we are in fact licensed to go after the power our innocence tells us we deserve. In this sense, *innocence is power.*"[47] According to Steele, black provocations of white racial guilt are often "*power* moves, little shows of power that try to freeze the 'enemy' in self-consciousness. They gratify and inflate the provocateur. They are the underdog's bite."[48]

Steele's power analysis of invocations of oppression has been echoed by critics of multiculturalism such as D'Souza. "By converting victimhood into a certificate of virtue," wrote D'Souza, "minorities acquire a powerful moral claim that renders their opponents defensive and apologetic, and immunizes themselves from criticism and sanction."[49] Reminiscent of Gates's "academic one-upmanship," D'Souza also noted the competition for victimhood's power within the multicultural coalition. "Even as they work in concert on some issues," wrote D'Souza, "these groups compete to establish themselves as the most oppressed of all. Everyone races to seize the lowest rung of the ladder."[50]

Robertson, it is interesting to note, has taken both sides in the debate over "victimism." Citing Charles J. Sykes's *A Nation of Victims,* Robertson denounced what he called the "cult" of victimization. "We find ourselves," he wrote, "living in a society that grants opportunities to the oppressed of every description, not because they are deserving, but because they are 'disadvantaged.'"[51] According to Robertson, victimism "encourages litigation, provides virtual license for certain kinds of character assassination and name calling, and breeds a dangerous splintering of society."[52]

Yet Robertson, Reed, and the literature of the CC have often offered claims of victimhood. These claims function in much the same ways they do for multiculturalism—building collective solidarity and gaining moral leverage against opponents.

The need for solidarity against persecution is an important theme in CC literature. In the Fall 1990 issue of *Christian American,* an advertisement for membership in the organization displayed a photograph of a lapel pin with the CC logo. The caption read, "If There's Safety in Numbers for Christians, This Is a Safety Pin."[53] One CC pamphlet stated, "Christian America has been a house divided for far too long. As such, we have been misrepresented, underrepresented and outright ignored. The time to stand together as Christians for our God-given rights is right now."[54] The need for collective action was stressed in a passage that often appeared in CC fund-raising letters signed by Robertson: "In other words, *anti-Christian bigotry* is no longer under the surface. It's now out in the open. It's now acceptable! And it will get worse—*unless* you and I continue to work together to organize millions of Christian voters to fight back."[55] The basic message, as a *Christian American* editorial put it, was simple: "Christians Must Stand Together."[56]

The necessity of standing together has sometimes been demonstrated by citing offensive statements by various critics of the CC— public officials, prominent Democrats, or liberal public policy organizations. "Opponents of conservative Christians," observed Reed, "use shrill charges to portray them as extremists. The National Abortion Rights Action League has charged that the movement has the 'potential for [the] destruction of our political, religious, and legal institutions.'"[57] To the CC's constituency, such a charge is so patently false that it could only be malicious in intent. Reed put this rather delicately when he wrote, "Their tendency to label the entire agenda of politically active Christians as dangerous is disingenuous."[58]

As I noted at the beginning of this chapter, the FEC's July 1996 lawsuit alleging violations of federal election laws by the CC was also seen as an example of anti-Christian bigotry. "This is a completely baseless and legally threadbare attempt by a reckless federal agency to silence people of faith and deny them their First Amendment rights," said Mike Russell, CC communications director.[59] Reed told Jerry Falwell's *National Liberty Journal* that "The motivation (of this FEC action) is to silence people of faith and to have a dangerous, chilling effect on their ability to exercise their rights as citizens and voters."[60] A letter sent to CC supporters, and signed by both Reed and Robertson, alleged that the lawsuit was the work of "the liberal bureaucrats at the Clinton-controlled Federal Election Commission." The letters pointed out that the "left-wing superbureaucrats at the FEC" were ignoring a $35 million campaign by "far-left union bosses" to elect liberal Democrats. "But they are singling out Christians, and using the power of the federal government to keep Christians uninformed."[61]

As I noted in Chapter 4, the CC claimed that these "left-wing superbureaucrats" did not succeed in "silencing people of faith." Reed maintained the CC's voter education efforts did better than ever in 1996, with 22,000 more churches participating than in 1994. According to Reed, "The FEC lawsuit has had no discernible impact whatsoever except in creating a backlash that has generated more support than ever."[62] It would be very hard to determine if the CC's claims of victimization elicited sympathetic cooperation at the grass roots, but by October, the FEC had received some 600 letters protesting the CC lawsuit—the most mail it had ever received regarding a single case.[63]

The news media has often been seen as an agent of anti-Christian attitudes.[64] The most notorious such anti-Christian statement appeared in the *Washington Post* on February 1, 1993. Staff writer Michael Weisskopf, in a front-page news story on the communications networks employed by the Christian Right, characterized the "followers" of Falwell and Robertson as "largely poor, uneducated and easy to command."[65] Weisskopf offered no evidence or attribution for this statement because, as he later said, "I try not to have to attribute every point in the story if it appears to be universally accepted."[66] After receiving hundreds of complaints, the next day the *Post* printed this correction: "There is no factual basis for that statement."[67] *Post* Managing Editor Robert G. Kaiser admitted, "We really screwed up."[68]

The immediate reaction of the CC to the *Post* story was indignation. "In other words," wrote CC Government Affairs Director Heidi Scanlon, "it is not awareness and involvement that motivates the Christian citizen, but ignorance and gullibility."[69] A *Christian American* editorial noted the *Post*'s correction but focused on Weisskopf's "unrepentant" stance and stated that "Weisskopf's unfortunate attitude reflects the thinking of most of the liberal media elite. Christians need to recognize this fact and act accordingly."[70] In another article, *Christian American* quoted Reed: "The article was prejudiced and bigoted and shows that *The Washington Post,* with the rest of the media, is insensitive as to who evangelicals are."[71] In a February 16, 1993, speech at the National Religious Broadcasters's convention, Robertson used the statement as proof that the biased media will not give evangelicals "a fair break."[72]

Despite the *Post*'s willingness to admit its mistake, the phrase "poor, uneducated and easy to command" has lived on in CC literature. Indeed, the admitted mistake by the *Post,* which Robertson has called "the official press arm of the liberal welfare state,"[73] is too valuable not to capitalize on. It has often been used simply as evidence of media bias. "Despite their protestations to the contrary," wrote Robertson, "such blatant prejudice makes the liberal media truly the most bigoted group in American society today."[74] A 1995 CC fund-raising letter stated, "I'm sure you've noticed how bold liberals in the media, in our schools and in our government have become in their attacks on Christians— especially when it comes to Christian involvement in politics. For example . . . THE WASHINGTON POST described conservative Christians as *'largely poor, uneducated and easy-to-command.'*"[75]

Weisskopf's infamous phrase has also been used, particularly by Reed, as a peg on which to hang assertions of the mainstream nature of the pro-family movement. Citing a commissioned survey, Reed held that, "the typical pro-family voter is a well-educated professional woman, usually a baby-boomer and a mother, whose political attitudes are largely shaped by her concerns for her family and children."[76] In the introduction to the CC's *Contract with the American Family,* Reed used Weisskopf's phrase as a reminder of how "the media has frequently caricatured people of faith active in the political process," but Reed asserted that "the reality is very different. People of faith in this country want . . . what almost everyone else wants."[77] Reed has also used it as a rhetorical tool with which to ridicule stereotypes about the CC constituency. "Some people view people of faith as latter-day Babbitts," wrote Reed, "who troop to churches in polyester suits, handle snakes, and pray in tongues for the return of Jim Crow and patriarchy. The *Washington Post* even labeled them 'poor, uneducated, and easy to command.'"[78]

Weisskopf's phrase has come to be used by the CC as a mocking salute to its critics and opponents. In 1993, *Time* reported that the CC had made buttons that said, "Poor, Uneducated and Easy to Command." Leaders and members of the CC were wearing them as a "defiant badge of honor."[79] In a 1993 *New York Times Magazine* article on the Oregon CC, writer Robert Sullivan noted that CC activists "hear all the talk about the poor, undereducated Christian voter and laugh."[80]

Eliciting triumphant laughter seems to have become a primary function of Weisskopf's phrase for the CC. At the CC's "Road to Victory" conference in 1995, Reed told his delighted audience: "The *Washington Post* called people like you, and this is a quote, 'poor, uneducated, and easy to command.' I think the reporter who wrote that story ought to come to Road to Victory and see what we have here today!" Reed happily went on to describe how "the fax machines at the *Post* were jammed for three days with people who were faxing in their college diplomas and their 1040 Forms to let them know that they're very well educated, and were middle class!"[81] At the same conference Robertson drew laughter with this: "Just think what these poor uneducated people have been able to accomplish in six years. Think what they could do if some of them ever got educated."[82] Reed, after telling the story again in his 1996 book, *Active Faith,* concluded, "No other episode from the early Clinton administration so heartened and awakened our supporters."[83]

While "poor, uneducated and easy to command" has become a humorous affirmation of internal solidarity, there are other invocations of oppression that elicit no amusement whatsoever. These invocations often take the form of "horror stories"—narratives of injustices perpetrated against ordinary and entirely innocent "people of faith," or demonstrations of hostility against religion. An absurd decision by a zealous government official is often involved. For example: "In Hayward, California, a pastor was told that he could not pray at a birthday for his wife at a rented hall in the city park."[84] The American Civil Liberties Union (ACLU) is also often the villain. "*Thanks to law suits filed by the ACLU,*" claimed Reed in a 1996 direct-mail piece, "students are being sent home from the schools for asking God's grace over their lunches and Christian symbols have been removed from public places all across America."[85]

These accusations, which never leave doubt as to the guilt or innocence of the parties involved, are sometimes presented in some detail, such as in the CC publication *Religious Rights Watch.* But they are more often cited, especially in speeches by Robertson and Reed, with few specifics. For the skeptical, this may create doubts about authenticity, but for those already inclined to believe, these stories gain rhetorical strength by not being too specific. By not tying oppressive actions to a particular context, CC members can be made to feel that such injustices can happen anywhere—"all across America"—at any time. Both Robertson and Reed have sought to strengthen the impression that such abuses are common. After recounting dozens of "horror stories" in *The Turning Tide,* Robertson told his readers, "These are but the tip of the iceberg."[86] Reed alleged that the "rights to freedom of speech and religion" of people of faith "are under constant attack whenever they enter the public arena."[87]

Robertson and Reed have often used nonspecific stories in which Christian children were the victims. Reed offered these instances in a 1995 speech: "In Missouri, for example, a child caught praying silently over lunch was sent to week-long detention. In southern Illinois, a fifteen-year-old girl was handcuffed, threatened with mace, and shoved into the back of a police car. Her crime? Praying around the flagpole before school hours."[88] Robertson presented this horror story: "In Michigan, a five-year-old girl in kindergarten tried to thank Jesus quietly before her Friday snack. Her teacher told her to stop because prayer is not allowed in school. The girl went home in tears."[89]

In each case, Robertson and Reed juxtaposed an innocent expression of Christian piety against a harsh and unreasonable exercise of secular authority. This juxtaposition was meant to elicit outrage. And this outrage, it was hoped, will lead to collective action through the CC. Reed, in his speech at the 1995 "Road to Victory" conference, appealed to this outrage. After recounting a horror story about a seven-year-old boy, Reed said, "You know, I have a six-year-old. I know something about the tenderness, and the innocence, and the vulnerability of a child that young. And I want you to know . . . that should never go on in America, and we're going to see that it stops—from one end of this country to the other!"[90]

It may be that the victim status of evangelicals has remained largely unrecognized, but the CC's aspiration to exercise the moral clout of victimhood—what Steele called "the underdog's bite"—is demonstrated in its tendency to draw parallels between anti-Christian bigotry and the prejudice and discrimination suffered by other groups in history. The African-American community has been the subject of most of these parallels. "In the 1930s," wrote Robertson bluntly, "African-Americans in the South were classified by bigots as 'niggers,' not worthy of respect; today it is evangelical Christians who are considered by the liberal media as 'niggers' and not worthy of respect."[91] Reed, however, has been more circumspect about making these parallels. Unlike African-Americans, Reed observed, "No one is denying people of faith the right to vote or to live where they choose."[92] Referring to the Civil Rights movement, Reed acknowledged, "We will never know the suffering and the indignity that they knew. . . . I am in no way, comparing our two movements."[93]

Yet Reed has continued to utilize such comparisons. Sometimes they are more implicit comparisons of historical significance. "The union of Roman Catholics and conservative Protestants could have a greater impact on American politics than any coalition since African-Americans and Jews came together during the civil rights movement."[94] As I observed above, Reed has appealed to the precedent of the religiously based civil rights movement to justify the political activism of religious conservatives. In particular, the name of Martin Luther King, Jr.'s organization, the Southern *Christian* Leadership Conference, has been used to justify the name *Christian* Coalition, as well as to accuse political liberals of using a double standard when it comes to conservative faith-based political activism.[95] And as I noted above, Reed has pointed to King's healing and inclusive rhetoric as the proper model for the pro-family movement.[96]

Reed's comparisons have also been more explicit and direct. Regarding the role of religious conservatives in the Republican party, Reed said, "We don't want to be asked to pick cotton in the fields and then be told we can't sit on the porch."[97] He has used the phrase "the Back of the Bus" to describe the marginalization of religion in American culture.[98] And according to Reed, the media has used "Amos-and-Andy-like caricatures of people of faith [to] reinforce our culture's phobia of religion."[99] Reed drew an explicit parallel between race and religion in describing the Democratic candidates's tactics in 1993 Virginia state elections. "George Wallace ran against blacks. Mary Sue Terry and Don Byer are running against Christians. Their campaign tactics are identical in their appeal to bald faced bigotry."[100]

The CC has also drawn comparisons between Christians in America and Jews in Nazi Germany. A 1990 *Christian American* advertisement for membership in the CC listed a series of anti-religious horror stories and then asked, "A look back at Hitler's Germany? An alarmist view of the future? Not at all. These outrages are here and now."[101] A 1993 *Christian American* editorial made the comparison more explicit: "But Christians are being boxed into a cultural ghetto in the eyes of the American public just as surely as Jews were boxed into a physical ghetto in Nazi Germany."[102] In 1990, Robertson, responding to the *Miami Herald*'s criticism of his involvement in the Florida governor's race, invoked images of the Holocaust. "Do you also have a ghetto chosen to herd the pro-life Catholics and evangelicals into? Have you designed the appropriate yellow patch that Christians should wear on their garments to make certain that no Florida politicians become polluted by associating with them?" Robertson concluded with, "You are not going to get away with it. This is America, not Nazi Germany. Christians are Americans too."[103]

A 1993 editorial cartoon by Pat Oliphant depicting a bewildered GOP elephant being dragged by rats into the "Fundamentalist Christian Mission" drew a sharp reaction from *Christian American*. The cartoon was likened to a Nazi-era propaganda film that juxtaposed images of praying Jews with images of sewer rats, "thereby conditioning the German people . . . to regard Jews as social parasites." *Christian American* asserted that "The same phenomenon is now being observed in America, but this time the group being demonized is Christians rather than Jews."[104]

Reed, again, has been more prudent than to call his critics "Nazis."[105] Rather than draw parallels between America and the Third Reich, Reed has concentrated on common threats to Jews and Christians in the American context. In a speech to the ADL, he said, "Jewish immigrants also encountered cultural stereotypes, a scowling intolerance that our community has only recently experienced. . . . Religious conservative candidates have been called 'snake handlers,' 'unfit for office,' 'extremists' because they were members of a particular church. This kind of religious bigotry is a threat to Jews and Christians alike."[106]

The CC has also drawn comparisons to other groups that have been victimized or excluded. Robertson, using the phrase "religious cleansing," compared secularization of the "public square" in America to genocidal "ethnic cleansing" in the former Yugoslavia.[107] When a South Carolina Republican was dismissed by an opponent as having no qualifications for office other than "handling snakes and being able to speak fluently in tongues," Reed said, "This comment is religious bigotry, pure and simple. It is no different than the kind of intolerance that John F. Kennedy faced in 1960 when he ran for President and faced anti-

Catholicism."[108] An article in *Christian American* alluded to nineteenth-century anti-Irish sentiment by charging that secular elites, "hope to intimidate both the Democratic and Republican parties into posting official notice that evangelicals need not apply."[109] "Like the 'separate sphere' once assigned to women," observed Reed, "religious people are now relegated to their churches and homes, where their faith poses no threat to the social order."[110] Using a phrase popularized by feminists, CC Field Director Guy Rodgers wrote of the liberal anti-religious media, "They just don't get it."[111] And Robertson has called the demeaning of religion "McCarthyism" and asserted that "it's just as foul a tactic when practiced against Christians as it was against purported Communists."[112]

As I noted in Chapter 4, when a series of arson attacks on African-American churches gained national attention in 1996, Reed announced a series of initiatives to help these churches as steps toward "racial reconciliation." The September/October 1996 issue of *Christian American,* however, also presented these attacks as part of a broader hostility toward all "people of faith." Based on information supplied by the Bureau of Alcohol, Tobacco, and Firearms (ATF) regarding 208 incidents of violence aimed at houses of worship in 35 states from May 1990 to June 1996, *Christian American* concluded: "In short, the wave of violence has been an attack on places of worship in general even more than an attack on certain ethnic, racial, or denominational groups."[113] African-American churches were burned not because they were African-American, but because they were churches. This analysis allowed the CC to claim for its constituency—white middle-class evangelicals—a place among the victimized in American society. This analysis also implied that anti-religious bigotry was a more serious problem than racism.

Reminiscent of the competition among multiculturalists for recognition as "most oppressed," the CC has implied that its constituency should be able to claim the "lowest rung on the ladder." It has done this through reminders of the intolerance toward evangelicals displayed by those who preach tolerance. Referring to Democratic criticisms of religious conservatives, Reed observed, "They demonstrate how intolerant some liberals can become when religion creeps beyond the stained-glass ghetto assigned to it."[114] When the African-American leader Reverend Jesse Jackson, in a newspaper interview, likened the CC to slaveholders in the antebellum South and to Nazis, CC spokesperson Mike Russell said, "It's sad and pathetic that Jesse Jackson, who has dedicated his life to combating bigotry, has now committed a brazen act of bigotry himself."[115] The CC's critique of the ADL's report *The Religious Right* lamented, "The Anti-Defamation League has committed defamation, not only against religious conservatives, but against its own stated purpose."[116] A 1992 *Christian American* editorial charged gay rights activists in Oregon with violence. "Churches have been defaced and burned. Cars, homes, and businesses have been vandalized. Peaceful citizens going about their lawful business have been brutalized by goon squads of militant homosexual 'bigot-busters.'"[117] And of course, "the liberal media" has also been hypocritical. Reed observed that it "celebrates feminist political involvement, but condemns Christians who exercise their civic responsibilities as fascists."[118]

These allegations of hypocrisy are, on one level, simple attacks on the credibility and moral standing of the CC's critics and opponents. But on another level, the CC is making a more powerful moral claim on behalf of its constituency. We are, the CC has implied, not only victims, but we have been victimized by all the other victim groups—the victim of victims. Thus they are the "bottom rung," the most innocent, and the most entitled to power. Reed has acknowledged the obvious difference between the victimization experienced by contemporary white middle-class evangelicals and African-Americans under Jim Crow laws. Yet he was willing to assert, "It is no exaggeration to say that Christian bashing is the last acceptable form of prejudice in America."[119] According to Reed, "As a society, we have become biased against bigotry itself except when that bias is directed at religion."[120] Anti-religious bigotry may not be the most severe form of bigotry in American history, Reed seemed to say, but it is the *final* form of bigotry we need to overcome. And the constituency of the CC, conservative evangelicals and pro-family Roman Catholics, are the final victims.

A Usable Past

A second parallel between the CC and multiculturalism is their pursuit of a "usable past" as a foundation for their respective invocations of oppression. Multiculturalism's usable past has been supplied, for the most part, by the unprecedented number of women and members of minority groups who have entered the academy as historians since the 1960s. Aside from shaping a more inclusive historiography, this new generation of historians has provided the evidence to support the invocations of oppression on behalf of various marginalized groups. By embedding these invocations in historical narratives, and clothing them with the authority of the historical profession, multiculturalist historians have created more powerful instruments of group solidarity and have sharpened the rhetorical teeth of the underdog's bite. This particular use of history by multiculturalists has *not* been paralleled in the literature of the CC. According to the restorationist jeremiads of Robertson and Reed, anti-Christian bigotry and discrimination against "people of faith" are relatively recent developments. The 1962-63 Supreme Court decisions on prayer and Bible-reading, a commonly cited turning point on America's "journey away from God," are simply too recent to be able to invoke the power of history. Yet the CC has appealed to history in a way that parallels the appeals of some advocates of multiculturalism.

Schlesinger, in *The Disuniting of America,* argued that much of the history being written in the name of multiculturalism is "compensatory history." Compensatory history, according to Schlesinger, "is underdog history, designed to demonstrate what Bertrand Russell called the 'superior virtue of the oppressed' by inventing or exaggerating past glories and purposes."[121] In reaction to Anglocentric dominance, excluded ethnic groups in America have sought "counter-affirmations of their own historical and cultural dignity, myths celebrating, and often exaggerating . . . their own unacknowledged contributions to the making of America." "Inspired by group resentment and pride," according to Schlesinger, "this literature very often succumbed to the Platonic temptation of 'noble lies.'"[122]

These noble lies have necessitated rewriting the historical record in order to give an oppressed group a central, if not *the* central, role. Schlesinger cited historian John V. Kelleher, who called this the "there's-always-an-Irishman-at-the-bottom-of-it-doing-the-real-work approach to American history."[123] Such an approach is not a disciplined search for knowledge but rather "social and psychological therapy whose purpose is to raise the self-esteem of children from minority groups."[124]

Schlesinger and other critics of multiculturalism have charged that history directed toward the production of self-esteem is particularly prone to distortion and myth-making. "Exhibit A" for these critics has been the Afrocentric notion of the ancient Greek "theft" of African culture from ancient Egypt, a black civilization—a debt the dominant white racist culture has been unwilling to acknowledge.[125] Whatever the intellectual merits of this Afrocentric interpretation of history, and they have been hotly disputed, one can see that this version of history has provided the grounds for group pride, nostalgia for a lost golden age, and resentment over the current order of things.

As I noted in the previous chapter, the restorationist version of American history that Robertson, Reed, and the CC present to their constituency has provided similar grounds for pride, nostalgia, and resentment. In their view, the nation was founded by Christians, governed by Christian leaders, and was based on Christian beliefs and morality. America grew to prosperity, power, and greatness, if not because of the blessings of God, who was well-pleased with His covenanted Christian nation, then because of the moral and social influence of Christianity. As Robertson wrote, "We simply will not let secularization crowd us out. After all, our forefathers founded this country, and we're not about to give it up!"[126]

But in contrast to many minority groups who have complained that their story has never been told in traditional histories of America, the CC has complained that the proud history of Christianity has been written *out* of contemporary history books. "Campus gurus and thought police," wrote Robertson, "have attempted to strip from our society all references to our Christian heritage, to the faith of our fathers, to the artistic and literary achievements of Western Christian civilization."[127] Reed asserted that those who denounce contemporary faith-based political activism "seek to redefine our national character and deny our past in a way that expresses not mere neutrality, but hostility, towards religion as a legitimate source of political ideas."[128] Reed cited examples of how history textbooks have slighted American religion, and he seemed to allege that this exclusion was intentional. "While some call for the inclusion of women, minorities, and native Americans in the discussion of our history," said Reed, "they present a highly inaccurate portrait of our national past by ignoring the contributions made by people of faith."[129]

Using his background in history, Reed has tried to demonstrate religious contributions to reform movements in American history. "The antislavery crusade, temperance movement, and civil rights struggle all owed their distinctive moral flavor to the messianic zeal of their adherents. Religion sparking political involvement is not an aberration of the American experience, but is perhaps its most persistent theme."[130] Reed also pointed to the importance of religious values in the American Revolution, the Populist, Progressive, Social Gospel, and Labor movements, and even in the New Deal.[131] Unlike Robertson, who has been deeply suspicious of the progressive reform movements,[132] Reed enlists the ancestors of modern liberalism into a "there's-always-a-Christian-at-the-bottom-of-it-doing-the-real-work approach to American history." In Reed's version of history, the mantle of social reform has passed to today's religious conservatives, not to the liberals of the Democratic party. "Far from being a sharp break with America's political past," asserted Reed, "the Christian Coalition represents a recovery of its most honored and noble traditions."[133]

It should be noted, however, that Reed departed significantly from the pattern of feel-good or compensatory history with reminders of the long and shameful association of the white evangelical community with racism. "The white evangelical church marched in the vanguard of the campaign to preserve segregation in the South," confessed Reed. "George Wallace may have stood in the schoolhouse door, but evangelical clergy provided the moral framework for his actions."[134] Reed even echoed criticisms of the hollowness of Christian Right appeals to the precedent of the Civil Rights movement. "We quote Martin Luther King to great effect, but how many of us marched with him, and how many of us bear the scars of Bull Connor's billy clubs and police dogs? Sadly, the answer is few."[135]

Other works distributed by the CC presented usable versions of American history. Some works explained, for instance, the Christian roots of the Declaration of Independence,[136] or provided a compilation of historical quotations that testify to the Christian character of American culture, society, and politics.[137] Another work distributed by the CC, David Barton's *The Myth of Separation,* was an especially clear attempt to enlist history in the Christian Right's cause. Barton, who has often spoken at CC events, attempted to demonstrate the antiseparationist character of the Constitution, the First Amendment, and American jurisprudence until 1947.[138] In the foreword, Barton explained that his work was a "'book of remembrance'—a record of those men who, in previous times, had 'feared God and honored his name' (Malachi 3:16)." Barton hoped that through "this 'book of remembrance,' the hearts of the nation may again be turned back to their fathers—their Founding Fathers."[139] Like Barton's work, the historical literature of the CC are "books of remembrance" that present a politically useful history in which evangelicals and evangelical faith have been unjustly displaced from the center of national life. In short, the constituency of the CC has been provided with historical grounds for pride, nostalgia, and resentment.

A Critique of Oppression

A third parallel between multiculturalism and the CC is a critique of oppression. The tactics of invoking oppression and creating a usable history would be insufficient to guide political activity without an understanding of their opponents-oppressors and how to overcome them. This common necessity for theoretical weapons, and their common functions, is easy to overlook because the intellectual tools employed are of such a starkly different nature and level of sophistication.

The multicultural perspective in higher education is not only the offspring of the "identity politics," of the 1960s. It is also the child of French postmodernist philosophical and literary theories. These postmodern theories have been called the "'68 Philosophy" because of their close association with the student radicalism that convulsed France that year.[140] According to author Paul Berman, the '68 theories involved a sharp rejection of epistemological realism and of the liberal humanist belief in the autonomy and freedom of individuals.[141]

These postmodernist ideas, which began to appear in American academic circles in the 1970s, were adapted to the purposes of civil rights and identity politics. This adaptation, according to Berman, was "an authentically American mutation of '68 Philosophy," which ought to be called "race/class/gender-ism."[142] Race, class, and gender were seen as the basic categories of analysis that could be used to break the oppressive power of the dominant culture. This analysis was especially brought to bear on the educational system, a primary means of securing the dominant position of rich white males. But oppression and injustice were not seen as the product of chance or the evil will of individuals. Instead, oppression was understood to be systemic, woven into the fabric of society and into our thinking in the form of "isms" of oppression—racism, capitalism, or sexism—based on hierarchical subordination of differences.

A common name for the entire system of oppression, domination, and hierarchical subordination is "cultural hegemony." A concept associated with the Italian Marxist Antonio Gramsci (1891-1937), cultural hegemony refers to the dominant group's ability to exercise "cultural, moral and ideological leadership over . . . subordinate groups."[143] This leadership is based on the successful propagation of the dominant group's worldview among subordinates, and the subordinates's voluntary acceptance of it, rather than through coercive power alone.[144]

"Dominants enjoy hegemony," wrote Merelman, "when their point of view becomes a 'common sense,' shared widely both within their own group and beyond. Hegemony thus undercuts the ability of subordinates to resist domination."[145] Systemic oppression can only be overcome by systemic "isms" of liberation, such as multiculturalism, which questions "common sense," contests the cultural hegemony of white heterosexual males, and demands they relinquish their power to subordinate groups.[146]

With its division of the world into dominants and subordinates, oppressors and oppressed, race/class/gender-ism can have a sharply dualistic moral structure. Because oppression is evil, goodness is on the side of the victims of oppression. "There are only two positions," Afrocentrist Molefi Kete Asante told *Newsweek* in 1990, "either you support multiculturalism in American education, or you support the maintenance of white supremacy."[147] Sharp moral dualisms, as so often seen in religious history, tend to treat criticism or dissent as the expression of an evil hidden agenda rather than an honest difference of opinion.

Such passionate moral dualism, and the equation of criticism with enmity, has been associated with one of America's most enduring political styles—what historian Richard Hofstadter called "the paranoid style."[148] According to Hofstadter, the paranoid style of politics is based on a model of the world in which "all our ills can be traced to a single center and hence can be eliminated by some final act of victory over the evil source."[149] Central to the paranoid style is an awareness of persecution directed against "a nation, a culture, a way of life." This awareness is "systematized in grandiose theories of conspiracy."[150] These theories regard "a 'vast' or 'gigantic' conspiracy as *the motive force* in historical events."[151] By their very nature, conspiracy theories tend toward totalization, the production of theories that explain *everything* without recourse to coincidence or accident. The paranoid style delineates the enemy as "a kind of amoral superman" who controls, but is not controlled by, the mechanism of history. "The paranoid's interpretation of history," wrote Hofstadter, "is in this sense distinctly personal: decisive events are not taken as part of the stream of history, but as the consequence of someone's will."[152]

Multiculturalism has also created a model of the world in which "all our ills can be traced to a single center." For race/class/gender-ism, the single center is a vast hidden structure of oppression, a cultural hegemony embodied in the traditional university curriculum that keeps whites, the rich, and men in positions of power and privilege throughout society. "By building racism, sexism, heterosexism, and class privilege into its [the curriculum's] very definition of 'reality,'" observed philosopher Paula S. Rothenberg, "it implies that the current distribution of wealth and power in the society, as well as the current distribution of time and space in the traditional curriculum, reflects the natural order of things."[153] The drive for hegemonic dominance through the power to define reality is, like the all-encompassing conspiracies that Hofstadter described, *the motive force* in historical events.

Hofstadter's practitioners of the paranoid style, however, depict the conspiracy as the work of a definite group of persons who consciously, intentionally, personally, and secretly work for evil ends. This personal quality stands in contrast to the impersonal and unconscious nature of oppression depicted by postmodernist race/class/genderism. According to Rothenberg, "Racism and sexism are not merely narrow but identifiable attitudes, policies and practices that affect individuals's lives. Rather they operate on a basic level to structure what we come to think of as 'reality.'"[154] Racism, sexism, and other ideologies of oppression, therefore, have no need of covert organizations or secret cabals for their perpetuation.

Multiculturalism, according to Berman's explanation, relies on postmodern intellectual tools provided by elite academics. These tools provided the basis for a stance of absolute rejection toward the liberal humanism of modernity as constructed by the Enlightenment.[155] Robertson has also taken a stance of absolute rejection toward the liberal humanism of modernity. He has not objected to the Enlightenment's monocultural universalism, as the multiculturalists have, but to its aggressive secularism. And Robertson's intellectual tools have not been postmodern and elitist, but premodern and populist.

Robertson's premodern tools have been the Bible and what he has referred to as "common sense."[156] In this he has been faithful to the worldview developed by nineteenth-century evangelicals—a synthesis of their Bible-centered faith and Scottish Common Sense epistemology.[157] Evangelical belief in the authority, reliability, practicality, and perspicuity of scripture was buttressed by an epistemology that held that human beings can have direct and reliable knowledge of reality, religious truth, and morality.

Common sense has been so important to Robertson that he even elevated it to a position of coequality with Christianity and liberty among the founding principles of America. "This country was founded on common sense. Our founding fathers came here to escape the unreasonable demands of bureaucrats and tyrants; they came here for free speech and free exercise of their religious beliefs." And the loss of this common sense has been incorporated into his jeremiad of American decline. "Common sense and plain truth have been lost in the halls of government, and violence and immorality stalk the land."[158]

Robertson has never defined common sense but has offered many examples instead. These examples often concentrate on a lack of common sense demonstrated by political leaders, bureaucrats, or social theorists in the academy. Robertson usually points to what he feels are the disastrous consequences of a particular public policy or social theory. The billions spent on welfare since the 1960s, according to Robertson, have not ended poverty but have only exacerbated the problem. For Robertson the consequences of welfare spending are *obvious*. "It doesn't take a rocket scientist to deduce that this system promotes illegitimacy, discourages stable families, and promotes dependency."[159] Robertson has likened the refusal to recognize these disastrous consequences to being "removed from reality" and to "madness."[160] Robertson's analysis of welfare policy is quite simple. Giving people money when they don't support themselves will only encourage them not to support themselves. The solution is equally simple. Cut off the money. It doesn't take a rocket scientist, Robertson believes, to figure this out. All it takes is a little common sense.

Robertson's view of truth—truth is simple and clear rather than complex and ambiguous—not only supports his religious beliefs and social analysis, it also displays an elective affinity for populist hostility to experts in all areas of life. Robertson's books are full of denunciations of "the plague of experts"[161] in government, law, the media, and education. These experts seem to violate common sense while claiming that the problems of society and their solutions are just too complex to be grasped by the average citizen.

Robertson's understandable resistance to the concentration of power in the hands of unaccountable elites has edged over into a powerful suspicion of the ideological and cultural agenda of experts. "Already we have compromised essential domestic and cultural values," wrote Robertson, "out of ignorance and out of a mistaken faith in the rule of 'experts.'"[162] His most complete description of this agenda, which he called "liberalism," can be found in his 1993 book, *The Turning Tide: The Fall of Liberalism and the Rise of Common Sense*. Robertson did not offer any precise definitions but, citing conservative columnist George F. Will, Robertson identified liberalism with the "desire to conscript the individual into collective undertakings."[163] Such collectivism, according to Robertson, has a spiritual dimension. "This is the belief that society—not personal faith, nor industry, nor even individual initiative—will lead individuals to transcendence and spiritual perfection, and this through the ministrations of more and bigger government."[164] Traditional Christianity and Judaism resist liberalism's "salvation by society" and the deification of the state. Therefore, statist liberalism has regarded traditional religion as an obstacle to social progress that must be restricted, if not eliminated. Citing the usual statistics of America's social pathologies, Robertson asserted that the "twin thrusts" of statist liberalism, "assault on religious faith and huge centralized government," have brought the nation to the brink of destruction.[165] The loss of religious faith has destroyed the basis of individual and public morality. Freedom without morality has become chaotic and intolerable. Social anarchy has made necessary a more powerful central government to keep order, according to Robertson, a trend that will culminate in totalitarianism.

Antireligious statist liberalism has been for Robertson the structure of oppression that must be exposed and opposed. It should not be surprising that Robertson's two intellectual tools, the Bible and common sense, are utilized to defeat the "twin thrusts" of liberalism. The teachings and prophecies of the Bible are used to understand the spiritual and eschatological significance of liberalism's "assault on religious faith," as well as to demonstrate the false, if not demonic, character of "salvation by society." In the same fashion, common sense, which is identified with political and economic conservatism, is used to reveal not only the oppressive evils, but the absurdities of liberalism's reliance on big government. As the subtitle of *The Turning Tide* implies, the "fall of liberalism" is connected to the "rise of common sense." But identifying the source of oppression has not been enough. It must be defeated. Here Robertson explicitly mimicked the objective of one of his opponents. "Gloria Steinem," wrote Robertson, "said that the goal of the feminists was not just to destroy capitalism but the entire patriarchy. Today the goal of common-sense conservatives is not only to tear down liberalism, but the entire socialist, welfare state."[166]

It may seem odd, if not mistaken, to compare the sophisticated intellectual tools of multiculturalism—postmodern philosophy and literary criticism—with the homely truths of the Bible and common sense. The Bible and common sense, however, have the same *instrumental* value to Robertson as postmodernism has for multiculturalism—providing a vocabulary for describing and fighting perceived oppression. In this way, Robertson's critique of oppression actually has a functional advantage over that of multiculturalism. While the multiculturalists must teach supporters a new, and sometimes obscure, vocabulary, Robertson has spoken in familiar terms and has merely called upon his constituency to employ tools that they already possess—Christian faith and common sense.

Another common feature of both multiculturalism's and Robertson's political rhetoric has been dualization. Just as multiculturalists have often divided the world into oppressors and oppressed, Robertson has laid out clear oppositions between Christians and secularists, conservatives and liberals, decent common sense Americans and radical elites. Those who hold dualistic worldviews are not receptive to criticism and tend to respond to critics as enemies. In a dualized world, there is no moral equivalence between "us" and "them"—we are good, and they are evil. Critics of multiculturalism, Afrocentrism, and feminism can therefore be dismissed as racists and sexists. Critics of the CC can therefore be denounced as anti-Christian bigots.

On one level, such dualization can be understood as part of the polarized style of political rhetoric that has become common in contemporary America. But moral dualism for Robertson has been more than a matter of rhetorical style. The battle between God and Satan— between the servants of God and Satan—has been the essence of Robertson's understanding of the development of human history. He has pointed to "the great cleavage that has existed in the human race since the early beginnings of civilization in the Tigris-Euphrates Valley. On the one side are the beliefs of a portion of humanity that flowed from Abraham to the Jewish race and to the Christians of the world. These are the people of faith, the people who are part of God's world order. On the other side are the people of Babel—those who build monuments to humanity under the inspiration of Satan."[167] In Robertson's reading of history, a reading that has uncritically blended secular and sacred accounts of history into a single narrative, the godly people of faith have been in a constant struggle with the Satanic people of Babel. This has been the basic dynamic of human history.

Robertson outlined this struggle in his 1991 book, *The New World Order,* in terms of an international conspiracy spanning centuries, directed by Satan, and involving Marxism, the Illuminati, the Rocke-fellers and Rothchilds, the Federal Reserve Board, the Council on Foreign Relations, the Trilateral Commission, the United Nations, Secular Humanism, and New Age religion. This conspiracy's purpose has been to bring about a godless socialist one-world government, the "new world order," under the leadership of Satan's emissary, the Antichrist. This conflict will culminate in a biblically prophesied final battle, resulting in the defeat of the forces of evil and the triumphant return of Christ.

While the manipulation of the world financial system has been an important vehicle of this conspiracy,[168] the crucial step in the establishment of this new world order has been the restriction, repression, and elimination of the influence of Christianity. Why? Robertson explained: "The institutions of the church, evangelical Christians (who actually believe what they profess), and any other recognition of God would be obstructions to his [Satan's] plan."[169] The persecution of Christians will therefore escalate with the establishment of the global order. "Whatever violation of freedom has taken place here [in the United States] will take place in a world body, only in a more blatant fashion."[170] Robertson has wanted his readers to understand that "Satan will launch a war against the Christian people." In fact, it has already begun with "false propaganda, ridicule, and demeaning comments—anything to ruin the influence of Christians and their ability to block Satan's plans."[171] He went on to liken this to Hitler's propaganda campaign against the Jews, a campaign that led to genocide. "This very technique," warned Robertson, "is being used already against Christian people."[172] Thus Robertson's explanation of anti-Christian bigotry, and his expectations of its escalation, has provided a powerful rationale for the CC to "protest anti-Christian bias and defend the legal rights of Christians."

For Robertson, the escalating persecution of people of faith and the increasing centralization of government have not been the result of impersonal social forces, the unintended consequences of ideas, acci-dents, or coincidences. Secularization and globalization have been the intentional result of actions that were personal, deliberate, and coordi-nated—a conspiracy.[173] "[I]t is my firm belief," wrote Robertson, "that the events of public policy are not the accidents and coincidences we are generally led to believe. They are planned."[174] For Robertson, the new world order conspiracy has been the motive force of history. Writing in the aftermath of the 1991 Gulf War, Robertson suggested, "Or perhaps some very powerful being or some very powerful group, somewhere, wanted it all to happen just the way it did to set the stage for something that indeed transcended Saddam Hussein, or Iraq, or Kuwait, or even Middle East Oil." Rather than these things, "Launching the new world order *was* the main thing."[175]

Robertson did not allege, however, that all advocates of global cooperation have been knowing co-conspirators—"the inner circle of a secret society." According to Robertson, "men of goodwill like Woodrow Wilson, Jimmy Carter, and George Bush, who sincerely want a larger community of nations living at peace in our world, are in reality unknowingly and unwittingly carrying out the mission and mouthing the phrases of a tightly knit cabal whose goal is nothing less than a new order for the human race under the domination of Lucifer and his followers."[176]

Robertson's model of the world has been one in which "all our ills can be traced to a single center and hence can be eliminated by some final act of victory over the evil source."[177] And this "tightly knit cabal"—"the Establishment"—the members of which cannot, of course, be named because of the effective cloak of secrecy that surrounds them, has been that "single center." This behind-the-scenes Establishment, through its most visible expression in government policy, the Council on Foreign Relations (CFR), has reached out through many centers of power in government, finance, business, education, the media, and private foundations to manipulate the events of history in the direction of global government.[178]

What motivates the members of the Establishment? According to Robertson, "Some members are genuinely idealistic and feel this is the only way to world peace. Others are simply greedy and power hungry. And some, I fear, are motivated by other powers."[179] Given these motives, especially the last, it has not been surprising that opponents of the Establishment are in for trouble. "Anyone who gets involved in the struggle for freedom can be assured of being branded by the Establishment as being narrow-minded, provincial, obstructionist, a defender of fortress America, out of touch with the global realities, unskilled in foreign policy and, of course, the usual 'bigoted, fundamentalist Christian, right-wing zealot.'"[180] This branding has been carried out by the "liberal press," which according to Robertson, "represents the Establishment in the United States and Europe."[181]

If Hofstadter were writing today, he would have no difficulty seeing in Robertson "the qualities of heated exaggeration, suspiciousness, and conspiratorial fantasy"—the qualities of the paranoid style of American politics.[182] He would also find in Robertson's writings many of the traditional elements of American conspiracy theories—suspicion of the Illuminati, the Masons, centralized banking, intellectuals, Communism, internationalism in foreign policy, and world government.[183] Hofstadter also found anti-Semitism to be a persistent element of these conspiracy theories.[184] But Robertson's conspiratorial speculations have lacked overt expressions of anti-Semitism.

Journalist Michael Lind, however, found an implicit but essential anti-Semitism in Robertson's references to conspiratorial "European" or "German" bankers—anti-Semitic code words for "Jews"—and in his reliance on the overtly anti-Semitic works of other conspiracy theorists.[185] Lind's well-documented essay in *The New York Review* touched off an extensive discussion of Robertson's alleged anti-Semitism throughout 1995.[186] Despite Robertson's reputation as a "friend of Israel," Lind did offer convincing proof that Robertson relied on anti-Semitic ideas and sources in explicating his conspiracy theory of history. And I agree with Lind's observation that Robertson's conspiracy theory "is central to his vision of his own destiny, his movement, and his ambitions for the American Right and the Republican party and the United States of America." But Lind was misleading when he asserted that "Robertson's theories about Jewish bankers and Jewish revolutionaries are central to his conspiracy theory."[187] What has been central to Robertson's conspiracy theory is not a hatred of Jews and Judaism but a contempt for liberals and liberalism. As neoconservative Norman Podhoretz observed in an essay on Robertson, "Jews as Jews have little cause to worry about the growing influence of the Christian Right. But liberals are another matter; and to the extent that Jews are liberals, they have every reason to be deeply troubled."[188] According to Robertson, if individual Jews—bankers, revolutionaries, and assorted members of the contemporary "cultural elite"—adopt such liberalism, then they become partners, knowingly or unknowingly, with Satan. For Robertson, just as liberalism and Christianity are incompatible, a liberal Jew is a contradiction in terms. As Robertson told the *New York Times,* "there are those who have embraced the New Deal and the Fair Deal and incorporated them into Judaism. And to me, they're not a part of Judaism."[189] Jews who are orthodox in religion and conservative in politics, however, become partners, again knowingly or unknowingly, with God. Such Jews stand on the right side of what Robertson called in the final chapter of

The New World Order "The Great Divide" between the people of God and the people of Satan.[190]

This basic dualism, combined with Robertson's understanding of end-times events, provides an explanation for Robertson's staunch advocacy of a pro-Israel foreign policy for the United States.[191] Indeed, Robertson has interpreted attacks on Jews and Israel, like attacks on Christians and Christian America, as an essential part of the new world order conspiracy. "It is also clear," wrote Robertson, "that Satan's strategy will include a frontal assault on Israel. Rest assured that the next objective of the presently constituted new world order, under the present United Nations, will be to make Israel its target."[192] While Robertson, who has called himself "one of the strongest friends of Israel anywhere in the world,"[193] was undoubtedly distressed by being labeled an anti-Semite, these accusation have probably functioned as a confirmation of his conspiratorial understanding of contemporary events. After all, if Satan plans to attack Israel, then the Establishment, through the "liberal media," must first strike at the friends of Israel, such as Robertson.

In great contrast to Robertson, Reed has not used a conspiratorial view of history. Rather than depicting evangelicals as entirely innocent victims of conspiratorial Satanic forces, Reed admits that evangelicals bear at least partial responsibility for their own marginalization.

At the highest level of generalization, Reed has argued that the social processes and developments associated with modernity have moved religion toward the margins of American culture.[194] Unlike Robertson, Reed has given no indication that these processes should be considered part of a deliberate coordinated effort to marginalize religion, or that they should be rejected categorically. Reed, for instance, has viewed new mass media technologies and greater racial and denominational diversity among evangelicals as developments that "bode well" for religious conservatives.[195]

Reed has also stressed deep changes in the role of political parties, businesses, labor unions, and the media. "The winds of change are howling across the American cultural landscape, uprooting old institutions that have controlled the culture and transforming how we live."[196] Politics, for instance, has ceased to be just a struggle between the Republicans and Democrats. "America has become a fragmented, fractious republic of what James Madison called 'factions'—citizen movements held together by shared values rather than party loyalty."[197] In the breakdown of old institutions, Reed saw new opportunities for religious conservatives. "People of faith," he wrote, "must build their own institutions that represent their views accurately."[198] Thus hostility toward religious conservatives was not rooted so much in the battle between evil and good as in the tension between old and new institutions. Even the *Washington Post*'s characterization of Robertson's "followers" as "poor, uneducated and easy to command," according to Reed, "signified a counter-assault by one of yesterday's powerbrokers (the metropolitan daily newspaper) against one of tomorrow's kingmakers (cable television)."[199]

Another important reason for the marginalization of religion, according to Reed, has been "that the Left has unilaterally surrendered invocations of God and religion to conservatives."[200] Reed lamented that religion has become a way to divide the electorate. "God has become a political football, used all too often by only one team on the field, usually the Republicans."[201] Reed, citing legal scholar Stephen Carter, pointed to the major role of abortion in the partisanization of religion. "Because of the evangelical idiom employed by many opponents of abortion," observed Reed, "the politics of abortion and church-state issues have become inextricably intertwined."[202]

In defiance of the conventional wisdom about the CC's takeover of the Republican party, Reed has portrayed religious conservatives as guiltless amateurs in this division of the electorate. He reported, for instance, that the overt religiosity of the 1992 Republican National Convention was the result of the Bush campaign's decision to "get God into the platform" to energize religious conservatives.[203] This was, in Reed's view, an empty and cynical gesture because Bush saw platform content as meaningless. But some religious conservatives, not knowing better, "showed their influence by lacing the platform with Bible verses and pro-family homilies."[204] Having criticized the Republicans, Reed added that "The Democrats have behaved even more irresponsibly, launching personal assaults on candidates because of their religious faith."[205]

More generally, Reed criticized the Left for raising the alarm over Right-wing religion while hypocritically forgetting how much it once relied on religious language and religious legitimation. Unlike Robertson, Reed has described liberalism sympathetically. Its "grand theme," traditionally expressed in moral and religious language, was originally "to guarantee equal opportunity for all Americans and a level playing field through government assistance to the disfranchised—the poor, the disabled, racial minorities, and women."[206] In the 1960s and 1970s, however, in Reed's view, liberalism became captive to the expansion of the federal welfare state, and to the satisfaction of special interest constituencies—twin imperatives that did not depend upon, or were hostile to, religious values. Liberalism thereafter became uncomfortable with religion in the political arena. And in the attempt to hold onto political power, according to Reed, it has even resorted to "the kind of religious bigotry that it had historically battled."[207]

Yet Reed has also admitted that evangelicals were partially responsible for their own marginalization. Most fundamentally, they became marginal because of acquiescence to secular domination. "After the Scopes trial of 1925," observed Reed, "people of faith withdrew to their churches, creating a cultural ghetto of their own making."[208] Reed has refused the option of portraying his constituency as powerless victims. But he has also made it clear that their attempt to leave the evangelical ghetto was not greeted with much encouragement. "Their recent reentry into civic life after decades of neglect has been greeted with what might be called a faith phobia: an irrational fear of the integration of religious people into public life."[209] Reed also charged there was an element of "class antagonism" in this phobia: "One gets the sneaking suspicion that if those religious folk shopped at Neiman-Marcus instead of Sears they would not encounter the same disfavor from the chattering class."[210]

While Reed called this fear "irrational" and a "phobia," he has been willing to admit that religious conservatives have sometimes exacerbated these fears by their political methods. "Too often those of devout faith have spoken in the public square with a scowl, using language that did not embrace all their listeners."[211] As I noted above, Reed had a rather poor opinion of the early Christian Right's tactics, rhetoric, and expectations. They combined, as Reed observed, "the skill of a novice with the temperament of a zealot."[212] He has argued that experience has taught religious conservatives, "not to expect a heaven on earth, to take defeat (and victory) with a grain of salt, and to respect the right of their political foes to play on the same field."[213] Reed's stress on activist training, more carefully modulated rhetoric, a wider issues agenda, a broader constituency, and strategic pragmatism have been attempts not only to become more effective but to calm the more rational fears about the Christian Right. Reed probably hoped to rob his critics of ammunition while strengthening his own claims that only an irrational bigotry, not unlike racism or anti-Semitism, has been behind opposition to his movement. But unlike Robertson, Reed has not presented the motives of his opponents as Satanic.

Beyond the excessive zeal and poor political manners of religious conservatives, which he has viewed as soluble problems, Reed also noted other self-inflicted wounds. These include immoral behavior by a few religious leaders and the use of violence to oppose abortion. Even when admitting these errors, Reed accused the news media and political liberals of using the behavior of a tiny minority to unfairly caricature and stigmatize all religious conservatives.

A more serious problem for Reed has been "the legacy of racism that religious conservatives carry like an albatross."[214] This legacy, according to Reed, has been one reason evangelicals still find themselves marginalized. Reed can easily maintain that the vast majority of CC members have not been flagrantly immoral or violent, but the racial homogeneity of the CC has been impossible to deny. Reed issued this blunt warning to religious conservatives: "If we flow out of lily-white churches into lily-white political organizations and support only lily-white candidates for elective office, we cannot expect the larger society to take us or our agenda seriously."[215] The CC's financial aid to African-American churches destroyed by arson and the proposals of "The Samaritan Project" have been part of Reed's efforts to deal with the taint of racism so that the religious conservative agenda could be taken seriously.

Thus Reed offered a distinctly different analysis than that of Robertson. The two men have identified the same opponents, liberals and secularists in the dominant institutions of American society. They have also agreed on a strategy of resistance—build alternative institutions based on religion and conservatism. But when Robertson has described his opponents, he has pointed to a solid phalanx of enemies manipulating the machinery of history for evil purposes. His analysis has been embedded in a total worldview in which events have ultimate causes and problems have ultimate answers. The only sin of which religious conservatives have been guilty has been one of omission, failing to act swiftly and decisively against obvious evils. Like the multiculturalists, Robertson has provided his constituency with a critique of systemic oppression.

Reed has opponents, and even enemies, but they have not been a solid phalanx—they too have been confused and blown about by the winds of social change. The enmity that some bear toward people of faith and religious conservatives was not explained as the product of an ultimate cause or a system, but by a combination of proximate causes: rational concern, flawed political opinions, self-interest, and irrational prejudice. And Reed has been willing to admit that religious conservatives need to put their own house in order before they can be full participants in American cultural and political life. Reed, unlike Robertson, has not presented an ideological critique of a system of oppression. Nor has he resorted to the paranoid style of American politics.

A Public Agenda

The fourth and final parallel between multiculturalism and the CC lies in the similar character of their public agendas. Again, their specific public policy objectives have been diametrically opposed at almost every point. But both engage in what philosopher Charles Taylor called "the politics of recognition." According to Taylor, "A number of strands in contemporary politics," including nationalist movements, minority rights, feminism, and multiculturalism, "turn on the need, sometimes the demand, for *recognition.*"[216]

The importance of recognition is based on what Taylor referred to as the dialogical formation of self-understanding or identity.[217] "The thesis is that our identity is partly shaped by recognition or its absence," wrote Taylor, "often by the *mis*recognition of others, and so a person or group of people can suffer real damage, real distortion, if the people or society around them mirror back to them a confining or demeaning or contemptible picture of themselves."[218] Subordinate groups will often internalize a demeaning self-image projected upon them by the culturally dominant group. This internalized image "becomes one of the most potent instruments of their own oppression."[219]

The notion that the oppressed must purge themselves of demeaning imposed identities has been widely applied. One such application has been in multicultural education. The features of multiculturalism I have already discussed—the invocation of oppression, the pursuit of a usable history, and the development of a critique of oppression—all aid in this project of revising the self-image of members of oppressed social groups.

But since human identity is, according to Taylor, created dialogically, a revised self-image or identity has to be recognized by others. Therefore, multiculturalists have had to obtain recognition of their new identities from the institutions of the dominant culture. Multiculturalism, to recall Merelman's description, "not only asserts the viability, merit, and durability of multiple cultures, but also calls for public support of these cultures within a democratic framework."[220] Again, the features of multiculturalism I have already discussed have all been enlisted to strengthen, both intellectually and emotionally, this demand for support and recognition.

Such demands for recognition, according to Taylor, have taken two somewhat contradictory forms: 1) the demand that members of disadvantaged groups be treated equally by ignoring their differences from other citizens; and 2) the demand that members of disadvantaged groups be given preferential treatment on the basis of their distinctive qualities.[221]

The first form, the demand for equal treatment of all citizens, has involved the decisive rejection of the legitimacy of any sort of "second-class citizenship" based on race, gender, or other personal characteristics. While it can hardly be argued that difference-blind equal treatment for all kinds of citizens, or in all areas of life, has been achieved *in fact,* equality and nondiscrimination have become accepted *in principle* as basic in American law and polity. "Every position," observed Taylor, "no matter how reactionary, is now defended under the colors of this principle."[222]

Yet the second form, as Taylor pointed out, springs from inadequacies in the first. On one level, equal treatment can do nothing to correct the consequences of a long history of unequal treatment in education or employment. "Affirmative action" programs, which mandate that some degree of preference in admissions, hiring, or promotion be given to members of minority groups and women, have been attempts to deal with legacies of discrimination. These programs have often been controversial because they seem to contradict the principle of difference-blindness. They have been justified as temporary measures that will only be used until the legacies of historical disadvantages have been eliminated.

On a deeper level, if all citizens have to be treated equally, then certain differential characteristics, often the basis of group identity, have to be ignored by the state. By ignoring characteristics that individuals or a group may deem essential to their identity, the state has failed to *fully* recognize or respect them. Because identity is linked to recognition, nonrecognition or misrecognition of a group's distinctive qualities can inflict damage. Thus, merely equal treatment, difference-blindness, can be a further injustice perpetrated against members of a disadvantaged group.

Difference-blindness can also be seen as a covert means of deracination and assimilation by the dominant social group. "The claim," observed Taylor, "is that the supposedly neutral set of difference-blind principles of the politics of equal dignity is in fact a reflection of one hegemonic culture. As it turns out, then, only the minority or suppressed cultures are being forced to take alien form."[223] Those who do not fit the imposed hegemonic mold have resisted conformity. And they have also contested, as Taylor put it, "the assumed superiority that powers this imposition."[224] Thus difference-blindness, which is seen by its mainstream advocates as neutral and fair, can be seen by marginalized "others" as an expression of contempt.

The proposed requirement, for instance, of conducting government business exclusively in a standard version of U.S. English, would impose a practical burden upon linguistic minorities to learn and use a new language. Nevertheless, the English-only requirement is, in principle, blind-to-difference because it demands the same public behavior of everyone and promises equal access. The exclusion, however, of other languages from public life implies that those languages are somehow inferior and those who speak them are unworthy of a place in public life. And by discouraging the children of linguistic minorities from using anything but English, and encouraging them to assimilate into the dominant group, English-only threatens the very survival of such linguistic minorities.

Multicultural, Afrocentric, and bilingual curricula in primary and secondary education, as well as women's, African-American, and Latino studies programs at many universities, have all been responses to the demand for differential recognition, the demand that implicit contempt be replaced with explicit respect and affirmation. In addition, so-called political correctness in speech has been part of this demand for differential recognition. Reforming the way in which groups or individuals have been labeled because of their differences, has been an effort to eliminate the attitudes of superiority and contempt embodied in traditional language. Thus someone using a wheelchair should be called "differently abled" rather than "disabled"—a term which implies deficiency and inferiority. The term "womyn" has sometimes been used to avoid the notion that the identity of "women" is dependent upon "men."

While political correctness has become an easy target for ridicule, it would be a mistake to regard victim groups's demands for respect and differential treatment as a passing campus fad. "The politics of nationalism," wrote Taylor, "has been powered for well over a century, in part, by the sense that people have had of being despised or respected by others around them. Multinational societies can break up, in large part because of a lack of (perceived) recognition of the equal worth of one group or another."[225] While questions of economic justice, legal rights, and political power have ostensibly been the "objective" matters of contention, the subjective factors of mutual respect and trust between groups may determine the future of a given national community.

The public agenda of the CC, like that of multiculturalism, is about the demand for recognition. The philosophical basis of their demand—that identity is created dialogically with others—stands in tension with basic evangelical notions about identity. For evangelicals, their identity as Christians is dialogically generated through a saving experience. But the "significant other" in this dialogue of identity generation is God himself. If God, the most significant other that can be, has "recognized" a Christian's identity, should there be any further need for human recognition? Shouldn't it be irrelevant whether society mirrors back to Christians a demeaning image of themselves? (If God loves me, why should I care what the *Washington Post* thinks of me?)

The literature of the CC has not dealt with this question directly. But an answer can be found in its appeals to the Augustinian notion of the Christian's dual citizenships as a justification for political participation. "While Christians are citizens of heaven," stated a manual distributed to participants at CC training seminars, "they are at the same time full-fledged citizens of the earth."[226] And as "full-fledged citizens" they have the same rights as everyone else in the "city of man." In a 1992 *Christian American* column, Reed reminded CC members, "The Bible tells us to exercise our rights under the law (Acts 25:11)."[227] Four years later, in *Active Faith,* Reed was even more adamant that "we must assert our full rights as American citizens." He argued that the notion that Christians should gladly endure persecutions "does a disservice to those who died that we may have those rights." He reminded his readers that "The Bible is filled with the accounts of heroes of the faith who served God and His people toward government service" and he appealed to the good ends that political involvement can bring. "To the unborn, the poor, the downtrodden, the persecuted minorities, people with faith who occupy high positions in government can bring mercy and deliverance."[228] These rights must not only be exercised, they must be recognized and respected by others. While irrelevant to the ultimate value and destiny of the Christian, nonrecognition or misrecognition are as harmful to the Christian as to any other citizen.

For Robertson and Reed, the politics of recognition have probably not been worked out on a theoretical level. It is far more likely that they have adapted to their political environment by mimicking the rhetoric and tactics of their opponents. Robertson hinted at this in a 1995 letter to CC members: "I saw that many of the interest groups on the Left (including *militant homosexuals, radical feminists,* and Big Government liberals) all have powerful organizations advancing their point of view in government. So, I thought, Christians need an organization that can take a stand for our values in the halls of government."[229]

The CC's practice of the politics of recognition, like that of multiculturalists, has utilized invocations of oppression, the pursuit of a usable history, and the development of a critique of oppression in the project of purging demeaning imposed identities and building a new positive identity. And like the multiculturalists, the CC has pursued the recognition of that new identity from the institutions of the dominant culture. This is one reason why the "poor, uneducated and easy to command" stories that I examined above have had such an enduring appeal. Weisskopf's infamous description was a blatant example of the demeaning identity imposed upon, and internalized by, evangelicals. The CC constituency assertively purged itself of that demeaning identity— "the fax machines at the *Post* were jammed for three days"—and forced one of the premier organizations of the "cultural elite" into a recognition of the revised identity of evangelicals. These stories have functioned as reminders of oppression, the necessity of demanding recognition from the dominant culture, and the possibility of success.

The CC and Equal Recognition

Like the politics of recognition as practiced by multiculturalists, the CC's pursuit of recognition has taken the form of demands for both equal recognition and differential recognition. The demand for equal treatment has been Reed's favorite way of explaining the intentions of religious conservatives. In *Politically Incorrect,* he told the story of being asked by a journalist, "'What is it you people *really* want?'" Reed answered, "'I would like to see a day when an evangelical Christian could stand next to the president of the United States and oversee his transition into office—in the same way that Vernon Jordan as an African-American led Bill Clinton's transition—and never have his religion become an issue.'"[230] In other words, evangelicals should be treated equally by ignoring their differences from other citizens. Reed also invoked the ideal of difference blindness, and the rejection of any form of second-class citizenship, in his introduction to *Contract with the American Family,* "We believe in an America where all citizens are judged on the content of their character, and not their gender, race, religion, or ethnic background."[231] Robertson also appealed to this ideal with the statement, "It's time to assert loud and clear, 'Christians are Americans, too.'"[232]

As implied by its name, the Religious Equality Amendment proposed by the CC also appealed to the ideal of equal treatment. Answering objections that such an amendment would lead to an established state religion, the *Contract* asserted, "A Religious Equality Amendment will simply restore the free-speech rights of religious Americans to equality with those already enjoyed by their nonreligious fellow citizens."[233] The *Contract* also promised that the amendment would respect the rights of others to equal treatment. "Such an amendment would ensure that all citizens, including students, would be free to express their faith in noncompulsory settings and in ways that affirm their convictions without infringing on the rights of others."[234] In May 1997, after two years of disagreements, religious conservative leaders seemed to unite behind a Religious Freedom Amendment proposed by Rep. Ernest Istook (R-OK). Despite the name change, Reed announced the CC's full support for the Istook proposal under the banner of equal rights: "We want to make it clear that we are no longer going to be treated as second-class citizens."[235]

Reed also appealed to the ideal of equal treatment in opposition to stereotypical media and popular culture portrayals of religious people. "Stereotypes by definition justify discrimination. Not everyone who howled at Amos and Andy was a racist. But the stereotype of black Americans fostered by popular culture before the 1960's undergirded Jim Crow laws precisely because society never accords full equality to those whom it ridicules. No one knows the pain of this reality more than people of faith."[236] Robertson, in a 1994 letter, claimed that with two million members the CC could "Make anti-Christian bigotry as unacceptable in American life as racism and anti-Semitism."[237] Reed stated a similar goal in *Politically Incorrect:* "Before their [people of faith's] voice can be heard, we must make attacks on religion as unacceptable as slurs against race or gender."[238] In short, "people of faith" want to be treated in a difference-blind fashion.

The CC has made its most sustained and ambitious demand for equal treatment in terms of access to and influence upon the political process. A 1994 CC letter asked, "Have you had enough of members of

Congress and the Clinton Administration ridiculing Bible-believing Christians as 'kooks' and 'fanatics'? If your answer is 'YES'—this is the chance to make the politicians in Washington *feel the power of the Christian vote*."[239] Rather than a demonstration of power, Reed preferred to describe what religious conservatives really want as "a place at the table in the conversation we call democracy."[240] This "place at the table" is necessary because people of faith are, according to Reed, "the only group in government whose role is almost inversely proportional to their numbers."[241]

Robertson, perhaps under Reed's influence, used the same "place at the table" image in a speech at the 1993 "Road to Victory" conference: "But if Christian believers or those of faith cannot enter into the public process, then by definition only those who don't have faith can participate, and that isn't American. It's not right. We want a place at the table to speak our views, so people will hear them."[242] Reed has been careful to point out that this is an image that is compatible with the pluralistic ethos of American politics. "Their [people of faith's] commitment to pluralism includes a place for faith among the many other competing interests in society."[243] Robertson echoed this sentiment: "We seek nothing more radical than to ensure a hearing for America's time honored values and to join with Americans of every cultural background to ensure for ourselves and our posterity the successful continuance of this great experiment in ordered liberty we call the United States of America."[244]

Despite the CC's ongoing use of invocations of oppression and fulminations against anti-Christian bigots in high places, there have been some indications that the right of religious conservatives to a place at the table has been recognized. One important and unexpected step toward such recognition came from the intellectual support for faith-based political activism provided in the 1993 book *The Culture of Disbelief* by Yale Law Professor Stephen L. Carter, a politically and theologically liberal African-American. As Reed acknowledged in *Politically Incorrect,* "I am indebted to him [Carter] for beginning a vital conversation on such a civil note."[245] Although Carter regarded the CC as an example of "religious fascism,"[246] he drew parallels between the religious basis of the Civil Rights movement and the Christian Right. Carter also supported the perception that religious believers in contemporary American were being unjustly asked to "leave their faith outside" when entering the public sphere.[247]

More surprising has been the willingness of one of the primary targets of the CC's criticism to admit that secularization of the public realm has gone too far. Carter's book apparently influenced President Clinton in 1993 to say, "Sometimes I think the environment in which we operate is entirely too secular. The fact that we have freedom of religion doesn't mean we need to try to have freedom from religion."[248] And Clinton concluded his remarks at the signing ceremony for the Religious Freedom Restoration Act of 1993 with a striking parallel to Reed's favorite "table" imagery: "Let us instead respect one another's faiths . . . but bring our values back to the table of American discourse to heal our troubled land."[249] Reed commended the President for these remarks but asserted that the record of his administration "hardly meets the test of civility and respect for religious beliefs of others."[250]

Robertson and Reed, understandably, have placed more emphasis on the achievement of recognition through political success. In a speech made in early 1995, Reed said, "The 1994 elections were also important because they gave people of faith what they have always sought: a place at the table, a sense of legitimacy, and a voice in the conversation that we call democracy. We have become a permanent fixture on the American political landscape, too large, too significant, and too diverse to be ignored by either major party."[251] The release of the CC's *Contract* on May 17, 1995, and the attention it attracted, according to Reed, "represented an historic day in American politics—a day where pro-family policies took center stage and were finally given the attention they deserve."[252]

Reed's 1996 book, *Active Faith,* was virtually a book-length announcement that "In political terms, we had arrived."[253] As one reviewer observed, "His [Reed's] prose hums with energy when he describes all the leading Republicans paying court to him, or the electrifying effect that he and his supporters have on big party gatherings, or his canny, high-status backroom dealings."[254] While Reed was delighted by recounting his own "wheeler-dealer" role in passage of important legislation, he also reminded his readers of how far, and how fast, the CC has had to travel to achieve respect. He put the book's first such reminder in the mouth of a grassroots CC activist,

> "When we first showed up at the local meeting of the Republican party, we were treated like pariahs," she said. "It was almost like we had leprosy. That was two years ago. Last week [November 1995] we went to a meeting and we were surrounded by candidates

and legislators seeking our help. We're no longer on the outside looking in. We're on the inside looking out."[255]

Reed pointed to the same transformation on the national level. "In the space of just two years, the pro-family community and the Christian Coalition had gone from being seen as the 'sponsors of hate' in Houston to being one of the most important and respected voting constituencies in the electorate."[256]

The impression that this recognition was an accomplished fact has been strengthened by the number of Republicans who have defended the Christian Right against the "anti-Christian bigotry" of liberal Democrats.[257] But Robertson and Reed would have to be fools to take these Republican affirmations at face value. Many of their political allies have continued to regard religious conservatives with disdain and cynicism. "Of course they're mad," an anonymously quoted conservative magazine editor said, "but we need their votes."[258] In 1995 Robertson reminded CC members of the continuation of many morally objectionable government policies and stated, "And even though Republicans now hold a majority in Congress, none of this will change . . . *so long as Christian voices remain silent on these issues.* That's because even the best members of Congress prefer not to discuss the moral issues. They would much prefer to talk about economic issues . . . which are not as controversial."[259] In preparation for the 1996 Republican presidential primaries Robertson warned: "If we fail to generate an impressive Christian voter turnout in Iowa and New Hampshire, the news media is sure to portray the Christian voter as a toothless tiger which the candidates can feel free to ignore. *We must not let this happen.*"[260] In a 1996 direct-mail piece sent out just as *Active Faith* was released, Reed warned, that attacks on Christian voters by "the extreme Left" have "intimidated and frightened even the best members of Congress."[261]

Rather than a mere celebration of self-importance by Reed, *Active Faith* also contained goading reminders to the CC constituency of the indignities they have suffered and could suffer again. Reed recalled how religious conservative delegates at the 1992 Houston convention were "treated as if they were horned monsters rising from the swamp."[262] For those who may have forgotten, he summarized the post-Houston conventional wisdom about the Christian Right: "religious conservatives had infiltrated the Republican party like termites, had seized control of the levers of power, and now aimed to impose their theocratic designs on an unwitting public."[263] Indeed, Reed's extensive rehearsal of the Houston convention and the mistakes of 1992 was not just self-congratulation for obstacles overcome, but these anecdote were "lessons of history" revealing what *not* to do at the San Diego convention and in the elections of 1996. Reed's poorly disguised efforts to steer religious conservatives away from Buchanan, and his well-publicized efforts to divorce the CC from extremism, demonstrated how fragile his hold upon mainstream status has remained. Perhaps Reed's assertion that "We're insiders" was not so much a statement of fact as a way of inducing in his constituency the mindset and behavior of insiders.

As I noted in Chapter 4, that insider identity was tested at the 1996 Republican National convention. Reed and other religious conservatives were clearly aware of the disparity between their large numbers and their small public role. At the CC's "Faith and Freedom Celebration," a rally held during the convention for their delegates, Reed said to much applause, "In case you haven't heard it from the podium the last two days, let me say it so there can be no doubt: The Republican Party is a pro-life party."[264] While some news reports played up the dissatisfaction among the rank and file of the CC, Reed dismissed the need for "rhetorical stroking."[265] He told one reporter, "At the end of the day, do we care more about speeches or about institutional strength? Clearly, institutional strength."[266] This fit with Reed's long-term thinking and his pragmatic willingness to cooperate with his Republican allies. It also fit with the "shut up and smile to win" lesson that Reed derived from the 1992 Houston convention.

Despite the pragmatic wisdom of Reed's willingness to accept a less visible role in order to avoid "scaring" moderate voters, the Republican leadership's nonrecognition of religious conservatives and their concerns still bothered Robertson. In remarks at the 1996 "Road to Victory" conference, Robertson observed that "The people who are manipulating, if I can use that term, the presidential campaign have persuaded themselves that evangelicals and pro-family values are something akin to leprosy." He recalled the exclusion of evangelicals from the podium in San Diego and noted, "They're not really terribly interested about having somebody say too much at this meeting here about those same issues."[267] Robertson was probably referring to Dole's rather conspicuous absence from the schedule of the CC's 1996 conference—a sharp contrast to Dole's open pursuit of religious conservative support at the same event in 1995.[268]

Almost as if in answer to Robertson's demand for recognition by the Republicans, Dole made a "surprise" appearance at the conference within hours of Robertson's speech. This appearance was the result of Reed's repeated entreaties to the Dole campaign. While Dole had reportedly decided to speak before Robertson voiced his complaints, most attendees were unaware of the change in plans and welcomed Dole's entrance with thunderous applause.[269] Dole's speech and a subsequent speech by Kemp, both laced with references to abortion, religion, and morality, especially Dole's pledge to sign a ban on "partial-birth" abortions, were well received.[270] But these speeches also seemed to be the kind of "rhetorical stroking" that Reed had dismissed as unnecessary in San Diego only a month before. The necessity of energetically soliciting such "stroking" demonstrated that Robertson and Reed knew, in pragmatic political terms, that their place at the table was not yet secure.

The CC and Differential Recognition

Like that of the multiculturalists, the public agenda of the CC goes beyond the principle of difference-blindness to a demand for the recognition of the differential characteristics of the CC constituency. These demands for differential treatment, however, have not been based on the need to compensate for any historical legacy of disadvantage. Since the CC has been so strident in affirming that its constituency is *not* poor or uneducated, it has not sought affirmative-action programs for evangelicals in hiring, promotion, or admissions.[271] What Robertson and Reed have sought to remedy are disadvantages only recently imposed upon evangelicals—disadvantages rooted in the dominant culture's consistent application of difference-blindness.

Some contemporary political theorists have argued that the way we must deal with the political problem of social diversity is the creation of a scrupulously neutral state in which the public discourse is based upon only the most widely held and most accessible moral premises.[272] "We should," suggested philosopher Bruce Ackerman, "put the moral ideals that divide us off the conversational agenda of the liberal state."[273] Legal scholar Sanford Levinson observed that "Such a constraint would certainly exclude any appeals to justifications that rest on a privileged *episteme* of revelation from a sovereign God and appointed messengers."[274] Restrictions on the availability of divorce, for instance, may be justified as a way of protecting children from psychological harm or economic deprivation. But Christ's injunction against divorce in Matthew 19:6, a teaching that not even all Christians interpret in the same way, should simply not be part of the public discussion.

In practical terms, according to these liberal theorists, public discourse in a religiously pluralistic society must be secular, and those who may be motivated by religious convictions must make their public arguments in secular terms. This ostensible neutrality, which burdens the religiously motivated with a requirement to translate their arguments into secular terms, or to find entirely new arguments, has seemed to many religious persons more like discrimination and exclusion from participation. As Carter observed, "[T]he effort to place limits on this kind of dialogue is less likely to move many citizens to restructure their arguments than to silence them—or, perhaps (if history is any fair teacher) to move them to revolution."[275]

Beyond the practical burdens that bracketing religious convictions out of public discourse would impose on those who hold such convictions, such bracketing would also inflict a very personal damage— the suppression and denial of essential aspects of the self. According to legal theorist Michael J. Perry, "And doing that would preclude her—the particular person she is—from engaging in moral discourse with other members of society."[276] To engage in such discourse a religious person would have to adopt an alien, inauthentic, and imposed identity.

Thus the nonrecognition of qualities essential to the identity of evangelicals would lead to not only their political marginalization but to requiring their acceptance of personal negation. Indeed, it is not hard to find in demands for neutral secularity in public discourse a not-so-subtle contempt for religious convictions and persons. A 1994 *New Republic* editorial, for example, argued for the exclusion of religious reasons from the debate over abortion.

> There are secular reasons not to recommend abortion, and those are the reasons that must be debated, if the opposition to abortion is to be more than a mere report of somebody else's certainty. The intensity of a conviction, moreover, says nothing about its merit.[277]

Religiously motivated opponents of abortion would have no difficulty in detecting that the writer regarded religious reasons inferior and unworthy of discussion—"a mere report of somebody else's certainty." And they might also infer that the editorialist regarded religious believers themselves as inferior and unworthy to join in the discussion of public issues.

One way Robertson and Reed have expressed the demand for differential recognition has been by calling for the inclusion of a "Christian voice" in "the conversation that we call democracy." Recognition should be extended not merely to the equal right of individual Christians to enter the political realm, but recognition should be extended to Christians as a group, without Christians having to bracket their distinctive Christian qualities. The logic of differential recognition requires that this "voice" be a distinctively and identifiably Christian voice that does not have to be translated into secular terms, or modulated to please secular ears. Such a voice should be able to call upon the authority of the Bible and to speak of God's will in reference to specific public policy initiatives.

Speaking in a distinctive Christian voice, however, was clearly *not* what Reed's "casting a wider net" strategy was about. Reed called upon the constituency of the CC to speak in a voice that the wider society can understand and even accept. Robertson, who has continued to function as a religious leader in addition to his political activities, has shown less willingness to consistently adopt the same discursive style as Reed. As a more distinctly religious voice, Robertson has provided opponents with proof of his "extremism" even as he has articulated the concerns and beliefs of those who feel themselves to be religious outsiders in a secular society. The distinctive voice that Reed has called for in principle, Robertson has come closer to using in practice.

Reed has been criticized for this by his allies. As I noted in Chapter 4, Reed has supported his "wider net" strategy by citing Paul in I Corinthians 9:22: "I have become all things to all people so that by all possible means I might save some."[278] At the 1993 "Road to Victory" conference final banquet, William Bennett used the same text to caution against compromise. "Don't ever forget what you are, where you came from or in whose name you come. . . . You cannot be all things to all people, and you shouldn't be."[279]

Alan Keyes, an unsuccessful candidate for the Republican presidential nomination in 1996, implicitly attacked Reed's pragmatism at that year's "Road to Victory" conference. The passionately pro-life Keyes was probably disappointed that Reed did not show as much support for his campaign as Reed did for the less-than-passionately pro-life candidacy of Dole. "What will happen," asked Keyes, "to that certain trumpet that must be sounded to awaken this nation's conscience if you decide that the most important thing to you is who wins and who loses?" Keyes, who had previously lost two bids for a U.S. Senate seat, told CC members that it did not matter if you lose an election for the sake of a righteous cause. But if you lose, he warned "having compromised what you believe because you thought someone would win and when they lose, what do you have left?" Noting that he ran the risk of not being invited back next year, Keyes singled out one of Reed's favorite political images in order to make his case against compromise. "So to what do we cling?" asked Keyes, "Do we cling to our place in the game and our seat at the table? Or do we cling to the words of almighty God?"[280]

Perhaps in response to such criticism, Reed said in his 1995 "Road to Victory" speech, "We do not bear the name of Ronald Reagan or Bob Dole or Newt Gingrich. We bear the name which is above every name." Calling politics "a mission field," Reed told attendees, "The responsibility is not ultimately to win, it is to be found faithful when He returns."[281] Reed also made his call for civility in *Active Faith* with explicitly Christian terminology: "Our political witness should reflect not only God's judgment but also His forgiveness. For He loves everyone—including our political foes."[282] Reed has also elected on occasion to emphasize the "Christian" in "Christian Coalition." At a San Antonio CC fund-raising event in June 1996, Reed reportedly brought the audience to its feet with, "We are Christians! And we honor and serve our God. We are not going to apologize for being Christians anymore. To anyone!"[283] Despite all this, some have suspected that Reed's religion has been secondary to his politics.[284]

Another expression of the CC's demand for differential recognition has been sensitivity to labels. Robertson, of course, has long been aware of the implications of labels—witness his strenuous objections during the 1988 presidential primaries to being called a "televangelist" and a "fundamentalist," rather than a "religious broadcaster" and an "evangelical." Reed also has engaged in verbal reform to resist the imposition of demeaning self-images and stereotypes: "I do not use 'the Religious Right' as a term of self-identification. . . . [I]t has become a pejorative term that connotes an intolerant and extremist political agenda. . . . I prefer 'religious conservative' and 'pro-family conservative' and will use these terms interchangeably."[285] Reed also favored the term "people of faith," to refer to the CC constituency—an interesting parallel to the term "people of color" used by multiculturalists. Perhaps mindful of these parallels, and the specter of the verbal reformism of campus P.C. speech codes, Reed asserted that, "People of faith must not adopt the status of 'victims' who seek special protection from the rough-and-tumble of civic life." Yet Reed immediately qualified this with a call for special protection. "But some blows are cheap shots, and attacks on religion are the rhetorical equivalent of kidney punches that should be against the rules."[286] Reed, however, did not clarify whether "rules" meant a legal code or merely unwritten norms of decent behavior.

Nowhere has the CC's demand for differential recognition been more powerfully expressed, or with greater significance, than in the area of education. Like multicultural education's resistance to assimilation by the dominant culture, the CC has called for resistance to liberal and secular values in education—values antithetical to evangelical identity and destructive to the survival of that community.

Robertson, as I have noted, regarded the dual thrusts of liberalism to be statism and secularism. Both are linked to education. Quoting conservative author Samuel Blumenfeld, Robertson in *The Turning Tide* told his readers, "'the most potent and significant expression of statism is a state educational system. Without it, statism is impossible. With it, the state can and has become everything.'"[287] The absolutism of the state has required the destruction of competing absolutes—religious beliefs— through education. "[T]heories of modern education," according to Robertson, "can be summed up as a basic denial of the value of Western tradition and a repudiation of the role of religion in the welfare of the community."[288] Robertson has called the "public school cartel" the "vehicle for socialism and anti-religious cleansing."[289] He has depicted the purposes of the National Education Association (NEA), "a radical, leftist organization," as part of the drive toward the anti-Christian new world order. "The prime thrust of the NEA," charged Robertson in *The New Millennium,* "is to wean children away from loyalty to 'the outdated religious superstitions,' loyalty to the family, loyalty to the United States, and belief in free market economics, and then to introduce them to socialism and world citizenship."[290]

On educational issues, Reed has emphasized the modest and essentially defensive character of religious conservative activism. "They [religious conservatives] are far less interested in legislating against the sins of others, and far more interested in protecting their own right to practice their religion and raise their children in a manner consistent with their values."[291] Reed's fundamental premise has been that "the rights of parents to mold and shape the souls of their children should be respected."[292] Religious conservatives who run for local school boards, according to Reed, "are parents with children in public schools who simply want the basic values instilled at home reinforced, rather than undermined, at school."[293] Without resorting to sensational language, Reed has still gotten across that these rights have sometimes been usurped, and these values undermined.

The CC's *Contract with the American Family* utilized Reed's language of the disrespect and undermining of parental rights and values, while combining it with more pointed jabs at the so-called educational establishment: "From its inception, the department [Department of Education] has functioned as a tool of the education establishment, a force for the status quo rather than for change, a friend of the bureaucrats and 'experts' rather than ordinary parents."[294] The *Contract* also discussed the usurpation of local control of education, rising violence, and falling test scores, but it stressed heavily the question of values: "Rather than handing out condoms and promoting homosexuality, providing psychological counseling without parental consent, and pushing the skewed values of Outcomes Based Education, schools should be reinforcing the values taught in homes, churches, and synagogues."[295]

The CC stress on values in education is often seen, and with some justice, as part of its restorationist agenda. But the specific demand that schools reinforce rather than undermine the values taught in a child's home and religious community bears substantial resemblance to the demands of multiculturalism. Multiculturalism, to recall Merelman's description once again, "not only asserts the viability, merit, and durability of multiple cultures, but also calls for public support of these cultures within a democratic framework."[296] These multiple cultures, which children have been taught in their homes, in their neighborhoods, and in their religious communities, should be—to use Reed's terminology—reinforced, not undermined, by the public schools. To Robertson and Reed, the distinctive religious and moral beliefs that are the basis of evangelical cultural identity ought to receive the kind of differential recognition that multiculturalism demands for the unique cultural identities of African-Americans, Latinos, and others.

Such differential recognition in education often manifests itself in demands for adjustments in school curricula and policies. Reed, for instance, drew this parallel between racial and religious sensitivities. "African-American parents do not want their third-grader learning language that denigrates their race. Deeply religious parents do not want their children taught ideas about morality that directly contradict their religious beliefs." He concluded that the school's "primary job is to reinforce the basic values taught at home, not experiment with alternative value systems."[297]

Carter noted the similarity between proponents of creationism and advocates of a multicultural curriculum. Both are, according to Carter, "Concerned that 'expert authority' is replete with distortions and evil influences," and therefore "insist that other points of view be included or in some cases, allowed to dominate."[298] Carter offered a defensive interpretation of the motives of creationist parents. "The parents are fighting to preserve their sense of community, a sense engendered in part through a shared religious faith."[299] Robertson and Reed have been able to call upon much the same defensive motive for resistance to in-school condom distribution and to various sex-ed programs that do not stress abstinence or the normative character of heterosexuality.

The practical implications of curricular accommodations to the sensitivities or values of parents have proven complex, difficult, and divisive. The CC's *Contract* noted these difficulties and observed, "So long as the public school system remains monopolistic in nature these debates will not be resolved to the satisfaction of all concerned."[300] The *Contract* used this as an argument for an even more thoroughgoing form of differential recognition in education—school choice or voucher programs in which public funds would be used by parents to send their children to the private or religious school of their choice. "By adopting a more decentralized and responsive approach to education, however, choice would permit families with differing personal preferences to enroll in public and private schools that reflect their interests."[301] While the CC also argued that there are other practical advantages to school choice, the central argument was "the satisfaction of personal preference."[302]

Carter observed that school choice "can be seen as a way of extending the principle of government-funded choice—a staple of the modern welfare state—into another important field of endeavor."[303] Robertson and Reed, as opponents of welfare state expansion, should actually oppose school choice programs.[304] Yet school choice programs fit perfectly into the CC's politics of differential recognition. Based on their understanding of evangelicals as a victim group in danger of assimilation, the CC has regarded the viability, merit, and durability of the cultural identity of evangelicals as something that *should* be affirmed and supported by public institutions. Their victimization entitled them to affirmation and support. In addition, religiously motivated parents to whom the CC has appealed want to protect their children and ensure the survival of their community. Compared to those imperatives, arguments about the principles of the welfare state would seem abstract and irrelevant.

Robertson was also unmoved by arguments that school choice or vouchers would be detrimental to public education. "They say," wrote Robertson, "vouchers would spell the end of public schools in America. To which we say, So what?"[305] He argued, of course, that free-market competition will make for better schools for everyone at a better price. (Reed, as usual, was more circumspect with his estimate that 70-80 percent of children would remain in the public schools. Public schools, he argued also, would be improved, yet not eliminated, by free-market competition.[306]) But it is not difficult to detect in Robertson's "So what?" a deep resentment against what he has seen as the education establishment's antireligious and collectivist agenda, an evil agenda that will rob the evangelical community of its children and its future. "[P]ublic education in America today is firmly in the grip of fanatical ideologues," asserted Robertson, "whose crackpot theories are fast destroying not only the public school system but an entire generation of our young."[307] Robertson has maintained that the NEA regards religious conservatives with fear and loathing—"their most hated enemy is the Religious Right"[308]—and he has responded in kind.

There is another reason that the CC's support of school choice is ironic. School choice, theoretically, could foster a greater diversity of cultural and lifestyle expressions in American society—a distinct educational experience for the children of each and every group within society. Some of these lifestyle expressions might be morally repugnant to religious conservatives. Consider, for example, what Robertson might say about a tax-supported gay and lesbian high school. But even more important, acceptance of such increased diversity would contradict the CC's monocultural restorationism that I examined in the previous chapter. Rather than an evangelical *reconquista* of American culture, or an expectation of the second coming of the de facto Protestant establishment, the CC's advocacy of school choice represents an acceptance of the priority and irreconcilability of difference. It also signals a willingness to play by the rules of interest group politics—"you can get yours if I get mine." Rather than restoring "one nation under God," the CC may be willing merely to be recognized as "one interest group under God."

CHAPTER 7

WHAT THEY
REALLY WANT

I BEGAN THIS STUDY OF THE CC WITH THE SIMPLE QUESTION, "What do they *really* want?" To answer that question I have examined two basic themes that are pervasive in the literature of the CC—restoration and recognition. But what do they really want? Does the CC want a restoration of Christian America? Or does it merely want a recognition of the right of religious conservatives to participate fully in American public life?

My answer is that they want both. They want "their place at the table" *and* they want everyone at the table to agree with them. They want a Christian nation *and* religious freedom. As contradictory as it may seem, they want to have their cake *and* to eat it too.

This seems an unsatisfactory resolution because restoration and recognition are fundamentally incompatible responses to the pluralistic reality of contemporary America. As I noted at the end of Chapter 5, the logic of restoration implies a rejection of diversity and the pluralistic ethos of contemporary American society. A restored Christian nation such as Robertson has called for would mean non-Christians would also be non-citizens or, at best, second-class citizens, who might not be allowed to hold public office or to offer their non-Christian views in public discussion. And Reed's desire to return to the moral-religious consensus of a less diverse American past would induce less respect for difference in a more diverse American future. For the restorationism of both Robertson and Reed, diversity has remained a threat and pluralism a problem.

In contrast, the recognition theme discussed in Chapter 6, particularly in the hands of Reed, has appealed to the pluralistic ethos and depended upon an acceptance of diversity to support its claims. This ethos has also legitimated the desire, so often expressed by Reed, for a "place at the table in the conversation we call democracy." That place must be granted to religious conservatives so long as they respect the right of others to their places at the table.

Restoration rejects the pluralistic ethos while recognition depends upon it. The tension between these two themes can be seen in the CC's position on school prayer. The CC's *Contract with the American Family* asserts that the passage of the Religious Equality Amendment "would not mean a return to the days of organized, sectarian prayer in public schools."[1] Reed has expressed the hope that "Voluntary, student-initiated prayer in the public schools would be treated as protected speech under the First Amendment."[2] Rather than a return to pre-1962 mandatory state-sponsored prayers, the CC's rights-based argument for voluntary school prayer involved an important concession to the pluralistic ethos—a recognition of the right of others *not* to pray. But if America's covenant with God, or its moral-religious consensus, was supposedly sustained throughout its history by mandatory state-sponsored school prayer, the logic of the restorationist argument would require that to "put God back in the schools" we need to return to mandatory state-sponsored prayer. Or if prayer is meant to support civic morality in public education, then student-initiated, student-led, voluntary prayer would seem to indicate that morality is a voluntary matter of personal preference—a contingent and relativistic view of morality that is unacceptable to the conservative evangelical constituency of the CC. Voluntarism would gut the restorationist moral and religious purpose of prayer in the schools. Restoration demands what recognition cannot accept. Recognition requires what restoration cannot abide.

As I have discussed this contradiction with my friends and colleagues, they have, almost universally, offered what I call the "Trojan horse" interpretation of the CC. According to this interpretation, there is only an apparent tension, because Robertson and Reed have not actually accepted the pluralistic ethos. Despite the CC's new image, its ugly antipluralistic goals remain. "Just behind Reed's carefully constructed facade," asserted one proponent of this interpretation, Joseph L. Conn of Americans United, "lurked the same old Christian Coalition."[3] What the CC *really* wants is the restoration of a Christian nation and the imposition of evangelical religion and morality on American society. Its use of the rhetoric of recognition and affirmations of the pluralistic ethos have been deceptions, a "Trojan horse" to gain access to the political power it needs to "take over." Some proponents of this interpretation have even charged that the final goal of the CC is the establishment of a totalitarian theocracy—a Christian fundamentalist version of Iran. I do not, however, find this understanding particularly convincing. Very popular with the political opponents of the CC, the "Trojan horse" interpretation proceeds from the assumption that the motives of Robertson and Reed are unambiguously malevolent. Anything they say that is not malevolent must be a deception for a malevolent purpose—they are liars, therefore, they lie. Unless one assumes what has yet to be proven—the bad intent of the CC and its leaders—this understanding is not persuasive. I believe human motivation to be more complex and ambiguous than allowed for in this interpretation. In the end, such cynical and reductive understanding will lead us to a demonization of the CC, an ironic mirror image of Robertson's paranoid speculations on the new world order conspiracy.

A more immediate problem with the "Trojan horse" interpretation concerns the evidence used for its support and proof. Proponents can pile up a small mountain of Robertson quotations demonstrating his "extremism," his "intolerance," and his "theocratic" intentions. *"The 700 Club,"* as Robert Boston of Americans United observed, "has been a gold mine for collectors of 'Pat-speak.'"[4] But the sheer volume of these quotations, and the consistent presence of what I have called restorationism in the literature of the CC, casts doubt on this interpretation. One must wonder, if Robertson has been clever enough to gain power through stealth and deception, why has he not been clever enough to stop talking about his true goals? If he has a "stealth agenda," why should he provide critics with such a huge quantity of publicly available evidence? This could only be the product of immense stupidity, an unconscious desire for failure, or suicidal arrogance. Whatever the reason, such relentless self-sabotage probably means the dangers posed by the CC have been exaggerated.

There is, however, another way of explaining the CC's tension between restoration and recognition. Popular among the political allies of the CC, this interpretation sees Reed's affirmations of diversity as honest, and his modest desire for "a place at the table" as what the CC *really* wants. This interpretation relies on an evolutionary understanding of the Christian Right. While early spokespersons may have used offensive rhetoric, as the Christian Right has moved toward "institutionalization" it has gradually accepted and adapted to the norms and practices of American politics and public life. Hard experience has taught them that there is no "moral majority" waiting to be mobilized to bring sweeping and sudden change, but that they could be a politically effective "moral minority" within a larger coalition by learning to compromise and cooperate. Restorationist rhetoric persists only as a means to energize and mobilize the least sophisticated elements of the Christian Right. In time, the Christian Right, guided by political pragmatism, will be a fully normalized and uncontroversial presence in American politics.

My understanding of the evolution of the Christian Right makes me more sympathetic to this second interpretation. I do not, however, find it convincing. Whereas the "Trojan horse" interpretation is reductive in its cynicism, this evolutionary understanding asks us to naively believe that the ambitions of CC leaders are straightforward and entirely benign. Reed, for instance, has depicted his movement as "an essentially defensive struggle by people seeking to sustain their faith and values."[5] Political allies of the CC have also adopted this image of religious conservatives. "They [evangelicals and orthodox Catholics] organized politically," wrote Congressman Dick Armey (R-TX), "after decades of shunning politics, not to impose their beliefs on others, but because the federal government was imposing its values on them."[6] Initially, the motives of religious conservatives may have been just that simple. But taking Reed's "a place at the table" image at face value ignores how political power, which the CC has acquired, vastly complicates the motives of those who exercise it.

The evolutionary interpretation can be supported by the prominence of what I have called the recognition theme in the literature of the CC, by the rise of Reed, and by the relative success of his pragmatic methods. As I demonstrated in Chapter 4, the CC represents an attempt at institutionalizing the Christian Right. Yet I cannot simply dismiss the restorationism of the CC as a lingering bad habit. This theme has *not* been left behind or minimized in the CC's "defensive" attempts to provide marginalized evangelicals with a political voice. The CC's restorationist jeremiad has not been found only in Robertson's diatribes on *The 700 Club* or in direct-mail pieces, but has been woven into carefully prepared statements of the CC's policy and political positions. Nor has Robertson been the only spokesman for restorationism in the

CC. Reed has not been citing Deuteronomy or issuing calls for a Christian nation, but restorationism in Reed's speeches and writings has been more than a minor theme that could be quietly eliminated at a later date. Reed's call for the restoration of a lost and better age has been as central as his call for a place at the table for marginalized evangelicals. The CC has shown no signs of abandoning its restorationism.

Proponents of both the "Trojan horse" theory and the evolutionary interpretation ask that we disbelieve or discount much of what the CC invariably says to its constituency. For purposes that may fit with their respective political commitments, proponents of each interpretation try to impose too much intellectual coherence on the dynamic and chaotic reality of the CC. Robertson and Reed are understood as either deceptive theocrats or unfairly maligned populists. Neither understanding by itself is fully accurate or particularly helpful.

Instead, I prefer to take seriously the CC's use of *both* themes, restoration *and* recognition. This does not provide the comfort of intellectual simplicity, but it has the virtue of being loyal to more of the facts. I am assuming that the things the leaders of a movement say consistently and persistently are significant—even when those things are confused and contradictory. Robertson and Reed are not, after all, developing a systematic theology of political activism, but seeking out ideas and rhetoric that "work"—that help accomplish their political goals. Thus far, it seems that restoration *and* recognition have worked for the CC.

Reed has embraced this ambiguous duality of purposes. In the January 1993 edition of *Christian American,* Reed asserted, "Our Judeo-Christian heritage and our religio-ethnic pluralism are the twin pillars of American society. Neither can be sacrificed without both suffering." He did not, however, explain how or why these two pillars were mutually dependent, or discuss their tendency toward mutual exclusion. Reed advised CC members to "affirm our faith while expressing tolerance of others"[7] but said nothing about the difficulty in doing so.

A similar ambiguity can be found in Reed's assertion of the importance of the public role of religion: "Until our culture begins to honor and affirm religion, civility may never return to American civic discourse."[8] But the meaning of "religion" was ambiguous. It can mean religious believers *or* religious beliefs. Did Reed mean that religious believers, if unrecognized and excluded from public life, would leave too large a demographic hole in the pluralistic tapestry of America for civic life to function properly? Or did Reed mean that religious beliefs themselves, specifically his own evangelical beliefs, hold the answer to what ails us and that we should restore their role in our civic life? Reed, perhaps wisely, has made no attempt to confront this ambiguity. I say "wisely" because restoration and recognition, despite their contradictions, have worked together in a complementary fashion to the benefit of the CC. Outrage over the unfair treatment of "people of faith" has been necessary to create a sense of shared identity, grievance, and entitlement, as well as to bring in direct-mail contributions and to motivate activism. The politics of recognition have provided the CC with a tactical program of productive involvement in contemporary American politics.

But outrage and a tactical program are not enough. The CC must also offer to its constituency some vision of what America ought to be. The restoration of a lost era of piety and morality is central to that vision. Whatever flaws it might have, the restoration of Christian America is a vision of the common good that allows its advocates to believe that they have not been merely seeking political power and a bigger piece of the public pie for themselves. They believe themselves to be idealists fighting unselfishly for a noble cause. Reed appealed to this idealism at the 1995 CC national convention:

> We will not, we must not, become to the Republicans, what the AFL-CIO, the feminists, and the radical left have become to the Democratic party. They are no longer servants, but power brokers. They seek no longer to heal; they seek influence. We will not become, as people of faith, what they have become—just another special interest group. Politics, for us, is a mission field, not a smoke-filled room.[9]

In seeking a voice in government, in pursuing "a place at the table," Reed, so far, has not forgotten what he originally wanted to say. The restoration theme, so far, has functioned alongside of the recognition theme.

But as many of the CC's conservative allies are fond of saying, ideas have consequences. And so the contradictions between the ideas of restoration and recognition have consequences for the CC. This has been expressed in the ongoing struggle for a sustainable balance between principle and pragmatism. Reed was once asked how he balanced the necessity of compromise in politics with the absolutes of the Bible. Reed responded, "We should never compromise our principles. But we should be willing to move gradually because that's how political changes takes place."[10] There is undoubtedly a segment of religious conservatives who accept the wisdom of Reed's pragmatism. But there are also those who find his gradualism a new name for old-fashioned worldliness. And as the Buchanan campaign in 1996 demonstrated, the struggle for the hearts and minds of grassroots religious conservatives is far from over.

Both Robertson and Reed have recognized the spiritual and moral dangers of political involvement, but they have done so in different ways. Robertson has shown concern with the danger to the spiritual lives of individuals. In his 1989 book *The Plan,* Robertson confessed the spiritual cost of his disappointing presidential campaign: "The one thing that I had told Him I would not give up to run for office was gone, the most precious thing in the world: my relationship with the Lord Himself."[11] He testified that he was able to restore that relationship, but his subsequent books, written as the CC has grown to prominence, do not caution readers about the dangers of politics. "Professional politicians say, Give on principle, but hold on offices," wrote Robertson in 1993. He urged Christians "to understand that the name of the game [in politics] is to win offices."[12]

Reed has been more focused on challenges faced by the entire movement. In *Active Faith,* he depicted the movement as being at a crossroads. "History has shown that people of faith can follow two paths in politics," explained Reed. "Either we can become inflamed with zeal, and make much sound and fury before our fervor and influence ultimately dissipate; or we can assume the role of a responsible player within the democratic polity, so that the voices of Christians will always be heard in public discourse."[13]

The first path is defined by, according to Reed, "its spiritual arrogance and by its faulty assumption that the most efficacious way to change the hearts of men and women is through the coercive power of the state."[14] This was the way chosen by the prohibitionists, advocates of the Social Gospel, and the other faith-based political movements in American history. Reed warned against this path for contemporary religious conservatism lest it become "just another of those brief, intense bursts of reformist enthusiasm that burn brightly but for only a short period, and leave little lasting legacy."[15]

The second path, that of responsible and permanent participation in the political system, is Reed's preference for religious conservatives.

And it is, according to Reed, an untried path. Previous faith-based political movements provide a precedent for activism, but few positive models for success. The CC, claimed Reed, "represents a new thing in American politics: the marriage of a sense of social justice with the practical world of modern politics."[16]

Reed's writing resonates with his sense of the historical destiny of religious conservatism. "The American revolutionaries in their day," he explained, "the Communists in their time, and the left in the 1960s all possessed a unique and powerful conviction that history was on their side. Today that conviction no longer belongs to liberals or their allies, but to the right and, more particularly, to religious conservatives." For Reed, we are entering "an era of American life in which moral issues, and the pro-family agenda, will predominate."[17] Reed seemed to be saying that religious conservatives are the chosen people of American politics entering their promised land of influence.

To Reed's credit, he admitted that the path of responsible participation is a "dim and dangerous one." The dangers, of course, are temptations to corruption that come with political power. Reed traced out these corrupting effects of power in the history of other religiously influenced reform movements, especially in the case of liberalism in the 1960s. "The sad truth is that involvement in politics has corrupted the religious faith of liberals." Reed argued that mainline denominations and the National Council of Churches "confused their liberal politics with the gospel, causing a mass exodus from the pews." Reed warned, "If we want to avoid the fate of the religious left, there are times when we will have to resist the temptation of political power instead of blindly pursuing it."[18]

Reed, however, clearly wanted to communicate to his constituency a confidence that they can avoid the mistakes of previous religious reformers, that they can remain uncorrupted and innocent. There is a hint of this in the way Reed used a quotation from *Beyond Tragedy* by theologian Reinhold Niebuhr: "Goodness, armed with power, is corrupted."[19] The lesson that Reed derived from Niebuhr, that the government should be kept small and limited, was a valid point and one that served Reed's political agenda. But it was *not* the point Niebuhr was making. Reed avoided Niebuhr's religious message of the inevitability of corrupting sin in *all* human endeavors that involve the exercise of power. Reed did not take note of another observation by Niebuhr that appeared only a few sentences later, "Thus every morality which begins by counting on the success of a pure action must end by reducing the purity of the action in the interest of success."[20] Instead of confronting his readers with Niebuhr's "hard teaching," Reed encouraged the illusion that political power can be exercised without the sacrifice of principle, that one can do good without becoming enmeshed in evil.

The way Reed has written history, however, indicates that he has seen through this illusion. His dissertation, after all, dealt with the unintended, if not ironic, consequences of the good but ambiguous intentions of nineteenth-century southern evangelical educators. The pages of *Active Faith* are filled with the stories of movements that had their moment, made their contribution, and then fell under the weight of their contradictions or corruptions. Original intentions, Reed seemed to recognize, are not determinative of final outcomes.

Yet Reed seemed to promote the notion that religious conservatism, led by the CC, will escape this historical pattern, that it will become, paradoxically, a "permanent movement." Reed called for a recognition of the limits and hazards of politics, and he asserted, "It is this recognition that will allow us to thrive in the future and not perish."[21] Appealing to the lessons of history, Reed apparently believed in the possibility of maintaining the difficult balance between the conflicting imperatives of religion and politics, the possibility that his movement will succeed where all others have failed.

His hopes seemed to rest heavily on the goodness of the CC constituency. "Religious conservatives have poured into politics in recent years," according to Reed, "not out of thirst for power but out of a sense of right and wrong, seeking to restore values that have been lost and hoping to heal deep spiritual wounds in society."[22] He asserted that their success will come from the practice of Christian love and warned that "If we fail, it will not be a failure of money or methods, but a failure of the heart and soul."[23]

The importance of the motives and intentions of his constituency may also be reflected in Reed's concern with racism within his movement. If religious conservatives are a historically or divinely "chosen people," the sin of racial prejudice may make them, just as the sin of slavery made Americans, in Lincoln's words, an "almost chosen people." Race, however, seems to be the only question on which Reed has taken a less than celebratory stance toward his constituency.

As I noted above, Reed asserted that people of faith will not become "just another special interest group." Why? Because for them, politics is "a mission field, not a smoke-filled room."[24] When asked about the danger of religious conservatives becoming part of the establishment, he affirmed his faith in their incorruptibility. "I view the establishment as the focus on power for the sake of power alone," he explained, "and primarily coming from a moderate-to-liberal philosophy. We won't become part of the establishment because our values and our views are never likely to become establishment values and views. Our viewpoint is conservative, traditional, religious and pro-family."[25] In other words, Reed was saying, we won't become like them because we aren't like them.

I do not know if Reed, intoxicated by unexpected success, believed that his movement and its destiny is really that different from its predecessors. Perhaps he was merely overstating his belief in the long-term significance of the Christian Right. Or perhaps Reed just knew that discussions of the irony of history will not energize CC activists, but that the conviction "that history is on their side" may move them to action. In any case, Reed's encouragement of this illusion of chosenness and incorruptible innocence may also encourage the kind of arrogant, uncompromising, crusading mentality that Reed has sought to replace with pragmatism and gradualism.

Given the short and complex history of the CC, it would be foolish to attempt to say much about its future. But assuming that what I have described bears some resemblance to reality, I want to consider the consequences for the CC of the choices it may have made in regard to restoration and recognition.

If indeed Robertson and Reed have settled on a "Trojan horse" strategy, playing the pluralistic political game in order to destroy diversity, the CC is probably doomed to become a footnote in American religious and political history. The pluralistic ethos that they would seek to destroy is too pervasive and deeply ingrained in American culture to be abolished by anything but a massive and radical cultural change— something far beyond the CC's, or perhaps anyone's, power to effect. If the destruction of diversity is what the CC *really* wants, then it will almost certainly be destined to disappointment and political irrelevance.

The pluralistic ethos of American society could possibly be repressed and destroyed by a totalitarian political regime. This of course would be the "theocracy" that some proponents of the "Trojan horse" interpretation warn of. Behind closed doors, Robertson, Reed, and their allies may be plotting a forcible overthrow of the government, but I have seen no credible evidence of this. And even more important, they have not been communicating any such ideas to the membership of the CC. To accept the totalitarian threat of CC political activism as real without evidence is to plunge through the looking glass into the intellectually bankrupt wonderland of conspiracy theories.

If the CC has chosen the path toward a consistent and institutionalized practice of the politics of recognition, they will probably experience a greater degree of short-term success and wider acceptance. By adopting the practices of interest-group and identity-group politics, the CC will be swimming with the political tide of this era. But like other movements, such as organized labor, that have pioneered this path of defending the rights, interests, and identities of their particular constituencies, the CC may lose touch with the idealism and energy that initially propelled it to prominence. The transition from the pro-family *movement* to the pro-family *lobby* will probably be accompanied by a cooling of enthusiasm and a leveling off, if not a decline, of membership and activity.

Whether or not the CC consciously chooses this second path, it is most likely to end up moving in that direction. The tide of politics in our era will encourage it to drift toward that option. Less likely is the possibility that the CC will be able to continue tolerating the tension between restoration and recognition. Up to this point in its development, a period of rapid expansion and relative success, it has been able to fuse its restorationist idealism with pragmatic demands for recognition. This fusion may even last for some time to come. But what has been called "Wesley's Law" is probably as operative at the juncture of religion and politics as it always has been at the juncture of religion and economics. "I fear, wherever riches have increased," observed John Wesley, the founder of Methodism, "the essence of religion has decreased in the same proportion."[26] Success, even when fueled by idealism, breeds the decline of idealism. In achieving a place at the table for religious conservatives, Robertson and Reed have not yet forgotten what they originally wanted to say to America, but it is probable that someday they, or their successors, will have trouble remembering.

EPILOGUE

AFTER RALPH

EVEN BEFORE RALPH REED'S political consulting firm, Century Strategies, was officially open for business, clients were lining up. "I just got my business cards a week ago," Reed told the *New York Times.* "I don't know how these people got my phone number. I'm averaging 30 to 40 calls a day, just coming in over the transom!"[1] By June 1998, Reed could claim involvement in "27 campaigns in 14 states" including at least three gubernatorial and two U.S. Senate races.[2] His immediate goal was helping grassroots religious conservatives. "Those guys need me because no one else is helping them."[3] His long-range goals, however, were more grandiose. "Our goal is to be involved in one out of every 10 or 15 (federal and state) campaigns in America" and to elect 100 "pro-family, pro-faith, pro-free enterprise" Congressmen in the next decade. "If we can do that," Reed said, "we'll transform the political landscape of the country."[4]

As soon as Reed announced he was leaving the CC, speculation began over which Republican presidential campaign he would join.[5] Political consultant Frank Luntz told the *Washington Times,* "Ralph Reed will probably be the most in demand of all of us for the year 2000."[6] Indeed, Reed confirmed that several candidates (he refused to say whom) had expressed interest in his services. In contrast to Pat Robertson's "coalesce early"-behind-a-single-candidate strategy (see page 84), Reed preferred to wait. "I don't think," he told an interviewer, "I'm going to be making a decision until after the 1998 elections."[7]

By keeping his role as free agent—someone to watch—Reed was able to maintain press interest in his activities and views. Reporters often sought him out for quotations, and he came more and more to be identified as, "Ralph Reed, Republican strategist," as well as the former executive director of the CC. Reed's name recognition, at least in political circles, was such that he was more prominent than many of his clients and he could be made into a campaign issue.[8] Reed maintained this was not a problem, "I just don't think most voters care about that. My name's not on the ballot."[9] But in June 1998, *Newsweek*'s "Conventional Wisdom Watch" noted Reed's potential overexposure. "Baby-faced Bible boy smooths GOP extremes. But watch the high profile, Ralphie."[10]

Managing too much success was not, however, the problem faced by the CC's new leadership team, president Donald Hodel and executive director Randy Tate. The public debut of Hodel and Tate at the 1997 "Road to Victory" conference was not particularly auspicious. Held in Atlanta, rather than in Washington, D.C., the conference garnered fewer attendees and less media attention than in previous years. And much of that attention focused on the CC's doubtful future without Reed and its problems, especially the Federal Election Commission (FEC) lawsuit against it.[11] Even worse, Americans United for Separation of Church and State released a tape of Pat Robertson giving a sharply partisan speech in a private meeting at the conference. The story appeared in all major media outlets, and critics of the CC used the opportunity to once more call for the revocation of CC's tax-exempt status. Put on the defensive, CC spokesperson Arne Owens could only maintain that Robertson was "speaking as a private individual, which he has a right to do."[12] Despite all this, potential Republican presidential candidates still came to the conference eager for the support of the CC membership in 2000.[13]

By year's end, the CC was facing problems far more serious than unflattering news reports. The most pressing problem was financial. From a record level of $26.4 million in 1996, CC revenue dropped to $17 million in 1997.[14] A principal reason for the decline was that 1997 was not a major election year, making it harder to motivate donors. The CC had also experienced a 12 percent decline in 1995, the last electoral off year (see page 54). But the 1997 decline was 35 percent, almost three times as large. Why?

Reed's departure, and the relative unfamiliarity of Hodel and Tate, probably depressed donations substantially.[15] Perhaps even more important, the generally complacent political environment of 1997, based on the health of the American economy, did not lend itself to CC fundraising appeals. Unlike 1993, it was much harder to accuse the Clinton administration of having a "radical" cultural agenda. Many CC supporters may also have been angry with what seemed to be the CC's cozy relations in 1996 with Dole and other Republican leaders who wanted the votes of religious conservatives but treated them as an embarrassment. Many former CC donors just kept their money or sent it to other organizations that had not been so visibly "Doled" in 1996.

There were also important problems in the management of the CC's financial and fundraising operations. In 1996, the CC's chief financial officer, Judy Liebert, was fired after reporting to federal prosecutors financial irregularities concerning a direct-mail vendor. While the CC initially minimized the seriousness of Liebert's accusations, in December 1997 the CC filed a federal lawsuit against the vendor, Hart Conover Inc., for fraudulently using the CC's mailing list. The CC alleged that this caused a decline in CC revenues. An undisclosed out-of-court settlement of the suit was reached in March 1998.[16] The CC's problems with financial management, however, did not end there. In September 1997, Liebert's successor, controller Jeanne K. DelliCarpini, plead guilty to charges that she had embezzled $40,000 from the CC.[17]

Robertson, who was supposedly moving into more of an "elder statesman" role as chairman of the CC Board, reportedly took an active role in demanding drastic measures to deal with the CC's financial crisis. In December 1997, one-fifth of the CC's 100-person staff were laid off. The CC's magazine, *Christian American*, ceased publication. Reed's outreach programs to Catholics and African Americans, the Catholic Alliance and the Samaritan Project, were defunded. And fundraising operations were brought under tighter control. "Our intent is to get back to our core mission of grass-roots activism and prepare for next year," said a CC spokesperson. "You might say we have put ourselves on a diet."[18]

These austere measures apparently contributed to the CC's fiscal recovery in 1998. In August, a CC spokesperson could claim the CC was "$1 million in the black now" versus a deficit of $1.2 million one year earlier.[19] By the 1998 election, CC membership claims also edged up from 1.9 to 2.1 million.[20] Hodel's extensive experience as an administrator in both business and government probably contributed to this turnaround as well. Beyond better fiscal policies, Hodel spoke of adopting a more focused, "back to basics, back to the grassroots" strategy. In an obvious allusion to Reed's fame, Hodel told the *Washington Times* that "a picture of me on the cover of *Time* magazine" mattered less than what Congressmen were hearing from people in their districts. Sounding very much like Reed in the early days of the CC,

Hodel explained, "A group like ours may in fact have greater impact if it is not visible. One of the strengths of a grass-roots campaign is that it doesn't show up on a radar screen."[21] In February 1998, as part of what it called its "core mission of grassroots activism," the CC announced "Families 2000," an initiative meant to recruit 100,000 CC Church Liaisons by November 2000.[22]

Tate's contribution to the fortunes of the post-Reed CC, however, has been harder to determine. Reed, the media star and *wunderkind,* would be a hard act for anyone to follow. But the fact that Robertson reportedly hired Tate as executive director and *then* brought in Hodel as president undermined Tate's credibility. Hodel, not Tate, initially stepped forward as the public voice of the CC. It was not until January 1998 that CC press releases began quoting Tate, and until May that Tate's signature began appearing on CC fundraising letters. While the division of labor between Hodel and Tate—the administrator and the spokesman— stabilized, Tate still seemed to have credibility problems. An unflattering August 1998 profile in the *New York Times Magazine* portrayed him as "a little too nice—and not too effective."[23]

Beyond the difficulties posed by the CC's financial difficulties and leadership transition, the FEC's civil lawsuit posed a fundamental threat to the CC, to its distribution of voter guides, and to its still-pending tax-exempt status. Filed in a U.S. District Court in July 1996, the FEC suit alleged that the CC had improperly aided and cooperated with Republican candidates in the 1990, 1992, and 1994 elections. The FEC asked that the CC be fined and prohibited from engaging in similar activities in the future.[24] As of this writing, *FEC v. Christian Coalition* remains unresolved. The CC has, of course, mounted a determined legal defense claiming that the FEC charges are "groundless" and that the FEC has exceeded its legal authority.[25] Should the FEC win this case, the CC would undoubtedly appeal, a process that might take months or even years to reach a final resolution.

Possibly because of the combination of financial and legal troubles, the new leadership of the CC briefly considered forming a political action committee which would allow for the support of specific candidates and other partisan activities. Perhaps this idea was rejected because it might be taken as an admission of guilt in the FEC lawsuit.[26] In any case, the CC leaders apparently decided that the best way out of their difficulties was to face them head on. As I observed in Chapter 6 above, the CC has used the FEC suit as yet another instance of anti-

Christian bigotry in order to motivate their constituency. In a June 1998 letter to CC members, Tate claimed the FEC lawsuit was "politically-motivated," and "an attempt by liberals to misuse the power of government *to destroy America's leading Christian voice* in government." Tate appealed for funds to pay the CC legal expenses and to get ready for the upcoming elections.[27]

As if to prove the old adage that politics makes for strange bedfellows, on September 28, 1998 the AFL-CIO and the ACLU filed a "friend of the court brief" urging U.S. District Court Judge Joyce Greene to dismiss *FEC v. Christian Coalition*. The brief argued that the FEC's legal position posed a threat to "protected speech by organizations throughout the ideological and political spectrum."[28] This sort of cooperation was not unprecedented. In 1997, Senator Fred Thompson's (R-TN) Committee on Governmental Affairs launched an investigation of illegal or improper campaign activities in the 1996 elections, including partisan activities by nonprofit groups. The CC followed the lead of the AFL-CIO in refusing to comply with committee subpoenas. Defiance of the subpoenas by these nonprofit groups was supported by the ACLU.[29] Because of a December 31, 1997 deadline on its activities, the Thompson committee could not pursue the lengthy process of citing these organizations for contempt of Congress.[30]

The fact that the FEC case was unresolved by election day 1998 provided the CC's critics and opponents with a useful tool against the distribution of voter guides. The CC announced that it would spend $3.1 million to distribute 35 million voter guides at churches on the Sunday prior to the election.[31] Just as in 1996, two organizations opposed to the CC, Americans United and Interfaith Alliance, began a well-publicized counter campaign to discourage churches from cooperating with the CC.[32] Calling the CC guides "campaign propaganda," Barry Lynn of Americans United warned that his organization would report churches distributing CC voter guides to the Internal Revenue Service.[33] In a letter sent to ministers, Tate called Lynn's statements a "false and misleading" attempt to "silence many Christians." He also declared that distributing CC voter guides would not jeopardize the tax-exempt status of churches.[34] As in 1996, it is impossible to determine the overall effectiveness of the anti–voter guide campaign. There was, however, anecdotal evidence of its success. Tate himself admitted that "Some pastors are scared off."[35]

The surprising outcome of the 1998 elections, however, quickly overshadowed all else. In contrast to the almost universal expectation of Republican gains in both houses of Congress, the Democrats picked up five seats in the House and lost none in the Senate. The conventional wisdom that the turnout of the Republican base of religious conservatives would be greater than the Democratic base of union and minority voters, proved false.[36] The election results led to the resignation of Rep. Newt Gingrich (R-GA) from his position as Speaker of the House. While the Republicans could point to some victories in state elections, many candidates who identified with the Christian Right lost.[37] "They [religious conservatives] saw some of their staunchest allies defeated," observed political scientist John C. Green. "And many of their challengers didn't win."[38]

Reed also had a bad night. He claimed victory for approximately 50 percent of his clients, some of whom he was contractually obligated not to name.[39] But I have only been able to identify three who won. All three were Republican incumbents, and only one, U.S. Senator Paul Coverdell of Georgia, faced any real competition.[40] Reed's best-known client, Fob James, incumbent Governor of Alabama and a well-known champion of Christian Right causes, was decisively defeated. *Newsweek*'s post-election "Conventional Wisdom Watch" delivered a harsh verdict on Reed. "Old: Divine consultant to the righteous. New: Hire him and lose."[41] While it is unlikely that Reed will have to look for a new line of work, his bid to "transform the political landscape" has gotten off to a slow start.

If the results of the 1998 election were unexpected, the immediate analyses of its meaning were more predictable. The usual critics of the CC and the Christian Right pointed to the electorate's rejection of extremism. "The embrace of the Religious Right was a kiss of death for candidates in many competitive races," Lynn of Americans United told reporters. "Simply put, narrow moralizing by the Coalition doesn't resonate with moderate voters."[42] James P. Pinkerton, a moderate Republican columnist, pointing to the landslide victory of Texas Governor George W. Bush, Jr., offered a similar interpretation: "If Republicans want to compete in 2000, they will have to loosen the stranglehold of the ideological fringe."[43] Whit Ayres, a Republican pollster, told the *Washington Post,* "Pragmatic Conservatism works, Ideological Conservatism doesn't."[44]

Tate's interpretation, paralleling those of other Christian Right leaders, was that the Republican leadership in Congress failed to talk about issues, other than the Clinton-Lewinsky scandal, that would appeal to religious conservatives.[45] "Republicans tried to win a campaign based solely on anti-Clinton sentiment. Democrats had an agenda, albeit a liberal agenda . . . and some agenda will beat no agenda every time." Citing an exit poll commissioned by the CC, Tate asserted that only 54 percent of religious conservatives voted Republican in 1998, down from 67 percent in 1994. "In 1994 there was the same anti-Clinton sentiment among conservatives as there was this year," explained Tate, "but there was also a clear conservative agenda in 1994 which did not exist in 1998."[46] Tate also warned, "If the 106th Congress does not immediately take up pro-family, conservative issues and talk about them, not just for one day but day in and day out; if they don't do these things, things will get worse before they get better for them."[47]

This interpretation defied the conventional wisdom that the Republicans were concentrating on the Clinton scandal largely because that was what religious conservatives were demanding.[48] Disapproval of President Clinton's policies and personal life has been, of course, a constant for the CC constituency. This was certainly the case at the September 1998 "Road to Victory" conference, held just days after the release of the Starr report. Those attending enthusiastically cheered repeated calls by the speakers for Clinton's resignation or impeachment.[49] In an October mailing, Robertson urged CC members to "flood the halls of the Capitol" with petitions urging Congress to remove Clinton from office if he did not immediately resign.[50] The day before the election, Tate's standard media soundbite was, "This election's going to be a national referendum on values. It's going to be a referendum on ethics and morality in government."[51]

Yet it should be noted that from January 21, when America first heard of Monica S. Lewinsky, until August 17, when the president publicly admitted his "inappropriate relationship" with her, there was little or no mention of the scandal in CC literature—direct-mail, press releases, action alerts, and Congressional scorecards. Instead, there was the usual mix of the CC's standard issues, such as abortion, homosexual rights, education, and taxes. Clinton was only mentioned for his opposition on these issues. Reed, who remains on the CC Board, seemed to have been responsible for this cautious approach.[52] As early as February, Reed was issuing a warning that anticipated Tate's post-election complaint. "The scandal does not absolve the Republican Party of its obligation going into an election, namely to present a compelling agenda on the issues."[53]

After August 17, however, the question of impeachment, as the saying goes, "sucked all the oxygen out of the room." Even if they had not wanted to, the CC had little choice but to accept the reality that impeachment was *the* issue on the Republican table. But when it came, they embraced the prospect of Clinton's disgrace with relish. One of Robertson's biggest applause lines in his speech at the "Road to Victory" conference was, "But we've been told it's not our place to express outrage and demand something better. Well ladies and gentlemen, I say to you today, we will be silent no longer!"[54] But the expressed outrage of Robertson ironically may have helped reenergize Democratic voters. When People for the American Way aired their "Let's Move On" anti-impeachment commercial in October, Robertson's picture appeared on-screen with those of House Speaker Newt Gingrich and Independent Counsel Ken Starr.[55]

The 1998 post-election blame game among Republicans was immediately seen as The Pragmatic Center v. The Ideological Right.[56] Just as in the aftermath of defeats in 1992 and 1996, the Center blamed the "Scary" Right, especially the Christian Right, for alienating swing voters, and the Right blamed the "Squishy" Center for compromising away a distinct and compelling message.

The outcome of these Center v. Right intra-party struggles will be influenced by a parallel and interrelated division among religious conservatives. While the situation remains fluid, this division seems to be among Pragmatists who adopt an insider identity toward the Republican party, and Purists who see themselves as outsiders. In 1996, the same fault line among religious conservatives appeared between the supporters of Pat Buchanan, the insurgent outsider, and Bob Dole, the establishment candidate.

In February 1998, psychologist James Dobson of Focus on the Family, whose radio broadcasts are heard by tens of millions of evangelicals, made this rift public again. Articulating the Purist position, Dobson warned that if the Republicans continued to "betray" religious conservatives he would leave the party and "do everything I can to take as many people with me as possible."[57] Dobson's warning marked the ascendancy of a more confrontational attitude. As Richard Land, an official with the Southern Baptist Convention, observed, "The go-along, get-along strategy is dead."[58] Republicans, fearing a revolt in an election year, paid attention and made more effort on Dobson's agenda, at least until the question of impeachment came to dominate all else in

Washington.[59] Dobson's personal ability to exert pressure on the Republicans was also curtailed when, on June 16, he suffered a stroke.[60] While Dobson soon returned to his duties at Focus on the Family, he abandoned high-profile political activity.

Reed, of course, criticized Dobson's threats. "If the pro-family movement leaves the Republican Party," he warned, "they will enter a no man's land in which they lose influence and lose the ability to use a major political party as a vehicle."[61] But true to form, he also found a way to strategically embrace the outsider upsurge of 1998. Using the analogy of positions on a football team, Reed observed that there was a role for those outside the system "pressing it and speaking with moral authority and urging more action." He explained that his role was different, "I'm more engaged inside, but I'm grateful that they're outside pressing, because it makes my job that much easier."[62]

The CC's new leadership team was in the midst of their rebuilding project when Dobson's outsider message became dominant, but it did not present an immediate problem. Hodel, a former executive vice president of Focus on the Family, had a cooperative relationship with Dobson.[63] Also, outsider rhetoric fit with the CC's "back to basics, back to the grassroots" strategy. A reemphasis on red-meat, core issues was just what CC fundraising efforts needed. This was also necessary to reclaim the more "bold" image that had been obscured by Reed's less confrontational style. Concern with homosexuality was particularly useful for these purposes. When Senate majority leader Trent Lott (R-MS) told an interviewer that homosexuality is a "sin," Tate praised Lott's "courageous leadership."[64] In contrast, Reed commented that "The Republican Party has tripped over its own shoelaces and found itself on the defensive."[65] In July 1998, the CC also joined with other Christian Right organizations to sponsor full-page ads in the *New York Times, Washington Post,* and *USA Today* promoting the controversial idea that homosexuality can be "healed" through religious faith.[66]

Taking a more controversial stance in public, however, was complemented by a more conciliatory pragmatic approach in private. After months of Dobson's saber-rattling about bolting the party, Robertson paid a low-profile visit in June 1998 to Republican leaders on Capitol Hill, reportedly reassuring them that he and the CC would remain supportive.[67] Also, Tate's experience in the 104th Congress as a Deputy Whip probably provides him with a greater measure of sympathy for the realities facing leaders and members, and he has gained the reputation of being cooperative.[68] At a press conference following the May 8, 1998 "Values Summit," (a meeting between Dobson, various Christian Right leaders, and the House leadership), it was Tate who stressed "the realization that the legislative process is slow."[69] Tate continues to use Reed's "a place at the table" image to describe the goal of the CC, but he also has another shorthand phrase for pragmatism: "Politics is a process, not an event."[70]

The CC's place in the national political process after the election of 1998 is, however, unclear. In 1998 it did not live up to its reputation for being able to turn out a constituency who would vote Republican, as the old saying goes, "early and often." Without the payoff of a large and reliable bloc of votes, the leadership of the Republican party may have less incentive to go the extra mile to keep the CC happy—especially if the broader electorate decides to punish the Republicans for the Clinton impeachment. While the CC leaders have positioned themselves more as cooperative Pragmatists than confrontational Purists, it remains to be seen how cooperative Congressional leaders will be.

The 1998 election was hardly over when speculation about the presidential race in 2000 began. Gov. George W. Bush, Jr. of Texas was immediately anointed as the Republican front-runner against the presumptive Democratic candidate, Vice President Al Gore. The popular governor of a vote-rich state with the name recognition that comes from being the son of a former president, Bush was known for his pragmatic implementation of a conservative agenda, and his ability to reach out to Hispanic and women voters.[71] Most of all, Bush had the sunny smell of heartland success, not the stench of repeated inside-the-beltway defeats.

The big question is whether Bush will be acceptable to the Ideological Right of his party, particularly to the Christian Right. He is "pro-life" but avoids talk of banning abortion. "We should talk about parental notification, adoption, abstinence," Bush has said. "Issues over which we can make a difference."[72] Cautious about being "Doled" by yet another establishment candidate, especially one named Bush, many religious conservatives will find him unacceptable. But for the more pragmatically inclined, Bush's lack of passion on abortion must be weighed against the prospect of a Democrat winning the White House in 2000. Even worse, a Democratic presidential victory might create enough of a "coattail effect" to return both houses of Congress to the control of the Democrats. For his part, Bush has not been unfriendly toward the Christian Right, but has stayed away from events such as the

CC's "Road to Victory" conference. Reed has had especially friendly relations with Bush, and it has often been suggested that he will work for Bush in 2000.[73]

Other candidates, such as Dan Quayle and Alan Keyes, will offer themselves to religious conservatives as the alternative to Bush. Pat Buchanan may run once again. And Steve Forbes has found unexpected support by adding anti-abortion rhetoric to his flat-tax message.[74] But many religious conservatives who reject Bush may turn to one of their own, Gary Bauer. As president of the Family Research Council, Bauer stood in the shadow of the younger, more telegenic Reed. But after Reed's 1997 departure from the CC, Bauer emerged as an advocate of outsider Purism second only to Dobson, with whom Bauer is closely allied. While Bauer has not officially declared his candidacy, he has created a political action committee, made frequent visits to primary states, and held a candidate-style reception at the CC's 1998 "Road to Victory" conference. By appealing to what he calls, "a yearning for unflinching leadership,"[75] Bauer pointedly distinguishes himself from Reed's pragmatism. "Nobody's going to put on your tombstone, 'He had a place at the table.'" Bauer once said. "The thing you want on your tombstone is, 'He liberated the slaves' or 'He stopped the slaughter of the innocents.'"[76]

Bauer's candidacy is comparable to Robertson's outsider campaign in 1988. Yet it is unlikely that Robertson will support Bauer, whom he probably regards as a threat to his leadership within the Christian Right. Robertson instead showed more interest in supporting U.S. Senator John Ashcroft (R-MO), who dropped out of the race in January 1999. Unlike Bauer, Ashcroft would have had to rely on Robertson as an intermediary to the CC constituency. Robertson, for instance, made a $10,000 contribution to Ashcroft's political action committee.[77] When Ashcroft delivered the 1998 commencement address at Robertson's Regent University, Robertson praised the senator and told a reporter, "I would love to see him as president."[78] After Ashcroft finished first in a presidential preference poll of CC state leaders, it was reported that Robertson ordered Tate to leak the supposedly secret results to the media.[79] Another presidential poll to be taken at the 1998 "Road to Victory" conference was canceled at the last minute, ostensibly because it might take attention away from the upcoming election. But it was rumored that Robertson canceled the poll in order to protect Ashcroft from a very public defeat by Bauer or Forbes.[80]

Robertson's sponsorship of Ashcroft, of course, reflects the "coalesce early" strategy he announced just after the 1996 election. While this strategy for magnifying the impact of the Christian Right is rational, it is unrealistic. Lacking a towering, charismatic leader, achieving consensus in grass roots-based social movements, like the Christian Right, is rather like "herding cats." Consensus may emerge but it cannot be orchestrated or ordained. And the withdrawal of Ashcroft, Robertson's favorite, makes it even less likely that the Christian Right will achieve an early consensus. Much to Robertson's frustration, religious conservatives will most likely bicker their way through the 2000 primary season only to discover that the Republican establishment has once again won the prize. And the Christian Right's Pragmatists, despite misgivings, will once again "go along, to get along."

If this is the scenario that plays out in 2000, regardless of victory or defeat on election day, it may be the Purists not the Pragmatists who are strengthened in its aftermath. Obviously, if the Republicans lose the White House *and* control of Congress, Purists like Bauer can make a strong case for the futility of compromise and the need for "unflinching leadership." If the Republicans win in 2000, religious conservatives will inevitability be frustrated by Republican compromise, delay, inaction, or betrayal. The frustrated and disillusioned may be more receptive to the argument that the real problem is a failure of nerve, and the only solution is the leadership of those who never compromise—the Purists.

It is not hard to imagine that the Purist strategy, a Goldwater-like capture of the Republican nomination, or the creation of a third party, could lead to electoral disaster and a collapse of the Christian Right's political credibility.[81] If so, it would be more pragmatic insiders like Robertson and Reed who would be positioned to pick up the pieces. This, of course, assumes that such a recovery is possible. But in looking at two decades of Christian Right history it is apparent that reports of its death, based on the most recent election results, have often been greatly exaggerated. The social base of religious conservatism, and dissatisfaction within that base with the direction of American culture, is not only intact but thriving. Particular figures or organizations come and go, but so long as that dissatisfaction continues, and so long as channels for expressing it through politics remain open, something like the Christian Right will be as perennial as the grass.

The argument between the Christian Right's Pragmatists and Purists will also be perennial. Their quarrel is most fundamentally about the problem of pluralism, about how to advance their ideals in a context in which religious conservatives are a minority. While the Purists make use of what I have called "demands for recognition," it is their "dreams of restoration" in which they place their ultimate trust. For the Purists it is the power of the Truth itself, the correctness of their vision of "Christian America," that will win. Dobson, for instance, has likened "modern liberalism" to the "evil empire" of the Soviet Union in its final days—seemingly so formidable yet in reality "a house of cards . . . ready to come down." According to Dobson, just as Ronald Reagan's unwavering conviction and courage pushed the "Evil Empire" to its sudden collapse, "We could win this thing and we could do it fairly quickly, in my view. And what we need are people of courage."[82] Only by proclaiming that Truth, the Purists argue, by refusing to compromise their vision, can the minority become a majority. Only by holding fast to the dream can the problem of pluralism be solved.

The Pragmatists, of course, would maintain they have no less faith in the ultimate power of the dream of restoration, but that the election results of 1998 do not hint of the imminent collapse of the opposition. Rather than Reagan's "evil empire" speech, Pragmatists might invoke John F. Kennedy's mid–Cold War call to "bear the burden of a long twilight struggle, year in and year out."[83] To let the perfect become the enemy of the good, to reject partial victories because they are also partial defeats, the Pragmatist would argue, demonstrates not only a lack of wisdom but a lack of faith in eventual victory. In America's two-party pluralistic democracy, the politics of recognition, of demanding and securing a place at the table, and of playing the insider game is the way to carry on that long struggle.

The danger for the Pragmatists, as it has always been for Christians engaged in culture, is that they will become part of the problem rather than part of the solution. In seeking to change the "world" they become "worldly." The CC will probably not solve the Christian Right's problem of pluralism because it depends too heavily on the norms of pluralism to legitimate its existence and guide its action. Success, as I noted in the original conclusion of this work, even when fueled by idealism, breeds the decline of idealism. Even more dangerous to idealism is the desperate attempt to hold onto success—its place at the table—as success begins to slip away. That is the danger facing the CC today.

Justin Watson
January 19, 1999
Tallahassee, FL

NOTES

Chapter 1

1. Barry W. Lynn, "Anti-Christian 'Bigotry': A Fundamentally Unfair Complaint," *Church & State,* February 1994: 23(47).

2. Matthew Moen, *The Transformation of the Christian Right* (Tuscaloosa: University of Alabama Press, 1992), 131; Steve Bruce, *The Rise and Fall of the Christian Right* (Oxford: Clarendon Press, 1988), 172.

3. Perry Miller, *Errand into the Wilderness* (Cambridge: Belknap Press, 1984), 101.

4. This movement has been referred to by a variety of names, "Christian Right," "Religious Right," "New Christian Right," "Religious New Right," "New Political Religious Right," "Radical Religious Right," and so on. While scholars have not arrived at a consensus on nomenclature, "Christian Right" has been a common, if not the most common, name for this movement. I also believe that "Christian" is a more precise way of describing the constituency of the movement than the broader term "Religious."

   Nomenclature that used "New," or that stressed connections to the secular "New Right," may have been accurate in the early 1980s but have become quite dated. Reference to the newness or the novelty of the movement may also obscure strong indications of its increasing institutionalization.

5. See Steve Bruce, "The Inevitable Failure of the New Christian Right," *Sociology of Religion* 55, no. 3 (Fall 1994): 229-42.

6. Matthew C. Moen, "From Revolution to Evolution: The Changing Nature of the Christian Right," *Sociology of Religion* 55, no. 3 (Fall 1994): 345.

7. Charles Taylor, "The Politics of Recognition," in *Multiculturalism and "The Politics of Recognition,"* ed. Amy Gutmann (Princeton: Princeton University Press, 1992), 25-73.

8. Ralph Reed, Jr., "Statement by Ralph Reed, Jr. Concerning His Resignation from the Christian Coalition," Christian Coalition press release, April 23, 1997.

9. Pat Robertson, "Pat Robertson Expresses Gratitude and Support for Ralph Reed," Christian Coalition press release, April 23, 1997.

10. "Christian Coalition Names New President and Executive Director," Christian Coalition press release, June 11, 1997; Peter Baker and Laurie Goodstein, "Christian Coalition Rearranges Top Posts," *Washington Post,* June 12, 1997: A15; Richard L. Berke, "From Cabinet to Leadership of Coalition," *New York Times,* June 12, 1997: A15.

Chapter 2

1. Jerry Falwell, "Future-Word: An Agenda For the Eighties," in *The Fundamentalist Phenomenon,* ed. Jerry Falwell (Garden City, NY: Doubleday & Company, Inc., 1981), 219.

2. There are some, of course, who would term my intention to avoid offending the subjects of this study as unnecessary and mistaken, as "bending over backward." I am merely extending the same respect that the academy offers to other social groups. No reputable scholar currently studying the African-American community, for instance, would use the term "Negro" except in the quotation of historical materials.

3. George M. Marsden, *Understanding Evangelicalism and Fundamentalism* (Grand Rapids, MI: William B. Eerdmans, 1991), 2.

4. Timothy L. Smith, "The Evangelical Kaleidoscope and the Call to Christian Unity." *The Christian Scholar's Review* 15 (1986): 125-40.

5. George M. Marsden, "The Evangelical Denomination," in *Piety and Politics,* eds. Richard John Neuhaus and Michael Cromartie (Washington, D.C.: Ethics and Public Policy Center, 1987), 57-58.

6. Marsden, "The Evangelical Denomination," 59.

7. Ibid., 61.

8. George M. Marsden, *Fundamentalism and American Culture* (New York: Oxford University Press, 1980), 6-7.

9. Sydney E. Ahlstrom, *A Religious History of the American People* (New Haven: Yale University Press, 1972), 387.

10. William G. McLoughlin, *Revivals, Awakenings, and Reform* (Chicago: University of Chicago Press, 1978), 98-140.

11. Martin E. Marty, *Righteous Empire* (New York: Dial Press, 1970), 67.

12. Mark A. Noll, *A History of Christianity in the United States and Canada* (Grand Rapids, MI: William B. Eerdmans Publishing Company, 1992), 243.

13. Perry Miller, "From the Covenant to the Revival," in *The Shaping of American Religion,* eds. James Ward Smith and A. Leland Jamison (Princeton: Princeton University Press, 1961), 355.

14. Ahlstrom, *A Religious History of the American People,* 387.

15. Noll, *A History of Christianity in the United States and Canada,* 243.

16. Marsden, *Understanding Fundamentalism and Evangelicalism,* 122-52.

17. Ahlstrom, *A Religious History of the American People*, 805.

18. Marsden, *Understanding Fundamentalism and Evangelicalism*, 13.

19. James Davison Hunter, *American Evangelicalism: Conservative Religion and the Quandary of Modernity* (New Brunswick, NJ: Rutgers University Press, 1983), 11-12.

20. Peter Berger, *The Sacred Canopy* (New York: Anchor Books, 1969), 107.

21. Hunter, *American Evangelicalism*, 15.

22. Ibid.

23. Nancy Ammerman, *Bible Believers: Fundamentalists in the Modern World* (New Brunswick, NJ: Rutgers University Press, 1987), 211.

24. Martin E. Marty and R. Scott Appleby, "Introduction," in *Fundamentalisms Observed*, eds. Martin E. Marty and R. Scott Appleby (Chicago: University of Chicago Press, 1991), ix.

    Fundamentalism has often been understood as a temporary aberration, the product of rural economic dislocation, status anxiety, or lack of education. See, for instance, Richard Hofstadter, *Anti-Intellectualism in American Life* (New York: Vintage Books, 1963). A distinctly different interpretation was advanced by historian Ernest R. Sandeen who stressed the theological/intellectual roots of fundamentalism. For Sandeen, "Fundamentalism ought to be understood partly if not largely as one aspect of the history of millenarianism." *The Roots of Fundamentalism* (Chicago: University of Chicago Press, 1970), xix.

25. Marsden, upon whom I will rely for my understanding of fundamentalism, found Sandeen's analysis correct when tracing the roots of those who have continued to call themselves fundamentalists. "Yet this approach," Marsden argued, "fails to deal adequately with the larger phenomenon of the militantly anti-modernist Evangelicalism of the 1920s, known at the time as 'fundamentalism'" (*Fundamentalism and American Culture*, 5).

26. Marsden, *Understanding Fundamentalism and Evangelicalism*, 1.

27. Nancy Ammerman, "North American Protestant Fundamentalism," *Fundamentalisms Observed*, eds. Martin E. Marty and R. Scott Appleby (Chicago: University of Chicago Press, 1991), 27.

28. For an account of these intradenominational struggles, see Marsden, *Fundamentalism and American Culture*, 171-83.

29. Ammerman, "North American Protestant Fundamentalism," 27.

30. Ammerman, "North American Protestant Fundamentalism," 29-33; Marsden, *Understanding Fundamentalism and Evangelicalism*, 66.

31. Ammerman, "North American Protestant Fundamentalism," 29-33; Marsden, *Understanding Fundamentalism and Evangelicalism*, 62-82.

32. Marsden, *Understanding Fundamentalism and Evangelicalism*, 68.

33. George M. Marsden, *Reforming Fundamentalism* (Grand Rapids, MI: William B. Eerdmans Publishing Company, 1987), 7.

34. Hunter, *American Evangelicalism,* 41.

35. Hunter, for instance, dates it from the creation of the National Association of Evangelicals (NAE)in 1942, an organization that consciously eschewed the strict separatism of Carl McIntire's American Council of Christian Churches (ACCC) founded in 1941 (*American Evangelicalism,* 41, 47). Marsden points to Billy Graham's willingness to cooperate with mainline churches in his 1957 New York City crusade as precipitating "a definitive split with hardline fundamentalists" (*Understanding Fundamentalism and Evangelicalism,* 73).

36. Hunter, *American Evangelicalism,* 46-47.

37. Marsden, *Understanding Fundamentalism and Evangelicalism,* 82.

38. Ibid., 39, 42-44.

39. Robert Mapes Anderson, *Vision of the Disinherited* (New York: Oxford University Press, 1979), 114-36.

40. Grant Wacker, "Pentecostalism," in *Encyclopedia of the American Religious Experience,* eds. Charles H. Lippy and Peter W. Williams (New York: Charles Scribner's Sons, 1988), 944, 942-43.

41. Richard Quebedeaux, "Conservative and Charismatic Developments of the Later Twentieth Century," in *Encyclopedia of American Religious Experience,* eds. Charles H. Lippy and Peter W. Williams (New York: Charles Scribner's Sons, 1988), 963.

42. Marsden, *Understanding Fundamentalism and Evangelicalism,* 105.

43. Marsden, *Fundamentalism and American Culture,* 92-93.

44. Hunter, *American Evangelicalism,* 30.

45. Marsden, *Fundamentalism and American Culture,* 91.

46. Quoted in Marsden, *Understanding Fundamentalism and Evangelicalism,* 31.

47. Marsden, *Fundamentalism and American Culture,* 85-93, 206-11. Ammerman has also observed: "When today's fundamentalists speak of tradition or orthodoxy . . . they are most likely referring, even if unknowingly, to ideas, images, and practices that were prevalent in the late nineteenth century" ("North American Protestant Fundamentalism," 8).

48. Marsden, *Understanding Fundamentalism and Evangelicalism,* 100.

49. Ibid., 94.

50. Ahlstrom, *A Religious History of the American People,* 926-29. These included Gerald Winrod, Gerald L. K. Smith, and J. Frank Norris. See also Leo P. Ribuffo, *The Old Christian Right: The Protestant Far Right from the Great Depression to the Cold War* (Philadelphia: Temple University Press, 1983).

51. Marsden, *Understanding Fundamentalism and Evangelicalism,* 102; Erling Jorstad, *The Politics of Doomsday* (Nashville: Abingdon Press, 1970), 44.

52. These included Billy James Hargis, Edgar Bundy, and Fred Schwartz. See Jorstad and Gary Clabaugh, *Thunder on the Right* (Chicago: Nelson-Hall, 1974).

53. Richard Hofstadter, *The Paranoid Style in American Politics* (New York: Alfred A. Knopf, 1966), 72-77.

54. Marsden, *Reforming Fundamentalism,* 80-82.

55. Marsden, *Understanding Fundamentalism and Evangelicalism,* 74.

56. James D. Fairbanks, "Politics and the Evangelical Press: 1960-1985," in *Religion and Political Behavior in the United States,* ed. Ted G. Jelen (New York: Praeger, 1989), 255.

57. Richard V. Pierard, "The New Religious Right in American Politics," in *Evangelicalism and Modern America,* ed. George M. Marsden (Grand Rapids, MI: William B. Eerdmans Publishing Company, 1984), 165-67. This era also saw the development of a notable politically liberal to radical evangelical left. See Quebedeaux, "Conservative and Charismatic Developments of the Later Twentieth Century," 968-69, and Hunter, *American Evangelicalism,* 107-12.

58. Martin E. Marty, "Fundamentalism as a Social Phenomenon," *Evangelicalism and Modern America,* ed. George M. Marsden (Grand Rapids, MI: William B. Eerdmans Publishing Company, 1984), 64.

59. Kevin P. Phillips, *Post-Conservative America* (New York: Random House, 1982), 35.

60. George H. Nash, *The Conservative Intellectual Movement in America Since 1945* (New York: BasicBooks, 1976), 292-95.

61. Phillips, *Post-Conservative America,* 30.

62. Ibid., 199.

63. Ibid., 22.

64. Ibid., 47. Phillips originated the term "New Right" in 1974 to describe populist-conservative groups aligned with Richard Viguerie.

65. Ibid., 3, 13.

66. Fritz Stern, *The Politics of Cultural Despair* (Berkeley: University of California Press, 1961), xvi. Quoted in Phillips, *Post-Conservative America,* 200-201.

67. Lyman A. Kellstadt and Mark A. Noll, "Religion, Voting for President, and Party Identification," in *Religion and American Politics,* ed. Mark A. Noll (New York: Oxford University Press, 1990), 359.

68. Richard A. Viguerie, *The New Right: We're Ready to Lead* (Falls Church, VA: The Viguerie Company, 1981), 124.

69. Ralph Reed, the CC Executive Director, writes that this was the "greatest spark of the movement" and that conservative evangelicals regarded it as "nothing less than a declaration of war on their schools, their churches, and

their children." Ralph Reed, *Active Faith* (New York: Free Press, 1996), 105.

70. Ammerman, "North American Protestant Fundamentalism," 42-43.

71. Kenneth D. Wald, *Religion and Politics in the United States* (New York: St. Martin's Press, 1987), 187.

72. Quoted in James Davison Hunter, "The Liberal Reaction to the New Christian Right," in *New Christian Right,* eds. Robert C. Liebman and Robert Wuthnow (New York: Aldine Publishing Company, 1983), 152.

73. John H. Garvey, "Fundamentalism and American Law," in *Fundamentalisms and the State,* eds. Martin E. Marty and R. Scott Appleby (Chicago: University of Chicago Press, 1993), 28-49.

74. Nathan Glazer, "Fundamentalists: A Defensive Offensive," in *Piety and Politics: Evangelicals and Fundamentalists Confront the World,* eds. Richard John Neuhaus and Michael Cromartie (Washington, D.C.: Ethics and Public Policy Center, 1987), 250-51.

75. John H. Garvey, "Introduction: Fundamentalism and Politics," in *Fundamentalisms and the State,* eds. Martin E. Marty and R. Scott Appleby (Chicago: University of Chicago Press, 1993), 21.

76. James Davison Hunter, *Evangelicalism: The Coming Generation* (Chicago: University of Chicago Press, 1987), 92, 76-93.

77. Allen Hunter, *Virtue with a Vengeance: The Pro-Family Politics of the New Right* (Ph.D. dissertation, Brandeis University, 1984).

78. Schaeffer was not the originator of this dualistic framework but a popularizer of the ideas of Dutch theologian Abraham Kuyper (1837-1920). This view of western history was further popularized and simplified by politicized fundamentalists, such as Tim LaHaye, who made discussion of a "secular humanist conspiracy" one of the hallmarks of Christian Right rhetoric in the early 1980s. Marsden, *Understanding Fundamentalism and Evangelicalism,* 108-109. See Tim LaHaye, *The Battle for the Mind* (Old Tappan, NJ: Fleming H. Revell, 1980).

79. Francis Schaeffer, *A Christian Manifesto* (Wheaton, IL: Crossway Books, 1993).

80. Ronald H. Nash, *Evangelicals in America,* (Nashville: Abingdon Press, 1987), 92.

81. Marsden, *Fundamentalism and American Culture,* 7.

82. Grant Wacker, "Uneasy in Zion: Evangelicals in Postmodern Society," in *Evangelicalism and Modern America,* ed. George M. Marsden (Grand Rapids, MI: William B. Eerdmans Publishing Company, 1984), 24.

83. Peter Marshall and David Manuel, *The Light and the Glory* (Grand Rapids, MI: Fleming H. Revell, 1977), 359.

84. Wald, *Religion and Politics in the United States,* 182.

85. Hunter, "The Liberal Reaction," 162.

86. On negative perception, see Matthew C. Moen, "From Revolution to Evolution: The Changing Nature of the Christian Right," *Sociology of Religion* 55, no. 3 (Fall 1994): 346-47. On public sympathy, see A. James Reichley, *Religion in American Public Life* (Washington, D.C.: Brookings Institution, 1985), 330.

87. Clyde Wilcox, *God's Warriors: The Christian Right in Twentieth-Century America* (Baltimore: The Johns Hopkins University Press, 1992), 21-40, 224-26. Quotation on 224.

88. Moen, "From Revolution to Evolution," 347.

89. Alan Brinkley, "The Problem of American Conservatism," *American Historical Review* 99, no. 2 (April 1994): 425.

90. Steve Bruce, "The Inevitable Failure of the New Christian Right," *Sociology of Religion* 55, no. 3 (Fall 1994): 229-42. Quotation on 240-41. See also Steve Bruce, *The Rise and Fall of the Christian Right* (Oxford: Clarendon Press, 1990).

91. Falwell, "Future-Word," in *The Fundamentalist Phenomenon,* 189.

92. Moen, "From Revolution to Evolution," 345.

93. Ibid., 348-49.

94. Ibid., 350-51.

95. Ibid., 351-53.

96. Ibid., 353. Moen later added a fourth phase of development. He called it the "devolutionary phase." This phase began in 1995 with the Republican-controlled 104th Congress. It has the same characteristics as the institutional phase but it was also marked by a willingness to accept compromises on social issues and by an attempt to return political authority to the states. Moen wondered how long this fourth phase would last because it was predicated on Republican control of the Congress. Matthew C. Moen, "The Evolving Politics of the Christian Right," *PS: Political Science and Politics,* September 1996: 461-62.

Chapter 3

1. Biographical material, unless otherwise noted, will be drawn from David Edwin Harrell, *Pat Robertson: A Personal, Political and Religious Portrait* (San Francisco: Harper & Row, 1987).

2. For recent discussions of the enterprises associated with Robertson and CBN, see William Prochnau and Laura Parker, "The Doomsday Man," *Vanity Fair,* July 1996: 82-88, 147-53; Robert Boston, *The Most Dangerous Man in America?* (Amherst, NY: Prometheus Books, 1996), 183-207; Alec Foege, *The Empire God Built: Inside Pat Robertson's Media Machine* (New York: John Wiley & Sons, Inc., 1996); Mark Robichaux, "Tim Robertson Turns TV's Family Channel Into a Major Business," *Wall Street Journal,*

August 29, 1996: A1; and Tim Stafford, "Robertson R Us: When Evangelicals Look in the Mirror, Do We See the Host of *The 700 Club* Staring Back?" *Christianity Today,* August 12, 1996: 26-33. For a complete description of the programs offered by Regent University, see *Regent University Graduate Catalog 1994-96* (Virginia Beach, VA: Regent University, 1994).

3. John B. Donovan, *Pat Robertson: The Authorized Biography* (New York: Macmillan Publishing Company, 1988), 20.

4. If Robertson, as critics have charged, avoided combat duty in Korea through his father's political influence, then his disillusionment in these years might have been far deeper. Raised in Lexington, where "Stonewall" Jackson and Robert E. Lee are venerated, Robertson might have felt that both he and his father had betrayed the southern gentleman's code of martial honor. Garry Wills presented the basis for such an interpretation in *Under God* (New York: Touchstone, 1990), 184-91.

5. Pat Robertson, *America's Dates with Destiny* (Nashville, TN: Thomas Nelson Publishers, 1986), 19.

6. Harrell, *Pat Robertson,* 45.

7. Ibid., 70.

8. Pat Robertson with Bob Slosser, *The Secret Kingdom* (Nashville, TN: Thomas Nelson Publishers, 1982); Pat Robertson with William Proctor, *Beyond Reason: How Miracles Can Change Your Life* (New York: William Morrow and Company, Inc., 1985).

9. Robertson, *The Secret Kingdom,* 43. Robertson discusses eight such laws: Reciprocity, Use, Perseverance, Responsibility, Greatness, Unity, Miracles, and Dominion. In a subsequent edition, *The Secret Kingdom: Your Path to Peace, Love, and Financial Security,* 2d ed. (Dallas: Word Publishing, 1992), Robertson added two laws: Fidelity (203-208) and Change (209-20).

10. In the second edition of *The Secret Kingdom,* Robertson added material denouncing, and distancing himself from, unnamed "Name-It-and-Claim-It" religious hucksters who promise instant riches and quick gratification. For Robertson it was the more traditional values of the Protestant ethic that lead to prosperity. "It's just that the normal consequence of godly, frugal living and generosity is to have more." *The Secret Kingdom,* 2d ed., 86.

11. Robertson, *The Secret Kingdom,* 44.

12. James Davison Hunter, *American Evangelicalism: Conservative Religion and the Quandary of Modernity* (New Brunswick, NJ: Rutgers University Press, 1987), 73-84.

13. Harrell attributed this to Robertson's reaction to doctrinal extremism and authoritarianism in the "discipleship controversy" among charismatics in the mid-1970s. "From the moment of that controversy," Harrell quoted

Robertson as saying, "I felt more comfortable identifying myself as an evangelical." Harrell, *Pat Robertson,* 126-28.

14. Beth Spring, "Pat Robertson's Network Breaks Out of the Christian Ghetto," *Christianity Today,* January 1, 1982: 37.
15. See Martin E. Marty and R. Scott Appleby, "Introduction," in *Fundamentalisms Observed* (Chicago: University of Chicago Press, 1991), vii-xiii.
16. Clyde Wilcox, *God's Warriors: The Christian Right in Twentieth Century America* (Baltimore: The Johns Hopkins University Press, 1992), 166.
17. Pat Robertson, *Answers to 200 of Life's Most Probing Questions* (Nashville, TN: Thomas Nelson Publishers, 1984), 153.
18. Mark G. Toulouse, "Pat Robertson: Apocalyptic Theology and American Foreign Policy," *Journal of Church and State* 31, no. 1 (Winter 1989): 80.
19. Harrell, *Pat Robertson,* 148; Toulouse, "Pat Robertson," 85-99.
20. Robertson, *Answers to 200 of Life's Most Probing Questions,* 155-56; Harrell, *Pat Robertson,* 148-49; and Hubert Morken, *Pat Robertson: Where He Stands* (Old Tappan, NJ: Fleming H. Revell, 1988), 213.
21. Pat Robertson, remarks on *The 700 Club,* Christian Broadcasting Network, January 4, 1993.
22. I will discuss Robertson's relationship with the postmillennial Christian reconstructionism of R. J. Rushdoony and others in Chapter 5.
23. Donovan, *Pat Robertson,* 24.
24. "I yearned to get into the fray," Robertson wrote in his 1972 autobiography, "but the Lord refused to give me the liberty. 'I have called you to my ministry,' he spoke to my heart. 'You cannot tie my eternal purposes to the success of any political candidate . . . not even your own father.'" Pat Robertson and Jamie Buckingham, *Shout It from the Housetops* (Plainfield, NJ: Logos International, 1972), 179. When the Robertson campaign reissued his autobiography, this passage had been excised. T.R. Reid, "Robertson Corrects Details of His Life," *Washington Post,* October 8, 1987, A6.
25. Robertson later claimed that after he interviewed Carter on *The 700 Club* shortly before the 1976 election he decided to vote for Gerald Ford, the Republican candidate. Donovan, *Pat Robertson,* 181.
26. Harrell, *Pat Robertson,* 177; Garrett Epps, "Voices of '88: A Surprising New Politics of Protest, Robertson's Evangelicals," *Washington Post,* February 14, 1988: C2; and Mark J. Rozell and Clyde Wilcox, *Second Coming: The New Christian Right in Virginia Politics* (Baltimore: The Johns Hopkins University Press, 1996), 37-39.
27. Quoted in "Preachers in Politics," *U.S. News & World Report,* September 24, 1979: 37.
28. Rally organizers put the figure at 500,000 and the National Park Service estimated 200,000. Harrell, *Pat Robertson,* 177.

29. Jeffrey K. Hadden and Anson Shupe, *Televangelism* (New York: Henry Holt and Company, 1988), 27.

30. Ben A. Franklin, "200,000 March and Pray at Christian Rally in Capital," *New York Times*, April 30, 1980: A1, A20.

31. Robertson, *America's Dates with Destiny,* 282. Reed described the 1980 "Washington for Jesus" event as a key event in Robertson's turn toward politics. "While the purpose of the march was spiritual," wrote Reed, "the political subtext was unmistakable." Reed also described Robertson's speech at that event as issuing "a call for political action to turn the nation back from the brink of disaster." Ralph Reed, *Active Faith* (New York: Free Press, 1996), 107.

32. Hadden and Shupe, *Televangelism,* 37.

33. Harrell, *Pat Robertson,* 187.

34. Quoted in Allan J. Mayer, "A Tide of Born-Again Politics," *Newsweek,* September 15, 1980: 36.

35. Quoted in Harrell, *Pat Robertson,* 187.

36. Quoted in Mayer, "A Tide of Born-Again Politics," 31.

37. Harrell, *Pat Robertson,* 187-88.

38. Sara Diamond, *Spiritual Warfare* (Boston: South End Press, 1989), 12.

39. Quoted in Hadden and Shupe, *Televangelism,* 249.

40. Ibid., 250-53. The Freedom Council was dissolved in 1986 amid an IRS audit based on accusations that it had violated its tax-exempt status by engaging in partisan activities on behalf of Robertson. Matthew Moen, *The Transformation of the Christian Right* (Tuscaloosa: University of Alabama Press, 1992), 38.

41. Dick Dabney, "God's Own Network," *Harper's Magazine,* August 1980: 37.

42. Pat Robertson, *The Plan* (Nashville, TN: Thomas Nelson Publishers, 1989), 20-23.

43. Donovan, *Pat Robertson,* 181; Dudley Clendinen, "TV Evangelists Assume Larger Convention Role," *New York Times,* August 19, 1984: A32.

44. Cory SerVaas and Maynard Good Stoddard, "CBN's Pat Robertson: White House Next?" *The Saturday Evening Post,* March 1985: 50(11).

45. Mary Matalin, an official of the Republican National Committee, which later purchased Robertson's campaign mailing list, said they were given only 1.8 million names. T. R. Reid, "'Invisible Army' Won Few Battles," *Washington Post,* December 17, 1988: A3.

46. Quoted in David Von Drehle and Thomas B. Edsall, "Life of the Grand Old Party," *Washington Post,* August 14, 1994: A23.

47. Philip Weiss, "The Cultural Contradictions of the G.O.P.," *Harper's Magazine,* January 1988: 48-57; James M. Penning, "Pat Robertson and the GOP: 1988 and Beyond," *Sociology of Religion* 55, no. 3 (Fall 1994): 327-

35; Allen D. Hertzke, "Harvest of Discontent: Religion and Populism in the 1988 Presidential Campaign," in *The Bible and the Ballot Box,* eds. James L. Guth and John C. Green (Boulder, CO: Westview Press, 1991), 18.

48. For a useful look at Robertson's relations with the media, see Lloyd Grove, "Robertson, Taking Aim At the Critics: A Campaign Plagued by Rocky Relations With the Press," *Washington Post,* February 22, 1988: B1, B9.

49. Garry Wills, "Robertson and the Reagan Gap," *Time,* February 22, 1988: 28.

50. Lisa Langenbach and John C. Green, "Hollow Core: Evangelical Clergy & the 1988 Robertson Campaign," *Polity* 25, no. 1 (Fall 1992): 147-58; John C. Green, "Pat Robertson and the Latest Crusade: Religious Resources and the 1988 Presidential Campaign," *Social Science Quarterly* 74, no. 1 (March 1993): 161.

51. John J. Fialka and Ellen Hume, "Pulpit and Politics: TV Preacher, Possibly Eyeing the Presidency, Is Polishing His Image," *Wall Street Journal,* October 17, 1985: 1.

52. Steve Bruce, *Pray TV* (London: Routledge, 1990), 175-78; Reid, "'Invisible Army' Won Few Battles," A3.

53. See Pat Robertson, "The Speech," *New York Times,* January 14, 1988: I20.

54. Robertson finished third in percentage of vote received and second in delegates out of a field of six. Moen, *Transformation of the Christian Right,* 110, 113.

55. Hertzke, "Harvest of Discontent," 17-18; Green, "Pat Robertson and the Latest Crusade," 159, 164-66.

56. Wilcox, *God's Warriors,* 16.

57. Quoted in Kim A. Lawton, "Pat's Big Surprise: The Army Is Still Invisible," *Christianity Today,* April 8, 1988: 44-45. See also Paul Cahu-Jiunn Shie, *Why the Robertson Campaign Failed: A Study of Political Mobilization of Evangelical Ministers in the 1988 Republican Presidential Primaries* (Ph.D. diss., University of Kansas, 1990), 205-11.

58. For an interesting discussion of Max Weber's concept of charismatic leadership and Robertson's presidential campaign, see Allen D. Hertzke, *Echoes of Discontent: Jesse Jackson, Pat Robertson, and the Resurgence of Populism* (Washington, D.C.: Congressional Quarterly Press, 1993), 17-21.

59. T. R. Reid, "Robertson Joins the Fray," *Washington Post,* October 2, 1987: A1; David Schribman, "Robertson Starts Presidential Campaign As Protestors Strive to Shout Him Down," *Wall Street Journal,* October 2, 1987: A44.

60. T. R. Reid, "Traditional Morality at Core of Robertson's Political Quest," *Washington Post,* March 2, 1988: A8.

61. In his study of populist themes in Robertson's 1988 presidential campaign, political scientist Allen D. Hertzke emphasized Robertson's religiously

based "communitarian" denunciations of "destructive individualism"—self-gratification unrestrained by morality—in economics and culture. Hertzke, *Echoes of Discontent,* 93-106.

62. Robertson, *The Secret Kingdom,* 28. This passage was retained in *The Secret Kingdom,* 2d ed., 29.

63. Robertson, *America's Dates With Destiny,* 15.

64. Ibid., 296.

65. Sharon A. Showman, *The Rhetoric of a "Holy Nation": A Fantasy Theme Analysis of the Rhetorical Vision of the Rev. Marion "Pat" Gordon Robertson* (Ph.D. diss., Bowling Green State University, 1988), 76.

66. Pat Robertson, interview by Marvin Kalb, *Meet the Press,* National Broadcasting Co., Inc., December 15, 1985.

67. Pat Robertson, "Evangelicals 'Reinforce Mainstream America,'" interview, *U.S. News & World Report,* November 4, 1985: 71.

68. Pat Robertson, "Thousands of People Say 'Go for it!'," interview, *U.S. News & World Report,* July 14, 1986: 25.

69. Robertson's resignation letter, quoted in Wayne King, "Robertson Quits as a Baptist Minister," *New York Times,* September 30, 1987: A20.

70. Pat Robertson, "Inquiry: I Can Keep Politics and Religion Apart," *USA Today,* July 1, 1986: 9A.

71. Marion G. "Pat" Robertson, "A New Vision for America," speech to a Political Rally in Constitution Hall, Washington, D.C., September 17, 1986.

72. Quoted in Wayne King, "The Record of Pat Robertson On Religion and Government," *New York Times,* December 27, 1987: 1.

73. King, "The Record of Pat Robertson On Religion and Government," 30.

74. Ellen Hume, "Pat Robertson Hopes to Turn Evangelical Fervor Into Political Constituency for a Presidential Bid," *Wall Street Journal,* July 16, 1986: 44.

75. Jim Castelli, *Pat Robertson: Extremist* (Washington, D.C.: People for the American Way, 1986), 11.

76. Quoted by Maralee Schwartz, "Politics: GOP's War of Words," *Washington Post,* October 3, 1986: A8.

77. Quoted in William Schneider, "The Republicans in '88," *Atlantic Monthly,* July 1987: 81; Donovan, *Pat Robertson,* 180.

78. On *Face the Nation,* October 4, 1987, Robertson added to the ambiguity by saying, "But I don't want to say no. And the reason is because if the people want this to be a Christian nation, it's up to the people. But they can't do it through law. It's got to be through their own beliefs." Quoted in "Robertson Backs View of a Separate Church," *New York Times,* October 5, 1987: B10.

79. E. J. Dionne, Jr., "Robertson's Victory in Ballot Shakes Rivals in G.O.P. Race," *New York Times,* September 14, 1987: B12.

80. Fritz Stern, *The Politics of Cultural Despair* (Berkeley: University of California Press, 1961), xvi. For a useful discussion of populist anger and frustration in the 1988 election see Hertzke, "Harvest of Discontent," 3-27.

81. Quoted in Jack W. Germond and Jules Witcover, "The Miracle Worker," *The Washingtonian*, November 1986: 119. On the "sense of siege" felt by Robertson and his supporters, see Hertzke, *Echoes of Discontent*, 187-88.

82. Kim A. Lawton, "A Democratic Fund-Raising Letter Rips Pat Robertson," *Christianity Today*, April 18, 1986: 48. Hadden and Shupe argued that Kirk's letter helped Robertson achieve national visibility (*Televangelism*, 182).

83. Quoted in Maralee Schwartz, "Politics: Tit for Tat," *Washington Post*, September 9, 1986: A8.

84. "With Little Time to Exult or Weep, Candidates Get Set for the Next Round," *New York Times*, February 10, 1988: I22.

85. Quoted in Maralee Schwartz, Thomas B. Edsall, and T. R. Reid, "Robertson Blasts Media," *Washington Post*, January 24, 1988: A10.

86. Laurence I. Barrett, "His Eyes Have Seen the Glory," *Time*, September 28, 1987: 23.

87. Quoted in John Corry, "In Iowa, Networks Address the Robertson Factor," *New York Times*, February 10, 1988: III26.

88. His opposition to the label, "television evangelist," however, preceded the Bakker and Swaggart scandals of 1987-88. He told *New York* magazine in 1986, "Calling someone a television evangelist is a convenient way to dismiss somebody, to lump him into two categories—(a) a fundamentalist, which means you don't know anything, and (b) an evangelical, which means there's something wrong with you." Quoted in Michael Kramer, "Are You Running With Me Jesus?," *New York*, August 18, 1986: 28.

89. Russell Baker, "It's Safe With Me, Pat," *New York Times*, February 13, 1988: I27; "What to Call Pat Robertson," *New York Times*, February 15, 1988: I20; and Tom Wicker, "Just a TV Evangelist," *New York Times*, February 16, 1988: I21.

90. Quoted in Jonathan Alter and Howard Fineman, "Pat Robertson: The TelePolitician," *Newsweek*, February 22, 1988: 19.

91. Quoted in Alter and Fineman, "Pat Robertson," 18.

92. Quoted in T. R. Reid, "Robertson's Recruits," *Washington Post*, February 8, 1988: A6. This was later changed to "Tom Brokaw's face" and "South Carolina." Maralee Schwartz, "Robertson-Rather Peace?," *Washington Post*, February 26, 1988: A8.

93. Phil Gailey, "A Bitter Struggle Splits South Carolina G.O.P.," *New York Times*, April 6, 1987: B9; Weiss, "The Cultural Contradictions of the G.O.P.," 53; James M. Perry and David Schribman, "Robertson's Showing

and Dole Triumph Change GOP Picture," *Wall Street Journal,* February 10, 1988: 1; and Hertzke, "Harvest of Discontent," 18.

94. Maralee Schwartz, "'Anti-Christian Bashing,'" *Washington Post,* February 2, 1988: A7. Neil Bush, the son of the vice president, allegedly called evangelicals "cockroaches." Bush later said that he meant "worker bees." Quoted in Fred Barnes, "Blessed Are The Kingmakers," *New Republic,* March 21, 1988: 13. See also Hertzke, *Echoes of Discontent,* 158-70.

95. T. R. Reid, "Robertson Links Bush to Swaggart Scandal," *Washington Post,* February 24, 1988: A1.

96. Robertson, *Answers to 200 of Life's Most Probing Questions,* 156.

97. Alter and Fineman, "Pat Robertson," 19.

98. Quoted in Mark Andrews, "Pat's People," *Charisma,* March 1988: 36.

99. Richard Hofstadter, *The Paranoid Style in American Politics and Other Essays* (New York: Alfred A. Knopf, 1966), 3-40.

100. Robertson, *Answers to 200 of Life's Most Probing Questions,* 262-63; Robertson, *Secret Kingdom,* 132-33; Robertson, *Secret Kingdom,* 2d ed., 148-49.

101. David Boaz, "Pat Robertson's Crackpopulism," *Wall Street Journal,* February 10, 1988: 20.

102. Hertzke found in the Jackson campaign of 1988 an economic populism that reflected another side of the religious heritage of populist tradition. The Jackson and Robertson campaigns, in Hertzke's view, "have much to teach us about the cultural and economic challenges of the age in which we live." Hertzke, *Echoes of Discontent,* xv.

103. Schneider, "The Republicans in '88," 78.

104. Richard N. Ostling, "A Jerry-Built Coalition Regroups," *Time,* November 16, 1987: 68.

105. Richard Brookhiser, "Pat Robertson Seeks Lower Office," *National Review,* August 29, 1986: 30.

106. Quoted in Harrison Rainie, "Robertson's Grand Design," *U.S. News & World Report,* February 22, 1988: 14. See Andrews, "Pat's People," 29-30: "the groundwork is already being laid for a post-1988 national political organization."

107. Reid, "'Invisible Army' Won Few Battles," A3. After the 1988 election season was over, Robertson came to believe that God's plan all along was not to put a Christian in the White House but to energize and organize a new movement of Christian activists. Hertzke, *Echoes of Discontent,* 170.

108. Basic biographical material on Reed has been drawn from many sources: John Nicols, "Christian Coalition Now a Lion in GOP," *(Toledo, Ohio) Blade,* August 16, 1992: 1-2; Ralph Reed, *An American Profile,* interview, C-SPAN, August 19, 1993; Thomas B. Edsall, "Christian Political Soldier Helps Revive Movement," *Washington Post,* September 10, 1993: A4;

Laurence I. Barrett, "Fighting For God and the Right Wing," *Time,* September 13, 1993, 58-60; Ralph Reed, *Politically Incorrect* (Dallas: Word Publishing, 1994); Kim Hubbard and Linda Kramer, "Ralph Reed," *People,* February 27, 1996: 60-64; Jeffery Birnbaum, "The Gospel According to Ralph," *Time,* May 15, 1995: 28-35; "Ralph Reed," *Current Biography,* March 1996: 34-37; Joe Conason, "Ralph Reed, Smart As The Devil," *Playboy,* November 1996: 90-92, 136, 140-42; and Reed, *Active Faith.*

109. Quoted in Birnbaum, "The Gospel According to Ralph," 33.

110. Quoted in Barrett, "Fighting for God and the Right Wing," 60.

111. Ralph E. Reed, Jr., "'Christian Right' Belongs in the GOP," interview by Allan Ryskind, *Human Events,* February 6, 1993: 11.

112. Reed, *Active Faith,* 22.

113. Edsall, "Christian Political Soldier Helps Revive Movement," A4.

114. Conason, "Ralph Reed, Smart As The Devil," 136. Reed allegedly plagiarized Richard Grenier, "The Gandhi Nobody Knows," *Commentary,* March 1983: 59-72.

115. Reed, *Politically Incorrect,* 25.

116. Ralph Reed, "'Fighting the Devil with Fire': Carl Vinson's Victory over Tom Watson in the 1918 Tenth District Democratic Primary," *Georgia Historical Quarterly* 67, no. 4 (Winter 1983): 451-79. On one side in this primary was an aging and ill Watson, the controversial populist leader of the 1890s, attempting to recapture lost glories and revive the spirit of agrarian discontent. On the other side was Vinson, the shrewd young incumbent who hammered Watson with charges of disloyalty in wartime. The campaign was marked by extreme rhetoric, dirty tricks, fistfights, vote buying, and burning of disputed ballots. The outcome of the primary was only settled when a state convention of the Democratic party rejected Watson's allegations of vote fraud by Vinson. Vinson never again faced serious electoral opposition and served in Congress until 1965. Watson won a U.S. Senate seat in a 1920 landslide victory but died in 1922. Reed ends his essay with a striking detail—Vinson was one of the first persons called to Watson's bedside when the old populist fell into his last illness.

117. Ralph Reed, *An American Profile,* interview, C-SPAN, August 19, 1993. Although Atwater was Reed's political model, Reed did not refer to him as a mentor because they only dealt with one another on a professional level.

118. Quoted in Barrett, "Fighting For God and the Right Wing," 60.

119. Reed, *Politically Incorrect,* 25-26; Birnbaum, "The Gospel According to Ralph," 33.

120. Edsall, "Christian Political Soldier Helps Revive Movement," A4.

121. Reed, *Politically Incorrect,* 26.

122. Nicols, "Christian Coalition Now a Lion in GOP," 1.

123. Reed, *Active Faith,* 122.
124. Information about Mt. Paran Church of God can be obtained from their Internet web site at http://www.mtparan.org. In his 1994 book, *Politically Incorrect,* Reed mentioned in passing that a church he attended regularly in Atlanta had more than 10,000 members, but he did not identify the denomination or the congregation. Reed, *Politically Incorrect,* 137.
125. John Sedgwick, "The GOP's Three Amigos," *Newsweek,* January 9, 1995: 40. There was no mention, however, of which Presbyterian denomination he belonged to.
126. Ralph Reed, *An American Profile,* interview, C-SPAN, August 19, 1993.
127. Quoted in Birnbaum, "The Gospel According to Ralph," 33.
128. Quoted in Edsall, "Christian Political Soldier Helps Revive Movement," A4.
129. Quoted in Barrett, "Fighting for God and the Right Wing," 58.
130. "A Campaign of Falsehoods: The Anti-Defamation League's Defamation of Religious Conservatives" (Chesapeake, VA: Christian Coalition, July 28, 1994), 3.
131. See Ernest B. Furgurson, *Hard Right: The Rise of Jesse Helms* (New York: W. W. Norton & Company, 1986).
132. Ralph Reed, *An American Profile,* interview, C-SPAN, August 19, 1993.
133. Quoted in Barrett, "Fighting for God and the Right Wing," 60.
134. Reed, *Active Faith,* 110. According to Conason, Reed created this organization in 1984 at the suggestion of Gary Jarmin, the legislative director of Christian Voice. Jarmin recalled telling Reed, "What we really need is an organization on campuses to mobilize conservative Christian students." Quoted in Conason, "Ralph Reed, Smart As The Devil," 136, 140.
135. "Students for America," pamphlet (Raleigh, NC: Students for America, undated.) SFA listed its activities as sponsoring demonstrations, picketing, writing letters to newspaper editors, and publishing a monthly newsletter. Members were also promised opportunities to win cash scholarships, to go on "fact finding trips to international hot spots," and to attend an annual national convention in Washington, D.C. It was at an SFA banquet in January 1989 that Robertson and Reed first discussed the creation of the CC. Ralph Reed, *An American Profile,* interview, C-SPAN, August 19, 1993.
136. *Encyclopedia of Associations,* 1986-1995 eds. s.v., "Students for America."
137. Reed, *Active Faith,* 110.
138. "People and Events: Ralph Reed Led Extreme Protests at North Carolina Clinic," *Church & State,* November 1995: 18 (234).
139. Reed, *Active Faith,* 13.
140. Quoted in Nichols, "Christian Coalition Now a Lion in GOP," 2.

141. Reed, *Politically Incorrect,* 26.
142. Reed, *Active Faith,* 116.
143. Ibid., 114.
144. Reed, *Politically Incorrect,* 192.
145. Barrett, "Fighting for God and the Right Wing," 60. In *Active Faith,* Reed stressed the detrimental effects of a career in politics on the personal lives of many religious conservative activists. "I saw the same sad tale repeated dozens of times. It was one of the reasons why I left politics in 1985 to begin a new life in academe." Reed, *Active Faith,* 114.
146. Quoted in Sedgwick, "The GOP's Three Amigos," 40.
147. Ralph E. Reed, Jr., "Emory College and the Sledd Affair of 1902: A Case Study in Southern Honor and Racial Attitudes," *Georgia Historical Quarterly* 72, no. 3 (Fall 1988): 463-92.
148. Ralph Eugene Reed, Jr., *Fortresses of Faith: Design and Experience at Southern Evangelical Colleges, 1830-1900* (Ph.D. diss., Emory University, 1991). Carter is the author of the Bancroft prize–winning *Scottsboro: A Tragedy of the American South* (Baton Rouge: Louisiana State University Press, 1969) and a biography of George Wallace, *The Politics of Rage* (New York: Simon & Schuster, 1995).
149. Reed, *Fortresses of Faith,* 1.
150. Ibid., 4.
151. Ferdinand Tonnies, *Community and Society: Gemeinschaft und Gesellschaft,* trans. and ed. Charles P. Loomis (East Lansing, MI: Michigan State University Press, 1957).
152. Reed, *Fortresses of Faith,* 8.
153. Ibid., 6.
154. Quoted in Barrett, "Fighting for God and the Right Wing," 60.
155. Reed, *Fortresses of Faith,* 470.

Chapter 4

1. James A. Barnes, "Revival Time," *National Journal,* January 23, 1993: 190.
2. Sean Wilentz, "God and Man at Lynchburg," *The New Republic,* April 25, 1988: 30.
3. Quoted in Jackie Calmes, "Tougher GOP Stance on Social Issues Reflects Surge of the Religious Right," *Wall Street Journal,* August 20, 1992: A1.
4. "Ralph Reed," *Current Biography,* March 1996: 36.
5. Ralph Reed, *Active Faith* (New York: Free Press, 1996), 129.
6. Ralph Reed, *Politically Incorrect* (Dallas: Word Publishing, 1994), 1. Robertson also described this meeting in *The Turning Tide* (Dallas: Word Publishing, 1993), 61-62.

7. Ralph Reed, *An American Profile,* interview, C-SPAN, August 19, 1993.

8. Just prior to this meeting Reed had been featured in "Rising Young Stars," an article in *Conservative Digest* about young conservative activists. Reed was quoted as saying, "I believe we are on the verge of a Christian revival that will change the American political landscape." He also described "the Evangelical movement as a huge, still largely untapped reservoir of political power 'ready to explode.'" Quoted in Ben Hart, "Rising Young Stars," *Conservative Digest,* January/February 1989: 19.

9. Also attending the meeting were former state leaders of the 1988 Robertson campaign, as well as Charles Stanley, D. James Kennedy, and Beverly LaHaye. Reed, *Politically Incorrect,* 3.

10. Reed, *Politically Incorrect,* 1-3.

11. Reed, *Active Faith,* 12.

12. Ibid., 13-14. Reed explained that many participants at the meeting, who already had established their own organizations, were reluctant to create yet another grassroots group to compete for money, members, and media attention. He also reported that he encountered suspicions that the CC was intended as a front for another presidential campaign by Robertson. Reed found these suspicions "slightly amusing." Reed, *Active Faith,* 13, 17, 132.

13. Ibid., 17-18.

14. Ibid., 14.

15. Reed, *Politically Incorrect,* 4.

16. Quoted in "Robertson Regroups 'Invisible Army' into New Coalition," *Christianity Today,* April 23, 1990: 35.

17. Michael Isikoff, "Christian Coalition Steps Boldly into Politics," *Washington Post,* September 10, 1992: A14.

18. "Christian Coalition Congressional Scorecard, 1993 Edition," pamphlet (Chesapeake, VA: Christian Coalition, 1993).

19. "Christian Americans Are Tired Of Getting Stepped On," pamphlet (Chesapeake, VA: Christian Coalition, 1992).

20. See Jim Drinkard, "Christian Coalition: Religious Advocate or Tax-Free Political Machine?" Associated Press, July 7, 1996; Larry J. Sabato and Glenn R. Simpson, *Dirty Little Secrets* (New York: Time Books, 1996), 310-11.

21. Statements to this effect are found on much CC literature, especially direct-mail pieces asking for contributions and on voter guides.

22. Sabato and Simpson, *Dirty Little Secrets,* 310-11.

23. The CC has kept its national headquarters "outside the beltway." Its offices, which reporters have described as "humble," are located in an industrial park. David Von Drehle and Thomas B. Edsall, "Life of the Grand Old Party," *Washington Post,* August 14, 1994: A22.

24. Form 990, Return of Organization Exempt From Income Tax for 1994, The Christian Coalition. Copies of this tax return can be obtained by writing to the Virginia State Division of Consumer Affairs, P.O. Box 1163, Richmond, VA 23209.

25. Form 990, Return of Organization Exempt From Income Tax for 1995, The Christian Coalition.

26. Ruth Marcus, "Christian Coalition Suspends Official," *Washington Post,* July 19, 1996: A30; Jim Drinkard, "Direct-Mail Contractor Says Prosecutors Have Questioned Him," Associated Press, July 20, 1996; Jim Drinkard, "Group Accepted Money From Businessman Wanting to Help Bush," Associated Press, August 3, 1996.

27. William L. Fisher, "State Affiliates and Their Chapters," *Christian Coalition Leadership Manual* (Chesapeake, VA: Christian Coalition, 1990), 3.1-3.3.

28. Mary Beth Regan and Richard S. Dunham, "Gimme that Old-Time Marketing," *Business Week,* November 6, 1995: 77.

29. Quoted in Jeffrey Birnbaum, "The Gospel According to Ralph," *Time,* May 15, 1995: 34.

30. "Robertson Regroups 'Invisible Army' into New Coalition," 35.

31. Reed, *Active Faith,* 136.

32. Mike Russell, "Millionth Member Joins Christian Coalition," *Christian American,* March 1994: 5.

33. Birnbaum, "The Gospel According to Ralph," 30.

34. 34."National Christian Voter Mobilization Campaign," Christian Coalition mailing, undated; "Inside Politics," *Washington Times,* September 7, 1995: A9.

35. Larry Witham, "Christian Coalition Steps Up Efforts as Election Nears," *Washington Times National Weekly Edition,* August 4, 1996: 13.

36. Ralph Reed, Jr., "Statement by Ralph Reed, Jr. Concerning His Resignation from the Christian Coalition," Christian Coalition press release, April 23, 1997.

37. Form 990, Return of Organization Exempt From Income Tax for 1995, The Christian Coalition; Form 990, Return of Organization Exempt From Income Tax for 1994, The Christian Coalition.

38. "Christian Group Raises $24.9M," Associated Press, December 10, 1996; "Christian Coalition Raises Record Funds in 1996," Christian Coalition press release, December 10, 1996.

39. Christian Coalition mailing, undated. This claim, however, is somewhat doubtful. *Christian American* claimed an average circulation per issue of 418,428 for the period October 1, 1994 through October 1, 1995. Average circulation *dropped* to 381,718 during the year ending October 1, 1996. "Statement of Ownership, Management and Circulation," *Christian Amer-*

ican, November/December 1995: 3; "Statement of Ownership, Management and Circulation," *Christian American,* November/December 1996: 6. In addition to the decline in readership, during this period the CC claimed a membership that was three to five times these circulation numbers. On the basis of this disparity, critics of the CC have questioned the CC's membership claims. See "Ralph Reed's Missing Million: Christian Coalition Numbers Drop," *Church & State,* January 1996: 15(15); "Christian Coalition Numbers Still Don't Add Up," *Church & State,* December 1996: 10(250). Spokespeople for the CC have maintained that *Christian American* is sent only to active financial donors. They argued that these circulation figures have not included conference attendees and activists in the CC's membership files who may not contributed funds. See "Coalition's Size Challenged," *Christian Century,* January 24, 1996: 68-69.

40. "Satellite Broadcast," Christian Coalition Web site at http://cc.org/cc/edu/sat.html, September 2, 1995. See also Carolyn Curtis, "High Tech Activism," *Christian American,* October 1995: 20-23.

41. Reed, *Politically Incorrect,* 158-59.

42. Mike Russell, "Coalition Opens D.C. Office," *Christian American,* March 1993: 3.

43. Louis Jacobson, "Washington's Five-Rolodex Lobbyist," *National Journal,* August 5, 1995: 2017.

44. Jim Drinkard, "Lobbyists Paid $400M in D.C.," Associated Press, September 22, 1996.

45. See Reed, *Politically Incorrect,* 157-69; Reed, *Active Faith,* 176-84; and Alicia Mundy, "The God Squad," *Adweek,* February 13, 1995: 20-26.

46. Carey Goldberg, "In Abortion War, High-Tech Arms," *New York Times,* August 9, 1996: A20.

47. Gustav Niebuhr, "The Christian Coalition Plans To Register One Million Voters," *New York Times,* September 14, 1996: I9.

48. Christian Coalition mailing dated July 15, 1997.

49. "Christian Coalition Leadership School," pamphlet (Chesapeake, VA: Christian Coalition, 1993).

In contrast to the usual training seminars, the CC announced in early 1996 a week-long "membership retreat/election strategy briefing," to be held on board a "luxurious cruise-ship" during a tour of Caribbean ports, May, 18-25, 1996. "Victory at Sea 1996," as it was called, was hosted by Reed. Prices for attendance varied from $1,236 to $4,476 (airfare not included), depending on accommodations. Christian Coalition mailing, undated.

50. "Christian Group Coaches School Board Candidates," *New York Times,* June 14, 1995: B8; "School Board Training Seminar," *Christian American,* March 1995: 31.

51. Ralph E. Reed, Jr., "Mobilizing the Christian Right," interview, *Campaigns & Elections,* October/November 1993: 36.

52. See "National Christian Voter Mobilization Campaign," and "Inside Politics," A9.

53. Judy Lundstrom Thomas, "The New GOP," *Wichita Eagle,* September 26, 1992: 1A.

54. Rob Boston, "'Thank God for Computers,'" *Church & State,* October 1996: 10(202).

55. In an early version of this phone survey, callers were asked: "Did you vote for Dukakis or Bush? Are you a Republican or a Democrat?" Reed is reported to have said in 1991, "If they answered 'Dukakis, Democrat' that was the end of the survey. . . . We don't even want them to know there is an election going on." Quoted in Frederick Clarkson, "The Christian Coalition: On The Road to Victory?" *Church & State,* January 1992: 5(5).

    In a 1995 version of a "Voter Identification Script," however, there were no questions about past voting or party identification. *Citizen Action Seminar Manual* (Chesapeake, VA: Christian Coalition, 1995), 29.

56. Ralph Reed, "Active Faith," speech at the 6th Annual Christian Coalition "Road to Victory" conference, Washington, D.C., September 13, 1996.

57. "Precinct Coordinator Handbook," pamphlet (Chesapeake, VA: Christian Coalition, 1993).

58. *Citizen Action Seminar Manual,* 8.

59. Niebuhr, "The Christian Coalition Plans To Register One Million Voters," I9.

60. See Sabato and Simpson, *Dirty Little Secrets,* 126-39; Rob Boston, "Stacked Deck," *Church & State,* July/August 1996: 4(148)-8(152).

61. Reed, *Active Faith,* 63. Sabato and Simpson, however, observed that the CC's guides were much less complicated than previous types of voter guides. Candidates were compared on fewer issues and differences were expressed in terms of very simple contrasts. And unlike previous voter guides the CC printed theirs on one-page handbills that gave them the appearance of campaign fliers. Sabato and Simpson asserted that these were "major innovations in the long tradition of voter guides" (*Dirty Little Secrets,* 127).

62. Reed, *Active Faith,* 132-33.

63. "Court Cases: New Litigation, FEC v. The Christian Coalition," *Federal Election Commission Record* 22, no. 9 (September 1996): 1-2; Ruth Marcus, "FEC Files Suit Over Christian Coalition Role," *Washington Post,* July 31, 1996: A1.

64. Jim Drinkard, "Christian Coalition Narrowly Avoids Second Suit on Campaign Spending," Associated Press, July 31, 1996; Ruth Marcus, "Elections Commission Accuses Christian Coalition," *Washington Post,* August 1, 1996: A10.

65. William Barr, "The FEC's War Against the First Amendment," *Wall Street Journal,* August 14, 1996: A13.

66. Barry W. Lynn, "An Open Letter to America's Churches About Politics," *Church & State,* October 1996: 15(207).

67. Quoted in Howard Kurtz, "Clinton Ad Counters Christian Coalition's Voter Guide," *Washington Post,* November 3, 1996: A32.

68. D. J. Gribbin, "Campaign to Derail Voter Guides Failed," *Christian American,* January/February 1997: 51.

69. *Citizen Action Seminar Manual,* 9-10.

70. Reed, *Active Faith,* 123. Reed learned this approach at Mt. Paran Church of God in Atlanta. In order to deal with the many requests from various causes, the congregation created a "Moral Concerns Ministry with lay leadership headed by a Chamber of Commerce executive." Reed called this innovation an "essential element in our national strategy." Reed, *Active Faith,* 122-23.

71. Ralph Reed, interview by David Gergen, *Lehrer News Hour,* Public Broadcasting System, June 6, 1996. The one minister Reed was referring to was probably Rev. Billy McCormack, state chairman of the Louisiana CC and a member of the CC Board of Directors.

72. *Citizen Action Seminar Manual,* 20.

73. Reed, *Politically Incorrect,* 197. See also Reed, *Active Faith,* 29.

74. Matthew C. Moen, "From Revolution to Evolution: The Changing Nature of the Christian Right," *Sociology of Religion* 55, no. 3 (Fall 1994): 351-53. For the purposes of this discussion, I will treat Moen's characteristics in a different order.

75. Form 990, Return of Organization Exempt From Income Tax for 1994, The Christian Coalition.

76. Glenn R. Simpson, "Christian Coalition's Low-Profile Event Seeks Big Donations From Conservatives," *Wall Street Journal,* September 16, 1996: A20.

77. "Robertson Regroups 'Invisible Army' into New Coalition," 35.

78. As one critic of the CC observed, "This amounts to an enormous in-kind contribution." Quoted in Regan and Dunham, "Gimme that Old-Time Marketing," 76-77.

79. This service accused major long-distance services such as AT&T of funding homosexual-rights and abortion-rights organizations, as well as sponsoring immoral television shows. Regan and Dunham, "Gimme that Old-Time Marketing," 77; and "LifeLine, Changing the World with Every Call,"

pamphlet (Oklahoma City: AmeriVision Communications, Inc., undated.); and "Dialing For Theocracy? 'LifeLine' Phone Group Favors Church Over State," *Church & State,* January 1996: 15(15)-16(16).

80. The items in the CC's "Family Resource Center" do not, strictly speaking, have a price. Items have "suggested donation" amounts.

81. Reed, "Mobilizing the Christian Right," 35.

82. Quoted in Reed, *Politically Incorrect,* 194.

83. See Allen D. Hertzke, *Echoes of Discontent: Jesse Jackson, Pat Robertson, and the Resurgence of Populism* (Washington, D.C.: Congressional Quarterly Press, 1993).

84. Reed, *Active Faith,* 126-27. Despite the fact that Reed supported Kemp, the Robertson forces did not exclude him. "The Robertson folks knew I was a committed Christian," explained Reed, "and they allowed me to attend the convention—as an alternate." Reed, *Active Faith,* 126. In describing this incident Reed was curiously unaware of how exclusionary this seemed to be to those who are not "committed Christians." By calling his realization an "epiphany," moreover, he seemed to be endorsing the exclusion of non-Christians from political activity.

85. Quoted in "Ex-Candidate Robertson Creates New Christian Political Group," *Washington Post,* March 14, 1990: A6.

86. Reed, *Active Faith,* 128; David Shribman, "Going Mainstream: Religious Right Drops High-Profile Tactics, Works on Local Level," *Wall Street Journal,* September 26, 1989: A1; Clyde Wilcox, *God's Warriors: The Christian Right in Twentieth-Century America* (Baltimore: The Johns Hopkins University Press, 1992), 222.

87. The New York City school board elections of 1993 were an excellent example of the dynamics of national visibility and local implementation. See Sam Dillon, "Lifting a Conservative Voice: Christian Group Views School Board Elections as a Test of Voter Support," *New York Times,* April 10, 1993: I23; Sam Dillon, "Spirited Race for Schools Accelerates," *New York Times,* April 28, 1993: B2.

88. Ralph Reed, "Priorities," *Christian American,* September/October 1996: 54.

89. Ralph Reed, "How People of Faith are Changing the Soul of American Politics," speech at the National Press Club, Washington D.C., October 22, 1996.

90. "Precinct Coordinator Handbook."

91. Quoted in Mark J. Rozell and Clyde Wilcox, *Second Coming: The New Christian Right in Virginia Politics* (Baltimore: The Johns Hopkins University Press, 1996), 85.

92. "Precinct Coordinator Handbook."

93. Duane M. Oldfield, *The Right and the Righteous* (Lanham, MD: Rowman & Littlefield Publishers, Inc., 1996), 190.

94. Kim A. Lawton, "A Republican God?" *Christianity Today,* October 5, 1992: 50. For a useful discussion of the Christian Right's influence on the 1992 Republican platform committee, see Oldfield, *The Right and the Righteous,* 197-207.

95. Thomas B. Edsall, "Christian Right Avoiding Spotlight," *Washington Post,* August 14, 1996: A1; Brooks Jackson, "Religious Right, Convention Might," *CNN Inside Politics,* Cable News Network, August 8, 1996.

96. For an explanation of the methods and terms used in this study, see John F. Persinos, "Has the Christian Right Taken Over the Republican Party," *Campaigns & Elections,* September 1994: 22.

     Oldfield, in his study of the Christian Right's relationship with the Republican party, cautioned against exaggerating the importance of Persinos's findings. "Control of state party organization," wrote Oldfield, "does not necessarily mean selection or control of the party's elected officials." Despite this caveat, he characterized the Christian Right's level of strength across the country as "very impressive." Oldfield, *The Right and the Righteous,* 211-12.

97. Quoted in Persinos, "Has the Christian Right Taken Over the Republican Party," 23.

98. People for the American Way, in a 1992 survey of 550 candidates in 33 states, reported that "the Radical Right's candidates were successful in more than 40 percent of the state and local races in which they were involved." PAW also reported that "the Christian Coalition's endorsed candidates prevailed in nearly half of their races." "The Radical Right and the 1992 Election: The Stealth Campaign" (Washington, D.C.: People for the American Way, 1993), 3-4.

99. Quoted in Seth Mydans, "Evangelicals Gain With Covert Candidates," *New York Times,* October 27, 1992.

100. Quoted in Carol Innerst, "Parents Labeled Religious Fanatics for Fighting Schools: Schools Learn Ways to Pin Labels on Parental Foes," *Washington Times,* April 13, 1994: A1.

101. Quoted in Joe Conason, "The Religious Right's Quiet Revival," *The Nation,* April 27, 1992: 555. See also Robertson, *The Turning Tide,* 62-63.

102. Quoted in Hertzke, *Echoes of Discontent,* 183.

103. Quoted in Barry M. Horstman, "Crusade for Public Office in 2nd Stage," *Los Angeles Times,* March 22, 1992: B5. This quotation has also appeared in "The Radical Right and the 1992 Election: The Stealth Campaign," 1; David Cantor, *The Religious Right: The Assault on Tolerance & Pluralism in America* (New York: Anti-Defamation League, 1994), 29; Robert

Boston, *The Most Dangerous Man in America? Pat Robertson and the Rise of the Christian Coalition* (Amherst, NY: Prometheus Books, 1996).

104. Ralph Reed, *Time Online,* interview on America Online Computer Network, May 10, 1995; Thomas B. Edsall, "Christian Political Soldier Helps Revive Movement," *Washington Post,* September 10, 1993: A4.

105. Reed, "Mobilizing the Christian Right," 34.

106. "A Campaign of Falsehoods: The Anti-Defamation League's Defamation of Religious Conservatives" (Chesapeake, VA: Christian Coalition, July 28, 1994), 10.

While the charges of stealth have undoubtedly been used as a "scare tactic" by the CC's opponents, a recent CC training manual was ambiguous on the use of stealth in voter identification procedures. The "Voter Identification Script," which was so detailed that it included a blank for the name of the volunteer, did not *explicitly* say that the survey was being conducted by the CC. Phone volunteers were also reminded by the manual, "Do not solicit membership in Christian Coalition. Your purpose is to identify voters only. Provide information on the Coalition only if the respondent asks." This could be taken to mean that volunteers were not to mention the CC at all unless asked *(Citizen Action Seminar Manual,* 29, 26). It should be noted, however, that the same manual reminded those conducting door-to-door canvasses to keep a pleasant demeanor. "The way you present yourself while conducting the canvass will leave a lasting impression of the Christian Coalition on that person." This implied that canvassers should identify themselves as CC volunteers. *Citizen Action Seminar Manual,* 27.

107. Sidney Blumenthal, "Christian Soldiers," *New Yorker,* July 18, 1994: 31.

108. Ralph E. Reed, Jr., "The Good News," *Christian American,* November/December 1992: 29.

109. See Reed, *Active Faith,* 136-50; Reed, *Politically Incorrect,* 72, 110.

110. Ralph Reed, Jr. "Casting a Wider Net," *Policy Review,* Summer 1993: 35.

111. Wilcox, *God's Warriors,* 19.

112. Richard L. Berke, "Christian Right Defies Categories," *New York Times,* July 22, 1994: A1.

113. Quoted in Michael Kagay, "Growth Area Seen for Religious Right," *New York Times,* August 10, 1996: I1; Tom W. Smith, "A Survey of the Religious Right" (New York: American Jewish Committee, 1996), 42-43.

114. "The Diminishing Divide . . . American Churches, American Politics" (Louisville, KY: The Pew Research Center for the People & the Press, 1996), 5.

115. "1996 Voters at a Glance," Associated Press, November 5, 1996.

116. Quoted in Thomas B. Edsall, "Christian Coalition Threatens GOP," *Washington Post,* February 11, 1995: A6.

117. Quoted in Mundy, "The God Squad," 26.

118. Quoted in Katherine Q. Seelye, "Christian Coalition Plans a Program for Inner-City Residents," *New York Times,* January 31, 1997: A15. See also Von Drehle and Edsall, "Life of the Grand Old Party," A23.

119. Reed has often pointed to the 1993 New York City school board elections as a model of such cooperation. See Reed, *Politically Incorrect,* 7-21; Reed, "Casting a Wider Net," 34; "A Campaign of Falsehoods," 12-13.

120. Pat Robertson, "Keynote Address," speech at the 6th Annual Christian Coalition "Road to Victory" conference, Washington, D.C., September 15, 1996.

121. Quoted in Reed, *Active Faith,* 219.

122. Ralph Reed, "Ralph Reed on Catholics," interview by Deal W. Hudson, *Crisis,* November 1995: 18.

123. Reed, *Active Faith,* 219. See Gustav Niebuhr, "Christian Coalition Sees Recruiting Possibilities Among Catholics," *New York Times,* October 7, 1995: 13; Carolyn Curtis, "The Crucial Catholic Vote," *Christian American,* November/December 1995: 12-15.

124. Laurie Goodstein, "Catholics Prove Hard to Convert to the Politics of Coalition," *Washington Post,* September 2, 1996: A1; Heidi Schlumpf, "How Catholic Is the Catholic Alliance?" *Christianity Today,* May 20, 1996: 76.

125. "Catholic Alliance Cites New Status and Names New Board," Catholic Alliance press release, September 10, 1996.

126. See Ralph Reed, Speech to the 17th National Leadership Conference of the Anti-Defamation League of B'nai B'rith, Washington, D.C., April 3, 1995; also Reed's chapter "The Curse of Ham," in *Politically Incorrect,* 235-48.

127. This was my impression when I attended the 1993, 1995, and 1996 "Road to Victory" conferences. African-American speakers at these meetings included Star Parker, Congressman J. C. Watts (R-OK), Dr. Alan Keyes, Kay Coles James, Dr. E. V. Hill, Rev. Earl Jackson, Armstrong Williams, and Roy Innis. Jewish speakers included Mona Charon, Michael Medved, Rabbi Yechiel Eckstein, Rabbi Daniel Lapin, Marshall J. Breger, and Don Feder. In some cases, such as Parker, Keyes, and Lapin, audience response could be described as wildly enthusiastic.

128. See Cantor, *The Religious Right.* I will discuss the CC's response to this report in Chapter 6.

129. See Michael Lind, "Rev. Robertson's Grand International Conspiracy Theory," *The New York Review,* February 2, 1995: 21-25. I will return to this topic in Chapter 6 in my discussion of Robertson's conspiracy theory of history.

130. Reed, *Active Faith,* 214. It was fortunate that Reed did not choose to launch this affiliate at the 1996 "Road to Victory" conference. The opening day of

the conference coincided with Rosh Hashanah, the Jewish New Year. A CC spokesman explained that the dates of the 1996 conference were determined by the availability of the Washington Hilton Hotel, the only hotel in Washington with the facilities large enough for their needs. Two Rabbis who spoke at the conference were scheduled with enough time to return to their homes by sundown Friday. Laurie Goodstein and Donald P. Baker, "Politics: Coalition Schedule Angers Some Jews," *Washington Post,* September 7, 1996: A4.

131. Reed also claimed "About 3 percent is Latino and about 2 percent or 3 percent is Native American." Reed, "Ralph Reed on Catholics," 22. And according to Reed, "more than two hundred African-American and Latino pro-family activists" attended the 1995 "Road to Victory" conference. Reed, *Active Faith,* 221. If Reed's claims were accurate, with over 4000 activists in attendance, the minority presence at the conference was 5 percent.

132. Description of "Satellite Broadcast," from CC Web site (http://cc.org/cc/edu/sat.html). See also Curtis, "High Tech Activism," 20-23.

133. D. J. Gribbin, "Bridge-Building Across Racial Lines," *Christian American,* September 1995: 20-21; Reed, *Active Faith,* 220.

134. "Christian Coalition Hires Black Liaison," *Christian Century,* April 24, 1996: 448.

135. "Coalition Posts Reward in Church Arson Cases," *Christian Century,* May 8, 1996: 504-05.

136. Hollis R. Towns, "Black Leaders Mixed Over Reed Pledge," *Atlanta Constitution,* June 19, 1996: B1. For the CC's view of the interracial and interdenominational response on this issue, see Carolyn Curtis, "Coming Together," *Christian American,* September/October 1996: 22-27.

137. Quoted in Michelle Crouch, "Coalition Aids Burned Churches," Associated Press, October 18, 1996.

138. Seelye, "Christian Coalition Plans a Program for Inner-City Residents," A15; John E. Yang, "Christian Coalition Revamps Agenda to Reach Out to Inner Cities," *Washington Post,* January 31, 1997: A3; "The Samaritan Project" (Chesapeake, VA: Christian Coalition, 1997).

139. Amy Argetsinger, "Christian Coalition Courts Black Churches," *Washington Post,* May 11, 1997: A18.

140. CC spokesperson Mike Russell claimed the sample had been prepared by an outside company and faxed to the CC for approval. "The photographs were so fuzzy and dark in the fax. We approved it. We're guilty of an honest mistake." Barbara Vobejda, "Politics: Coalition Contrite Over Voter Guide," *Washington Post,* October 12, 1996: A17.

141. Quoted in Angie Cannon, "Christian Coalition Woos Blacks," *Tallahassee Democrat,* June 17, 1996: 3A.

142. Seelye, "Christian Coalition Plans a Program for Inner-City Residents," A15.

143. James M. Perry, "Soul Mates: The Christian Coalition Crusades to Broaden Rightist Political Base," *Wall Street Journal,* July 19, 1994: A1.

144. Quoted in Seelye, "Christian Coalition Plans a Program for Inner-City Residents," A15.

145. These include Ione Dilley (State Chairman, Iowa), Roberta Combs (State Chairman, South Carolina), and Maureen Roselli (the first executive director of Catholic Alliance). Both Dilley and Combs have been associated with Robertson since his presidential campaign. See James R. Wallis, Jr., "Mobilizing Christians Excites Her," *Christian American,* April 1995: 30; Barbara J. Woerner, "Top Organizer On A Roll," *Christian American,* October 1994: 12.

146. I base this assertion on my observation of "Road to Victory" conferences in 1993, 1995, and 1996.

147. "Survey Dashes Stereotypes," *Christian American,* April 1993: 5; Mike Russell, "Poll Shows GOP Exodus," *Christian American,* April 1993: 1, 4. According to this poll, these churchgoing voters, 61 percent female, were twice as likely to be Republicans as Democrats. See also Reed, *Active Faith,* 193.

148. Tom W. Smith, "A Survey of the Religious Right" (New York: American Jewish Committee, 1996), 19.

149. John C. Green, James L. Guth, Lyman A. Kellstedt, and Corwin E. Smidt, "Evangelical Realignment: The Political Power of the Christian Right," *Christian Century,* July 5-12, 1996: 678.

150. Ralph Reed, interview by Tony Snow, *Fox News Sunday,* Fox Television Network, November 10, 1996. See also "Religious Conservative Firewall Protects Pro-Family Candidates," Christian Coalition press release, November 6, 1996.

151. For a discussion of the partisanship of the CC, see Sabato and Simpson, *Dirty Little Secrets,* 103-50.

152. Ralph Reed, "One Lord, One Faith, One Voice?" symposium with Tony Campolo and Charles Colson, *Christianity Today,* October 7, 1996: 37. Of these two issues, only gambling has received much attention in CC publications. See Ronald A. Reno, "Gambling with America," *Christian American,* July/August 1996: 24-27; Reed, *Active Faith,* 222-24.

153. Robertson winked at this formal stance in his 1995 keynote speech at the "Road to Victory" conference when he recalled a goal he set for the organization in 1991: "that we would have a significant voice—actually I said something else, but Ralph [Reed] said I can't say that here tonight because we've got press—that we would have a significant voice in one of the political parties by 1994." Quoted in Thomas B. Edsall, "Robertson

Urges Christian Activists to Take Over GOP State Parties," *Washington Post,* September 10, 1995: A24. Robertson was inaccurately recalling his 1991 statement, which was "We want . . . as soon as possible to see a working majority of the Republican Party in the hands of pro-family Christians by 1996." Quoted in Thomas B. Edsall, "Christian Coalition Steps Boldly into Politics," *Washington Post,* September 10, 1992: A14.

154. Ralph Reed, "A Strategy for Evangelicals," *Christian American,* January 1993: 15.

155. At the 1993 "Road to Victory" conference, the chairman of the Democratic National Committee, David Wilhelm, gave a speech that was so critical of the CC that he was booed by many in the audience. Thomas B. Edsall, "Democratic Party Chief's Fiery Words Stir Wrath as Christian Coalition Meets," *Washington Post,* September 11, 1993: A4. For Reed's account of the Wilhelm speech, see *Active Faith,* 174-75.

In 1994, Rep. Vic Fazio (D-CA), chairman of the Democratic Congressional Campaign Committee, called religious conservatives the "fire-breathing Christian radical right." Quoted in Richard L. Berke, "Is Suffering in Silence the Democrats' Cross?" *New York Times,* August 21, 1994: IV4. For Reed's account of the press conference during which Fazio made this comment and the CC's response, see *Active Faith,* 79-80.

Also in 1994, the Rev. Jesse Jackson charged that there was "an ideological and historical connection" between the CC and Nazi Germany and southern slave holders. Quoted in Laurie Goodstein, "Jackson Offers No Apology For Blast at Christian Right," *Washington Post,* December 9, 1994: A2.

156. Reed, *Active Faith,* 234.

157. Quoted in Andrew Stern, "Christian Coalition Rallies Anti-abortion Democrats," Reuter News Service, August 26, 1996.

158. Lloyd Grove, "Ralph Reed's Invisible Army," *Washington Post,* August 28, 1996: C1.

159. Oldfield, *The Right and the Righteous,* 190.

160. Reed, *Active Faith,* 224-28.

161. Ernest Tollerson, "Christian Coalition Give Perot a Mostly Cool Reception," *New York Times,* September 14, 1996: 9.

162. Reed, "A Strategy for Evangelicals," 15.

163. Reed, "Casting a Wider Net," 32.

164. Ibid., 31.

165. Ibid., 35.

166. Much of Reed's "wider net" or mainstreaming strategy was outlined in Thomas C. Atwood, "Through a Glass Darkly," *Policy Review* (Fall 1990) 44-53. Atwood, now associated with the conservative Heritage Foundation,

served as controller of Robertson's presidential campaign. He also spoke at the 1993 "Road to Victory" conference.

167. "Winning Political Victories: Pat Robertson's Four Point Plan," *Christian American,* January/February 1991: 10. Quotation from an address to a CC Leadership School in Virginia Beach, Virginia, in November 1990.

168. Richard L. Berke, "The 'Contract' Gets New Ally On the Right," *New York Times,* January 18, 1995: A13.

169. Quoted in Catherine S. Manegold, "The New Congress: Some on Right See a Tactical Misstep on School Prayer," *New York Times,* November 19, 1994: 1. In *Active Faith,* in Reed's discussion on Gingrich's school prayer proposal, he emphasized that his opposition was based on his rejection of compulsory school prayer. Reed did not mention his statement to Manegold about tax relief and welfare (196-97).

170. Gustav Niebuhr, "The Religious Right Readies Agenda for Second 100 Days," *New York Times,* May 16, 1995: A1.

171. Ralph E. Reed, Jr.,"'Christian Right' Belongs in the GOP," interview with Allan Ryskind, *Human Events,* February 6, 1993: 11.

172. Ralph Reed, Jr., "Introduction," in *Contract with the American Family* (Nashville: Moorings, 1995), xi-xii.

173. Reed, *Active Faith,* 198.

174. Gerald F. Seib, "GOP's Religious Conservatives Poised For Campaign to Get Action on Their Agenda," *Wall Street Journal,* May 8, 1995: A16; Reed, *Active Faith,* 199-201.

175. Ira Glasser, "Open Letter to Bill Clinton, President of the United States," dated May 15, 1995 (New York: American Civil Liberties Union).

176. "Whose American Family?" (Washington, D.C.: American Jewish Congress, 1995), 1.

177. Carolyn Curtis, "Putting Out a Contract," *Christianity Today,* July 17, 1995: 54.

178. Quoted in Reed, *Active Faith,* 203.

179. Randall Terry, "Selling Out the Law of Heaven," *Washington Post,* September 18, 1994: C9.

180. Martin Mawyer, "Martin Mawyer," interview by Karen Augustine, *Rutherford,* March 1994: 12.

181. Quoted in Mike Hertenstein, "Casting the Net Overboard: Is the Religious Right FINDING or ABANDONING the Mainstream?" *Rutherford,* March 1994: 9-10.

182. Quoted in Reed, *Active Faith,* 203.

183. Quoted in Thomas B. Edsall, "Powell Proving Divisive Among Conservatives," *Washington Post,* October 23, 1995: A8. Dobson's letter, quickly made public, was also addressed to William Bennett. See also Reed, *Active Faith,* 252-53.

184. Reed, "Casting a Wider Net," 32.
185. Thomas B. Edsall, "Conservatives Seek to Revise GOP's Call for Amendment Banning Abortion," *Washington Post,* September 18, 1994: A6.
186. See Howard Fineman, "The Fight Inside the Tent," *Newsweek,* May 13, 1996: 24-27.
187. See Reed, *Active Faith,* 250-55.
188. Kevin Galvin, "Buchanan Forces Gearing Up For Abortion Battle," Associated Press, May 3, 1996.
189. Reed probably had Robertson's support in the attempt to revise the abortion plank. Robertson has discounted the importance of political party platforms. "Christians who are novices in politics," observed Robertson, "have been concerned about party platforms as statements of faith because that's the way they operate as Christians." He called it "ridiculous to spend a lot of time arguing over the arcane points of a platform" when "the name of the game is to win offices." Robertson, *The Turning Tide,* 284.

   Robertson has also signaled his willingness to de-emphasize the pursuit of a constitutional amendment outlawing abortion. In a 1993 television interview he reiterated his conviction that abortion was wrong, but he added, "It's something else, though, in the political arena to go out on a quixotic crusade when you know you'll be beaten continuously. So I say let's do what is possible. What is possible is parental consent." Quoted in Rozell and Wilcox, *Second Coming,* 81.
190. Reed, *Active Faith,* 272; Ralph Reed, "'We Stand at a Crossroads,'" *Newsweek,* May 13, 1996: 29.
191. Reed, *Active Faith,* 271.
192. Reed was also seen as cooperating with Dole campaign manager Scott Reed (no relation) to get intraparty conflicts regarding abortion out in the open and over with long before the San Diego convention in August. As Scott Reed told *Newsweek* in May 1996, "We were going to have to face this debate anyway. So why not have it now?" Fineman, "The Fight Inside the Tent," 25.
193. Reed, "'We Stand at a Crossroads,'" 29. Michael Cromartie of the Ethics and Public Policy Center in Washington, D.C., speculated that Reed had to make this distinction because of "a little internal struggle" within the CC. Quoted in "Abortion Foes Differ on Tactics," *Christian Century,* May 22-29, 1996: 567.
194. Quoted in James Bennet, "Christian Coalition Leader Denies Shifting on Abortion," *New York Times,* May 5, 1996: A1.
195. Quoted in Jason DeParle, "A Fundamental Problem," *New York Times Magazine,* July 14, 1996: 32.
196. Reed soon claimed that he had ironed out his difficulties with the Buchanans and stated "the official position of the Christian Coalition" was that "there

can be no retreat, no backpedaling, no watering down, no signal of equivocation" on the pro-life plank. Ralph Reed, interview by Judy Woodruff, *CNN Inside Politics,* Cable News Network, May 6, 1996.

197. "Pro-abortion Republicans Push for Platform Showdown," *Christian American,* July/August 1996: 16.

198. Thomas B. Edsall, "By Overriding Hyde, Dole Invited Setback on Abortion Language," *Washington Post,* August 9, 1996: A12.

199. See Jane Mayer, "Lonely Guy: Why President Clinton is Partying Alone," *New Yorker,* October 30, 1995: 58-62.

200. Reed, *Active Faith,* 212. Reed happily cited Clinton's use of triangulation as a model: "Just as Bill Clinton's denunciation of the violent lyrics of Sister Souljah—and the flap with Jesse Jackson that followed—allowed him to appeal to the middle in 1992, our willingness to address the tax issue and weather a few barbs from friends on the right gained us new admirers and grudging respect even from critics." Reed, *Active Faith,* 174.

201. Quoted in DeParle, "A Fundamental Problem," 24.

202. Quoted in ibid., 32, 38.

203. Moen, "From Revolution to Evolution," 345.

204. "To the Congress of the United States," advertisement, *USA Today,* June 25, 1990: 8A.

205. "Pro-Family Candidates Capture Key Posts," *Christian American,* Winter 1990: 1. Next to this news story, *Christian American* printed a large picture of the smiling Helms with the caption, "Conservative Champion Senator Jesse Helms." The CC gave Helms its "Defender of Freedom Award" in 1991 and its "Friend of the Family Award" in 1993 at the CC's "Road to Victory" conferences. Paul English, "Quayle and Helms Rally Religious Right," *Christian American,* January/February 1992: 1; Paul English and Connie Zhu, "Road to Victory '93," *Christian American,* October 1993: 14.

206. "Confirm Clarence Thomas to the Court," *Christian American,* September/October 1991: 12.

207. Reed, *Politically Incorrect,* 198. See also Reed, *Active Faith,* 134-36.

208. This particular quotation has appeared innumerable times in various publications. The earliest appearance seems to have been in "Robertson Regroups 'Invisible Army' into New Coalition," 35. Reed, however, has stated flatly, "I never made this statement." Reed, *Active Faith,* 297, n. 12. But when I contacted the *Christianity Today* writer, Kim A. Lawton, who had interviewed Reed, she confirmed that Reed had made this statement.

209. Quoted in Russell Chandler, "Robertson Moves to Fill Christian Right Vacuum," *Los Angeles Times,* May 15, 1990: A5.

210. Quoted in Cantor, *The Religious Right,* 30.

211. Pat Robertson, "Address to the Republican National Convention," Houston, TX, August 19, 1992.

212. Quoted in Maralee Schwartz and Kenneth J. Cooper, "Politics," *Washington Post,* August 23, 1992: A15. Robertson's statement was in a fundraising letter and referred specifically to an Equal Rights Initiative in Iowa.

213. Laurence I. Barrett, "Fighting for God and the Right Wing," *Time,* September 13, 1993: 58.

214. Some critics of the CC see this as a tactic to hide the well-known Robertson's extremism. See, for instance, Frank Rich, "Bait and Switch," *New York Times,* March 2, 1995: A15 and "Bait and Switch II," *New York Times,* April 6, 1995: A15.

215. Robertson quoted in Birnbaum, "The Gospel According to Ralph," 33. The CC is but one of many projects in Robertson's extensive complex of ministries and businesses. Reed was responsible for the day-to-day operations of the CC. But it was unlikely, however, that Reed had an entirely free hand in developing the CC's strategy and policy positions. In the absence of contrary evidence, I must assume that Robertson gave at least tacit approval to Reed's initiatives.

216. Ralph Reed, remarks at beginning of *Contract with the American Family* presentation, Washington, D.C., May 17, 1995.

217. Yet Reed's reasoning on this subject may have indicated a change of tactics rather than a change of heart. He urged members to avoid phrases "like 'religious war' and 'take over'" because of "the media's propensity to twist the meaning of our words and report them out of context. Part of this reflects our own relative inexperience; part of it betrays the worst kind of media bias. Nevertheless, we can never win until we learn to communicate effectively." Reed, "A Strategy for Evangelicals," 14. In other words, the real problem was media bias.

218. Ibid.

219. Albert Hunt, "Christian Coalition's Problem Is Secular, Not Religious," *Wall Street Journal,* July 28, 1994: A13. Reed later confirmed this. "We kicked around some alternative names, such as Citizens for a Better America and the Family Values Coalition. I liked the former, but in the end we decided that no secular-sounding organization would pacify either the media or our critics. We were Christians, and we would be wise to wear that label proudly rather than appear to be ashamed of either our faith or our mission." Reed, *Active Faith,* 129.

220. Reed, "A Strategy for Evangelicals," 14.

221. Reed, *Politically Incorrect,* 27.

222. Ibid., 135.

223. Reed, Speech to the Anti-Defamation League.

224. Rich, "Bait and Switch II," A15.

225. Reed, "Introduction," in *Contract with the American Family,* xi-xii.

226. Reed attributed the *Contract*'s unthreatening character to the Catholic "natural law training" of Susan Moska, the CC staffer who drafted the *Contract*. According to Reed, "the Roman Catholic idiom" in debating social issues is "more amenable and less abrasive against the democratic ear of Americans." The rhetoric of evangelicals, in contrast, tends "to be triumphalistic and arrogant, kingdom-oriented rather than natural law based." Reed, "Ralph Reed on Catholics," 20.

227. Reed, "Introduction," in *Contract with the American Family*, xiii.

228. "Christian Coalition Pledge Card" (Chesapeake, VA: Christian Coalition, 1995); Reed, "The Role of Religious Conservatives in the '96 Elections." See also Reed, *Active Faith*, 280-81.

229. Reed, *Politically Incorrect*, 222.

230. Reed, *Active Faith*, 255.

231. Ibid., 119.

232. Ibid., 124.

233. Ibid., 258.

234. Ibid., 261.

235. According to Reed, the government should "tolerate but not encourage homosexual conduct." Granting minority status to homosexuals, in his view, would be encouragement. Reed, *Active Faith*, 264-66.

236. "Ralph Reed Calls on Religious Conservatives to Repent of Harsh Language about Clinton, Abortion, and Gays, but His Boss Pat Robertson and the Christian Coalition Just Keep On Sinning," Washington, D.C.: Americans United for the Separation of Church and State Media Advisory, May 17, 1996.

237. Ralph Reed, "One Lord, One Faith, One Voice?" symposium with Ralph Reed, Tony Campolo, and Charles Colson, *Christianity Today*, October 7, 1996: 43.

238. Quoted in Laura Meckler, "Christian Coalition Leader Wades into Dangerous Waters," Associated Press, May 21, 1996.

239. Quoted in DeParle, "A Fundamental Problem," 24.

240. Phyllis Schlafly, "What's Going On with Bob Dole's Friends?" column, Copley News Service, May 16, 1996.

241. Although he cited no specific incidents or evidence, Oldfield observed that, "Members [of the CC] have not proven particularly enthusiastic about Reed's attempts to move beyond the social issues; local activists continue to express themselves in language that scares off potential allies. Nor have coalition members easily accepted compromising their demands to advance the interests of the party" (*The Right and the Righteous*, 223).

242. See, for example, Robin Toner, "The Right Thinkers: Some Voices in the New Political Conversation," *New York Times*, November 22, 1994: B7;

John Sedgwick, "The GOP's Three Amigos," *Newsweek,* January 9, 1995: 38-40; and Birnbaum, "The Gospel According to Ralph," 28-33.

243. "A 'Contract with the Family,'" *Christian Century,* May 24-31, 1995: 559-60; Jeffrey M. Peyton, "Family Agenda Rolls Ahead," *Christian American,* July/August 1995: 1, 4.

244. Only Governor Pete Wilson and Senator Arlen Specter, both pro-choice on abortion, did not attend.

245. Reed, "The Role of Religious Conservatives in the '96 Elections."

246. Reed, "Active Faith."

247. Richard L. Berke, "For G.O.P., Religious Right Plays Waiting Game in Iowa," *New York Times,* April 17, 1995: A1, A12; Ralph Reed, interview by Bernard Shaw, *CNN Inside Politics,* Cable News Network, February 8, 1996.

248. Ralph Reed, interview by Bernard Shaw, *CNN Inside Politics,* Cable News Network, February 8, 1996.

249. It was natural that Robertson and Reed were resistant to Buchanan, a candidate who could *directly* energize and mobilize much of the CC membership *without* Robertson or Reed as intermediaries. Other Republican candidates, such as Dole, would have to get the blessing of the CC leaders.

250. Reed, *Active Faith,* 249. Four years earlier Robertson and Reed took the same stance toward Buchanan's challenge to President George Bush. See also Oldfield, *The Right and the Righteous,* 196-97. Prior to the 1992 South Carolina primary, Reed said that it was "time to stop sending a message and wounding the President." Quoted in Ronald Smothers, "Bush Less Than Loved among the Christian Right," *New York Times,* March 10, 1992: A21.

251. Reed explained Buchanan's basic appeal to religious conservatives in terms of his unequivocal pro-life stance, rather than his economic or foreign policy views. Reed, *Active Faith,* 244. While acknowledging the diversity of economic views within the CC, Reed, a supporter of supply-sider Jack Kemp in 1988, condemned Buchanan's economic nationalism and protectionism as an "inward-turning, backward-looking economic agenda" that "would have taken the pro-family community down the failed road of Bryanism" (*Active Faith,* 246).

Reed also found that "Buchanan's opposition to aid to Israel is in sharp contrast to the staunchly pro-Israel stance of conservative evangelicals" (*Active Faith,* 248-49).

252. Reed, *Active Faith,* 241.

253. Ibid., 243-44. Reed recounted a 1993 dinner meeting with Pat and "Bay" Buchanan at which Reed promised that the CC would remain neutral in the 1996 Republican primaries but predicted that Dole would win the nomination. An "intrigued and disappointed" Pat Buchanan, according to Reed,

jokingly told him, "You just keep working on those school board races and leave the presidency to me." Reed, *Active Faith,* 238-39. According to *Newsweek,* "The Buchanans don't dispute the account." Fineman, "The Fight Inside the Tent," 26.

254. Quoted in James Bennet, "Foes of Abortion Unite on a Warning to Dole," *New York Times,* March 17, 1996: I28.

255. Reed, *Active Faith,* 243; DeParle, "A Fundamental Problem," 23.

256. Quoted in Dan Balz and Ann Devroy, "Dole Shifts Attack, Drops 'Extremist' Tag," *Washington Post,* February 23, 1996: A12.

257. Paul A. Gigot, "The Religious Right Shows Its Own Strains," *Wall Street Journal,* March 1, 1996: A14.

258. Reed, *Active Faith,* 242.

259. Edsall, "Christian Right Avoiding Spotlight," A1.

260. Mark Z. Barabak and Amy Bayer, "An Interview with the Republican Challenger: Dole 'Not Bound' By Unread Platform," *San Diego Union-Tribune,* August 11, 1996: A1.

261. The Dole campaign reportedly had to work hard to reconcile Robertson to the selection of Kemp. According to *Newsweek,* there was "a river of bad blood between Kemp and Robertson" dating from bitter clashes during the 1988 presidential primaries. Robertson and Reed had also been told previously that Kemp was not under consideration. Dole, according to *Newsweek's* unnamed sources, did not make the offer to Kemp until the CC leaders had been pacified. Howard Fineman, "Just the Ticket?" *Newsweek,* August 19, 1996: 25.

262. There were a handful of speakers, including Quayle, who articulated themes important to religious conservatives. A brief videotape excerpt from Reed's presentation of the *Contract with the American Family* was shown. None of this appeared during prime-time coverage by the networks. See Calvin Woodward, "'Values' Theme Makes Brief Comeback with Quayle On Stage," Associated Press, August 15, 1996.

263. "Conventional Wisdom Watch: The Great GOP Beach Volleyball Bounce Edition," *Newsweek,* August 26, 1996: 6.

264. At the September "Road to Victory" conference, Robertson had observed, "This campaign for the presidency is far behind. Twenty-three points is about as insurmountable an obstacle as I can think of. And in my personal opinion there's got to be a miracle from Almighty God to pull it out." Robertson quickly added: "And that could happen." Quoted in Thomas B. Edsall, "Dole Vows to Sign 'Partial-Birth' Abortion Ban," *Washington Post,* September 15, 1996: A16.

　　Three weeks later, Robertson said, "I believe that without question, we're going to have a blowout this November, maybe like unto the Goldwater matter that took place when he ran against Lyndon Johnson."

Pat Robertson, remarks on *The 700 Club*, Christian Broadcasting Network, October 7, 1996.

265. "Despite Losses, Religious Right Retains Hold on Congress; Suffers Stunning Defeat in Colorado," People for the American Way press release, November 6, 1996.

266. "Christian Coalition Campaign Influence Seems to Have Peaked," Americans United for Separation of Church and State press release, November 6, 1996.

267. Quoted in John Dart, "Vote Buoys, Bothers Local Faith Activists," *Los Angeles Times,* November 9, 1996: A1.

268. "Religious Conservative Firewall Protects Pro-Family Candidates," Christian Coalition press release, November 6, 1996.

269. "Conservative Firewall Stops Ballot Meltdown," *Christian American,* January/February 1997: 24. Emphasis in original.

270. David S. Broder, "'Five Republican Parties' Seek Leader," *Washington Post,* November 7, 1996: A23.

271. Ralph Reed, interview by Pat Robertson, *The 700 Club,* Christian Broadcasting Network, November 6, 1996.

272. Ralph Reed, "Priorities," *Christian American,* September/October 1996: 54.

273. Pat Robertson, remarks on *The 700 Club*, Christian Broadcasting Network, November 6, 1996.

274. Quoted in Gustav Niebuhr, "Christian Group Vows to Exert More Influence on the G.O.P.," *New York Times,* November 7, 1996: B10.

275. Ralph Reed, interview by Tony Snow, *Fox News Sunday,* Fox Television Network, November 10, 1996.

276. Quoted in Cal Thomas, "Should Conservatives Abandon the Republican Ship?" Los Angeles Times Syndicate, November 21, 1996.

277. For a survey of some of the post-election finger-pointing among religious conservatives, see Kim A. Lawton, "Back to the Future?" *Christianity Today,* January 6, 1996: 54-56, 69-70.

278. Quoted in Richard Lacayo, "The Next Act," *Time,* November 18, 1996: 69.

279. Reed, "Statement by Ralph Reed, Jr. Concerning His Resignation from the Christian Coalition."

280. Pat Robertson, "Pat Robertson Expresses Gratitude and Support for Ralph Reed," Christian Coalition press release, April 23, 1997.

281. John E. Yang and Laurie Goodstein, "Reed Stepping Down as Christian Coalition Leader," *Washington Post,* April 24, 1997: A6.

282. Quoted in ibid.

283. "Americans United for Separation of Church and State Deplores Ralph Reed Contribution to U.S. Politics," Americans United for Separation of Church and State press release, April 23, 1997.

284. Dan Balz, "Ralph Reed Wants to Take Movement to New Political Level," *Washington Post,* April 25, 1997: A11.

285. Mike Mills, "Murdoch to Buy Half of Family Channel," *Washington Post,* June 12, 1997: E1; Peter Baker and Laurie Goodstein, "Christian Coalition Rearranges Top Posts," *Washington Post,* June 12, 1997: A15; "CBN to Further Worldwide Evangelism with Proceeds from IFE Stock Sale," Christian Broadcasting Network press release, June 11, 1997.

286. Quoted in Richard L. Berke, "From Cabinet to Leadership of Coalition," *New York Times,* June 12, 1997: A15.

287. Ibid.; Baker and Goodstein, "Christian Coalition Rearranges Top Posts," A15.

288. Eun-Kyung Kim, "From GOP to Christian Coalition," Associated Press, June 11, 1997.

289. Oldfield, *The Right and the Righteous,* 1.

290. Rozell and Wilcox, *Second Coming,* 242-43, n. 59.

291. Ibid., 20, 25.

Chapter 5

1. Mircea Eliade, *The Sacred and the Profane* (New York: Harper & Row, 1961), 20-113.

2. See Jesse Curtis Pope, *The Restoration Ideal in American Religious Thought* (Ph.D. diss., Florida State University, 1990).

3. David Edwin Harrell, Jr., "Epilogue" in *The American Quest for the Primitive Church,* ed. Richard T. Hughes (Chicago: University of Illinois Press, 1988), 239.

4. Richard T. Hughes and C. Leonard Allen, *Illusions of Innocence* (Chicago: University of Chicago Press, 1988), 2.

5. T. Dwight Bozeman, *To Live Ancient Lives: The Primitivist Dimension of Puritanism* (Chapel Hill, NC: University of North Carolina Press, 1988).

6. Hughes and Allen, *Illusions of Innocence,* 7-14.

7. Ibid., 14.

8. Ibid., 17.

9. Mark A. Noll, Nathan O. Hatch, and George M. Marsden, *The Search for Christian America* (Westchester, IL: Crossway Books, 1984), 17.

10. Pat Robertson, *America's Dates With Destiny* (Nashville: Thomas Nelson Publishers, 1986), 36.

11. Arthur Schlesinger, Jr., *The Cycles of American History* (Boston: Houghton Mifflin Company, 1986), ix, 3.

12. The Christian Right also seeks to discredit and demonize its opponents. For a look at this polarized style of public discourse, see James Davison Hunter,

Culture Wars (New York: BasicBooks, 1991), 135-58; and James Davison Hunter, *Before the Shooting Begins* (New York: Free Press, 1994), 45-67.

13. Ralph Reed, *Active Faith* (New York: Free Press, 1996), 119.

14. Quoted in Peggy Wehmeyer, "Christian Coalition Gaining Strength," *ABC World News Tonight,* American Broadcasting Company, November 3, 1994.

15. Ralph Reed, *Politically Incorrect* (Dallas: Word Publishing, 1994), 133-35.

16. Pat Robertson, interview by Robert Novak and Fred Barnes, *Evans & Novak,* Cable News Network, April 15, 1995.

17. Pat Robertson, "A Reply to My Critics," *Wall Street Journal,* April 12, 1995: A14.

18. Pat Robertson, "The Turning Tide," *Christian American,* October 1993: 19.

19. Pat Robertson, "Power to Change America and the World," tape 4, in *Living Successfully in the '90s* (Virginia Beach, VA: Christian Broadcasting Network tape series, 1993).

20. Ralph Reed, "Active Faith: The Role of Religious Conservatism in America," address at the Town Hall, Los Angeles, California, February 12, 1996, printed in *Vital Speeches of the Day,* March 15, 1996: 331.

21. Michael Ebert, "Godly Principles Will Restore Our Independence," *Christian American,* July/August 1996: 6.

22. *Citizen Action Seminar Manual* (Chesapeake, VA: Christian Coalition, 1995), 7.

23. Christian Coalition mailing, undated.

24. It should be noted, however, that not all the proposals argued for the return of a lost and better past. The argument for "Encouraging Support for Private Charities" was based on the greater efficiency of private charities versus government welfare program. Despite the long and notable history of religious charities in America the *Contract* proposal made no appeal to the past. *Contract with the American Family* (Nashville: Moorings, 1995), 85-96.

25. Ibid., 9. In response to the CC's call for such an amendment, two versions were introduced during the 104th Congress (1995-96). With support for an amendment divided, neither version came to a vote. As of this writing, only Rep. Ernest Istook's (R-OK) so-called Religious Freedom Amendment had been reintroduced in the 105th Congress (1997-98). Reed announced that the CC would work for the passage of the Amendment. Laurie Goodstein and John E. Yang, "Separation of Church, State Targeted," *Washington Post,* March 25, 1997: A4.

      Despite differences over which version should be passed, all support-ers of an amendment justify it as a restoration of the original meaning of the First Amendment. As Istook put it, "We wouldn't need a constitutional amendment, except that un-elected judges have changed the Constitution for us. This is our only way to change it back." Quoted in "Istook and More Than 100 Co-Sponsors Introduce Religious Freedom Amendment," press release from the office of Rep. Ernest Istook (R-OK), May 8, 1997.

26. Ibid., 26.

27. Ibid., 52-56.

28. Ibid., 63.

29. Ibid., 121.

30. "Winning Political Victories: Pat Robertson's Four Point Plan," *Christian American*, January/February 1991: 10.

31. Pat Robertson, *The Turning Tide* (Dallas: Word Publishing, 1993), 302.

32. Pat Robertson, "Time to Bring America Back," *Christian American*, October 1994: 19.

33. Pat Robertson, "Law Must Embrace Morality," *Christian American*, April 1995: 17.

34. Ralph Reed, Jr., "What Religious Conservatives Really Want," in *Disciples and Democracy*, ed. Michael Cromartie (Washington, D.C.: Ethics and Public Policy Center, 1994), 3-4.

35. Ralph Reed, Jr. "Faith Essential to Democracy," *Christian American*, November/December 1994: 11.

36. Reed, *Politically Incorrect*, 39.

37. Ibid., 36-37.

38. Ibid., 137. Reed's unqualified "everyone" was particularly surprising coming from a trained historian who wrote his dissertation on nineteenth-century material. Perhaps the "everyone" was merely an oversight on Reed's part, but more likely he was surrendering to restorationism's rhetorical imperative of drawing a stark contrast between the good past and the bad present.

39. Reed, "Faith Essential to Democracy," 11.

40. See Perry Miller, *Errand into the Wilderness* (Cambridge, MA: Harvard University Press, 1984), 1-15; Sacvan Bercovitch, *The American Jeremiad* (Madison: University of Wisconsin Press, 1978).

41. Michael Lienesch, *Redeeming America* (Chapel Hill, NC: University of North Carolina Press, 1993), 141-45. Lienesch provided an interesting discussion of difficulties and confusions occasioned by the Pilgrim-Puritan duality.

42. Locating the birthplace of Christian America in tidewater Virginia was unusual but useful. Robertson is a native Virginian who claimed ancestors, including Hunt, among the early settlers. Cape Henry is, as Robertson pointed out, "just twelve air miles from my office at CBN center." Robertson, *America's Dates with Destiny*, 27. Thus by heritage, blood, and proximity Robertson connected himself, his ministry, and his politics to the foundations of Christian America. Who, therefore, could be better qualified

NOTES 241

to understand the intentions of the founders, or a better leader of Christian America's restoration? See Anne Proffitt, *Religious Rhetoric in American Political Discourse: An Examination of Pat Robertson's "America's Dates with Destiny"* (M.A. Thesis: Eastern Michigan University, 1990), 39.

43. Robertson, *America's Dates with Destiny*, 25-26.

44. Pat Robertson, *The New Millennium* (Dallas: Word Publishing, 1990), 313. Robertson also linked this date to the fulfillment of biblical prophecy. "Four hundred years from the beginning of America—ten full biblical generations—takes place on April 29, 2007. By some amazing coincidence—or might we not say foresight of God—the 400th anniversary of the greatest Gentile power that the world has ever known coincides precisely with the 40th year conclusion of the generation of the 'end of the Gentile power'" (313). He was referring, of course, to the Israeli capture of Jerusalem in the June 1967 war as the fulfillment of Luke 21:24: "And Jerusalem shall be trodden under foot of the Gentiles until the times of the Gentiles are fulfilled." Robertson made no firm predictions about 2007, "but this scenario," he wrote, "is fascinating to contemplate." (313) Robertson also presented this interpretation in his novel, *The End of the Age* (Dallas: Word Publishing, 1995), 139-40, 180-83.

45. Robertson, *America's Dates with Destiny*, 275.

46. Robertson, *The Turning Tide*, 294.

47. Quoted in "Clinton Inaugural: Celebration or Tragedy?" *Christian American,* January 1993: 28.

48. "Clinton Inaugural: Celebration or Tragedy?" 28.

49. The quoted source for these views, Gary Amos, has long connections to Robertson and the CC. He has taught at Robertson's CBN (now Regent) University School of Law and Government, and in the Winter 1990 issue of *Christian American,* Amos was listed as a "Contributing Writer." "Christian American Staff," *Christian American,* Winter 1990: 2; Gary T. Amos, *Defending the Declaration* (Brentwood, TN: Wolgemuth & Hyatt Publishers Inc., 1989) 235. The CC distributed *Defending the Declaration,* in which Amos argued for the biblical and Christian character of the Declaration.

50. Robertson also took particular exception to Clinton's "new covenant" speech at the 1992 Democratic Convention. On *The 700 Club* Robertson told viewers, "If it isn't blasphemous, it certainly borders on it." Quoted in John Wheeler, Jr., "New Covenant or Old Heresy?" *Christian American,* September/October 1992: 12.

51. See Conrad Cherry, ed., *God's New Israel* (Englewood Cliffs, NJ: Prentice-Hall, 1971).

52. Pat Robertson, "Pat's View," *Christian American,* February 1994: 2.

53. Robertson, *The Turning Tide,* 291.

54. Ibid., 300.

55. "If my people, who are called by my name, shall humble themselves, and pray, and seek my face, and turn from their wicked ways; then will I hear from heaven, and will forgive their sin, and will heal their land." Quoted in Robertson, *The New Millennium,* 93. Robertson also attributed the same significance to the "Washington for Jesus" rally in his novel *The End of the Age,* 139-40.

56. Reed, *Politically Incorrect,* 63.

57. Reed, "Faith Essential to Democracy," 10.

58. Reed, *Politically Incorrect,* 134.

59. Ibid., 266.

60. Reed, *Active Faith,* 27.

61. Pat Robertson, *The Secret Kingdom: Your Path to Love, Peace, and Financial Security,* 2d ed. (Dallas: Word Publishing, 1992), 48.

62. See Reed's discussion on how Irish Catholics forged a strong identification with the Democratic party. Reed, *Active Faith,* 214-15.

63. Robertson, *The Turning Tide,* 233.

64. Ibid., 234.

65. Robertson, *America's Dates with Destiny,* 173.

66. Robertson, *The New Millennium,* 166-67.

67. Robertson, *The Turning Tide,* 272.

68. Pat Robertson, *The New World Order* (Dallas: Word Publishing, 1991), 250. For a more detailed discussion of Robertson's conspiracy theory of history, see Chapter 6.

69. See, for instance, Thomas B. Edsall, "Powell Proving Divisive Among Conservatives, *Washington Post,* October 23, 1995: A8; Randall A. Terry, "Selling Out the Law of Heaven," *Washington Post,* September 18, 1994: C9; Mike Hertenstein, "Casting the Net Overboard: Is the Religious Right FINDING or ABANDONING the Mainstream?" *Rutherford,* March 1994: 3, 8-10, 18; and Paul A. Gigot, "The Religious Right Shows Its Own Strains," *Wall Street Journal,* March 1, 1996: A14.

70. Reed, "What Do Religious Conservatives Really Want?" 5-6.

71. Reed, *Active Faith,* 72. For a fuller discussion, see Reed's chapter "Liberalism's Hollow Core" in *Active Faith,* 70-103.

72. Ibid., 6.

73. Ralph Reed, Jr., "We Want Washington to Value Families," *Christian American,* February 1995: 16.

74. Reed, *Politically Incorrect,* 74.

75. Reed, *Active Faith,* 9.

76. Christian Coalition mailings, undated. Capitalization and emphasis in originals.

77. "Violence in America: Symptoms and Causes," *Christian American,* October 1993: 28.

78. Robertson, *The Turning Tide,* 68.

79. Robertson, *The New World Order,* 246.

80. Robertson, *The New Millennium,* 167.

81. M. G. "Pat" Robertson, "Squeezing Religion Out of the Public Square," *William & Mary Bill of Rights Journal* 4, no. 1 (1995): 224.

82. Pat Robertson, interview by Robert Novak and Fred Barnes, *Evans & Novak,* Cable News Network, April 15, 1995.

83. Robertson, "Squeezing Religion Out of the Public Square," 225.

84. *Lemon v. Kurtzmann,* 403 U.S. 602 (1971). "First, the statute must have a secular legislative purpose; second, its principal or primary effect must be one that neither advances nor inhibits religion; finally, the statute must not foster 'an excessive entanglement with religion.'"

85. Robertson, "Squeezing Religion Out of the Public Square," 240. Robertson was quoting Michael W. McConnell, "Religious Freedom at a Crossroads," *University of Chicago Law Review* 59 (1992): 144.

86. Robertson, "Squeezing Religion Out of the Public Square," 238-39.

87. Ibid., 236. For Robertson's other criticisms, see 235-57.

88. Ibid., 224.

89. Ibid., 271-73.

90. Robertson, *The Turning Tide,* 306.

91. Robertson, "Squeezing Religion Out of the Public Square," 231.

92. Amos, *Defending the Declaration,* 24, 35-74.

93. Robertson, *America's Dates with Destiny,* 91. For Robertson's explanation of the Christian origin and character of this concept, see *America's Dates with Destiny,* 66-67. The immediate source for this interpretation was probably Herbert Titus, the Dean of CBNU (later Regent University) Law School. "I am," wrote Robertson, "indebted to him for his insight and assistance in preparing *America's Dates with Destiny*" (305, n. 4). Robertson also used as a source "The Christian Legacy of America's Declaration of Independence," an unpublished work by Titus in the preparation of the discussion of "laws of nature and nature's God" (308, n. 11). I will return to the link between Robertson and Titus below in a discussion of Christian reconstructionist connections with Robertson's Regent University.

94. Robertson's view mirrors what Hughes and Allen described as the nineteenth-century American amalgamation of Enlightenment nature restorationism and Puritan restoration of the primitive church. This amalgamation, as I noted above, provided the basis for identifying the nation with the original ideal and with the possibility of its restoration (*Illusions of Innocence,* 17).

95. Robertson, "Squeezing Religion Out of the Public Square," 231-33.

96. Ibid., 234.; Robertson, *The Turning Tide,* 37; Robertson, *The New Millennium,* 297; and Robertson, *America's Dates with Destiny,* 115.

97. Pat Robertson, "Faith and Democracy," *Christian American,* November/ December 1993: 16.

98. Reed, *Active Faith,* 25.

99. Reed, *Politically Incorrect,* 79.

100. Moore's refusal to obey the court order made his case a cause célèbre for the Christian Right and its political allies. See Joseph L. Conn, "'Tear Down the Wall,'" *Church & State,* May 1997: 9(105)-13(109).

101. Reed, *Politically Incorrect,* 77.

102. Ibid., 78.

103. *Contract with the American Family,* 8.

104. Reed, *Politically Incorrect,* 79.

105. Robertson, "Squeezing Religion Out of the Public Square," 240. Robertson was quoting McConnell, "Religious Freedom at a Crossroads," 144.

106. Reed, *Politically Incorrect,* 79.

107. Reed, *Active Faith,* 9.

108. Quoted in Tim Stafford, "Move Over, ACLU," *Christianity Today,* October 25, 1993: 24.

109. Robertson, "Squeezing Religion Out of the Public Square," 276. Also see Robertson, *America's Dates with Destiny,* 92: ". . . we are a republic, ruled by representatives chosen in free elections by the people. We are not a theocracy, ruled outright by God. Nor are we a theocracy ruled by godly prophets, priests, or elders in His name. The framers did not intend that we strive to be a theocracy in any form."

110. Reed, *Active Faith,* 273.

111. Mircea Eliade, ed. *Encyclopedia of Religion* (New York: Macmillan, 1986), s.v. "Theocracy," by Dewey D. Wallace, Jr.

112. Jerald C. Brauer, "The Rule of the Saints in American Politics," *Church History* 27, no. 3 (September 1958): 241-48.

113. Brauer, "The Rule of the Saints in American Politics," 249-54.

114. See, for example, Rob Boston, *Why the Religious Right Is Wrong* (Buffalo: Prometheus Books, 1993), 181-94; Fred Clarkson, "HardCOR," *Church & State,* January 1991: 9(9)-12(12); Sara Diamond, *Spiritual Warfare: The Politics of the Christian Right* (Boston: South End Press, 1989), 130-41.

115. The best single scholarly treatment of the origins and character of Christian reconstructionism or dominion theology is Bruce Barron, *Heaven on Earth?: The Social & Political Agendas of Dominion Theology* (Grand Rapids: Zondervan Publishing House, 1992).

116. Barron, *Heaven on Earth?,* 10.

117. Anson Shupe, "The Reconstructionist Movement on the New Christian Right," *Christian Century,* October 4, 1989: 881.

118. Greg L. Bahnsen, foreword to Gary DeMar, *The Debate Over Christian Reconstruction* (Atlanta: American Vision, 1988), xvi.

119. Barron, *Heaven on Earth?,* 30-31, 37-39; Gary DeMar, "Questions Frequently Asked About Christian Reconstruction," in Gary North and Gary DeMar, *Christian Reconstruction: What It Is, What It Isn't* (Tyler, TX: Institute For Christian Economics, 1991), 90.

120. Gary North, "Preface," in Gary North and Gary DeMar, *Christian Reconstructionism: What It Is, What It Isn't,* xi; Cornelius Van Til, *The Defense of the Faith,* 2nd ed. (Phillipsburg, NJ: Presbyterian & Reformed, 1963.)

121. Rousas John Rushdoony, *The Institutes of Biblical Law* (Nutley, NJ: The Craig Press, 1973), 10.

122. Greg Bahnsen, *Theonomy in Christian Ethics* (Phillipsburg, NJ: Presbyterian and Reformed, 1977), 82. While reconstructionists have never claimed that the law justifies the Christian before God, law-keeping is clearly the means of progressive personal and social sanctification. Barron, *Heaven on Earth?,* 24-25; Rushdoony, *The Institutes of Biblical Law,* 732-38; and DeMar, "Questions Frequently Asked About Christian Reconstruction," 103-05.

123. See Rushdoony, *The Institutes of Biblical Law,* 235 for a full listing of capital offenses. Willingness to expand application of the death penalty is often offered by critics as proof of the dangers of reconstructionism, and by implication, the dangers of the reconstructionist-influenced Christian Right. See Clarkson, "HardCOR," 10; Boston, *Why the Religious Right Is Wrong,* 184; Diamond, *Spiritual Warfare,* 138; and David Cantor, *The Religious Right: The Assault on Tolerance & Pluralism in America* (New York: Anti-Defamation League, 1994), 119.

124. Barron, *Heaven on Earth?,* 25; Greg Bahnsen, "The Theonomic Position," in *God and Politics: Four Views of the Transformation of Civil Government,* ed. Gary Scott Smith (Phillipsburg, NJ: Presbyterian and Reformed, 1989), 40-42.

125. Rushdoony, *The Institutes of Biblical Law,* 1-2; North, "Preface," in *Christian Reconstructionism: What It Is, What It Isn't,* xii; and DeMar, "Questions Frequently Asked About Christian Reconstruction," 152-53.

126. David A. Rausch and Douglas E. Chismar, "The New Puritans and Their Theonomic Paradise," *Christian Century,* August 3-10, 1983: 712-15.

127. Rushdoony, *The Institutes of Biblical Law,* 4.

128. Barron, *Heaven on Earth?,* 28-29; Rushdoony, *The Institutes of Biblical Law,* 14.

129. Barron, *Heaven on Earth?,* 144-46; DeMar, "Questions Frequently Asked About Christian Reconstruction," 140-43.

130. Quoted in Lienesch, *Redeeming America,* 226.

131. See Barron, *Heaven on Earth?,* 46-52, 165-86, for a thoughtful evaluation and response to reconstructionism.

132. Rushdoony, *The Institutes of Biblical Law,* 5.

133. Barron, *Heaven on Earth?,* 135-49.

134. Ibid., 100-01.

135. Diamond, *Spiritual Warfare,* 138. Diamond also claimed that "Reconstructionism can become an ideological bridge between the Christian Right and the extremist right" such as the John Birch Society, white-supremacy groups, and neo-Nazism (*Spiritual Warfare,* 139).

136. Cantor, *The Religious Right,* 120. Cantor did not provide a source for the quotation.

137. The same quotation was given in Barron, *Heaven on Earth?,* 9. Barron cited Gary North, "The Intellectual Schizophrenia of the New Christian Right," in *The Failure of American Baptist Culture,* ed. James B. Jordan (Tyler, TX: Geneva Divinity School, 1982), 12.

138. Reconstructionists have asserted that Francis Schaeffer was influenced by Rushdoony's analysis of social problems. As I noted above, Schaeffer's intellectual influence has been widely acknowledged by Christian Right leaders and activists. Reconstructionists, therefore, are claiming to be the real intellectual source behind the Christian Right. Ronald A. Wells, "Schaeffer on America," in *Reflections on Francis Schaeffer,* ed. Ronald W. Ruegsegger (Grand Rapids: Academie, 1986), 234-35.

139. See Barron's chapter, "Go Away, You're Embarrassing Me," in *Heaven on Earth?,* 107-34.

140. Rodney Clapp, "Democracy as Heresy," *Christianity Today,* February 20, 1987: 21.

141. Cantor, *The Religious Right,* 125.

142. Shupe, "The Reconstructionist Movement on the New Christian Right," 882.

143. Clapp, "Democracy as Heresy," 21; Barron, *Heaven on Earth?,* 12.

144. *Regent University Graduate Catalog, 1992-94* (Virginia Beach, VA: Regent University, 1992), 7.

145. Ibid., 10.

146. Barron, *Heaven on Earth?,* 19.

147. "Our Christian Duty to Vote," *Christian American,* September/October 1992: 24.

148. Quoted in "Robertson Bullish on Family Channel, UPI," *Christianity Today,* June 22, 1992: 51-52.

149. Gary DeMar, "Letters," *Christianity Today,* August 17, 1992: 10.

150. Barron, *Heaven on Earth?,* 14.

151. Ibid., 64. For some rather pointed expressions of reconstructionist contempt for the Christian Right in general, and Robertson in particular, see Jeanne Pugh, "Righter Than Thou," *Church & State,* June 1996: 12(132).

152. John Lofton, "Why Is Ralph Reed Saying He Would Vote for and Actively Support a Politically Correct Atheist Against a Politically Incorrect Christian?" one-page flier (P.O. Box 1142, Laurel, MD 20707). By "quietly distributed," I mean that a lone individual handed me this piece of literature but did not try to engage me in conversation about its contents.

        Lofton has his own publication, *The Lofton Letter,* and is a staff writer for Rushdoony's monthly publication, *Chalcedon Report.*

153. Gary DeMar, "Oh, Brother!" *Biblical Worldview,* May 1995: 4. DeMar was referring specifically to Reed's April 1995 speech to the Anti-Defamation League.

154. Gary DeMar, "What's Wrong with the Christian Coalition?" *Biblical Worldview,* October 1996: 11-12. Emphasis in original.

155. Jay Rogers, "A Book Review: *Politically Incorrect* by Ralph Reed," *Chalcedon Report,* February 1995: 38-40.

156. Barron, *Heaven on Earth?,* 53-66.

157. Ibid., 55.

158. See Robertson, *America's Dates with Destiny,* 305, n. 4, 308, n. 11.

159. See David Margolick, "At the Bar," *New York Times,* October 10, 1993: B10; Mark O'Keefe, "Ex-regent Dean: His Views Got Him Fired," *The Virginian-Pilot & The Ledger-Star,* January 23, 1994: B1; Roy Maynard, "Titus Breaks His Silence," *World,* February 5, 1994: 22-24; and Jennifer Ferranti, "Regent University Wins Faculty Tenure Lawsuit," *Christianity Today,* October 2, 1995: 104.

160. Quoted in Maynard, "Titus Breaks His Silence," 24. Reconstructionist Gary North interpreted Titus's firing as Robertson's willingness to sell out to the secular humanist American Bar Association in order to get accreditation for the Regent Law School. Gary North, "Letter to Institute for Christian Economics Subscribers," (Tyler, TX: Institute for Christian Economics, April 1994).

161. Reed, *Active Faith,* 261-62.

162. The USTP has been seen as being strongly influenced by reconstructionism. Mary Jacoby, "Another Convention: Tiny U.S. Taxpayers Party Represents a Minority within a Minority," *Chicago Tribune,* August 15, 1996: 1,1. Reconstructionist founder Rushdoony was a scheduled speaker at their national convention, August 15-18, 1996, in San Diego. See the USTP Web site at http://www.USTaxpayers.org.

163. Stephen Coakley, "Messages from the USTP Campaign News Hotline," September 14, 1996, USTP Web site at http://www.USTaxpayers.org.

164. "Christian Coalition 'Excludes' Pro-Life Presidential Candidate," U.S. Taxpayers Party Press Release, September 13, 1996. The "exclusion" of Phillips was far from total. The USTP campaign bus was parked on the street in front of the conference hotel, the Washington Hilton. This permitted Phillips easy access to conference participants as they entered or left the hotel. And on several occasions, I personally observed Phillips inside the hotel wearing an official conference name tag and talking with participants.

165. Titus became the vice-presidential nominee of the U.S. Taxpayers Party (USTP) at their national convention, August 15-18, 1996 in San Diego. See the USTP Web site at http://www.USTaxpayers.org.

166. See, for example, Laurence R. Iannaccone, "Heirs to the Protestant Ethic? The Economics of American Fundamentalists," in *Fundamentalisms and the State,* eds. Martin E. Marty and R. Scott Appleby (Chicago: University of Chicago Press, 1993), 349, 363, n. 35.

167. Robertson, *The Secret Kingdom,* 2d ed., 243.

168. Ibid., 245.

169. See, for instance, Harvey Cox, "The Warring Visions of the Religious Right," *The Atlantic Monthly,* November 1995: 66-68.

170. Pat Robertson with Bob Slosser, *The Secret Kingdom* (Nashville: Thomas Nelson Publishers, 1982), 210-23; Robertson, *The Secret Kingdom,* 2d ed., 251-65.

171. Robertson, *The End of the Age,* 133-52.

172. Robertson's inductive formulation of these universal "laws" from biblical texts clearly owed its method to the traditions of Baconian science and Common Sense Realism that reconstructionist presuppositionalism has rejected.

173. Robertson, *The Secret Kingdom,* 45; *The Secret Kingdom,* 2d ed., 49.

174. Barron, *Heaven on Earth?,* 86-88.

175. Robertson, *The Secret Kingdom,* 45; *The Secret Kingdom,* 2d ed., 49.

176. Reed, *Politically Incorrect,* 27.

177. Ralph Reed, "The Role of Religious Conservatives in the '96 Elections," speech at the 5th Annual Christian Coalition "Road to Victory" conference, Washington, D.C., September 8, 1995.

178. Ralph Reed, "Active Faith," speech at the 6th Annual Christian Coalition "Road to Victory" conference, Washington, D.C., September 13, 1996.

179. Evidence that both pre- and postmillennialists have been involved in the CC can be found in a study by Steven G. Dyer, an M.A. student in Regent University's School of Public Policy. Dyer's 1992 M.A. thesis was based on a survey of thirty regional and state leaders of the CC. He found that 10 percent of these leaders identified themselves as postmillennialists, adherents of Christian reconstruction or kingdom now teachings. A majority (58

percent) were premillennialist or dispensationalist, and, perhaps most interesting, 30 percent were undecided or uncertain of their eschatological views. Steven G. Dyer, "The Effect of Eschatology on the Christian Right: A Survey of Christian Coalition Leaders" (M.A. Thesis: Regent University, 1992), 35.

      While Dyer's study cannot tell us about eschatological views within the CC today, it suggests that in its early phases, at least, the CC did not depend on appeals to a particular eschatological viewpoint.

180. Rogers, "A Book Review," 40. Rogers, however, offered no evidence to support this assertion.
181. Gary DeMar, "Where Do We Go from Here?" *Biblical Worldview,* December 1996: 2.
182. Reed, "What Do Religious Conservatives Really Want?," 4.
183. Robertson, *The New World Order,* 205.
184. Robertson, *The Secret Kingdom,* 2d ed., 200.
185. Robertson, *The New Millennium,* 64.
186. Robertson, *The Secret Kingdom,* 2d ed., 11.

Chapter 6

1. It is a common accusation that Christian Right complaints about anti-Christian discrimination are put forward without specifics and are probably propagandistic fabrications. The CC's *Religious Rights Watch,* however, has always provided the name, address, and phone number of a specific public official or organizational executive to contact regarding a given incident. Whether there is any substance to an allegation needs to be investigated on a case-by-case basis, but the CC has provided enough specific information to at least begin such investigation.
2. John Wheeler, Jr., "Assault on Faith: Liberals Launch Campaign of Bigotry," *Christian American,* September 1994: 1.
3. "ADL Guilty of Defamation," *Christian American,* September 1994: 5; David Cantor, *The Religious Right* (New York: Anti-Defamation League, 1994).
4. "A Campaign of Falsehoods: The Anti-Defamation League's Defamation of Religious Conservatives" (Chesapeake, VA: Christian Coalition, July 28, 1994), 1.
5. "Christian Americans Are Tired of Getting Stepped On," pamphlet (Chesapeake, VA: Christian Coalition, 1992).
6. Christian Coalition mailing, undated.
7. Christian Coalition mailing, undated. Emphasis in original.
8. Christian Coalition mailing, undated. Emphasis in original.
9. Christian Coalition mailing, July 30, 1996.

10. Ralph Reed, "Active Faith," speech at the 6th Annual Christian Coalition "Road to Victory" conference, Washington, D.C., September 13, 1996.

11. *Contract with the American Family* (Nashville: Moorings, 1995), 2.

12. Ibid., 6.

13. Pat Robertson, *The New Millennium* (Dallas: Word Publishing, 1990), 63.

14. Pat Robertson, *The Turning Tide* (Dallas: Word Publishing, 1993), 305-20. Robertson claimed these stories were "just a sampling of the incidents that have taken place over the past few years." (307) The appendix concentrated on the accomplishments of the American Center for Law and Justice (ACLJ), an organization created by Robertson in 1990 as a Christian counterpart to the American Civil Liberties Union (ACLU). The ACLJ is headquartered on the campus of Robertson's Regent University.

15. See Pat Robertson, "Law Must Embrace Morality," *Christian American,* April 1995: 16-17.

16. Ralph Reed, *Politically Incorrect* (Dallas: Word Publishing, 1994), 43.

17. Ralph Reed, *Active Faith* (New York: Free Press, 1996), 25. Reed may have been referring to a biography of Wallace by his dissertation director, Dan T. Carter, *The Politics of Rage* (New York: Simon & Schuster, 1996). Carter argued that Wallace was "the most influential loser in twentieth-century American politics," (468) whose "politics of rage" paved the way for the social conservatism of Ronald Reagan and the Christian Right. Carter also noted that the Christian Right, as represented by Reed, had "resisted identification with the legacy of George Wallace." (466) Carter did not mention that Reed is his former student.

18. See Reed, *Politically Incorrect,* 53-65.

19. Ibid., 6.

20. On the significance of martyrdom in religious traditions, as well as in political movements, see Mircea Eliade, *Encyclopedia of Religion* (New York: Macmillan, 1986), s.v. "Martyrdom," by Samuel Z. Klausner.

21. Robertson, *The New Millennium,* 7. Robertson did not give credit to the author of this aphorism, the second-century church father, Tertullian.

22. Pat Robertson, *Answers to 200 of Life's Most Probing Questions* (Nashville: Thomas Nelson Publishers, 1984), 22-23.

23. Ibid., 156.

24. Ibid.

25. "Hate Crimes Against Christians," *Christian American,* November/December 1992: 28.

26. See Robertson, *Answers to 200 of Life's Most Probing Questions,* 156; Pat Robertson, *The New World Order* (Dallas: Word Publishing, 1991), 256-57; Pat Robertson, *The End of the Age* (Dallas: Word Publishing, 1995), 297-300.

27. These parallels have been noted by Steve Bruce, *The Rise and Fall of the Christian Right* (Oxford: Clarendon Press, 1988), 172; Matthew Moen, *The Transformation of the Christian Right* (Tuscaloosa: University of Alabama Press. 1992), 131; Stephen L. Carter, *The Culture of Disbelief* (New York: BasicBooks, 1993), 180-81; Sanford Levinson, "Some Reflections on Multiculturalism, 'Equal Concern and Respect,' and the Establishment Clause of the First Amendment," *University of Richmond Law Review* 27 (1993): 989-1021.

28. See Christine E. Sleeter and Carl A. Grant, "An Analysis of Multicultural Education in the United States," *Harvard Educational Review* 57, 4 (November 1987): 421-44. For a useful collection of essays demonstrating the variety of interpretations of multiculturalism, see David Theo Goldberg, ed., *Multiculturalism: A Critical Reader* (Oxford, UK: Blackwell, 1994).

29. "No One Model American: A Statement on Multicultural Education," *The Journal of Teacher Education,* Winter 1973: 264.

30. Richard M. Merelman, "Racial Conflict and Cultural Politics in the United States," *The Journal of Politics* 56, no. 1 (February 1994): 12.

31. Susan Auberbach, ed. *Encyclopedia of Multiculturalism.* (New York: Marshall Cavendish, 1994), s.v. "Multiculturalism," by Susan D. Greenbaum.

32. Merelman, "Racial Conflict and Cultural Politics in the United States," 12.

33. Arthur Schlesinger, Jr., "The Cult of Ethnicity, Good and Bad," *Time,* July 8, 1991: 21.

34. Richard Rorty, "The Unpatriotic Academy," *New York Times,* February 13, 1994: IV15.

35. In an essay responding to Ravitch, Molefi Kete Asante, a professor of African American Studies at Temple University, rejected this distinction. "She posits a *pluralist* multiculturalism—a redundancy—then suggests a *particularistic* multiculturalism—an oxymoron—in order to beat a dead horse." Molefi Kete Asante, "Multiculturalism: An Exchange," *American Scholar,* Spring 1991: 269. Emphasis in original. Asante argued that Ravitch's insistence on a common culture was merely a way to perpetuate white supremacy—the dead horse. "The real division on the question of multiculturalism," wrote Asante, "is between those who truly seek to maintain a Eurocentric hegemony over the curriculum and those who truly believe in cultural pluralism without hierarchy. Ravitch defends the former view" (271).

36. Diane Ravitch, "Multiculturalism: E Pluribus Plures." *American Scholar,* Summer 1990: 340-42.

37. Diane Ravitch, "Multiculturalism: An Exchange," *American Scholar,* Spring 1991: 276.

38. Robertson, *The Turning Tide,* 199.

39. Dinesh D'Souza, *Illiberal Education* (New York: Free Press, 1991), 13.

40. "A Curriculum of Inclusion: Report of the Commissioner's Task Force on Minorities: Equity and Excellence,"(New York: New York State Special Task Force on Equity and Excellence in Education, July 1989), iii. Quoted in Arthur Schlesinger, Jr., *The Disuniting of America* (New York: Norton, 1992), 66.

41. Henry Louis Gates, Jr., *Loose Canons* (New York: Oxford University Press, 1992), 188.

42. Henry Louis Gates, Jr., "A Bad Case of Academic Altruism," *New York Times,* December 9, 1990: IV5.

43. Keith A. Roberts, *Religion in Sociological Perspective,* 3d ed. (Belmont, CA: Wadsworth Publishing Company, 1995), 71.

44. See Luther P. Gerlach and Virginia H. Hine, *People, Power, Change: Movements of Social Transformation* (Indianapolis: Bobbs-Merrill Company, Inc., 1970) 183-97. Opposition was one of five key factors that Gerlach and Hine described. The other four were decentralized organization, face-to-face recruitment, a personal commitment experience, and an ideology. (xvii)

45. Gerlach and Hine, *People, Power, Change,* 185-86.

46. David Gates, "White Male Paranoia: New Victims or Just Bad Sports?" *Newsweek,* March 29, 1993: 3.

47. Shelby Steele, *The Content of Our Character: A New Vision of Race in America* (New York: St. Martin's Press, 1990), 8. Emphasis in original.

48. Steele, *The Content of Our Character,* 4. Emphasis in original.

49. D'Souza, *Illiberal Education,* 243.

50. Ibid., 242-43.

51. Robertson, *The Turning Tide,* 211-12.

52. Ibid., 117.

53. "If There's Safety in Numbers for Christians, This Is a Safety Pin," advertisement, *Christian American,* Fall 1990: 7.

54. "Christian Americans Are Tired of Getting Stepped On."

55. Christian Coalition mailing, undated. Emphasis in original.

56. "Christians Must Stand Together," *Christian American,* March 1993: 28.

57. Reed, *Politically Incorrect,* 24.

58. Ibid.

59. Quoted in "Christian Coalition Opposes Federal Election Commission's Attempt to Suppress First Amendment Rights of People of Faith," Christian Coalition press release, July 30, 1996.

60. Quoted in "Christian Coalition Sued by FEC," *National Liberty Journal,* September 1996: 8.

61. Christian Coalition mailing, dated July 30, 1996.

62. Quoted in Laurie Goodstein, "Christian Coalition Set For Voter Guide Blitz," *Washington Post,* November 2, 1996: A3.

63. While many of these letters were rather polite protests, many letters were outpourings of anger and outrage—name calling, harsh judgments upon the souls of the FEC commissioners, and dire apocalyptic warnings. Toni Locy, "FEC Lawsuit Against Christian Coalition Triggers Avalanche of Protest Letters," *Washington Post,* October 17, 1996: A9.

64. See, for example, Reed, *Politically Incorrect,* 53-57, 61; Robertson, *The Turning Tide,* 129-48.

65. Michael Weisskopf, "Energized by Pulpit or Passion, the Public is Calling," *Washington Post,* February 1, 1993: A10. Robertson took exception to the term "followers." In *The Turning Tide* he wrote: "most television talk show hosts have viewers—in *Post*-speak I have 'followers'" (143).

66. Quoted in Jon Meacham, "What the Religious Right Can Teach the New Democrats," *Washington Monthly,* April 1993: 43.

67. "Corrections," *Washington Post,* February 2, 1993: A3.

68. Quoted in "Washington Post Retracts," *Christian American,* March 1993: 7. The following Sunday, *Post* editorial page columnist Joann Byrd lamented the "stereotypical thinking," "blind spots," and "unexamined assumptions" that permitted Weisskopf's offensive statement to go unchallenged by the newspaper's editors. Byrd urged journalists to "get serious about their presumptions regarding any group whose backgrounds and beliefs and back-yard fences they do not share." Joann Byrd, "Blind Spots," *Washington Post,* February 7, 1993: C6.

69. Heidi Scanlon, "Fashionable Bigotry Against Evangelicals," *Christian American,* March 1993: 7.

70. "Liberal Media Elite Stigmatizes Evangelicals," *Christian American,* March 1993: 28. According to *Christian American,* Weisskopf was only willing to admit that evangelicals should be described as "relatively" rather than "largely" poor, uneducated, and easy to command. Quoted in "Washington Post Retracts," 7.

71. Quoted in "Washington Post Retracts," 7.

72. Quoted in Gustav Niebuhr, "Broadcasters Urged To Wage 'Cultural War,'" *Washington Post,* February 20, 1993: D8.

73. Robertson, *The Turning Tide,* 106.

74. Ibid., 144.

75. Christian Coalition mailing, undated. Emphasis in original.

76. Ralph Reed, Jr., "Putting a Friendly Face on the Pro-family Movement," *Christian American,* April 1993: 29. See also Ralph Reed, "Ralph Reed on Catholics," interview by Deal W. Hudson, *Crisis,* November 1995: 20; Reed, *Active Faith,* 193.

77. Ralph Reed, Jr., "Introduction," in *Contract with the American Family* (Nashville: Moorings, 1995), ix.

78. Reed, *Politically Incorrect,* 9. This phrase has been used so often that Reed, who was usually careful with his notes, did not bother to provide a citation.

79. "Religious Right Fashion Trends," *Time,* March 15, 1993: 15.

80. Robert Sullivan, "An Army of the Faithful," *New York Times Magazine,* April 25, 1993: 44.

81. Ralph Reed, "The Role of Religious Conservatives in the '96 Elections," speech at the 5th Annual Christian Coalition "Road to Victory" conference, Washington, D.C., September 8, 1995.

82. Quoted in Thomas B. Edsall, "Robertson Urges Christian Activists to Take Over GOP State Parties," *Washington Post,* September 10, 1995: A24.

83. Reed, *Active Faith,* 165.

84. Robertson, *The Turning Tide,* 309.

85. Christian Coalition mailing, undated. Emphasis in the original.

86. Robertson, *The Turning Tide,* 312.

87. Reed, *Politically Incorrect,* 41.

88. Ralph Reed, "Remarks to the Detroit Economic Club, January 17, 1995: Christian Coalition and an Agenda for the New Congress," *Contract with the American Family,* 143.

89. Robertson, *The Turning Tide,* 305.

90. Reed, "The Role of Religious Conservatives in the '96 Elections."

91. Robertson, *The Turning Tide,* 144.

92. Reed, *Politically Incorrect,* 41.

93. Ralph Reed, "The Role of Religious Conservatives in the '96 Elections," speech at the 5th Annual Christian Coalition "Road to Victory" conference, Washington, D.C., September 8, 1995. See also Reed, *Active Faith,* 63-65, 281.

94. Reed, *Politically Incorrect,* 13.

95. Ralph Reed, "A Strategy for Evangelicals," *Christian American,* January 1993: 14. See also Reed, *Active Faith,* 70-103.

96. See Reed, *Politically Incorrect,* 222.

97. Reed quoted in Steven V. Roberts, "Onward Christian Soldiers," *U.S. News & World Report,* June 6, 1994: 43.

98. Reed, *Politically Incorrect,* 41.

99. Ibid., 55.

100. "Religious Bigotry Backfires in Virginia," *Christian American,* November/ December 1993: 8.

101. "What's Happening to Religious Freedom Is Enough to Make You Gag," *Christian American,* Summer 1990: 6.

102. "The 'Ghettoizing of the Gospel," *Christian American,* January 1993: 28.

103. Pat Robertson, "'Earned the right to speak . . . without being savaged,'" *Miami Herald,* July 18, 1990: 11A. Robertson was responding to an editorial entitled, "Yield Not, Governor to Political Temptation," *Miami Herald,* July 8, 1990: 2E, and to columnist Carl Hiaasen, "Rev. Pat Goes to Bat for Martinez," *Miami Herald,* July 11, 1990: 1B.

104. "Cartoon Portrays Christians as Rats," *Christian American,* April 1993: 6.

105. Instead, Reed has recounted how that epithet has been unfairly applied to religious conservatives. See Reed, *Politically Incorrect,* 60-61; Ralph Reed, "Speech to the 17th National Leadership Conference of the Anti-Defamation League of B'nai B'rith," Washington, D.C., April 3, 1995.

106. Reed, "Speech to the 17th National Leadership Conference of the Anti-Defamation League of B'nai B'rith."

107. M. G. "Pat" Robertson, "Squeezing Religion Out of the Public Square," *William & Mary Bill of Rights Journal* 4, no. 1 (1995): 227-28. Robertson borrowed this term from Keith A. Fournier with William D. Watkins, *A House United? Evangelicals and Catholics Together—A Winning Alliance for the 21st Century* (Colorado Springs, CO: NavPress; Virginia Beach, VA: Liberty, Life and Family, 1994), 152. Fournier was the Executive Director of the American Center for Law and Justice (ACLJ), a public-interest law firm founded by Robertson. In March 1997, Fournier became the President of the CC's affiliate, Catholic Alliance.

108. Quoted in Wheeler, "Assault on Faith," 4.

109. Scanlon, "Fashionable Bigotry Against Evangelicals," 7.

110. Reed, *Politically Incorrect,* 42.

111. Guy Rodgers, "The Media Just Doesn't Get It," *Christian American,* April 1993: 31. The phrase was originally used to describe the all-male Senate Judiciary Committee during the Thomas-Hill sexual harassment controversy in 1991. Rodgers's use of the phrase is ironic in light of the CC's staunch support for Thomas's nomination to the Supreme Court.

112. Pat Robertson, "Faith and Democracy," *Christian American,* November/December 1993: 17.

113. Carolyn Curtis, "Coming Together," *Christian American,* September/October 1996: 27.

114. Reed, *Politically Incorrect,* 73.

115. Quoted in "Christian Coalition and Jewish Leaders Denounce Jackson Slur," Christian Coalition press release, December 7, 1994. See also James R. Wallis, Jr., "Reed Refutes Jackson Slander," *Christian American,* January 1995: 6; Laurie Goodstein, "Jackson Offers No Apology for Blast at Christian Right," *Washington Post,* December 9, 1994: A2.

116. "A Campaign of Falsehoods," 22.

117. "Hate Crimes Against Christians," 28. See also "Radical Attacks on Churches Increasing," *Christian American,* July/August 1994: 18.

118. Reed, "A Strategy For Evangelicals," 15.

119. Reed, "Putting a Friendly Face on the Pro-Family Movement," 28.

120. Reed, *Politically Incorrect,* 6.

121. Schlesinger, *The Disuniting of America,* 49.

122. Ibid., 55.

123. John V. Kelleher, "A Long Way from Tipperary," review of *To the Golden Door* by George Potter, *Reporter,* May 12, 1960: 44. Quoted in Schlesinger, *The Disuniting of America,* 56.

124. Schlesinger, *The Disuniting of America,* 68.

125. Works that present this view of history include George G. M. James, *Stolen Legacy* (New York: Philosophical Library, 1954; repr., San Francisco: Julian Richardson Associates, 1988); Martin Bernal, *Black Athena: The Afro-Asian Roots of Classical Civilization* (London: Free Association Press, 1987).

126. Robertson, *The New Millennium,* 68.

127. Pat Robertson, *The Secret Kingdom: Your Path to Peace, Love, and Financial Security,* 2d ed. (Dallas: Word Publishing, 1992), 60.

128. Reed, *Politically Incorrect,* 154.

129. Ibid.

130. Ibid., 141.

131. Ibid., 141-55; Reed, *Active Faith,* 27-69.

132. Compare Reed's evaluation of the Social Gospel movement and the New Deal in *Active Faith* (40-44, 52-55) with that of Robertson in *America's Dates with Destiny* (Nashville: Thomas Nelson Publishers, 1986), 181, 208-19.

133. Reed, *Active Faith,* 26.

134. Reed, *Politically Incorrect,* 237.

135. Reed, *Active Faith,* 68.

136. Gary T. Amos, *Defending the Declaration: How the Bible and Christianity Influenced the Writing of the Declaration of Independence* (Brentwood, TN: Wolgemuth & Hyatt, 1989).

137. William J. Federer, ed. *America's God and Country Encyclopedia of Quotations* (Coppell, TX: Fame Publishing Inc., 1994).

138. David Barton, *The Myth of Separation* (Aledo, TX: Wallbuilder Press, 1992), 145.

139. Ibid., 9.

140. See Luc Ferry and Alain Renaut, *French Philosophy of the Sixties: An Essay on Antihumanism* (Amherst: University of Massachusetts Press, 1990).

141. Paul Berman, "Introduction," in *Debating P.C.,* ed. Paul Berman (New York: Dell Publishing, 1992), 6-7.

142. Berman, "Introduction," in *Debating P.C.,* 13-14.

143. Antonio Gramsci, *A Gramsci Reader: Selected Writings 1916-1935,* ed. David Forgacs (London: Lawrence and Wishart, 1988), 423.

144. For a discussion of the nature of consent, see Thomas R. Bates, "Gramsci and the Theory of Hegemony," *Journal of the History of Ideas* 36 (April-June 1975): 351-66.

145. Richard M. Merelman, *Representing Black Culture: Racial Conflict and Cultural Politics in the United States* (New York: Routledge, 1995), 6.

146. Merelman, "Racial Conflict and Cultural Politics," 11.

147. Quoted in Jerry Adler, "Taking Offense," *Newsweek,* December 24, 1990: 54.

148. Richard Hofstadter, *The Paranoid Style in American Politics and Other Essays* (New York: Alfred A. Knopf, 1965).

149. Ibid., xii.

150. Ibid., 4.

151. Ibid., 29.

152. Ibid., 32.

153. Paula S. Rothenberg, "Critics of Attempts to Democratize the Curriculum Are Waging a Campaign to Misrepresent the Work of Responsible Professors," in *Debating P.C.,* ed. Paul Berman (New York: Dell Publishing, 1992), 266.

154. Paula S. Rothenberg, ed. *Racism and Sexism: An Integrated Study* (New York: St. Martin's Press, 1988), 4.

155. Paul Berman, "Intellectuals After the Revolution: What's Happened Since the Sixties?" *Dissent,* Winter 1989: 92.

156. Robertson used this term throughout *The Turning Tide.*

157. George Marsden, *Understanding Fundamentalism and Evangelicalism* (Grand Rapids: William B. Eerdmans, 1991) 122-52.

158. Robertson, *The Turning Tide,* 22-23.

159. Ibid., 181.

160. Ibid., 180.

161. Ibid., 69.

162. Ibid., 196.

163. George Will, "Here Come the Eager Beavers," *Newsweek,* November 16, 1992: 100. Quoted in Robertson, *The Turning Tide,* 17.

164. Robertson, *The Turning Tide,* 17.

165. Ibid., 20.

166. Ibid., 302.

167. Robertson, *The New World Order,* 257.

168. See ibid., 117-43.

169. Ibid., 176.

170. Ibid., 213.

171. Ibid., 257.

172. Ibid.

173. Robertson, however, has denied that he holds a conspiracy theory of history. "I do not believe," wrote Robertson, "in a 'conspiracy theory of world history.'" Pat Robertson, "Our Foreign Policy Should Put U.S. First," *New York Times,* March 5, 1995: IV4; see also Pat Robertson, "A Reply to My Critics," *Wall Street Journal,* April 12, 1995: A14.

　　But it is hard to see how Robertson's ideas in *The New World Order* could be described as anything else but a conspiratorial interpretation of events. Even a review of *The New World Order* published in the CC publication *Christian American* identified Robertson as an advocate of a conspiracy theory of history. "One cannot discuss this book without discussing the conspiracy view of history." Steven W. Fitschen, "The Not So New World Order," *Christian American,* January/February 1992: 12. This review appeared *in Christian American* directly above an advertisement that offered a copy of *The New World Order* to new members of the CC.

174. Robertson, *The New World Order,* 9.

175. Ibid., 13-14.

176. Ibid., 37.

177. Hofstadter, *Paranoid Style,* xii.

178. For a list of such power centers, see Robertson, *The New World Order,* 96.

179. Ibid., 97.

180. Ibid., 263.

181. Ibid., 243.

182. Hofstadter, *Paranoid Style,* 3.

183. Ibid., 3-28.

184. Richard Hofstadter, *The Age of Reform: From Bryan to F.D.R.* (New York: Alfred A. Knopf, 1955), 77-81.

185. Michael Lind, "Rev. Robertson's Grand International Conspiracy Theory," *New York Review,* February 2, 1995: 21-25. See also Michael Lind, "On Pat Robertson: His Defenders," *New York Review,* April 20, 1995: 67-68; Jacob Heilbrunn, "His Anti-Semitic Sources," *New York Review,* April 20, 1995: 68-71. Lind's charges had been anticipated in Cantor, *The Religious Right,* 23-25.

186. See Gustav Niebuhr, "Pat Robertson Says He Intended No Anti-Semitism in Book He Wrote Four Years Ago," *New York Times,* March 4, 1995: 10; Jonathan Kaufman, "Some Liberal Jews, to Their Own Surprise, See a Rise in Bigotry," *Wall Street Journal,* March 8, 1995: A1; Frank Rich, "Bait and Switch," *New York Times,* March 2, 1995: A23; Frank Rich, "Bait and Switch II," *New York Times,* April 6, 1995: A15; and Norman Podhoretz, "In the Matter of Pat Robertson," *Commentary,* August 1995: 27-32.

187. Lind, "Rev. Robertson's Grand International Conspiracy Theory," 25.

188. Podhoretz, "In the Matter of Pat Robertson," 31.

189. Quoted in Niebuhr, "Pat Robertson Says He Intended No Anti-Semitism in Book He Wrote Four Years Ago," 10.

190. Robertson, *The New World Order,* 249-68.

191. It can be argued that support for Israel, such as Robertson's, that is based on the prophetic role of the Jews, their future suffering, and their eventual conversion to Christianity, is a subtle form of anti-Semitism. For a useful overview of the essential ambivalence toward Jews in American evangelical prophecy belief, see Paul Boyer, *When Time Shall Be No More* (Cambridge, MA: Belknap Press, 1992), 181-224.

192. Robertson, *The New World Order,* 256.

193. Pat Robertson, "Two Letters and Excerpts from Book," *New York Times,* March 4, 1995: 10; Pat Robertson, "Anti-Semitism Not Acceptable," *Christian American,* April 1995: 27.

194. Reed, *Politically Incorrect,* 74.

195. Ibid., 75.

196. Ibid., 115.

197. Reed, *Active Faith,* 8.

198. Reed, *Politically Incorrect,* 130.

199. Ibid., 167.

200. Ibid., 71.

201. Ibid., 72.

202. Ibid., 58.

203. Ibid., 72.

204. Reed, *Active Faith,* 148.

205. Reed, *Politically Incorrect,* 72.

206. Reed, *Active Faith,* 75.

207. Ibid., 79.

208. Reed, *Politically Incorrect,* 71.

209. Ibid.

210. Reed, *Active Faith,* 193.

211. Reed, *Politically Incorrect,* 67.

212. Reed, *Active Faith,* 278.

213. Reed, *Politically Incorrect,* 25.

214. Ibid., 235.

215. Ibid., 241.

216. Charles Taylor, "Multiculturalism and the Politics of Recognition," in *Multiculturalism and the Politics of Recognition,* ed. Amy Gutmann (Princeton: Princeton University Press, 1992), 25.

217. For a full discussion of Taylor's theory of identity formation, see Charles Taylor, *Sources of the Self* (Cambridge: Harvard University Press, 1989).

218. Taylor, "Multiculturalism and the Politics of Recognition," 25.

219. Ibid., 26.

220. Merelman, "Racial Conflict and Cultural Politics in the United States," 12.

221. Taylor, "Multiculturalism and the Politics of Recognition," 37-44.

222. Ibid., 38.

223. Ibid., 43.

224. Ibid., 63.

225. Ibid., 64.

226. William L. Fisher, "Christian Responsibility for Government," *Christian Coalition Leadership Manual* (Chesapeake, VA: Christian Coalition, 1990), 2.9. See also Robertson, *Answers,* 185-99; Robertson, *The Secret Kingdom* 2d ed., 19-67; Robertson, *The Turning Tide* 157-58; and Reed, *Politically Incorrect,* 26-27.

227. Ralph E. Reed, Jr., "You Can Make a Difference," *Christian American,* July/August 1992: 25.

228. Reed, *Active Faith,* 256-57.

229. Christian Coalition mailing, undated.

230. Reed, *Politically Incorrect,* 23.

231. Reed, "Introduction," in *Contract with the American Family,* ix-x.

232. Robertson statement in the CC pamphlet, "Christian Americans are Tired of Getting Stepped On." The statement "Christians are Americans, too" also appeared in Robertson, "'Earned the right to speak . . . without being savaged,'" 11A; and was quoted in Paul English, "Quayle and Helms Rally Religious Right," *Christian American,* January/February 1992: 4.

233. *Contract with the American Family,* 10.

234. Ibid., 4. Two such constitutional amendments were introduced in the 104th Congress. For an analysis of these amendments, see Derek H. Davis, "Editorial: A Commentary on the Proposed 'Religious Equality/Liberties' Amendment," *Journal of Church and State* 38, no. 1 (Winter 1996): 5-23.

235. Quoted in Cassandra Burrell, "Christian Group Backs School Prayer," Associated Press, May 22, 1997.

236. Reed, "Putting A Friendly Face on the Pro-Family Movement," 28.

237. Christian Coalition mailing, undated.

238. Reed, *Politically Incorrect,* 40.

239. Christian Coalition mailing, undated. Emphasis in original.

240. Reed, *Politically Incorrect,* 24.

241. Ibid., 40. Reed did not offer any statistical evidence to support this assertion.

242. Pat Robertson, "The Turning Tide," *Christian American,* October 1993: 19.

243. Reed, *Politically Incorrect,* 24.

244. Robertson, "A Reply to My Critics," A14.

245. Reed, *Politically Incorrect,* xv-xvi.

246. Carter, *The Culture of Disbelief,* 263-74.

247. Ibid., 3. For a critique of Carter's arguments that the Christian Right has used to its own advantage, see David McKenzie, "Stephen Carter, the Christian Coalition, and the Civil Rights Analogy," *Journal of Church and State* 38, no. 2 (Spring 1996): 297-319.

248. "Remarks by the President in Photo Opportunity During White House Interfaith Breakfast," White House Press Office, August 30, 1993. President Clinton also specifically recommended to his audience that they read Carter's book.

249. "Remarks by the President at the Signing Ceremony for the Religious Freedom Restoration Act," White House Press Office, November 16, 1993.

250. Reed, *Active Faith,* 96. See also Reed, *Politically Incorrect,* 135-36. In a speech at the National Press Club just before the 1996 elections, Reed asserted that the Clinton administration's "record on the political participation of people of faith" was "bizarre." Reed cited news reports that a Democratic National Committee event at a Buddhist temple in Los Angeles took in $140,000 in illegal contributions. "This by the same Democratic National Committee," observed Reed, "that has attempted to intimidate conservative people of faith into silence and deny them their First Amendment right to distribute nonpartisan voter guides prior to an election." Ralph Reed, "How People of Faith are Changing the Soul of American Politics," speech at the National Press Club, Washington D.C., October 22, 1996.

251. Reed, "Remarks to the Detroit Economic Club," 135.

252. Reed, "Introduction," in *Contract with the American Family,* ix.

253. Reed, *Active Faith,* 3.

254. Nicholas Lemann, "Reed in the Wind," review of *Active Faith* by Ralph Reed and *The Godless Constitution* by Isaac Kramnick and R. Laurence Moore, *New Republic,* July 8, 1996: 33.

255. Reed, *Active Faith,* 2.

256. Ibid., 207.

257. See "Statement by RNC Chairman Haley Barbour on Democrat Christian-Bashing," Republican National Committee press release, June 21, 1994; Dick Armey, "Freedom's Choir," *Policy Review,* Winter 1994: 27-34; Newt Gingrich, "Renewing America," speech at the 5th Annual Christian Coalition "Road to Victory" conference, Washington, D.C., September 8, 1995; and Irving Kristol, "Conservative Christians: Into the Fray," *Wall Street Journal,* December 22, 1995: A8.

258. Anonymous quotation in Lind, "Rev. Robertson's Grand International Conspiracy Theory," 21. See also James Atlas, "The Counter Counterculture," *New York Times Magazine,* February 12, 1995: 34, 37, 65.

259. Christian Coalition mailing, undated. Emphasis in original.

260. Christian Coalition mailing, undated. Emphasis in original.

261. Christian Coalition mailing, undated.

262. Reed, *Active Faith,* 5.

263. Ibid., 149.

264. Quoted in Sam Howe Verhovek, "With Abortion Scarcely Uttered, Its Opponents Are Feeling Angry," *New York Times,* August 15, 1996: A1.

265. Thomas B. Edsall, "Christian Right Avoiding Spotlight," *Washington Post,* August 14, 1996: A1.

266. Quoted in Lisa Anderson, "Speaking Softly, GOP's Right Still Carries Big Stick," *Chicago Tribune,* August 16, 1996: 1,1.

   On August 15th on *The 700 Club,* Robertson said much the same: "I said, look, the object is to get people elected, who will in turn put in legislation which will further the goals of our organization. And rhetoric is not really that important at this point in time." Quoted in "The Christian Coalition Lawsuit: Shining Some Light in The Darkness," *Church & State,* September 1996: 14(182).

267. Pat Robertson, remarks to the 6th Annual Christian Coalition "Road to Victory" conference, Washington, D.C., September 14, 1996.

268. Richard L. Berke, "Politicians Woo Christian Group," *New York Times,* September 9, 1995: I1, I9.

269. Ralph Z. Hallow, "Activists Hail Gingrich, Save Hoots for Perot," *Washington Times,* September 14, 1996: A1; Jim Drinkard, "Robertson: Dole Needs Miracle," Associated Press, September 14, 1996.

270. Gustav Niebuhr, "Dole Gets Christian Coalition's Trust and Prodding," *New York Times,* September 16, 1996: A1, A12; Thomas B. Edsall, "Dole Vows to Sign 'Partial-Birth' Abortion Ban," *Washington Post,* September 15, 1996: A16; Ralph Z. Hallow, "Dole Visit Energizes Christian Coalition," *Washington Times,* September 15, 1996: A1, A5.

271. Reed, for instance, ridiculed as "comical" the demand of one Christian Right group that the Reagan administration "appoint evangelicals to political posts equal to their numbers in the U.S. population—a kind of quota system for Christians." Reed, *Active Faith,* 123.

272. See John Rawls, *A Theory of Justice* (Cambridge: Belknap Press, 1971); Bruce Ackerman, *Social Justice in the Liberal State* (New Haven: Yale University Press, 1980). Michael J. Perry presented a critique of this view in *Love and Power* (New York: Oxford University Press, 1991).

273. Ackerman quoted in Sanford Levinson, "Religious Language and the Public Square," review of *Love and Power* by Michael J. Perry, *Harvard Law Review,* 105 (June 1992): 2064.

274. Levinson, "Religious Language and the Public Square," 2064.

275. Carter, *The Culture of Disbelief,* 55-56.

276. Michael J. Perry, *Morality, Politics, and Law: A Bicentennial Essay* (New York: Oxford University Press, 1988), 181-82. Perry quoted in Carter, *The Culture of Disbelief,* 56.

277. "Demagoguery in America," *New Republic,* August 1, 1994: 7.

278. Ralph Reed, Jr., "Casting a Wider Net," *Policy Review,* Summer 1993: 35.

279. Quoted in Ralph Z. Hallow, "Bennett Wins Cheers with Call for Traditional Values," *Washington Times,* September 12, 1993: A3.

280. Alan Keyes, "America's Yearning for Spiritual Renewal," speech at the 6th Annual Christian Coalition "Road to Victory" conference, Washington, DC, September 14, 1996.

281. Reed, "The Role of Religious Conservatives in the '96 Elections."

282. Reed, *Active Faith,* 258.

283. Quoted in Jason DeParle, "A Fundamental Problem," *New York Times Magazine,* July 14, 1996: 42. This event was held in connection with the convention of the Texas Republican party. At that convention, religious conservatives were attempting to block the selection of pro-choice U.S. Senator Kay Bailey Hutchinson as a Texas delegate to the Republican national convention. Reed, who publicly supported efforts to deny delegate slots to other pro-choice delegates, was reportedly involved in behind-the-scenes negotiations to allow Hutchinson to become a delegate. Richard L. Berke, "News Analysis: Chaotic Message to Dole on Abortion," *New York Times,* June 24, 1996: A8.

284. One such person seems to be Gary Bauer. He did not appear at the 1996 "Road to Victory" conference, as he had at all five previous meetings, 1991-1995. The reason for his absence is not known, but Bauer's harsh characterization of Reed has probably not improved their relationship. Bauer's organization, the Family Research Council (FRC), did have a display table and a representative in the conference exhibition area. FRC advertisements have continued to appear in *Christian American.*

285. Ralph Reed, Jr., "What Do Religious Conservatives Really Want?" in *Disciples & Democracy,* ed. Michael Cromartie (Washington, D.C.: Ethics and Public Policy Center, 1994), 2.

286. Reed, *Politically Incorrect,* 48.

287. Samuel Blumenfeld, *Is Public Education Necessary?* (Old Greenwich, CN: Devin-Adair, 1981), 95. Quoted in Robertson, *The Turning Tide,* 229.

288. Robertson, *The Turning Tide,* 231.

289. Ibid., 219, 227-28.

290. Robertson, *The New Millennium,* 174-75.

291. Reed, *Politically Incorrect,* 18.

292. Ibid., 257.

293. Ibid., 34.

294. *Contract with the American Family,* 14-15.

295. Ibid., 20.
296. Merelman, "Racial Conflict and Cultural Politics in the United States," 12.
297. Reed, *Politically Incorrect,* 70.
298. Carter, *The Culture of Disbelief,* 180.
299. Ibid., 179.
300. *Contract with the American Family,* 30.
301. Ibid.
302. Ibid., 29.
303. Carter, *The Culture of Disbelief,* 193.
304. See Levinson, "Some Reflections on Multiculturalism," 999-1002. The legal right to choose a private or religious education for one's children will remain a largely hollow or formal right without the economic means of realization. This, of course, has been the logic behind taxpayer funding for a woman's right to choose an abortion—that it remains merely a formal right without the economic means for its realization—a measure that religious conservatives oppose.
305. Robertson, *The Turning Tide,* 239.
306. Reed, *Politically Incorrect,* 33.
307. Robertson, *The Turning Tide,* 216.
308. Ibid., 220.

Chapter 7

1. *Contract with the American Family* (Nashville: Moorings, 1995), 1.
2. Ralph Reed, *Politically Incorrect* (Dallas: Word Publishing, 1994), 36.
3. Joseph L. Conn, "Behind the Mask," *Church & State,* November 1994: 4(218). The subtitle of this article is, "Despite Attempts to Moderate Their Image, Pat Robertson and His Christian Coalition Still Want to Take Dominion in America."
4. Robert Boston, *The Most Dangerous Man in America?* (Amherst, NY: Prometheus Books, 1996), 150. For Boston's compilation of such quotations, see 149-82.
5. Reed, *Politically Incorrect,* 18.
6. Dick Armey, "Freedom's Choir," *Policy Review,* Winter 1994: 30.
7. Ralph Reed, "A Strategy for Evangelicals," *Christian American,* January 1993: 14
8. Reed, *Politically Incorrect,* 65.
9. Ralph Reed, "The Role of Religious Conservatives in the '96 Elections," speech at the 5th Annual Christian Coalition "Road to Victory" conference, Washington, D.C., September 8, 1995.
10. Ralph Reed, "Active Faith," interview by Michael Ebert, *Christian American,* May/June 1996: 13.

11. Pat Robertson, *The Plan* (Nashville: Thomas Nelson Publishers, 1989), 168.
12. Pat Robertson, *The Turning Tide* (Dallas: Word Publishing, 1993), 284.
13. Reed, *Active Faith,* 280.
14. Ibid., 255.
15. Ibid., 29.
16. Ibid., 28.
17. Ibid., 9-10.
18. Ibid., 279.
19. Reinhold Niebuhr, *Beyond Tragedy* (New York: Charles Scribner's Sons, 1937), 185. Quoted in Reed, *Active Faith,* 256.
20. Niebuhr, *Beyond Tragedy,* 185.
21. Reed, *Active Faith,* 279.
22. Ibid., 103.
23. Ibid., 65.
24. Reed, "The Role of Religious Conservatives in the '96 Elections." But in *Active Faith,* Reed did state that "religious conservatives in the United States are properly understood as an interest group within a democratic order." Reed, *Active Faith,* 25. The difference seems to be that they are not "just another special interest group."
25. Reed, "Active Faith," interview, 13.
26. Quoted in Max Weber, *The Protestant Ethic and the Spirit of Capitalism,* trans. Talcott Parsons with introduction by Anthony Giddens (New York: Charles Scribner's Sons, 1976), 175.

Epilogue

1. Quoted in Richard L. Berke, "To See Ralph Reed, Take a Number," *New York Times,* September 14, 1997: I18.
2. Ralph Reed, interview by Larry King, *Larry King Live,* Cable News Network, June 23, 1998; Kevin Sack, "Religious Right's Tactician on Wider Crusade," *New York Times,* June 12, 1998: A1.
3. Quoted in Berke, "To See Ralph Reed, Take a Number," I18.
4. Quoted in Peter H. Stone, "Spreading the GOP Gospel—And Thriving," *National Journal,* December 6, 1997: 2470; Sack, "Religious Right's Tactician," A1.
5. Gloria Borger, "The Ralph Reed Primary," *U.S. News & World Report,* December 29, 1997/January 5, 1997: 41.
6. Quoted in Ralph Z. Hallow, "At Last Minute, Reed Softens Farewell Speech to Coalition," *Washington Times,* September 13, 1997: A4.
7. Reed, *Larry King Live,* June 23, 1998.
8. For example, see Cynthia Tucker, "Skandalakis, Reed Show True Colors," *Atlanta Journal and Constitution,* October 18, 1998: 7G.

9. Quoted in Sack, "Religious Right's Tactician," A1.

10. "Conventional Wisdom Watch," *Newsweek*, June 22, 1998: 6.

11. See, for example, Ceci Connolly, "Political Machine Loses a Wheel," *Washington Post*, September 12, 1997: A4.

12. Quoted in "Robertson Speech Shows Partisanship, Group Says," *Chicago Tribune*, September 18, 1997: 14. See also Thomas B. Edsall, "Robertson: Christian Coalition Should Emulate Tammany Hall," *Washington Post*, September 18, 1997: A2.

13. Richard L. Berke, "For Christian Coalition, A Reaffirmation of Power," *New York Times*, September 15, 1997: A18.

14. Form 990, Return of Organization Exempt from Income Tax for 1996 and 1997, The Christian Coalition.

15. Michael J. Gerson, "Christian Coalition in Unprecedented Crisis," *U.S. News & World Report*, February 16, 1998: 33.

16. Bill Sizemore, "Fired Official is a Key Player in Christian Coalition Troubles," *Virginian-Pilot*, July 27, 1997: A1; Bill Sizemore, "Coalition Sues, Saying Ally Raided Mailing List," *Virginian-Pilot*, January 15, 1998: A1; Bill Sizemore, "Christian Coalition Settles Suit with Vendor," *Virginian-Pilot*, March 24, 1998: A4.

17. "Christian Coalition Names Finance Director," *Virginian-Pilot*, October 2, 1997: B5.

18. Ceci Connolly and Dan Balz, "Christian Coalition Is Reorganizing," *Washington Post*, December 20, 1997: A6. See also Gerson, "Christian Coalition," 33.

19. Quoted in Melinda Henneberger, "Ralph Reed Is His Cross to Bear," *New York Times Magazine*, August 9, 1998: 24-27.

20. Randy Tate, "News Briefing with Randy Tate, Executive Director of the Christian Coalition," press conference at the National Press Club, Washington, D.C., November 4, 1998.

21. Quoted in Ralph Z. Hallow, "Christian Coalition Goes Back to Core Principles," *Washington Times*, January 7, 1998: A1.

22. "'Families 2000' Strategy Announced by Christian Coalition," Christian Coalition press release, February 18, 1998.

23. Henneberger, "Ralph Reed," 24. Robertson appeared to share this view of Tate. "He's constantly up, always cheery, and it seemed he could help mobilize the troops." Robertson's use of the past tense, "seemed," may have been unintentional. Henneberger, "Ralph Reed," 26.

24. "Court Cases: New Litigation, FEC v. The Christian Coalition," *Federal Election Commission Record* 22, no. 9 (September 1996): 1-2; Ruth Marcus, "FEC Files Suit Over Christian Coalition Role," *Washington Post*, July 31, 1996: A1.

25. "FEC Case Groundless—Christian Coalition Files for Dismissal," Christian Coalition press release, September 8, 1998.

26. See for instance, "Christian Coalition Reorganization Proposal Is Act of Legal Desperation, Says Americans United," Americans United for Separation of Church and State press release, January 9, 1998.

27. Christian Coalition mailing, June 8, 1998. Emphasis in original.

28. Quoted in Kevin Galvin, "Unions Back Christian Coalition," Associated Press Online, September 29, 1998. See also "ACLU, AFL-CIO Support Christian Coalition in Battle over Free Speech and Public Advocacy," ACLU Press Release, September 30, 1998.

29. Neil A. Lewis, "Nonprofit Groups to Defy Subpoenas in Senate Inquiry," *New York Times,* September 4, 1997: A16; Helen Dewar, "7 Groups Join to Resist Panel Subpoenas," *Washington Post,* September 4, 1997: A12.

30. Senate Governmental Affairs Committee, *Investigation of Illegal or Improper Activities in Connection with 1996 Federal Election Campaigns,* 105th Cong., 2d sess., March 10, 1998, S. Rept. 105-167. See Section 27, "Compliance by Nonprofit Groups with Committee Subpoenas," 1-7, 27-29.

31. "Coalition Announces Nationwide Efforts for Election '98," Christian Coalition press release, October 28, 1998.

32. Laurie Goodstein, "Church Debate over Voter Guides," *New York Times,* October 29, 1998: A27.

33. "Churches that Hand Out Christian Coalition 'Voter Guides' Will Be Reported to the IRS Watchdog Group Warns," Americans United for Separation of Church and State press release, October 28, 1998.

34. Randy Tate, "Pastor's Letter from Randy Tate," Christian Coalition Web site at http://www.cc.org/voter/legal/rights.html, October 8, 1998. Tate's analysis of Lynn was somewhat contradictory. He called Lynn "the ACLU's hand-picked mouthpiece" yet also cited the ACLU's support for the CC's position in the FEC case as evidence against Lynn's position.

35. Quoted in Larry Witham, "Faithful Await Deluge of Voter Guides," *Washington Times,* October 27, 1998: A8.

36. David Goldstein, "Turnout a Key for Democrats," *Kansas City Star,* November 5, 1998: A1.

37. Laurie Goodstein, "Religious Conservatives, Stung by Vote Losses, Blame G.O.P. for Focusing on Clinton," *New York Times,* November 5, 1998: B3.

38. Quoted in Richard N. Ostling, "Religious Right Had Tough Election," AP Online, November 6, 1998.

39. Tom Baxter, "Reed's 'Tough' Election Day Probably a Maturing Experience," Cox News Service, November 4, 1998.

40. See "People for the American Way: Right Wing Watch Online," November 5, 1998. People For the American Way Web site at http://www.pfaw.org.

Reed's other victorious clients were Congressman Jay Dickey (R-AR) and Senator Richard Shelby (R-AL).

41. "Conventional Wisdom Watch," *Newsweek,* November 16, 1998: 6.

42. "American Voters Reject Religious Right Extremism," Americans United for Separation of Church and State press release, November 4, 1998. See also "The Religious Right Called the Tune, But Voters Wouldn't Dance," People For the American Way press release, November 4, 1998.

43. James P. Pinkerton, "Pragmatism Yes, Moralism No," *Los Angeles Times,* November 5, 1998: B9.

44. Quoted in Dan Balz and David S. Broder, "Gingrich Could Face Leadership Challenge," *Washington Post,* November 5, 1998: A1.

45. See, for example, Goodstein, "Religious Conservatives," B3; Judy Packer-Tursman, "Right Wing: GOP Too Wishy Washy," *Pittsburgh Post-Gazette,* November 5, 1998: A-18.

46. "Christian Coalition Exit Poll Reveals Pro-Family Voters Can't Be Taken for Granted," Christian Coalition press release, November 4, 1998.

47. Tate, "News Briefing."

48. See, for example, Elizabeth Drew, "Why Clinton Will Be Impeached," *Washington Post,* September 23, 1998: A25.

49. See Thomas B. Edsall, "Resignation 'Too Easy,' Robertson Tells Coalition," *Washington Post,* September 19, 1998: A8.

50. Christian Coalition mailing, October 13, 1998.

51. Quoted in John King, "Christian Coalition Uses Pulpits for Politics," *CNN Inside Politics,* Cable News Network, November 2, 1998.

52. Chuck Raasch, "Bennett Asks: Where's the Religious Right in Clinton Fight?" Gannett News Service, February 28, 1998; John Hall, "A Tentative Sort of Crusade," *Tampa Tribune,* October 2, 1998: 17.

53. Ralph Reed, interview by Judy Woodruff, *CNN Inside Politics,* Cable News Network, February 20, 1998.

54. Pat Robertson, "Remarks at Morning Plenary Session," speech at the 8th Annual Christian Coalition "Road to Victory" conference, Washington, D.C., September 18, 1998.

55. Ken Foskett, "National Campaign Ad Targets Clinton," Cox News Service, October 7, 1998.

56. See, for example, Richard L. Berke, "The Republican Middle Looks for an Edge," *New York Times,* November 8, 1998: IV1.

57. James Dobson, Speech to the Spring 1998 Council for National Policy meeting, Phoenix, AZ, February 7, 1998. See also, Laurie Goodstein, "Conservative Christian Leader Accuses Republicans of Betrayal," *New York Times,* February 12, 1998: A22.

58. Quoted in Laurie Goodstein, "Religious Right, Frustrated, Trying New Tactic on G.O.P.," *New York Times,* March 23, 1998: A1.

59. Benjamin Domenech, "Dobson's Choice, Why the Conservative Outsider's Agenda Worries GOP Leaders," *Washington Post,* April 19, 1998: C2; Grover G. Norquist, "Dobson and the GOP," *The American Spectator,* July 1998: 60-62; Thomas B. Edsall, "GOP's Agenda Pleases Backers," *Washington Post,* July 19, 1998: A6.

60. Dick Foster, "Focus on Family Leader Has Stroke," *Rocky Mountain News,* June 18, 1998: 14A.

61. Quoted in Sack, "Religious Right's Tactician," A1.

62. Reed, *Larry King Live,* June 23, 1998. It is interesting to note that Reed referred to "people like Pat Robertson, the Christian Coalition, Jim Dobson and others, who are outside the system."

63. Megan Rosenfeld, "Don Hodel: A Belief in Belief," *Washington Post,* May 4, 1998: D1; Joseph L. Conn, "Double Trouble," *Church & State,* July/August 1997: 4(148).

64. "Christian Coalition Commends Senate Leader for Strong Stand on Biblical Morality," Christian Coalition press release, June 17, 1998.

65. Quoted in Richard L. Berke, "Flurry of Anti-Gay Remarks Has G.O.P. Fearing a Backlash," *New York Times,* June 30, 1998: A1.

66. "Christian Coalition Joins Other Groups with Message of Hope for Homosexuals," Christian Coalition press release, July 13, 1998; Caryle Murphy, "Gays React to Ads that Call Them Sinners," *Washington Post,* July 19, 1998: B1.

67. Ron Fournier, "Pat Robertson Visits Capitol Hill," AP Online, June 10, 1998.

68. Henneberger, "Ralph Reed," 27.

69. Randy Tate, "Remarks After Attending the Values Summit," news conference, Washington, D.C., May 8, 1998. Tate was one of 13 speakers.

70. Randy Tate, "National Press Club Luncheon Address by Randy Tate, Executive Director of the Christian Coalition," speech at the National Press Club, Washington, D.C., September 16, 1998.

71. See, for example, Evan Thomas, "The Sons Also Rise," *Newsweek,* November 16, 1998: 44-48.

72. Quoted in Sam Howe Verhovek, "Riding High, Bush Eases into 2000 Election," *New York Times,* May 25, 1998: A1.

73. Berke, "To See Ralph Reed," 118; Borger, "Ralph Reed Primary," 41.

74. Dana Milbank, "The Conversion of Steve Forbes," *New Republic,* April 27, 1998: 21-25.

75. Quoted in "Campaign for Working Families, A Political Action Committee," pamphlet, Washington, D.C.: Campaign for Working Families, 1998. See also Fred Barnes, "Bauer Power," *Weekly Standard,* December 22, 1997: 18-23.

76. Quoted in Linda Feldmann, "Religious Right's New Mandarin," *Christian Science Monitor,* March 18, 1998: 1.

77. Thomas B. Edsall, "Christian Right Lifts Ashcroft," *Washington Post,* April 14, 1998: A1.

78. Quoted in Jon Sawyer, "Pat Robertson Says He Would 'Love to See' Ashcroft as President," *St. Louis Post-Dispatch,* May 10, 1998: B1.

79. Edward Walsh, "Christian Coalition Leaders Back Ashcroft," *Washington Post,* February 17, 1998: A4; Ralph Z. Hallow, "Christian Coalition Simmers Over Leak," *Washington Times,* February 19, 1998: A4.

80. "Christian Coalition Road to Victory '98 Update," Christian Coalition press release, September 14, 1998; Ralph Z. Hallow, "Canceling of Straw Poll Seen as Face-Saving Move," *Washington Times,* September 18, 1998: A4.

81. Paul A. Gigot, "Potomac Watch: Why Liberals Secretly Love James Dobson," *Wall Street Journal,* June 5, 1998: A14.

82. Dobson, Speech at the Spring 1998 Council for National Policy meeting.

83. John F. Kennedy, "Presidential Inaugural Address," Washington, D.C., January 20, 1961.

BIBLIOGRAPHY

BOOKS, DISSERTATIONS, AND THESES

Ackerman, Bruce. *Social Justice in the Liberal State.* New Haven: Yale University Press, 1980.

Ahlstrom, Sydney E. *A Religious History of the American People.* New Haven: Yale University Press, 1972.

Ammerman, Nancy. *Bible Believers: Fundamentalists in the Modern World.* New Brunswick, NJ: Rutgers University Press, 1987.

————."North American Protestant Fundamentalism." In *Fundamentalisms Observed,* eds. Martin Marty and Scott Appleby, 1-65. Chicago: University of Chicago Press, 1991.

Amos, Gary T. *Defending the Declaration: How the Bible and Christianity Influenced the Writing of the Declaration of Independence.* Brentwood, TN: Wolgemuth & Hyatt, 1989.

Anderson, Robert Mapes. *Vision of the Disinherited.* New York: Oxford University Press, 1979.

Auberbach, Susan, ed. *Encyclopedia of Multiculturalism.* New York: Marshall Cavendish, 1994. S.v. "Multiculturalism," by Susan D. Greenbaum.

Bahnsen, Greg L. Foreword to *The Debate Over Christian Reconstruction,* by Gary DeMar. Atlanta: American Vision, 1988.

————. "The Theonomic Position." In *God and Politics: Four Views of the Transformation of Civil Government,* ed. Gary Scott Smith, 21-54. Phillipsburg, NJ: Presbyterian and Reformed, 1989.

————. *Theonomy in Christian Ethics.* Phillipsburg, NJ: Presbyterian and Reformed, 1977.

Barron, Bruce A. *Heaven on Earth? The Social and Political Agendas of Dominion Theology.* Grand Rapids, MI: Zondervan, 1992.

Barton, David. *The Myth of Separation.* Aledo, TX: Wallbuilder Press, 1992.

Bercovitch, Sacvan. *The American Jeremiad.* Madison: University of Wisconsin Press, 1978.

Berger, Peter. *The Sacred Canopy.* New York: Anchor Books, 1969.

Berman, Paul. "Introduction." In *Debating P.C.,* ed. Paul Berman, 1-26. New York: Dell Publishing, 1992.

Bernal, Martin. *Black Athena: The Afro-Asian Roots of Classical Civilization.* London: Free Association Press, 1987.

Blumenfeld, Samuel. *Is Public Education Necessary?* Old Greenwich, CT: Devin-Adair, 1981.

Boston, Robert. *The Most Dangerous Man in America? Pat Robertson and the Rise of the Christian Coalition.* Amherst, NY: Prometheus Books, 1996.

————. *Why the Religious Right is Wrong.* Buffalo, NY: Prometheus Books, 1993.

Boyer, Paul. *When Time Shall Be No More.* Cambridge, MA: Belknap Press, 1992.

Bozeman, T. Dwight. *To Live Ancient Lives: The Primitivist Dimension of Puritanism.* Chapel Hill, NC: University of North Carolina Press, 1988.

Bruce, Steve. *Pray TV.* London: Routledge, 1990.

————. *The Rise and Fall of the Christian Right.* Oxford: Clarendon Press, 1988.

Cantor, David. *The Religious Right: The Assault on Tolerance & Pluralism in America.* New York: Anti-Defamation League, 1994.

Carter, Dan T. *The Politics of Rage.* New York: Simon & Schuster, 1995.

————. *Scottsboro: A Tragedy of the American South.* Baton Rouge: Louisiana State University Press, 1969.

Carter, Stephen L. *The Culture of Disbelief.* New York: BasicBooks, 1993.

Cherry, Conrad, ed. *God's New Israel.* Englewood Cliffs, NJ: Prentice-Hall, 1971.

Clabaugh, Gary. *Thunder on the Right.* Chicago: Nelson-Hall, 1974.

Contract with the American Family. Nashville: Moorings, 1995.

DeMar, Gary. "Questions Frequently Asked About Christian Reconstruction." In *Christian Reconstruction: What It Is, What It Isn't,* by Gary North and Gary DeMar, 79-143. Tyler, TX: Institute For Christian Economics, 1991.

Diamond, Sara. *Spiritual Warfare.* Boston: South End Press, 1989.

Donovan, John B. *Pat Robertson: The Authorized Biography.* New York: Macmillan Publishing Company, 1988.

D'Souza, Dinesh. *Illiberal Education.* New York: Free Press, 1991.

Dyer, Steven G. *The Effect of Eschatology on the Christian Right: A Survey of Christian Coalition Leaders.* M.A. thesis, Regent University, 1992.

Eliade, Mircea, ed. *Encyclopedia of Religion.* New York: Macmillan, 1986. S.v. "Martyrdom," by Samuel Z. Klausner.

————, ed. *Encyclopedia of Religion.* New York: Macmillan, 1986. S.v. "Theocracy," by Dewey D. Wallace, Jr.

————. *The Sacred and the Profane.* New York: Harper & Row, 1961.

Encyclopedia of Associations, 1986-1995 eds. S.v. "Students for America."

Fairbanks, James D. "Politics and the Evangelical Press: 1960-1985." In *Religion and Political Behavior in the United States,* ed. Ted G. Jelen, 243-57. New York: Praeger, 1989).

Falwell, Jerry. "Future-Word: An Agenda for the Eighties." In *The Fundamentalist Phenomenon,* ed. Jerry Falwell, 186-223. Garden City, NY: Doubleday & Company, Inc., 1981.

Federer, William J., ed. *America's God and Country Encyclopedia of Quotations.* Coppell, TX: Fame Publishing Inc., 1994.

Ferry, Luc and Alain Renaut. *French Philosophy of the Sixties: An Essay on Antihumanism.* Amherst: University of Massachusetts Press, 1990.

Foege, Alec. *The Empire God Built: Inside Pat Robertson's Media Machine.* New York: John Wiley & Sons, Inc., 1996.

Fournier, Keith A. with William D. Watkins. *A House United? Evangelicals and Catholics Together—A Winning Alliance for the 21st Century.* Colorado

Springs, CO: NavPress; Virginia Beach, VA: Liberty, Life and Family, 1994.

Furgurson, Ernest B. *Hard Right: The Rise of Jesse Helms.* New York: W. W. Norton & Company, 1986.

Garvey, John H. "Fundamentalism and American Law." In *Fundamentalisms and the State,* eds. Martin E. Marty and R. Scott Appleby, 28-49. Chicago: University of Chicago Press, 1993.

———. "Introduction: Fundamentalism and Politics." *Fundamentalisms and the State,* eds. Martin E. Marty and R. Scott Appleby, 13-27. Chicago: University of Chicago Press, 1993.

Gates, Henry Louis, Jr. *Loose Canons.* New York: Oxford University Press, 1992.

Gerlach, Luther P. and Virginia H. Hine. *People, Power, Change: Movements of Social Transformation.* Indianapolis: Bobbs-Merrill Company, Inc., 1970.

Glazer, Nathan. "Fundamentalists: A Defensive Offensive." In *Piety and Politics: Evangelicals and Fundamentalists Confront the World,* eds. Richard John Neuhaus and Michael Cromartie, 245-58. Washington, D.C.: Ethics and Public Policy Center, 1987.

Goldberg, David Theo, ed. *Multiculturalism: A Critical Reader.* Oxford, UK: Blackwell, 1994.

Gramsci, Antonio. *A Gramsci Reader: Selected Writings, 1916-1935,* ed. David Forgacs. London: Lawrence and Wishart, 1988.

Green, John C. "The Christian Right and the 1994 Elections: An Overview." In *God at the Grass Roots,* eds. Mark J. Rozell and Clyde Wilcox, 1-18. Lanham, MD: Rowman & Littlefield Publishers, Inc., 1995.

Hadden, Jeffrey K., and Anson Shupe. *Televangelism.* New York: Henry Holt and Company, 1988.

Harrell, David Edwin, Jr. "Epilogue." In *The American Quest for the Primitive Church,* ed. Richard T. Hughes, 239-45. Chicago: University of Illinois Press, 1988.

———. *Pat Robertson: A Personal, Political and Religious Portrait.* San Francisco: Harper & Row, 1987.

Hertzke, Allen D. *Echoes of Discontent: Jesse Jackson, Pat Robertson, and the Resurgence of Populism.* Washington, D.C.: Congressional Quarterly Press, 1993.

———. "Harvest of Discontent: Religion and Populism in the 1988 Presidential Campaign." In *The Bible and the Ballot Box,* eds. James L. Guth and John C. Green, 3-27. Boulder, CO: Westview Press, 1991.

Hofstadter, Richard. *The Age of Reform: From Bryan to F.D.R.* New York: Alfred A. Knopf, 1955.

———. *Anti-Intellectualism in American Life.* New York: Vintage, 1963.

———. *The Paranoid Style in American Politics and Other Essays.* New York: Alfred A. Knopf, 1966.

Hughes, Richard T. and C. Leonard Allen. *Illusions of Innocence.* Chicago: University of Chicago Press, 1988.

Hunter, Allen. *Virtue with a Vengeance: The Pro-Family Politics of the New Right.* Ph.D. diss., Brandeis University, 1985.

Hunter, James Davison. *American Evangelicalism: Conservative Religion and the Quandary of Modernity.* New Bruswick, NJ: Rutgers University Press, 1983.

————. *Before the Shooting Begins.* New York: Free Press, 1994.

————. *Culture Wars.* New York: BasicBooks, 1991.

————. *Evangelicalism: The Coming Generation.* Chicago: University of Chicago Press, 1987.

————. "The Liberal Reaction to the New Christian Right." In *The New Christian Right,* eds. Robert C. Liebman and Robert Wuthnow, 150-63. New York: Aldine Publishing Company, 1983.

Iannaccone, Laurence R. "Heirs to the Protestant Ethic? The Economics of American Fundamentalists." In *Fundamentalisms and the State,* eds. Martin E. Marty and R. Scott Appleby, 342-66. Chicago: University of Chicago Press, 1993.

James, George G. M. *Stolen Legacy.* New York: Philosophical Library, 1954; reprint, San Francisco: Julian Richardson Associates, 1988.

Jorstad, Erling. *The Politics of Doomsday.* Nashville: Abingdon Press, 1970.

Kellstadt, Lyman A. and Mark A. Noll. "Religion, Voting for President, and Party Identification." In *Religion and American Politics,* ed. Mark A. Noll, 355-79. New York: Oxford University Press, 1990.

LaHaye, Tim. *The Battle for the Mind.* Old Tappan, NJ: Fleming H. Revell, 1980.

Lienesch, Michael. *Redeeming America.* Chapel Hill, NC: University of North Carolina Press, 1993.

Marsden, George M. "The Evangelical Denomination." In *Piety and Politics,* eds. Richard John Neuhaus and Michael Cromartie, 55-68. Washington, D.C.: Ethics and Public Policy Center, 1987.

————. *Fundamentalism and American Culture.* New York: Oxford University Press, 1980.

————. *Reforming Fundamentalism.* Grand Rapids, MI: William B. Eerdmans, 1987.

————. *Understanding Fundamentalism and Evangelicalism.* Grand Rapids, MI: William B. Eerdmans, 1991.

Marshall, Peter and David Manuel. *The Light and the Glory.* Old Tappan, NJ: Fleming H. Revell, 1977.

Marty, Martin E. "Fundamentalism as a Social Phenomenon." *Evangelicalism and Modern America,* ed. George M. Marsden, 56-70. Grand Rapids, MI: William B. Eerdmans, 1984.

————. *Righteous Empire.* New York: Dial Press, 1970.

Marty, Martin E. and R. Scott Appleby. "Introduction." In *Fundamentalisms Observed,* eds. Martin E. Marty and R. Scott Appleby, vii-xiii. Chicago: University of Chicago Press, 1991.

McLoughlin, William G. *Revivals, Awakenings, and Reform.* Chicago: University of Chicago Press, 1978.

Merelman, Richard M. *Representing Black Culture: Racial Conflict and Cultural Politics in the United States.* New York: Routledge, 1995.

Miller, Perry. *Errand into the Wilderness.* Cambridge: Belknap Press, 1984.

————. "From the Covenant to the Revival." In *The Shaping of American Religion* eds. James Ward Smith and A. Leland Jamison, 322-68. Princeton: Princeton University Press, 1961.

Moen, Matthew. *The Transformation of the Christian Right.* Tuscaloosa: University of Alabama Press, 1992.

Morken, Hubert. *Pat Robertson: Where He Stands.* Old Tappan, NJ: Fleming H. Revell, 1988.

Nash, George H. *The Conservative Intellectual Movement in America Since 1945.* New York: BasicBooks, 1976.

Nash, Ronald H. *Evangelicals in America.* Nashville: Abingdon Press, 1987.

Niebuhr, Reinhold. *Beyond Tragedy.* New York: Charles Scribner's Sons, 1937.

Noll, Mark. *A History of Christianity in the United States and Canada.* Grand Rapids, MI: William B. Eerdmans, 1992.

Noll, Mark, Nathan Hatch, and George Marsden. *The Search for Christian America.* Westchester, IL: Crossway Books, 1983.

North, Gary. "The Intellectual Schizophrenia of the New Christian Right." In *The Failure of American Baptist Culture,* ed. James B. Jordan, 1-37. Tyler, TX: Geneva Divinity School, 1982.

————. "Preface." In *Christian Reconstructionism: What It Is, What It Isn't,* by Gary North and Gary DeMar, ix-xxi. Tyler, TX: Institute For Christian Economics, 1991.

Oldfield, Duane M. *The Right and the Righteous.* Lanham, MD: Rowman & Littlefield Publishers, Inc., 1996.

Perry, Michael J. *Love and Power.* New York: Oxford University Press, 1991.

————. *Morality, Politics, and Law: A Bicentennial Essay.* New York: Oxford University Press, 1988.

Phillips, Kevin P. *Post-Conservative America.* New York: Random House, 1982.

Pierard, Richard V. "The New Religious Right in American Politics." *Evangelicalism and Modern America,* ed. George M. Marsden, 161-74. Grand Rapids, MI: William B. Eerdmans, 1984.

Pope, Jesse Curtis. *The Restoration Ideal in American Religious Thought.* Ph.D. diss., Florida State University, 1990.

Proffitt, Anne. *Religious Rhetoric in American Political Discourse: An Examination of Pat Robertson's "America's Dates with Destiny."* M.A. thesis, Eastern Michigan University, 1991.

Quebedeaux, Richard. "Conservative and Charismatic Developments of the Later Twentieth Century." In *Encyclopedia of American Religious Experience,* eds. Charles H. Lippy and Peter W. Williams, 963-76. New York: Charles Scribner's Sons, 1988.

Rawls, John. *A Theory of Justice.* Cambridge: Belknap Press, 1971.

Reed, Ralph. *Active Faith.* New York: Free Press, 1996.

————. *Politically Incorrect.* Dallas: Word Publishing, 1994.

————. "Remarks to the Detroit Economic Club, January 17, 1995: Christian Coalition and an Agenda for the New Congress." In *Contract with the American Family,* 133-45. Nashville: Moorings, 1995.

Reed, Ralph, Jr. "Introduction." In *Contract with the American Family,* ix-xiii. Nashville: Moorings, 1995.

————. "What Do Religious Conservatives Really Want?" In *Disciples & Democracy,* ed. Michael Cromartie, 1-15. Washington, D.C.: Ethics and Public Policy Center, 1994.

Reed, Ralph Eugene, Jr. *Fortress of Faith: Design and Experience at Southern Evangelical Colleges, 1830-1900.* Ph.D. diss., Emory University, 1990.

Reichley, A. James. *Religion in American Public Life.* Washington, D.C.: Brookings Institute, 1985.

Ribuffo, Leo P. *The Old Christian Right: The Protestant Far Right from the Great Depression to the Cold War.* Philadelphia: Temple University Press, 1983.

Roberts, Keith A. *Religion in Sociological Perspective.* 3d ed. Belmont, CA: Wadsworth Publishing Company, 1995.

Robertson, Pat. *America's Dates with Destiny.* Nashville: Thomas Nelson, 1986.

————. *Answers to 200 of Life's Most Probing Questions.* Nashville: Thomas Nelson Publishers, 1984.

————. *The End of the Age.* Dallas: Word Publishing, 1995.

————. *The New Millennium.* Dallas: Word Publishing, 1990.

————. *The New World Order.* Dallas: Word Publishing, 1991.

————. *The Plan.* Nashville: Thomas Nelson Publishers, 1989.

————. *The Secret Kingdom: Your Path to Peace Love and Financial Security.* 2d ed. Dallas: Word Publishing, 1992.

————. *The Turning Tide.* Dallas: Word Publishing, 1993.

Robertson, Pat and Jamie Buckingham. *Shout It from the Housetops.* Plainfield, NJ: Logos International, 1972.

Robertson, Pat with William Proctor. *Beyond Reason: How Miracles Can Change Your Life.* New York: William Morrow and Company, Inc., 1985.

Robertson, Pat with Bob Slosser. *The Secret Kingdom.* Nashville: Thomas Nelson Publishers, 1982.

Rothenberg, Paula S. "Critics of Attempts to Democratize the Curriculum Are Waging a Campaign to Misrepresent the Work of Responsible Professors," In *Debating P.C.,* ed. Paul Berman, 262-68. New York: Dell Publishing, 1992.

————, ed. *Racism and Sexism: An Integrated Study.* New York: St. Martin's Press, 1988.

Rozell, Mark J. and Clyde Wilcox. *Second Coming: The New Christian Right in Virginia Politics.* Baltimore, MD: Johns Hopkins University Press, 1996.

Rushdoony, Rousas John. *The Institutes of Biblical Law.* Nutley, NJ: The Craig Press, 1973.

Sabato, Larry J. and Glenn R. Simpson. *Dirty Little Secrets.* New York: Times Books, 1996.

Sandeen, Ernest R. *The Roots of Fundamentalism.* Chicago: University of Chicago Press, 1970.

Schaeffer, Francis. *A Christian Manifesto.* Wheaton, IL: Crossway Books, 1993.

Schlesinger, Arthur, Jr. *The Cycles of American History.* Boston: Houghton Mifflin Company, 1986.

————. *The Disuniting of America.* New York: W. W. Norton, 1992.

Shie, Paul Chau-Jiunn. *Why the Robertson Campaign Failed: A Study of Political Mobilization of Evangelical Ministers in the 1988 Republican Presidential Primaries.* Ph.D. diss., University of Kansas, 1991.

Showman, Sharon A. *The Rhetoric of a "Holy Nation": A Fantasy Theme Analysis of the Rhetorical Vision of the Rev. Marion "Pat" Gordon Robertson.* Ph.D. diss., Bowling Green State University, 1988.

Steele, Shelby. *The Content of Our Character: A New Vision of Race in America.* New York: St. Martin's Press, 1990.

Stern, Fritz. *The Politics of Cultural Despair.* Berkeley: University of California Press, 1961.

Taylor, Charles. "The Politics of Recognition." In *Multiculturalism and the Politics of Recognition,* ed. Amy Gutmann, 25-73. Princeton: Princeton University Press, 1992.

———. *Sources of the Self.* Cambridge: Harvard University Press, 1989.

Tonnies, Ferdinand. *Community and Society: Gemeinschaft und Gesellschaft.* Trans. and ed. Charles P. Loomis. East Lansing: Michigan State University Press, 1957.

Van Til, Cornelius. *The Defense of the Faith.* 2d ed. Phillipsburg, NJ: Presbyterian & Reformed, 1963.

Viguerie, Richard. *The New Right: We're Ready to Lead.* Falls Church, VA: The Viguerie Co., 1980.

Wacker, Grant. "Pentecostalism." In *Encyclopedia of the American Religious Experience,* eds. Charles H. Lippy and Peter W. Williams, 933-45. New York: Charles Scribner's Sons, 1988.

———. "Uneasy in Zion: Evangelicals in Postmodern Society." In *Evangelicalism and Modern America,* ed. George M. Marsden, 17-28. Grand Rapids, MI: William B. Eerdman's, 1984.

Wald, Kenneth. *Religion and Politics in the United States.* New York: St. Martins Press, 1987.

Weber, Max. *The Protestant Ethic and the Spirit of Capitalism,* trans. Talcott Parsons with introduction by Anthony Giddens. New York: Charles Scribner's Sons, 1976.

Wells, Ronald A. "Schaeffer on America." In *Reflections on Francis Schaeffer,* ed. Ronald W. Ruegsegger, 221-42. Grand Rapids: Academie Books, 1986.

Wilcox, Clyde. *God's Warriors: The Christian Right in Twentieth-Century America.* Baltimore, MD: The Johns Hopkins University Press, 1992.

Wills, Garry. *Under God.* New York: Simon & Schuster, 1990.

PERIODICALS

"1996 Voters at a Glance." Associated Press, November 5, 1996.

"Abortion Foes Differ on Tactics." *Christian Century,* May 22-29, 1996: 566-67.

"ADL Guilty of Defamation." *Christian American,* September 1994: 5.

Adler, Jerry. "Taking Offense." *Newsweek,* December 24, 1990: 48-55.

Alter, Jonathan and Howard Fineman. "Pat Robertson: The TelePolitician." *Newsweek,* February 22, 1988: 18-19.

Anderson, Lisa. "Speaking Softly, GOP's Right Still Carries Big Stick." *Chicago Tribune,* August 16, 1996: 1,1.

Andrews, Mark. "Pat's People." *Charisma,* March 1988: 26-36.

Argetsinger, Amy. "Christian Coalition Courts Black Churches." *Washington Post,* May 11, 1997: A18.

Armey, Dick. "Freedom's Choir." *Policy Review,* Winter 1994: 27-34.

Asante, Molefi Kete. "Multiculturalism: An Exchange." *American Scholar,* Spring 1991: 267-72.

Atlas, James. "The Counter Counterculture." *New York Times Magazine,* February 12, 1995: 32-39, 54, 61-65.

Atwood Thomas C. "Through a Glass Darkly." *Policy Review,* Fall 1990: 44-53.

Baker, Peter and Laurie Goodstein. "Christian Coalition Rearranges Top Posts." *Washington Post,* June 12, 1997: A15.

Baker, Russell. "It's Safe with Me, Pat." *New York Times,* February 13, 1988: I27.

Balz, Dan. "Ralph Reed Wants to Take Movement to New Political Level." *Washington Post,* April 25, 1997: A11.

———, and David S. Broder. "Gingrich Could Face Leadership Challenge." *Washington Post,* November 5, 1998: A1.

———, and Ann Devroy. "Dole Shifts Attack, Drops 'Extremist' Tag." *Washington Post,* February 23, 1996: A1, A12.

Barabak, Mark Z. and Amy Bayer. "An Interview with the Republican Challenger: Dole 'Not Bound' by Unread Platform." *The San Diego Union- Tribune,* August 11, 1996: A1.

Barnes, Fred. "Bauer Power." *Weekly Standard,* December 22, 1997: 18-23.

———. "Blessed are the Kingmakers." *New Republic,* March 21, 1988: 13.

Barnes, James A. "Revival Time." *National Journal,* January 23, 1993: 189-91.

Barr, William. "The FEC's War Against the First Amendment." *Wall Street Journal,* August 14, 1996: A13.

Barrett, Laurence I. "Fighting for God and the Right Wing." *Time,* September 13, 1993: 58-60.

———. "His Eyes Have Seen the Glory." *Time,* September 28, 1987: 22-23.

Bates, Thomas R. "Gramsci and the Theory of Hegemony." *Journal of the History of Ideas* 36 (April-June 1975): 351-66.

Baxter, Tom. "Reed's 'Tough' Election Day Probably a Maturing Experience." Cox News Service, November 4, 1998.

Bennet, James. "Christian Coalition Leader Denies Shifting on Abortion." *New York Times,* May 5, 1996: A1.

———. "Foes of Abortion Unite on a Warning to Dole." *New York Times,* March 17, 1996: I28.

Berke, Richard L. "Christian Right Defies Categories." *New York Times,* July 22, 1994: A1.

———. "The 'Contract' Gets New Ally on the Right." *New York Times,* January 18, 1995: A13.

———. "Flurry of Anti-Gay Remarks Has G.O.P. Fearing a Backlash." *New York Times,* June 30, 1998: A1.

——. "For Christian Coalition, A Reaffirmation of Power." *New York Times,* September 15, 1997: A18.

——. "For G.O.P., Religious Right Plays Waiting Game in Iowa." *New York Times,* April 17, 1995: A1, A12.

——. "From Cabinet to Leadership of Coalition." *New York Times,* June 12, 1997: A15.

——. "Is Suffering in Silence the Democrats' Cross?" *New York Times,* August 21, 1994: IV4.

——. "News Analysis: Chaotic Message to Dole on Abortion." *New York Times,* June 24, 1996: A8.

——. "Politicians Woo Christian Group." *New York Times,* September 9, 1995: I1, I9.

——. "The Republican Middle Looks for an Edge." *New York Times,* November 8, 1998: IV1.

——. "To See Ralph Reed, Take a Number." *New York Times,* September 14, 1997: I18.

Berman, Paul. "Intellectuals After the Revolution: What's Happened Since the Sixties?" *Dissent.* Winter 1989: 86-94.

Birnbaum, Jeffery. "The Gospel According to Ralph." *Time,* May 15, 1995: 28-35.

Blumenthal, Sidney. "Christian Soldiers." *New Yorker,* July 18, 1994: 31-37.

Boaz, David. "Pat Robertson's Crackpopulism." *Wall Street Journal,* February 10, 1988: 20.

Borger, Gloria. "The Ralph Reed Primary." *U.S. News & World Report,* December 29, 1997/January 5, 1997: 41.

Boston, Rob. "Stacked Deck." *Church & State,* July/August 1996: 4(148)-8(152)

——. "'Thank God for Computers.'" *Church & State,* October 1996: 10(202).

Brauer, Jerald C. "The Rule of the Saints in American Politics." *Church History* 27, no. 3 (September 1958): 240-55.

Brinkley, Alan. "The Problem of American Conservatism." *American Historical Review* 99, no. 2 (April 1994): 409-52.

Broder, David S. "'Five Republican Parties' Seek Leader." *Washington Post,* November 7, 1996: A23.

Brookheiser, Richard. "Pat Robertson Seeks Lower Office." *National Review,* August 29, 1986: 30.

Bruce, Steve. "The Inevitable Failure of the New Christian Right." *Sociology of Religion* 55, no. 3 (Fall 1994): 229-42.

Burrell, Cassandra. "Christian Group Backs School Prayer." Associated Press, May 22, 1997.

Byrd, Joan. "Blind Spots." *Washington Post,* February 7, 1993: C6.

Calmes, Jackie. "Tougher GOP Stance on Social Issues Reflects Surge of the Religious Right." *Wall Street Journal,* August 20, 1992: A1.

Cannon, Angie. "Christian Coalition Woos Blacks." *Tallahassee Democrat,* June 17, 1996: 3A.

"Cartoon Portrays Christians as Rats." *Christian American,* April 1993: 6.

Chandler, Russell. "Robertson Moves to Fill Christian Right Vacuum." *Los Angeles Times,* May 15, 1990: A5.

"Christian American Staff." *Christian American,* Winter 1990: 2.

"Christian Coalition Hires Black Liaison." *Christian Century,* April 24, 1996: 448.

"The Christian Coalition Lawsuit: Shining Some Light in the Darkness." *Church & State,* September 1996: 14(182).

"Christian Coalition Names Finance Director." *Virginian-Pilot,* October 2, 1997: B5.

"Christian Coalition Numbers Still Don't Add Up." *Church & State,* December 1996: 10(250).

"Christian Coalition Sued by FEC." *National Liberty Journal,* September 1996: 1, 8.

"Christian Group Coaches School Board Candidates." *New York Times,* June 14, 1995: B8.

"Christian Group Raises $24.9M." Associated Press, December 10, 1996.

"Christians Must Stand Together." *Christian American,* March 1993: 28.

Clapp, Rodney. "Democracy as Heresy." *Christianity Today,* February 20, 1987: 17-23.

Clarkson, Frederick. "The Christian Coalition: On the Road to Victory?" *Church & State,* January 1992: 4(4)-7(7).

———. "HardCOR." *Church & State,* January 1991: 9(9)-12(12).

Clendinen, Dudley. "TV Evangelists Assume Larger Convention Role." *New York Times,* August 19, 1984: A32.

"Clinton Inaugural: Celebration or Tragedy?" *Christian American,* January 1993: 28.

"Coalition Posts Reward in Church Arson Cases." *Christian Century,* May 8, 1996: 504-05.

"Coalition's Size Challenged." *Christian Century,* January 24, 1996: 68-69.

Conason, Joe. "Ralph Reed, Smart As The Devil." *Playboy,* November 1996: 90-92, 136, 140-42.

———. "The Religious Right's Quiet Revival." *The Nation,* April 27, 1992: 551, 553-59.

"Confirm Clarence Thomas to the Court." *Christian American,* September/ October 1991: 12.

Conn, Joseph L. "Behind the Mask." *Church & State,* November 1994: 4(218)-8(222).

———. "Double Trouble." *Church & State,* July/August 1997: 4(148)-6(150).

———. "'Tear Down the Wall.'" *Church & State,* May 1997: 9(105)-13(109).

Connolly, Ceci. "Political Machine Loses a Wheel." *Washington Post,* September 12, 1997: A4.

———, and Dan Balz. "Christian Coalition Is Reorganizing." *Washington Post,* December 20, 1997: A6.

"Conservative Firewall Stops Ballot Meltdown." *Christian American,* January/ February 1997: 24.

"A 'Contract with the Family.'" *Christian Century,* May 24-31, 1995: 559-60.

"Conventional Wisdom Watch." *Newsweek,* June 22, 1998: 6.

"Conventional Wisdom Watch." *Newsweek,* November 16, 1998: 6.

"Conventional Wisdom Watch: The Great GOP Beach Volleyball Bounce Edition." *Newsweek,* August 26, 1996: 6.

"Corrections." *Washington Post,* February 2, 1993: A3.

Corry, John. "In Iowa, Networks Address the Robertson Factor." *New York Times,* February 10, 1988: III26.

"Court Cases: New Litigation, FEC v. The Christian Coalition." *Federal Election Commission Record* 22, no. 9 (September 1996): 1-2.

Cox, Harvey. "The Warring Visions of the Religious Right." *The Atlantic Monthly,* November 1995: 59-69.

Crouch, Michelle. "Coalition Aids Burned Churches." Associated Press, October 18, 1996.

Curtis, Carolyn. "Coming Together." *Christian American,* September/October 1996: 22-27.

———. "The Crucial Catholic Vote." *Christian American,* November/December 1995: 12-15.

———. "High Tech Activism." *Christian American,* October 1995: 20-23.

———. "Putting Out a Contract." *Christianity Today,* July 17, 1995: 54.

Dabney, Dick. "God's Own Network." *Harper's Magazine,* August 1980: 33-52.

Dart, John. "Vote Buoys, Bothers Local Faith Activists." *Los Angeles Times,* November 9, 1996: A1.

Davis, Derek H. "Editorial: A Commentary on the Proposed 'Religious Equality/ Liberties' Amendment." *Journal of Church and State* 38, no. 1 (Winter 1996): 5-23.

DeMar, Gary. "Letters." *Christianity Today,* August 17, 1992: 10.

———. "Oh, Brother!" *Biblical Worldview,* May 1995: 4.

———. "What's Wrong with the Christian Coalition?" *Biblical Worldview,* October 1996: 9-12.

———. "Where Do We Go from Here?" *Biblical Worldview,* December 1996: 2.

"Demagoguery in America." *New Republic,* August 1, 1994: 7.

DeParle, Jason. "A Fundamental Problem." *New York Times Magazine,* July 14, 1996: 18-25, 32, 38, 42-43.

Dewar, Helen. "7 Groups Join to Resist Panel Subpoenas." *Washington Post,* September 4, 1997: A12.

"Dialing For Theocracy? 'LifeLine' Phone Group Favors Church Over State." *Church & State,* January 1996: 15(15)-16(16).

Dillon, Sam. "Lifting a Conservative Voice: Christian Group Views School Board Elections as a Test of Voter Support." *New York Times,* April 10, 1993: I23.

———. "Spirited Race for Schools Accelerates." *New York Times,* April 28, 1993: B2.

Dionne, E. J., Jr. "Robertson's Victory in Ballot Shakes Rivals in G.O.P. Race." *New York Times,* September 14, 1987: B12.

Domenech, Benjamin. "Dobson's Choice, Why the Conservative Outsider's Agenda Worries GOP Leaders." *Washington Post,* April 19, 1998: C2.

Drew, Elizabeth. "Why Clinton Will Be Impeached." *Washington Post,* September 23, 1998: A25.

Drinkard, Jim. "Christian Coalition Narrowly Avoids Second Suit On Campaign Spending." Associated Press, July 31, 1996.

———. "Christian Coalition: Religious Advocate or Tax-Free Political Machine?" Associated Press, July 7, 1996.

————. "Direct-Mail Contractor Says Prosecutors Have Questioned Him." Associated Press, July 20, 1996.

————. "Group Accepted Money From Businessman Wanting to Help Bush." Associated Press, August 3, 1996.

————. "Lobbyists Paid $400M in DC." Associated Press, September 22, 1996.

————. "Robertson: Dole Needs Miracle." Associated Press, September 14, 1996.

Ebert, Michael. "Godly Principles Will Restore Our Independence." *Christian American,* July/August 1996: 6.

Edsall, Thomas B. "By Overriding Hyde, Dole Invited Setback on Abortion Language." *Washington Post,* August 9, 1996: A12.

————. "Christian Coalition Steps Boldly into Politics." *Washington Post,* September 10, 1992: A1, A14.

————. "Christian Coalition Threatens GOP." *Washington Post,* February 11, 1995: A6.

————. "Christian Political Soldier Helps Revive Movement." *Washington Post,* September 10, 1993: A4.

————. "Christian Right Avoiding Spotlight." *Washington Post,* August 14, 1996: A1.

————. "Christian Right Lifts Ashcroft." *Washington Post,* April 14, 1998: A1.

————. "Conservatives Seek to Revise GOP's Call for Amendment Banning Abortion." *Washington Post,* September 18, 1994: A6.

————. "Democratic Party Chief's Fiery Words Stir Wrath as Christian Coalition Meets." *Washington Post,* September 11, 1993: A4.

————. "Dole Vows to Sign 'Partial-Birth' Abortion Ban." *Washington Post,* September 15, 1996: A16.

————. "GOP's Agenda Pleases Backers." *Washington Post,* July 19, 1998: A6.

————. "Powell Proving Divisive Among Conservatives." *Washington Post,* October 23, 1995: A8.

————. "Resignation 'Too Easy,' Robertson Tells Coalition." *Washington Post,* September 19, 1998: A8.

————. "Robertson: Christian Coalition Should Emulate Tammany Hall." *Washington Post,* September 18, 1997: A2.

————. "Robertson Urges Christian Activists to Take Over GOP State Parties." *Washington Post,* September 10, 1995: A24.

Edsall, Thomas B. and David S. Broder. "Robertson Accuses Kirk Of Bigotry." *Washington Post,* March 2, 1986: A4.

English, Paul. "Quayle and Helms Rally Religious Right." *Christian American,* January/February 1992: 1, 4.

English, Paul and Connie Zhu. "Road to Victory '93." *Christian American,* October 1993: 14.

Epps, Garrett. "Voices of '88: A Surprising New Politics of Protest, Robertson's Evangelicals." *Washington Post,* February 14, 1988: C2.

"Ex-Candidate Robertson Creates New Christian Political Group." *Washington Post,* March 14, 1990: A6.

Feldmann, Linda. "Religious Right's New Mandarin." *Christian Science Monitor,* March 18, 1998: 1.

Ferranti, Jennifer. "Regent University Wins Faculty Tenure Lawsuit." *Christianity Today,* October 2, 1995: 104.

Fialka, John J. and Ellen Hume. "Pulpit and Politics: TV Preacher, Possibly Eyeing the Presidency, Is Polishing His Image." *Wall Street Journal,* October 17, 1985: A1.

Fineman, Howard. "The Fight Inside the Tent." *Newsweek,* May 13, 1996: 24-27.

———. "Just the Ticket?" *Newsweek,* August 19, 1996: 22-27.

Fitschen, Steven W. "The Not So New World Order." *Christian American,* January/February 1992: 12.

Foskett, Ken. "National Campaign Ad Targets Clinton." Cox News Service, October 7, 1998.

Foster, Dick. "Focus on Family Leader Has Stroke." *Rocky Mountain News,* June 18, 1998: 14A.

Fournier, Ron. "Pat Robertson Visits Capitol Hill." AP Online, June 10, 1998.

Franklin, Ben A. "200,000 March and Pray at Christian Rally in Capital." *New York Times,* April 30, 1980: A1, A20.

Gailey, Phil. "A Bitter Struggle Splits South Carolina G.O.P." *New York Times,* April 6, 1987: B9.

Galvin, Kevin. "Buchanan Forces Gearing Up for Abortion Battle." Associated Press, May 3, 1996.

———. "Unions Back Christian Coalition." Associated Press Online, September 29, 1998.

Gates, David. "White Male Paranoia: New Victims or Just Bad Sports?" *Newsweek,* March 29, 1993: 3, 48-53.

Gates, Henry Louis, Jr. "A Bad Case of Academic Altruism." *New York Times,* December 9, 1990: IV5.

Germond, Jack W. and Jules Witcover. "The Miracle Worker." *The Washingtonian,* November 1986: 106-20.

Gerson, Michael J. "Christian Coalition in Unprecedented Crisis." *U.S. News & World Report,* February 16, 1998: 33.

"The 'Ghettoizing' of the Gospel." *Christian American,* January 1993: 28.

Gigot, Paul A. "Potomac Watch: Why Liberals Secretly Love James Dobson." *Wall Street Journal,* June 5, 1998: A14.

———. "The Religious Right Shows Its Own Strains." *Wall Street Journal,* March 1, 1996: A14.

Goldberg, Carey. "In Abortion War, High-Tech Arms." *New York Times,* August 9, 1996: A20.

Goldstein, David. "Turnout a Key for Democrats." *Kansas City Star,* November 5, 1998: A1.

Goodstein, Laurie. "Catholics Prove Hard to Convert to the Politics of Coalition." *Washington Post,* September 2, 1996: A1.

———. "Christian Coalition Set for Voter Guide Blitz." *Washington Post,* November 2, 1996: A3.

———. "Church Debate over Voter Guides." *New York Times,* October 29, 1998: A27.

———. "Conservative Christian Leader Accuses Republicans of Betrayal." *New York Times,* February 12, 1998: A22.

————. "Jackson Offers No Apology for Blast at Christian Right." *Washington Post,* December 9, 1994: A2.

————. "Religious Conservatives, Stung by Vote Losses, Blame G.O.P. for Focusing on Clinton." *New York Times,* November 5, 1998: B3.

————. "Religious Right, Frustrated, Trying New Tactic on G.O.P." *New York Times,* March 23, 1998: A1.

Goodstein, Laurie and Donald P. Baker. "Politics: Coalition Schedule Angers Some Jews." *Washington Post,* September 7, 1996: A4.

Goodstein, Laurie and John E. Yang. "Separation of Church, State Targeted." *Washington Post,* March 25, 1997: A4.

Gray, Paul. "Whose America?" *Time,* July 8, 1991: 12-17.

Green, John C. "Pat Robertson and the Latest Crusade: Religious Resources and the 1988 Presidential Campaign." *Social Science Quarterly* 74, no. 1 (March 1993): 156-68.

————, James L. Guth, Lyman A. Kellstedt, and Corwin E. Smidt. "Evangelical Realignment: The Political Power of the Christian Right." *Christian Century,* July 5-12, 1995: 676-79.

Grenier, Richard. "The Gandhi Nobody Knows." *Commentary,* March 1983: 59-72.

Gribbin, D. J. "Bridge-Building Across Racial Lines." *Christian American,* September 1995: 20-21.

————. "Campaign to Derail Voter Guides Failed." *Christian American,* January/February 1997: 51.

Grove, Lloyd. "Ralph Reed's Invisible Army." *Washington Post,* August 28, 1996: C1.

————. "Robertson, Taking Aim at the Critics: A Campaign Plagued by Rocky Relations with the Press." *Washington Post,* February 22, 1988: B1, B9.

Hall, John. "A Tentative Sort of Crusade." *Tampa Tribune,* October 2, 1998: 17.

Hallow, Ralph Z. "Activists Hail Gingrich, Save Hoots for Perot." *Washington Times,* September 14, 1996: A1, A6.

————. "At Last Minute, Reed Softens Farewell Speech to Coalition." *Washington Times,* September 13, 1997: A4.

————. "Bennett Wins Cheers with Call for Traditional Values." *Washington Times,* September 12, 1993: A3.

————. "Canceling of Straw Poll Seen as Face-Saving Move." *Washington Times,* September 18, 1998: A4.

————. "Christian Coalition Goes Back to Core Principles." *Washington Times,* January 7, 1998: A1.

————. "Christian Coalition Simmers Over Leak." *Washington Times,* February 19, 1998: A4.

————. "Dole Visit Energizes Christian Coalition." *Washington Times,* September 15, 1996: A1, A5.

Hart, Ben. "Rising Young Stars." *Conservative Digest,* January/February 1989: 18-22.

"Hate Crimes Against Christians." *Christian American,* November/December 1992: 28.

Heilbrunn, Jacob. "His Anti-Semitic Sources." *New York Review,* April 20, 1995: 68-71.

Henneberger, Melinda. "Ralph Reed Is His Cross to Bear." *New York Times Magazine,* August 9, 1998: 24-27.

Hertenstein, Mike. "Casting the Net Overboard: Is the Religious Right FINDING or ABANDONING the Mainstream?" *Rutherford,* March 1994: 3, 8-10, 18.

Hiaasen, Carl. "Rev. Pat Goes to Bat for Martinez." *Miami Herald,* July 11, 1990: 1B.

Horstman, Barry M. "Crusade for Public Office in 2nd Stage." *Los Angeles Times,* March 22, 1992: B5.

Hubbard, Kim and Linda Kramer. "Ralph Reed." *People,* February 27, 1996: 60- 64.

Hume, Ellen. "Pat Robertson Hopes to Turn Evangelical Fervor into Political Constituency for a Presidential Bid." *Wall Street Journal,* July 16, 1986: A44.

Hunt, Albert. "Christian Coalition's Problem Is Secular, Not Religious." *Wall Street Journal,* July 28, 1994: A13.

"If There's Safety in Numbers for Christians, This Is a Safety Pin." advertisement. *Christian American,* Fall 1990: 7.

Innerst, Carol. "Parents Labeled Religious Fanatics for Fighting Schools: Schools Learn Ways to Pin Labels on Parental Foes." *Washington Times,* April 13, 1994: A1.

"Inside Politics." *Washington Times,* September 7, 1995: A9.

Isikoff, Michael. "Christian Coalition Steps Boldly into Politics." *Washington Post,* September 10, 1992: A1, A14.

Jacobson, Louis. "Washington's Five-Rolodex Lobbyist." *National Journal,* August 5, 1995: 2017.

Jacoby, Mary. "Another Convention: Tiny U.S. Taxpayers Party Represents a Minority within a Minority." *Chicago Tribune,* August 15, 1996: 1,1.

Kagay, Michael. "Growth Area Seen for Religious Right." *New York Times,* August 10, 1996: I1.

Kaufman, Jonathan. "Some Liberal Jews, to Their Own Surprise, See a Rise in Bigotry." *Wall Street Journal,* March 8, 1995: A1.

Kelleher, John V. "A Long Way from Tipperary," review of *To the Golden Door,* by George Potter. *Reporter,* May 12, 1960: 44-46.

Kim, Eun-Kyung. "From GOP to Christian Coalition." Associated Press, June 11, 1997.

King, Wayne. "The Record of Pat Robertson On Religion and Government." *New York Times,* December 27, 1987: 1, 30.

———. "Robertson Quits as a Baptist Minister." *New York Times,* September 30, 1987: A20.

Kramer, Michael. "Are You Running with Me Jesus?" *New York,* August 18, 1986: 22-29.

Kristol, Irving. "Conservative Christians: Into the Fray." *Wall Street Journal,* December 22, 1995: A8.

Kurtz, Howard. "Clinton Ad Counters Christian Coalition's Voter Guide." *Washington Post,* November 3, 1996: A32.

Lacayo, Richard. "The Next Act." *Time,* November 18, 1996: 69.

Langenbach, Lisa and John C. Green. "Hollow Core: Evangelical Clergy & the 1988 Robertson Campaign." *Polity* 25, no. 1 (Fall 1992): 147-58.

Lawton, Kim A. "Back to the Future?" *Christianity Today,* January 6, 1996: 54- 56, 69-70.

———. "A Democratic Fund-Raising Letter Rips Pat Robertson." *Christianity Today,* April 18, 1986: 48.

———. "Pat's Big Surprise: The Army Is Still Invisible." *Christianity Today,* April 8, 1988: 44-45.

———. "A Republican God?" *Christianity Today,* October 5, 1992: 50.

Lemann, Nicholas. "Reed in the Wind," review of *Active Faith,* by Ralph Reed and *The Godless Constitution,* by Isaac Kramnick and R. Laurence Moore. *New Republic,* July 8, 1996: 32-36.

Levinson, Sanford. "Religious Language and the Public Square," review of *Love and Power,* by Michael J. Perry. *Harvard Law Review* 105 (June 1992): 2061-79.

———. "Some Reflections on Multiculturalism, 'Equal Concern and Respect,' and the Establishment Clause of the First Amendment." *University of Richmond Law Review* 27 (1993): 989-1021.

Lewis, Neil A. "Nonprofit Groups to Defy Subpoenas in Senate Inquiry." *New York Times,* September 4, 1997: A16.

"Liberal Media Elite Stigmatizes Evangelicals." *Christian American,* March 1993: 28.

Lind, Michael. "On Pat Robertson: His Defenders." *The New York Review,* April 20, 1995: 67-68.

———. "Rev. Robertson's Grand International Conspiracy Theory." *New York Review,* February 2, 1995: 21-25.

Locy, Toni. "FEC Lawsuit Against Christian Coalition Triggers Avalanche of Protest Letters." *Washington Post,* October 17, 1996: A9.

Lynn, Barry W. "Anti-Christian 'Bigotry': A Fundamentally Unfair Complaint." *Church & State,* February 1994: 23(47).

———. "An Open Letter To America's Churches About Politics." *Church & State,* October 1996: 15(207).

Manegold, Catherine S. "The New Congress: Some on Right See a Tactical Misstep on School Prayer." *New York Times,* November 19, 1994: I1.

Marcus, Ruth. "Christian Coalition Suspends Official." *Washington Post,* July 19, 1996: A30.

———. "Elections Commission Accuses Christian Coalition." *Washington Post,* August 1, 1996: A10.

———. "FEC Files Suit Over Christian Coalition Role." *Washington Post,* July 31, 1996: A1.

Margolick, David. "At the Bar." *New York Times,* October 10, 1993: B10.

Mawyer, Martin. "Martin Mawyer," interview by Karen Augustine. *Rutherford,* March 1994: 12.

Mayer, Allan J. "A Tide of Born-Again Politics." *Newsweek,* September 15, 1980: 28-36.

Mayer, Jane. "Lonely Guy: Why President Clinton Is Partying Alone." *New Yorker,* October 30, 1995: 58-62.

Maynard, Roy. "Titus Breaks His Silence." *World,* February 5, 1994: 22-24.

McConnell, Michael W. "Religious Freedom at a Crossroads." *University of Chicago Law Review* 59 (1992): 115-94.

McKenzie, David. "Stephen Carter, the Christian Coalition, and the Civil Rights Analogy." *Journal of Church and State* 38, no. 2 (Spring 1996): 297-319.

Meacham, Jon. "What the Religious Right Can Teach the New Democrats." *The Washington Monthly,* April 1993: 42-48.

Meckler, Laura. "Christian Coalition Leader Wades into Dangerous Waters." Associated Press, May 21, 1996.

Merelman, Richard. "Racial Conflict and Cultural Politics in the United States." *The Journal of Politics* 56, no. 1 (1994): 1-20.

Milbank, Dana. "The Conversion of Steve Forbes." *New Republic,* April 27, 1998: 21-25.

Mills, Mike. "Murdoch to Buy Half of Family Channel." *Washington Post,* June 12, 1997: E1.

Moen, Matthew C. "The Evolving Politics of the Christian Right." *PS: Political Science and Politics* 39, no. 3 (September 1996): 461-64.

———. "From Revolution to Evolution: The Changing Nature of the Christian Right." *Sociology of Religion* 55, no. 3 (Fall 1994): 345-58.

Mundy, Alicia. "The God Squad." *Adweek,* February 13, 1995: 20-26.

Murphy, Caryle. "Gays React to Ads that Call Them Sinners." *Washington Post,* July 19, 1998: B1.

Mydans, Seth. "Evangelicals Gain With Covert Candidates." *New York Times,* October 27, 1992: A1, A9.

Nicols, John. "Christian Coalition Now a Lion in GOP." *(Toledo, Ohio) The Blade,* August 16, 1992: 1-2.

Niebuhr, Gustav. "Broadcasters Urged to Wage 'Cultural War.'" *Washington Post,* February 20, 1993: D8.

———. "Christian Coalition Sees Recruiting Possibilities Among Catholics." *New York Times,* October 7, 1995: 13.

———. "The Christian Coalition Plans to Register One Million Voters." *New York Times,* September 14, 1996: I9.

———. "Christian Group Vows to Exert More Influence on the G.O.P." *New York Times,* November 7, 1996: B10.

———. "Dole Gets Christian Coalition's Trust and Prodding." *New York Times,* September 16, 1996: A1, A12.

———. "Pat Robertson Says He Intended No Anti-Semitism in Book He Wrote Four Years Ago." *New York Times,* March 4, 1995: I10.

———. "The Religious Right Readies Agenda for Second 100 Days." *New York Times,* May 16, 1995: A1.

"No One Model American: A Statement on Multicultural Education." *The Journal of Teacher Education* 24, no. 1 (Winter 1973): 264-65.

Norquist, Grover G. "Dobson and the GOP." *The American Spectator,* July 1998: 60-62.

O'Keefe, Mark. "Ex-regent Dean: His Views Got Him Fired." *The Virginian- Pilot & The Ledger-Star,* January 23, 1994: B1.

Ostling, Richard N. "A Jerry-Built Coalition Regroups." *Time,* November 16, 1987: 68-69.

————. "Religious Right Had Tough Election." *AP Online,* November 6, 1998.

"Our Christian Duty to Vote." *Christian American,* September/October 1992: 24.

Packer-Tursman, Judy. "Right Wing: GOP Too Wishy Washy." *Pittsburgh Post-Gazette,* November 5, 1998: A-18.

Penning, James M. "Pat Robertson and the GOP: 1988 and Beyond." *Sociology of Religion* 55, no. 3 (Fall 1994): 327-35.

"People and Events: Ralph Reed Led Extreme Protests at North Carolina Clinic." *Church & State,* November 1995: 18(234).

Perry, James M. "Soul Mates: The Christian Coalition Crusades to Broaden Rightist Political Base." *Wall Street Journal,* July 19, 1994: A1.

Perry, James M. and David Schribman, "Robertson's Showing and Dole Triumph Change GOP Picture." *Wall Street Journal,* February 10, 1988: A1.

Persinos, John F. "Has the Christian Right Taken Over the Republican Party." *Campaigns & Elections,* September 1994: 20-24.

Peyton, Jeffrey M. "Family Agenda Rolls Ahead." *Christian American,* July/August 1995: 1, 4.

Pinkerton, James P. "Pragmatism Yes, Moralism No." *Los Angeles Times,* November 5, 1998: B9.

Podhoretz, Norman. "In the Matter of Pat Robertson." *Commentary,* August 1995: 27-32.

"Preachers in Politics." *U.S. News & World Report,* September 24, 1979: 37-41.

"Pro-Abortion Republicans Push for Platform Showdown." *Christian American,* July/August 1996: 16.

Prochnau, William and Laura Parker. "The Doomsday Man." *Vanity Fair,* July 1996: 82-88, 147-53.

"Pro-Family Candidates Capture Key Posts." *Christian American,* Winter 1990: 1.

Pugh, Jeanne. "Righter than Thou." *Church & State,* June 1996: 12(132).

Raasch, Chuck. "Bennett Asks: Where's the Religious Right in Clinton Fight?" Gannett News Service, February 28, 1998.

"Radical Attacks on Churches Increasing." *Christian American,* July/August 1994: 18.

Rainie, Harrison. "Robertson's Grand Design." *U.S. News & World Report,* February 22, 1988: 14-18.

"Ralph Reed." *Current Biography,* March 1996: 34-37.

"Ralph Reed's Missing Million: Christian Coalition Numbers Drop." *Church & State,* January 1996: 15(15).

Rausch, David A. and Douglas E. Chismar. "The New Puritans and Their Theonomic Paradise." *Christian Century,* August 3-10, 1983: 712-15.

Ravitch, Diane. "Multiculturalism: An Exchange." *American Scholar,* Spring 1991: 272-76.

————. "Multiculturalism: E Pluribus Plures." *American Scholar,* Summer 1990: 337-54.

Reed, Ralph. "Active Faith: The Role of Religious Conservatism in America," address at the Town Hall, Los Angeles, California, February 12, 1996. *Vital Speeches of the Day,* March 15, 1996: 329-31.

————. "Active Faith," interview by Michael Ebert. *Christian American,* May/June 1996: 12-13.

———. "'Fighting the Devil with Fire': Carl Vinson's Victory over Tom Watson in the 1918 Tenth District Democratic Primary." *Georgia Historical Quarterly* 67, no. 4 (Winter 1983): 451-79.

———. "One Lord, One Faith, One Voice?" symposium with Tony Campolo and Charles Colson. *Christianity Today,* October 7, 1996: 34-43.

———. "Priorities." *Christian American,* September/October 1996: 54.

———. "Ralph Reed on Catholics," interview by Deal W. Hudson. *Crisis,* November 1995: 18-22.

———. "A Strategy for Evangelicals." *Christian American,* January 1993: 15.

———. "'We Stand at a Crossroads.'" *Newsweek,* May 13, 1996: 28-29.

Reed, Ralph, Jr. "Casting a Wider Net." *Policy Review,* Summer 1993: 31-35.

———. "Faith Essential to Democracy." *Christian American,* November/ December 1994: 10-11.

———. "Putting a Friendly Face on the Pro-Family Movement." *Christian American,* April 1993: 29.

———. "We Want Washington to Value Families." *Christian American,* February 1995: 16-17.

Reed, Ralph E., Jr. "'Christian Right' Belongs in the GOP," interview by Allan Ryskind. *Human Events,* February 6, 1993: 10-12.

———. "Emory College and the Sledd Affair of 1902: A Case Study in Southern Honor and Racial Attitudes." *Georgia Historical Quarterly* 72, no. 3 (Fall 1988): 463-92.

———. "The Good News." *Christian American,* November/December 1992: 29.

———. "Mobilizing the Christian Right," interview. *Campaigns & Elections,* October/November 1993: 33-36.

———. "You Can Make a Difference." *Christian American,* July/August 1992: 25.

Regan, Mary Beth and Richard S. Dunham. "Gimme that Old-Time Marketing." *Business Week,* November 6, 1995: 76-77.

Reid, T. R. "'Invisible Army' Won Few Battles." *Washington Post,* December 17, 1988: A3.

———. "Robertson Corrects Details of His Life." *Washington Post,* October 8, 1987: A6.

———. "Robertson Joins the Fray." *Washington Post,* October 2, 1987: A1.

———. "Robertson Links Bush to Swaggart Scandal." *Washington Post,* February 24, 1988: A1.

———. "Robertson's Recruits." *Washington Post,* February 8, 1988: A6.

———. "Traditional Morality at Core of Robertson's Political Quest." *Washington Post,* March 2, 1988: A8.

"Religious Bigotry Backfires in Virginia." *Christian American,* November/ December 1993: 8.

"Religious Right Fashion Trends." *Time,* March 15, 1993: 15.

Reno, Ronald A. "Gambling with America." *Christian American,* July/August 1996: 24-27.

Rich, Frank. "Bait and Switch." *New York Times,* March 2, 1995: A15.

———. "Bait and Switch II." *New York Times,* April 6, 1995: A15.

Roberts, Steven V. "Onward Christian Soldiers." *U.S. News & World Report,* June 6, 1994: 43.

"Robertson Backs View of a Separate Church." *New York Times,* October 5, 1987: B10.

"Robertson Bullish on Family Channel, UPI." *Christianity Today,* June 22, 1992: 51-52.

Robertson, M. G. "Pat." "Squeezing Religion out of the Public Square." *William & Mary Bill of Rights Journal* 4, no. 1 (1995): 223- 76.

Robertson, Pat. "Anti-Semitism Not Acceptable." *Christian American,* April 1995: 27.

———. "'Earned the right to speak . . . without being savaged.'" *Miami Herald,* July 18, 1990: 11A.

———. "Evangelicals 'Reinforce Mainstream America,'" interview. *U.S. News & World Report,* November 4, 1985: 71.

———. "Faith and Democracy." *Christian American,* November/December 1993: 16-17.

———. "Inquiry: I Can Keep Politics and Religion Apart," interview. *USA Today,* July 1, 1986: 9A.

———. "Law Must Embrace Morality." *Christian American,* April 1995: 16-17.

———. "Our Foreign Policy Should Put U.S. First." *New York Times,* March 5, 1995: IV4.

———. "Pat's View." *Christian American,* February 1994: 2.

———. "A Reply to My Critics." *Wall Street Journal,* April 12, 1995: A14.

———. "The Speech." *New York Times,* January 14, 1988: I20.

———. "Thousands of People Say 'Go for It!'" interview. *U.S. News & World Report,* July 14, 1986: 25.

———. "The Turning Tide." *Christian American,* October 1993: 18-19.

———. "Two Letters and Excerpts from Book." *New York Times,* March 4, 1995: I10.

"Robertson Regroups 'Invisible Army' into New Coalition." *Christianity Today,* April 23, 1990: 35.

"Robertson Speech Shows Partisanship, Group Says." *Chicago Tribune,* September 18, 1997: 14

Robichaux, Mark. "Tim Robertson Turns TV's Family Channel into a Major Business." *Wall Street Journal,* August 29, 1996: A1.

Rodgers, Guy. "The Media Just Doesn't Get It." *Christian American,* April 1993: 31.

———. "Out Of The Pews, into The Precincts." *Christian American,* March 1993: 31.

———. "Setting New Year's Goals." *Christian American,* January 1993: 31.

Rogers, Jay. "A Book Review: *Politically Incorrect* by Ralph Reed." *Chalcedon Report,* February 1995: 38-40.

Rorty, Richard. "The Unpatriotic Academy." *New York Times,* February 13, 1994: IV15.

Rosenfeld, Megan. "Don Hodel: A Belief in Belief." *Washington Post,* May 4, 1998: D1.

Russell, Mike. "Coalition Opens D.C. Office." *Christian American,* March 1993: 3.

———. "Millionth Member Joins Christian Coalition." *Christian American,* March 1994: 5.

———. "Poll Shows GOP Exodus." *Christian American,* April 1993: 1, 4.

Sack, Kevin. "Religious Right's Tactician on Wider Crusade." *New York Times,* June 12, 1998: A1.

Sawyer, Jon. "Pat Robertson Says He Would 'Love to See' Ashcroft as President." *St. Louis Post-Dispatch,* May 10, 1998: B1.

Scanlon, Heidi. "Fashionable Bigotry Against Evangelicals." *Christian American,* March 1993: 7.

Schlafly, Phyllis. "What's Going On with Bob Dole's Friends?" column. Copley News Service, May 16, 1996.

Schlesinger, Arthur, Jr. "The Cult of Ethnicity, Good and Bad." *Time,* July 8, 1991: 21.

Schlumpf, Heidi. "How Catholic Is the Catholic Alliance?" *Christianity Today,* May 20, 1996: 76.

Schneider, William. "The Republicans in '88." *Atlantic Monthly,* July 1987: 58- 82.

"School Board Training Seminar." *Christian American,* March 1995: 31.

Schribman, David. "Robertson Starts Presidential Campaign as Protestors Strive to Shout Him Down." *Wall Street Journal,* October 2, 1987: A44.

Schwartz, Maralee. "'Anti-Christian Bashing.'" *Washington Post,* February 2, 1988: A7.

———. "Politics: GOP's War of Words." *Washington Post,* October 3, 1986: A8.

———. "Politics: Tit for Tat." *Washington Post,* September 9, 1986: A8.

———. "Robertson-Rather Peace?" *Washington Post,* February 26, 1988: A8.

Schwartz, Maralee and Kenneth J. Cooper. "Politics." *Washington Post,* August 23, 1992: A15.

Schwartz, Maralee, Thomas B. Edsall, and T. R. Reid, "Robertson Blasts Media." *Washington Post,* January 24, 1988: A10.

Sedgwick, John. "The GOP's Three Amigos." *Newsweek,* January 9, 1995: 38-40.

Seelye, Katharine Q. "Christian Coalition Plans a Program for Inner-City Residents." *New York Times,* January 31, 1997: A15.

Seib, Gerald F. "GOP's Religious Conservatives Poised For Campaign to Get Action on Their Agenda." *Wall Street Journal,* May 8, 1995: A16.

SerVaas, Cory and Maynard Good Stoddard. "CBN's Pat Robertson: White House Next?" *Saturday Evening Post,* March 1985: 50(11).

Shribman, David. "Going Mainstream: Religious Right Drops High-Profile Tactics, Works on Local Level." *Wall Street Journal,* September 26, 1989: A1.

Shupe, Anson. "The Reconstructionist Movement on the New Christian Right." *Christian Century,* October 4, 1989: 880-82.

Simpson, Glenn R. "Christian Coalition's Low-Profile Event Seeks Big Donations from Conservatives." *Wall Street Journal,* September 16, 1996: A20.

Sizemore, Bill. "Christian Coalition Settles Suit with Vendor." *Virginian-Pilot,* March 24, 1998: A4.

———. "Coalition Sues, Saying Ally Raided Mailing List." *Virginian-Pilot,* January 15, 1998: A1.

———. "Fired Official is a Key Player in Christian Coalition Troubles." *Virginian-Pilot,* July 27, 1997: A1.

Sleeter, Christine E. and Carl A. Grant. "An Analysis of Multicultural Education in the United States." *Harvard Educational Review* 57, no. 4 (November 1987): 421-44.

Smith, Timothy L. "The Evangelical Kaleidoscope and the Call to Christian Unity." *Christian Scholar's Review* 15 (1986): 125-40.

Smothers, Ronald. "Bush Less than Loved among the Christian Right." *New York Times,* March 10, 1992: A21.

Spring, Beth. "Pat Robertson's Network Breaks Out of the Christian Ghetto." *Christianity Today,* January 1, 1982: 36-37.

Stafford, Tim. "Move Over, ACLU." *Christianity Today,* October 25, 1993: 20- 24.

————. "Robertson R Us: When Evangelicals Look in the Mirror, Do We See the Host of *The 700 Club* Staring Back?" *Christianity Today,* August 12, 1996: 26-33.

"Statement of Ownership, Management and Circulation." *Christian American,* November/December 1995: 3.

"Statement of Ownership, Management and Circulation." *Christian American,* November/December 1996: 6.

Stern, Andrew. "Christian Coalition Rallies Anti-Abortion Democrats." Reuter News Service, August 26, 1996.

Stone, Peter H. "Spreading the GOP Gospel—And Thriving." *National Journal,* December 6, 1997: 2470.

Sullivan, Robert. "An Army of the Faithful." *New York Times Magazine,* April 25, 1993: 32-34, 40-44.

"Survey Dashes Stereotypes." *Christian American,* April 1993: 5.

Terry, Randall. "Selling Out the Law of Heaven." *Washington Post,* September 18, 1994: C9.

Thomas, Cal. "Should Conservatives Abandon the Republican Ship?" *Los Angeles Times* Syndicate, November 21, 1996.

Thomas, Evan. "The Sons Also Rise." *Newsweek,* November 16, 1998: 44-48.

Thomas, Judy Lundstrom. "The New GOP." *Wichita Eagle,* September 26, 1992: 1A.

"To the Congress of the United States," advertisement. *USA Today,* June 25, 1990: 8A.

Tollerson, Ernest. "Christian Coalition Give Perot a Mostly Cool Reception." *New York Times,* September 14, 1996: 9.

Toner, Robin. "The Right Thinkers: Some Voices in the New Political Conversation." *New York Times,* November 22, 1994: B7.

Toulouse, Mark G. "Pat Robertson: Apocalyptic Theology and American Foreign Policy." *Journal of Church and State* 31, no. 1 (Winter 1989): 73-99.

Towns, Hollis R. "Black Leaders Mixed over Reed Pledge." *Atlanta Constitution,* June 19, 1996: B1.

Tucker, Cynthia. "Skandalakis, Reed Show True Colors." *Atlanta Journal and Constitution,* October 18, 1998: 7G.

Verhovek, Sam Howe. "Riding High, Bush Eases into 2000 Election." *New York Times,* May 25, 1998: A1.

————. "With Abortion Scarcely Uttered, Its Opponents Are Feeling Angry." *New York Times,* August 15, 1996: A1.

"Violence in America: Symptoms and Causes." *Christian American,* October 1993: 28.

Vobejda, Barbara. "Politics: Coalition Contrite Over Voter Guide." *Washington Post,* October 12, 1996: A17.

Von Drehle, David and Thomas B. Edsall. "Life of the Grand Old Party." *Washington Post,* August 14, 1994: A1, A22-A23.

Wallis, James R., Jr. "Mobilizing Christians Excites Her." *Christian American,* April 1995: 30.

————. "Reed Refutes Jackson Slander." *Christian American,* January 1995: 6.

Walsh, Edward. "Christian Coalition Leaders Back Ashcroft." *Washington Post,* February 17, 1998: A4.

"Washington Post Retracts." *Christian American,* March 1993: 7.

Weiss, Philip. "The Cultural Contradictions of the G.O.P." *Harper's Magazine,* January 1988: 48-57.

Weisskopf, Michael. "Energized by Pulpit or Passion, the Public is Calling." *Washington Post,* February 1, 1993: A1, A10.

"What to Call Pat Robertson." *New York Times,* February 15, 1988: I20.

"What's Happening to Religious Freedom Is Enough to Make You Gag." *Christian American,* Summer 1990: 6.

Wheeler, John, Jr. "Assault on Faith: Liberals Launch Campaign of Bigotry." *Christian American,* September 1994: 1, 4.

————. "New Covenant or Old Heresy?" *Christian American,* September/ October 1992: 12.

Wicker, Tom. "Just a TV Evangelist." *New York Times,* February 16, 1988: I21.

Wilentz, Sean. "God and Man at Lynchburg." *New Republic,* April 25, 1988: 30.

Will, George. "Here Come the Eager Beavers." *Newsweek,* November 16, 1992: 100.

Wills, Garry. "Robertson and the Reagan Gap." *Time* February 22, 1988: 27-28.

"Winning Political Victories: Pat Robertson's Four Point Plan." *Christian American,* January/February 1991: 10.

"With Little Time to Exult or Weep, Candidates Get Set for the Next Round." *New York Times,* February 10, 1988: I22.

Witham, Larry. "Christian Coalition Steps up Efforts as Election Nears." *Washington Times National Weekly Edition,* August 4, 1996: 13.

————. "Faithful Await Deluge of Voter Guides." *Washington Times,* October 27, 1998: A8.

Woerner, Barbara J. "Top Organizer on a Roll." *Christian American,* October 1994: 12.

Woodward, Calvin. "'Values' Theme Makes Brief Comeback with Quayle on Stage." Associated Press, August 15, 1996.

Yang, John E. "Christian Coalition Revamps Agenda to Reach Out to Inner Cities." *Washington Post,* January 31, 1997: A3.

Yang, John E. and Laurie Goodstein. "Reed Stepping Down as Christian Coalition Leader." *Washington Post,* April 24, 1997: A6.

"Yield Not, Governor to Political Temptation." *Miami Herald,* July 8, 1990: 2E.

OTHER MATERIALS

"A Campaign of Falsehoods: The Anti-Defamation League's Defamation of Religious Conservatives." Chesapeake, VA: Christian Coalition, July 28, 1994.

"ACLU, AFL-CIO Support Christian Coalition in Battle over Free Speech and Public Advocacy." ACLU Press Release, September 30, 1998.

"American Voters Reject Religious Right Extremism." Americans United for Separation of Church and State press release, November 4, 1998.

"Americans United for Separation of Church and State Deplores Ralph Reed Contribution to U.S. Politics." Americans United for Separation of Church and State press release, April 23, 1997.

"Campaign for Working Families, A Political Action Committee," Pamphlet. Washington, D.C.: Campaign for Working Families, 1998.

Castelli, Jim. *Pat Robertson: Extremist.* Washington, D.C.: People for the American Way, 1986.

"Catholic Alliance Cites New Status and Names New Board." Catholic Alliance press release, September 10, 1996.

"CBN to Further Worldwide Evangelism with Proceeds from IFE Stock Sale." Christian Broadcasting Network press release, June 11, 1997.

"Christian Americans Are Tired of Getting Stepped On," pamphlet. Chesapeake, VA: Christian Coalition, 1992.

"Christian Coalition Campaign Influence Seems to Have Peaked." Americans United for Separation of Church and State press release, November 6, 1996.

"Christian Coalition Commends Senate Leader for Strong Stand on Biblical Morality." Christian Coalition press release, June 17, 1998.

"Christian Coalition Congressional Scorecard, Spring 1993 Edition," pamphlet. Chesapeake, VA: Christian Coalition, 1993.

"Christian Coalition 'Excludes' Pro-Life Presidential Candidate." U.S. Taxpayers Party press release, September 13, 1996.

"Christian Coalition Exit Poll Reveals Pro-Family Voters Can't Be Taken for Granted." Christian Coalition press release, November 4, 1998.

"Christian Coalition and Jewish Leaders Denounce Jackson Slur." Christian Coalition press release, December 7, 1994.

"Christian Coalition Joins Other Groups with Message of Hope for Homosexuals." Christian Coalition press release, July 13, 1998.

"Christian Coalition Leadership School," pamphlet. Chesapeake, VA: Christian Coalition, 1993.

Christian Coalition mailings, undated.

Christian Coalition mailing, dated June 8, 1998.

Christian Coalition mailing, dated October 13, 1998.

Christian Coalition mailing, dated July 30, 1996.

Christian Coalition mailing, dated July 15, 1997.

"Christian Coalition Names New President and Executive Director." Christian Coalition press release, June 11, 1997.

"Christian Coalition Opposes Federal Election Commission's Attempt to Suppress First Amendment Rights of People of Faith." Christian Coalition press release, July 30, 1996.

"Christian Coalition Pledge Card." Chesapeake, VA: Christian Coalition, 1995.

"Christian Coalition Raises Record Funds in 1996." Christian Coalition press release, December 10, 1996.

"Christian Coalition Reorganization Proposal Is Act of Legal Desperation, Says Americans United." Americans United for Separation of Church and State press release, January 9, 1998.

"Christian Coalition Road to Victory '98 Update." Christian Coalition press release, September 14, 1998.

"Churches that Hand Out Christian Coalition 'Voter Guides' Will Be Reported to the IRS Watchdog Group Warns." Americans United for Separation of Church and State press release, October 28, 1998.

Citizen Action Seminar Manual. Chesapeake, VA: Christian Coalition, 1995.

Coakley, Stephen. "Messages from the USTP Campaign News Hotline." U.S. Taxpayer Party Web site at http://www.ustaxpayers.org/peg01.html, September 14, 1996.

"Coalition Announces Nationwide Efforts for Election '98." Christian Coalition press release, October 28, 1998.

"A Curriculum of Inclusion, Report of the Commissioner's Task Force on Minorities: Equity and Excellence." New York: New York State Special Task Force on Equity and Excellence in Education, July 1989.

"Despite Losses, Religious Right Retains Hold on Congress; Suffers Stunning Defeat in Colorado." People for the American Way press release, November 6, 1996.

"The Diminishing Divide . . . American Churches, American Politics." Louisville, KY: The Pew Research Center for the People & the Press, 1996.

Dobson, James. Speech to the Spring 1998 Council for National Policy meeting. Phoenix, AZ, February 7, 1998.

"'Families 2000' Strategy Announced by Christian Coalition." Christian Coalition press release, February 18, 1998.

"FEC Case Groundless—Christian Coalition Files for Dismissal." Christian Coalition press release, September 8, 1998.

Fisher, William L. "Christian Responsibility for Government." In *Christian Coalition Leadership Manual,* 2.1-2.11. Chesapeake, VA: Christian Coalition, 1990.

———. "State Affiliates and Their Chapters." In *Christian Coalition Leadership Manual,* 3.1-3.3. Chesapeake, VA: Christian Coalition, 1990.

Form 990, Return of Organization Exempt from Income Tax for 1994, 1995, 1996, and 1997, The Christian Coalition. Copies of these tax returns can be obtained by writing to Virginia State Division of Consumer Affairs, P.O. Box 1163, Richmond, VA 23209.

Gingrich, Newt. "Renewing America," speech at the 5th Annual Christian Coalition "Road to Victory" conference. Washington, D.C., September 8, 1995;

Glasser, Ira. "Open Letter to Bill Clinton, President of the United States." New York: American Civil Liberties Union, May 15, 1995.

"Istook and More Than 100 Co-Sponsors Introduce Religious Freedom Amendment," press release from the office of Rep. Ernest Istook (R-OK). May 8, 1997.

Jackson, Brooks. "Religious Right, Convention Might." *CNN Inside Politics.* Cable News Network, August 8, 1996.

Kennedy, John F. "Presidential Inaugural Address." Washington, D.C., January 20, 1961.

Keyes, Alan. "America's Yearning for Spiritual Renewal," speech at the 6th Annual Christian Coalition "Road to Victory" conference. Washington, D.C., September 14, 1996.

King, John. "Christian Coalition Uses Pulpits for Politics." *CNN Inside Politics.* Cable News Network, November 2, 1998.

Lemon v. Kurtzmann, 403 U.S. 602 (1971).

"LifeLine, Changing the World with Every Call," pamphlet. Oklahoma City: AmeriVision Communications, Inc., undated.

Lofton, John. "Why Is Ralph Reed Saying He Would Vote for and Actively Support a Politically Correct Atheist Against a Politically Incorrect Christian?" one-page flier. P.O. Box 1142, Laurel, MD 20707.

"National Christian Voter Mobilization Campaign," undated Christian Coalition mailing.

North, Gary. "Letter to Institute for Christian Economics Subscribers." Tyler, TX: Institute for Christian Economics, April 1994.

"People for the American Way: Right Wing Watch Online." November 5, 1998. People For the American Way Web site at http://www.pfaw.org.

"Precinct Coordinator Handbook," pamphlet. Chesapeake, VA: Christian Coalition, 1993.

"The Radical Right and the 1992 Election: The Stealth Campaign." Washington, D.C.: People for the American Way, 1993.

"Ralph Reed Calls on Religious Conservatives to Repent of Harsh Language about Clinton, Abortion, and Gays, but His Boss Pat Robertson and the Christian Coalition Just Keep On Sinning." Washington, D.C.: Americans United for the Separation of Church and State media advisory, May 17, 1996.

Reed, Ralph. "Active Faith," speech at the 6th Annual Christian Coalition "Road to Victory" conference. Washington, D.C., September 13, 1996.

———. *An American Profile,* interview. C-SPAN, August 19, 1993.

———. "How People of Faith are Changing the Soul of American Politics," speech at the National Press Club. Washington D.C., October 22, 1996.

———. Interview by David Gergen. *Lehrer News Hour.* Public Broadcasting System, June 6, 1996.

———. Interview by Larry King. *Larry King Live.* Cable News Network, June 23, 1998.

———. Interview by Pat Robertson. *The 700 Club.* Christian Broadcasting Network, November 6, 1996.

———. Interview by Bernard Shaw. *CNN Inside Politics.* Cable News Network, February 8, 1996.

———. Interview by Tony Snow. *Fox News Sunday.* Fox Television Network, November 10, 1996.

———. Interview by Judy Woodruff. *CNN Inside Politics.* Cable News Network, May 6, 1996.

———. Interview by Judy Woodruff. *CNN Inside Politics.* Cable News Network, February 20, 1998.

———. Remarks at beginning of *Contract with the American Family* presentation. Washington, D.C., May 17, 1995.

———. "The Role of Religious Conservatives in the '96 Elections," speech at the 5th Annual Christian Coalition "Road to Victory" conference. Washington, D.C., September 8, 1995.

———. Speech to the 17th National Leadership Conference of the Anti- Defamation League of B'nai B'rith. Washington, D.C., April 3, 1995.

———. *Time Online,* interview, American Online Computer Network, May 10, 1995.

Reed, Ralph, Jr. "Statement by Ralph Reed, Jr. Concerning His Resignation from the Christian Coalition." Christian Coalition press release, April 23, 1997.

Regent University Graduate Catalog 1992-94. Virginia Beach, VA: Regent University, 1992.

Regent University Graduate Catalog 1994-1996. Virginia Beach, VA: Regent University, 1994.

"Religious Conservative Firewall Protects Pro-Family Candidates." Christian Coalition press release, November 6, 1996.

"The Religious Right Called the Tune, But Voters Wouldn't Dance." People For the American Way press release, November 4, 1998.

"Remarks by the President at the Signing Ceremony for the Religious Freedom Restoration Act." Washington, D.C.: White House Press Office, November 16, 1993.

"Remarks by the President in Photo Opportunity During White House Interfaith Breakfast." Washington, D.C.: White House Press Office, August 30, 1993.

Robertson, Marion G. "Pat." "A New Vision for America," speech to a political rally in Constitution Hall. Washington, D.C., September 17, 1986.

Robertson, Pat. "Address to the Republican National Convention." Houston, TX: August 19, 1992.

———. Interview by Robert Novak and Fred Barnes. *Evans & Novak.* Cable News Network, April 15, 1995.

———. "Keynote Address," speech at the 6th Annual Christian Coalition "Road to Victory" conference. Washington, D.C., September 15, 1996.

———. Interview by Marvin Kalb. *Meet the Press.* National Broadcasting Co., Inc., December 15, 1985.

———. "Pat Robertson Expresses Gratitude and Support for Ralph Reed." Christian Coalition press release, April 23, 1997.

———. "Power to Change America and the World." In *Living Successfully in the '90s,* tape 4, Virginia Beach, VA: Christian Broadcasting Network tape series, 1993.

———. "Remarks at Morning Plenary Session." Speech at the 8th Annual Christian Coalition "Road to Victory" conference. Washington, D.C., September 18, 1998.

———. Remarks to the 6th Annual Christian Coalition "Road to Victory" conference. Washington, D.C., September 14, 1996.

———. Remarks on *The 700 Club*. Christian Broadcasting Network, January 4, 1993.

———. Remarks on *The 700 Club*. Christian Broadcasting Network, October 7, 1996.

———. Remarks on *The 700 Club*. Christian Broadcasting Network, November 6, 1996.

"The Samaritan Project." Chesapeake, VA: Christian Coalition, 1997.

"Satellite Broadcast." Christian Coalition Web site at http://www.cc.org/cc/edu/sat.html, September 2, 1995.

Senate Governmental Affairs Committee. *Investigation of Illegal or Improper Activities in Connection with 1996 Federal Election Campaigns.* 105th Cong., 2d sess., March 10, 1998. S. Rept. 105-167.

Smith, Tom W. "A Survey of the Religious Right." New York: American Jewish Committee, 1996.

"Statement by RNC Chairman Haley Barbour on Democrat Christian-Bashing." Washington, D.C.: Republican National Committee press release, June 21, 1994.

"Students for America," pamphlet. Raleigh, NC: Students for America, undated.

Tate, Randy. "National Press Club Luncheon Address by Randy Tate, Executive Director of the Christian Coalition." Speech at the National Press Club, Washington, D.C., September 16, 1998.

———. "News Briefing with Randy Tate, Executive Director of the Christian Coalition." Press conference at the National Press Club, Washington, D.C., November 4, 1998.

———. "Pastor's Letter from Randy Tate." Christian Coalition Web site at http://www.cc.org/voter/legal/rights.html, October 8, 1998.

———. "Remarks After Attending the Values Summit." News conference, Washington, D.C., May 8, 1998.

Wehmeyer, Peggy. "Christian Coalition Gaining Strength." *ABC World News Tonight.* American Broadcasting Company, November 3, 1994.

"Whose American Family?" Washington, D.C.: American Jewish Congress, 1995.

INDEX